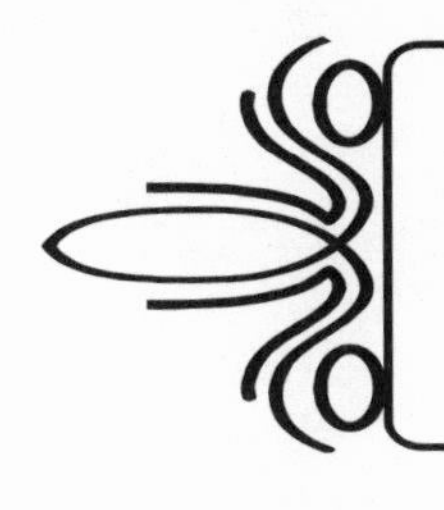

From the Flame of Battle to the Fiery Cross

From the Flame of Battle to the Fiery Cross

The 3rd Tennessee Infantry with Complete Roster

James Van Eldik

Yucca Tree Press

 Yucca Tree Press, 2130 Hixon Drive, Las Cruces, New Mexico 88005-3305.

First printing September 2001

Van Eldik, James
FROM THE FLAME OF BATTLE TO THE FIERY CROSS
1. United States - History - Civil War, 1861-1865; 2. Third Tennessee Infantry Regiment - History; 3. John C. Brown
I. James Van Eldik. II. Title

Library of Congress Catalog Card Number: 2001093586
ISBN: 1-881325-47-4

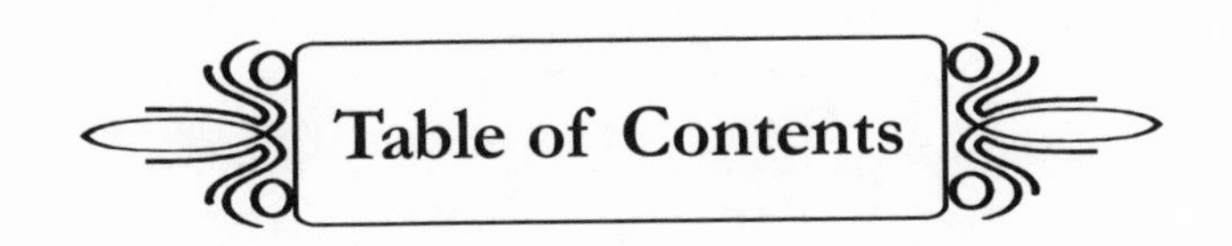

Table of Contents

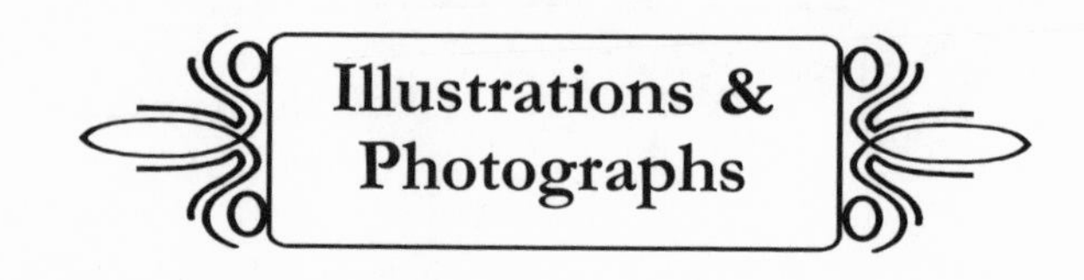

Illustrations & Photographs

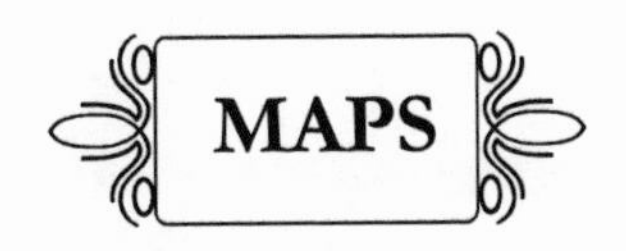

MAPS

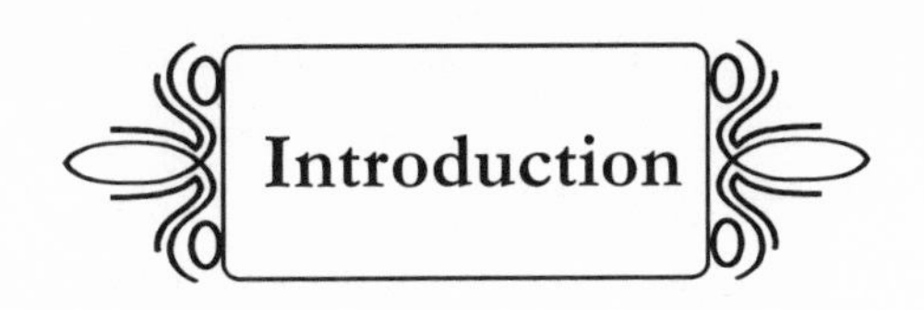

Introduction

For the past hundred plus years the United States has had a fascination with its great Civil War. Most of the attention has traditionally been given to the war in the east, and much of that to Robert E. Lee's Army of Northern Virginia. Lee's army was a superb fighting organization, and scored some remarkable victories in the face of great odds. Until recently its sister army west of the Appalachians, the Army of Tennessee, has been given short shrift. That is a disservice to the men of that army who, man for man, were every bit the equals of their counterparts in Virginia.

Beginning with Stanley Horn's *The Army of Tennessee*, and continuing with Thomas Connelly's two-volume set, *Army of the Heartland*, and *Autumn of Glory*, Civil War literature has come a long way in redressing this imbalance. The hard-luck Army of Tennessee fought some of the war's toughest battles— Shiloh, Stone's River, Chickamauga, and throughout the fabled Atlanta campaign. The head on charge it conducted at Franklin, Tennessee, was equal in size and intensity to the much more famous charge made by George Pickett at Gettysburg, and was certainly as bloody. Recent publications have finally given these desperate struggles the attention they deserve. The inescapable fact is that while the South fought and often won spectacular battles in the east, it lost the Civil War in the west.

Much more remains to be done. There is still a perspective of the western war that has not been adequately examined—that of the small fighting unit. There are a few good Confederate regimental histories, but these provide little detailed analysis of precisely what the unit did during each battle, and what sort of internal changes were going on within the organization as a result of heavy combat and the myriad other factors affecting the health and morale of a Civil War regiment. This narrative seeks to redress this shortfall.

To address the Confederate small unit experience, the author sought a regiment that was consistently in the thick of things, and also one that left behind an adequate record of exactly who they were and what they did. The 3rd Tennessee Infantry seemed an ideal selection.

The 3rd Tennessee was a part of the Confederate Army from the inception of the Civil War, and was present at Greensboro, North Carolina, at its very end. It fought in fierce battles at Fort Donelson, Chickasaw Bayou, Vicksburg, Port Hudson, Chickamauga, Chattanooga, and throughout the Atlanta campaign. An extremely proficient outfit, it was often positioned at the hottest or the most important part of the battlefield, and frequently used for skirmish duty where the norm was to be alone, outnumbered, and reliant on one's own wits. It scored impressive victories over the Federals at Fort Donelson, Chickasaw Bayou, Chickamauga, and Resaca, but was badly mauled at Raymond, Mississippi. By late 1864 it dropped to less than a dozen men and ended the war with barely the strength of one company still with the colors. It was one of the South's true fighting regiments, a good representative of the high-qualtity, low-numbered regiments that were the backbone of the Army of Tennessee.

It is the intent of this narrative to provide the reader with a true sense of what combat was like for these men—how they fit into the scheme of each battle—how the battle looked, sounded, and felt. There is an old saying that no plan survives the first minute of battle. That premise is more than validated in the chaos surrounding the 3rd Tennessee in each of the actions about to be described. Many of the most familiar battles of the western theater take on a new texture when viewed through the eyes of the small fighting unit.

In so far as his activities related to the actions of the 3rd Tennessee, this study will also provide insights into the military career of John C. Brown, the regiment's original commander.

Brown entered the war with no military experience, but was elected colonel of the regiment. He had a knack for military leadership and was soon elevated to temporary brigade command. By late 1862 he had been promoted to brigadier general and from then to the end of 1864 he was a permanent brigade commander, frequently assigned to the temporary command of full divisions. He finished the war a major general. Despite his rapid rise, Brown maintained a close relationship with the 3rd Tennessee throughout most of the conflict. He was the regiment's commander for the first year, was absent with Bragg during late 1862 to the end of 1863, then rejoined the regiment as brigade commander for most of 1864. He was absent again during the early months of 1865, but rejoined the army in time to welcome the regiment back to the army on their return from a harrowing experience in the wilds of North Carolina in the war's final days. Brown was one of the South's 'fighting' generals, and some of the absences were due to his taking time out to convalesce from bullet wounds.

The narrative will conclude with a brief summation of the post-war experiences of several members of the regiment and of Brown. Several of the regiment's soldiers have the notoriety of being part of the small group of men who founded the notorious Ku Klux Klan. Begun as a benign social club, it soon evolved into the vicious terrorist organization it is known as today. Brown had a spectacular post-war career serving two terms as governor of Tennessee, and going on to become a successful railroad baron.

This is a battle history. While considerable information on the

3rd Tennessee provides a concise idea as to the human material comprising the regiment and defining the character of the organization, the day-to-day camp life of the regiment is not here. If the reader desires information along these lines, Bell Wiley's, *The Life of Johnney Reb*, and more recently, Larry Daniel's, *Soldiering in the Army of Tennessee*, do a splendid job fulfilling this need.

Second, this study is based on primary sources—the 3rd Tennessee Rollbook, accounts written by regimental soldiers, and official reports by the regiment's commanders, by their more senior officers, and by their enemies in blue. Battle accounts are as 'clean' as possible reflecting as accurately as possible what the troops themselves said they actually saw and experienced.

And third, there were two 3rd Tennessee regiments in the Confederate Army. This narrative is about the volunteer regiment organized in central Tennessee and later transferred into Confederate service. Another regiment, the Third Confederate, was organized in Knoxville at the same time as the subject of this study. The Third Confederate, under the command of John C. Vaughan, fought with Lee in Virginia, with Pemberton in Vicksburg at the same time the other 3rd Tennessee was fighting outside the city, then with Longstreet at Knoxville, and finally with Lee again in Virginia at the final surrender. Both regiments are commonly referred to as the '3rd Tennessee' in Civil War literature, and the reader should be conscious of this factor when seeking additional information.

Chronology of John C. Brown and the 3rd Tennessee

1860

December 20	South Carolina seceeds from Union

1861

February 8	Confederate government formed
April 12	Confederates attack Fort Sumter
April 15	Lincoln calls for 100,000 troops; 3rd Tennessee companies begin organizing
May 16	3rd Tennessee is organized at Lynnville; John C. Brown elected colonel
May 17	Tennessee joins Confederacy
May 20	3rd Tennessee moves to Camp Cheatham in Robertson County
May 21	3rd Tennessee sworn into state service
July 26	3rd Tennessee moves to Camp Trousdale in Sumner County
August 7	3rd Tennessee transferred to Confederate service
September 17	3rd Tennessee moves to Bowling Green, Ky.
September 22	3rd Tennessee participates in sortie against Kentucky Unionists

1862

February 8	3rd Tennessee moves to Fort Donelson
February 8-15	Battle of Fort Donelson
February 16	Fort Donelson defenders surrender, Brown and 3rd Tennessee included
February 23	Most 3rd Tennesseans arrive at Camp Douglas, Il., POW facility
August 30	Brown exchanged sometime in August/promoted to brigadier general
September 1	Officers shipped to Vicksburg for exchange (Brown goes to Chattanooga to join Bragg's army for Kentucky invasion)
September 7	Enlisted men shipped to Vicksburg
September 23	Exchange process completed
September 26	3rd Tennessee reorganized

October 8	Brown shot in leg leading a charge at Battle of Perryville, Ky.
December 29	3rd Tennessee participates in Battle of Chickasaw Bayou
December 31-January 2	Brown commands army rear at First Battle of Murfreesboro

1863

March 14	3rd Tennessee subjected to naval bombardment at Port Hudson on Mississippi River
May 11	3rd Tennessee trounced in Battle of Raymond
July 15-16	3rd Tennessee in Johnston's retreat from Jackson, Ms.
September 19-20	Brown and 3rd Tennessee in Battle of Chickamauga
November 24	Brown and 3rd Tennessee reunited in Battle of Lookout Mountain
November 25	Brown and 3rd Tennessee in Battle of Missionary Ridge

1864

May 8-11	Brown and 3rd Tennessee in Battle of Rocky Face Ridge/Dalton
May 13-15	Brown and 3rd Tennessee in Battle of Resaca
May 25	3rd Tennessee in Battle of New Hope Church
June 22	3rd Tennessee in Battle of Kolb's Farm; Col. Calvin Walker killed
July 22	Brown and 3rd Tennessee in Battle of Atlanta; Brown commands Hindman's Division
July 28	Brown, still commanding Hindman's Division, fights Battle of Ezra Church
August 1	Brown promoted to major general
August 31-September 1	Brown and 3rd Tennessee in Battle of Jonesboro; Brown commands Bate's Division; Lt. Col. Calvin Clack killed
November	Hood moves army into Tennessee; Sherman begins march to sea
November 29	3rd Tennessee assaults Columbia; Brown contibutes to fiasco at Spring Hill

November 30	Brown severly wounded leading assault on Franklin
December 7	3rd Tennessee trounced in Second Battle of Murfreesboro

1865

March 19	Remnant of 3rd Tennessee in Battle of Bentonville, N.C.
April 26	Brown and 3rd Tennessee surrender
May 1	Brown and 3rd Tennessee paroled at Greensboro, North Carolina

1

THE REGIMENT

The 3rd Tennessee Infantry Regiment was officially organized on May 16, 1861. It started as a robust outfit of 1105 young men from Giles County and vicinity. Had they known that by December 21, 1864, the 3rd and 18th Infantry Regiments consolidated could muster only "17 [men] plus three colored servants," they no doubt would have been appalled. The 3rd Tennessee did recover, slightly, mustering out 79 men at war's end, but for all practical purposes the human meat grinder known as the American Civil War completely consumed this hopeful group of American soldiery.[1]

The 3rd Tennessee was one of the Civil War's fighting regiments. It experienced the gamut of combat action and delivered violent attacks against its enemies in blue at Fort Donelson, Raymond, Chickamauga, Resaca, and Kolb's Farm. It was stolid on the defense at Chickasaw Bayou, at Missionary Ridge, and throughout the Atlanta campaign, but was decimated at Raymond, at Chickamauga, and at the second battle of Murfreesboro. Often its best efforts were squandered by inept leadership, as at Fort Donelson and Chickamauga.[2]

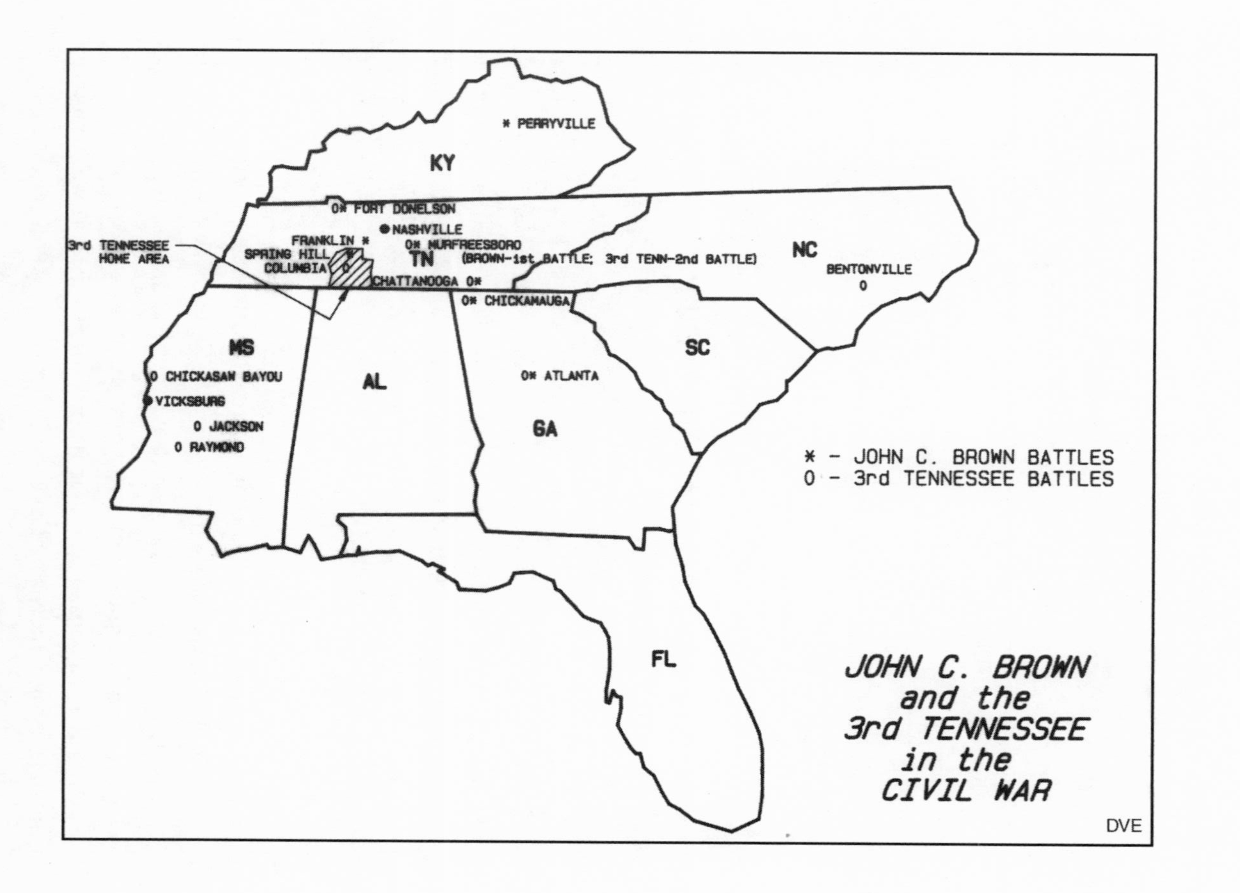
* PERRYVILLE
KY
0* FORT DONELSON
● NASHVILLE
FRANKLIN *
SPRING HILL
COLUMBIA
0* MURFREESBORO
TN
(BROWN-1st BATTLE; 3rd TENN-2nd BATTLE)
CHATTANOOGA 0*
3rd TENNESSEE
HOME AREA
NC
BENTONVILLE
0
0* CHICKAMAUGA
MS
0 CHICKASAW BAYOU
● VICKSBURG
0 JACKSON
0 RAYMOND
AL
0* ATLANTA
GA
SC
FL
* - JOHN C. BROWN BATTLES
0 - 3rd TENNESSEE BATTLES
JOHN C. BROWN
and the
3rd TENNESSEE
in the
CIVIL WAR
DVE

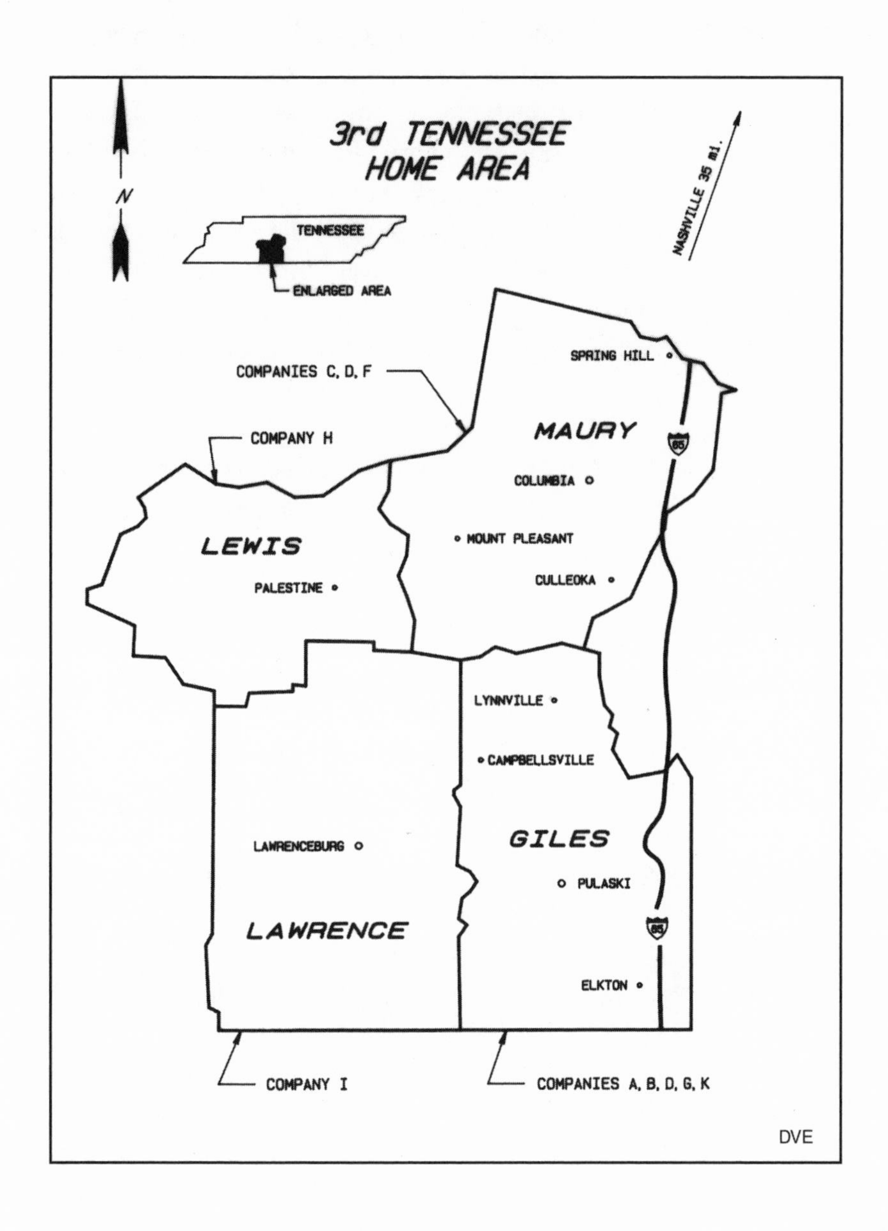
3rd TENNESSEE
HOME AREA
N
TENNESSEE
ENLARGED AREA
NASHVILLE 35 mi.
SPRING HILL
COMPANIES C, D, F
MAURY
COMPANY H
COLUMBIA
LEWIS
MOUNT PLEASANT
PALESTINE
CULLEOKA
LYNNVILLE
CAMPBELLSVILLE
LAWRENCEBURG
GILES
PULASKI
LAWRENCE
ELKTON
COMPANY I
COMPANIES A, B, D, G, K
DVE

For most of the war the 3rd Tennessee was a formidable fighting force. When it was teamed with the rangy frontiersmen of the 7th Texas, it was nearly unbeatable. For a considerable period, Southern independence was very much a viable possibility.

Specific reasons for the battlefield prowess of the 3rd Tennessee would, in all likelihood, also apply to many of the volunteer regiments both north and south. First, the 3rd was composed of volunteers from the same geographic area; the men were friends and neighbors. Five companies were from Giles County (A, B, C, D, E), three from Maury County (D, E, F), one from Lewis County (H), and one from Lawrence County (K). The men knew and trusted each other.[3]

Second, many of the men were related by blood or marriage. A characteristic of 19th century southern society was the large size of the clans, often extending across state lines. Five-hundred and eight out of 1098 3rd Tennesseans shared the same surname with at least one person in the same company. In all there were as many as two-hundred and eleven family relationships in the regiment.[4]

This family orientation had a direct bearing on the regiment's consistent success on the battlefield. While generals (and historians) generally gauge victory or defeat on the basis of ground gained or lost, numbers of casualties, integrity of battlefield forces, social and political repercussions, etc., the viewpoint of the individual Civil War soldier was much simpler. It was first and foremost focused on his own survival. Once that was assured his focus quickly shifted to the well being of his relatives. When his life and the lives of his kin were on the line he was capable of spectacular accomplishments. There was a distinct possibility that in times of mortal combat he might consider his commander's views unimportant, or even irrelevant.

Last, but by no means least, was a characteristic of the regiment itself. The real backbone of a regiment was 'mess,' informal groupings, usually of six to eight men, formed throughout the regiment. This group ate together, slept together, fought together, and sometimes died together. This small group developed an intense loyalty to each other which was intensified by the many family relationships also present. Once a soldier came under life-threatening fire, abstract concepts such as the rightness of his cause, or the honor of his regiment, or the honor of his country no longer seemed that important. When his own death and that of those near him became real possibilities, his concern shifted to himself and his own circle of close comrades, his mess or squad. It was the esteem of these comrades that the man most valued and was willing to risk his life to sustain. More than anything else, it was the esteem of blood relatives and close friends standing nearby that motivated the soldiers of the 3rd Tennessee to fight well.[5]

Origins of the regimental organization can be traced to the days when the infantryman's primary weapon was the spear. Sometime during antiquity a practitioner of the military arts discovered that a thousand men fashioned into two lines of five-hundred men each, all standing elbow to elbow, can hear the man in charge if that man stands in the approximate center and shouts out his orders at the top of his lungs. It was also determined that a second line of troops helps assure that the first line adheres to the task at hand.

In 1861 an infantry regiment was structured to operate as an independent tactical unit in the field as it often did during various Indian wars. It was possible to create three maneuver battalions from a regiment, or employ the ten companies separately, but this rarely occurred during the Civil War because of the massive size of the armies, and because disease and the frightful casualty rates decimated regimental strength so quickly. In fact, by the time the war was half over the average regiment on both sides had dwindled to about three-hundred men, about one-third of its original strength.

The next higher tactical unit, the brigade, composed of two to five regiments, evolved as the basic field maneuver unit. Divisions were formed by combining two or more brigades, and two or more divisions comprised a corps. One or more corps made up an army. While the Union numbered its brigades, divisions, and corps, the Confederates numbered only regiments. Everything else was designated by the name of its commander. This sometimes led to confusion when casualties and transfers necessitated new

THE 3RD TENNESSEE

FAMILY LINK

COMPANY	NUMBER OF SOLDIERS	NUMBER OF SOLDIERS SHARING SURNAME	%	NUMBER OF SHARED SURNAMES	SURNAMES SHARED BY 3 OR MORE SOLDIERS
A	120	49	41%	20	ABERNATHY (5) BUFORD (4) BUNCH (3) HOLT (3) REYNOLDS (4)
B	113	48	42%	21	BRICKEEN (3) FRY (4) MARTIN (3) MITCHELL (3) THOMPSON (3)
C	119	61	51%	27	BARNES (3) INGRAM (3) JUNE (3) KITTRELL (3) MATTHEWS (4) WATKINS (3)
D	108	57	53%	27	COMPTON (3) ENGLISH (3) HICKMAN (3)
E	100	33	33%	13	JOHNSON (4) OWEN (3) ROUNTREE (3) THOMPSON (4) TUCKER (3)
F	98	57	58%	22	CREWS (3) COFFEY (3) DAVIS (5) JARRETT (3)

PART ONE OF TWO PARTS

THE 3RD TENNESSEE
FAMILY LINK

COMPANY	NUMBER OF SOLDIERS	NUMBER OF SOLDIERS SHARING SURNAME	%	NUMBER OF SHARED SURNAMES	SURNAMES SHARED BY 3 OR MORE SOLDIERS
G	110	50	45%	23	BURGESS (3) CHILES (3) ORR (3) WILLIAMS (3)
H	99	60	61%	19	CLAYTON (3) CONDOR (4) COOPER (6) DAVIS (3) HENSLEY (3) DEEN (5) FITE (3) GRINDER (3) HINSON (3) POPE (4) PEAVYHOUSE (3) SHARP (3) STRICKLAND (3) SIMS (3) LANKFORD (3)
I	121	49	40%	20	GREEN (4) HUBBARD (3) JOHNSON (3) LITTLETON (4) McALLISTER (3) SMITH (4)
K	110	44	40%	19	ABERNATHY (4) BASS (3) BRUCE (3) DUNGY (3)

PART TWO OF TWO PARTS

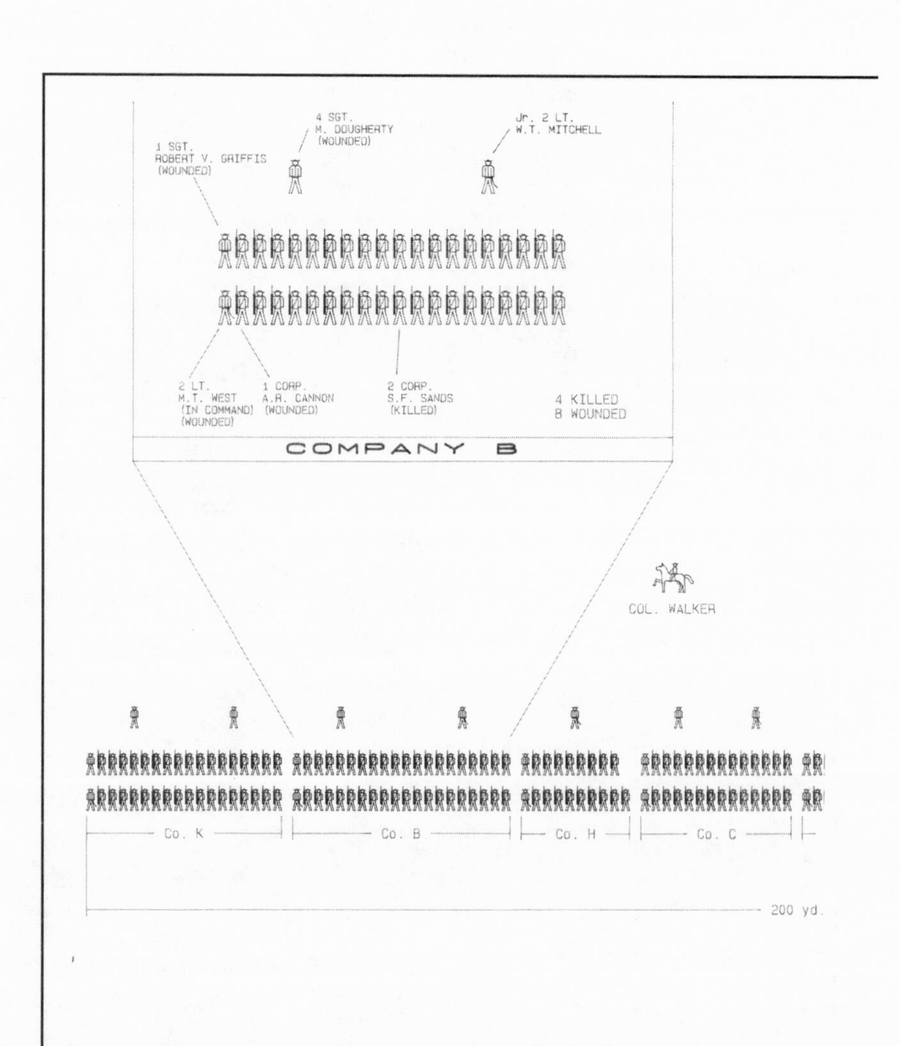
4 SGT.
M. DOUGHERTY
(WOUNDED)
Jr. 2 LT.
W.T. MITCHELL
1 SGT.
ROBERT V. GRIFFIS
(WOUNDED)
2 LT.
M.T. WEST
(IN COMMAND)
(WOUNDED)
1 CORP.
A.R. CANNON
(WOUNDED)
2 CORP.
S.F. SANDS
(KILLED)
4 KILLED
8 WOUNDED
COMPANY B
COL. WALKER
Co. K
Co. B
Co. H
Co. C
200 yd.

THE 3rd TENNESSEE AT CHICKAMAUGA

SEPTEMBER 19, 1863

LT. COL. CLACK

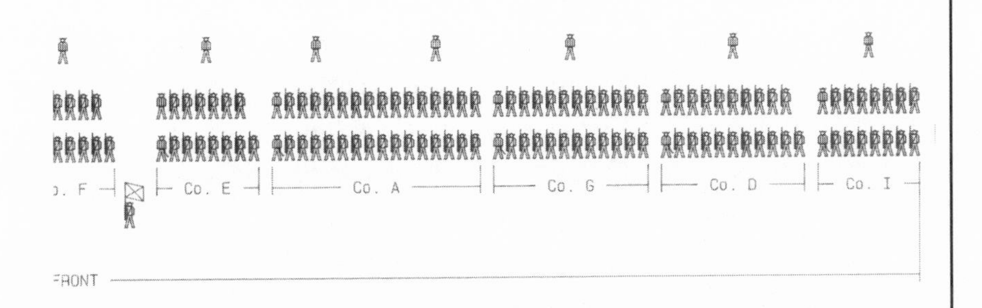

DVE

assignments, or when a new organization was created on the spot. For example, at Chickamauga John C. Brown, by this time a brigade commander, was head of Brown's Brigade. Simple enough. However, on Brown's flank was Johnson's Brigade commanded by J.S. Fulton. Johnson's Brigade (3rd Tennessee included) was part of Johnson's Provisional Division: same Johnson. Johnson's Provisional Division was assigned to Longstreet's Corps, commanded by J.B. Hood. Also assigned to this corps was Hood's Division. Similar confusing relationships existed throughout the army.

Of course an organization with more than a thousand men required a sizable bureaucracy to keep it operating smoothly. A Confederate army was commanded by a full general, a corps a lieutenant general, and a brigade by a brigadier general. Colonels commanded regiments including the 3rd Tennessee. Also performing command roles were the lieutenant colonel and a major. Support staff included an adjutant, two quartermasters, a commissary officer, two surgeons, an assistant surgeon, a chaplain, a sergeant major, two quartermaster sergeants, two ordnance sergeants, and a hospital steward.[6]

The 3rd Tennessee contained ten companies designated A through K (there was no J) with one-hundred privates each. Each company was led by a captain assisted by first and second lieutenants, a junior second lieutenant, first, second, third, fourth, and fifth sergeants, and first, second, third and fourth corporals. A company could be divided into two platoons led by the lieutenants. This was sometimes done to provide men for the thin line of skirmishers deployed several hundred yards in front of the regiment during an advance.

The officers of the 3rd Tennessee were well-educated and many were leaders in their communities. Of the three primary commanders, Brown and Calvin Clack were both lawyers while Calvin Walker was a physician. Most were lacking in military training, and often had an unrealistic and romanticized image of a combat leader. They were elected to command by virtue of personal popularity, and envisioned "meeting a hated foe in deadly combat" on "some well fought battlefield" as a part of a "great and noble undertaking."

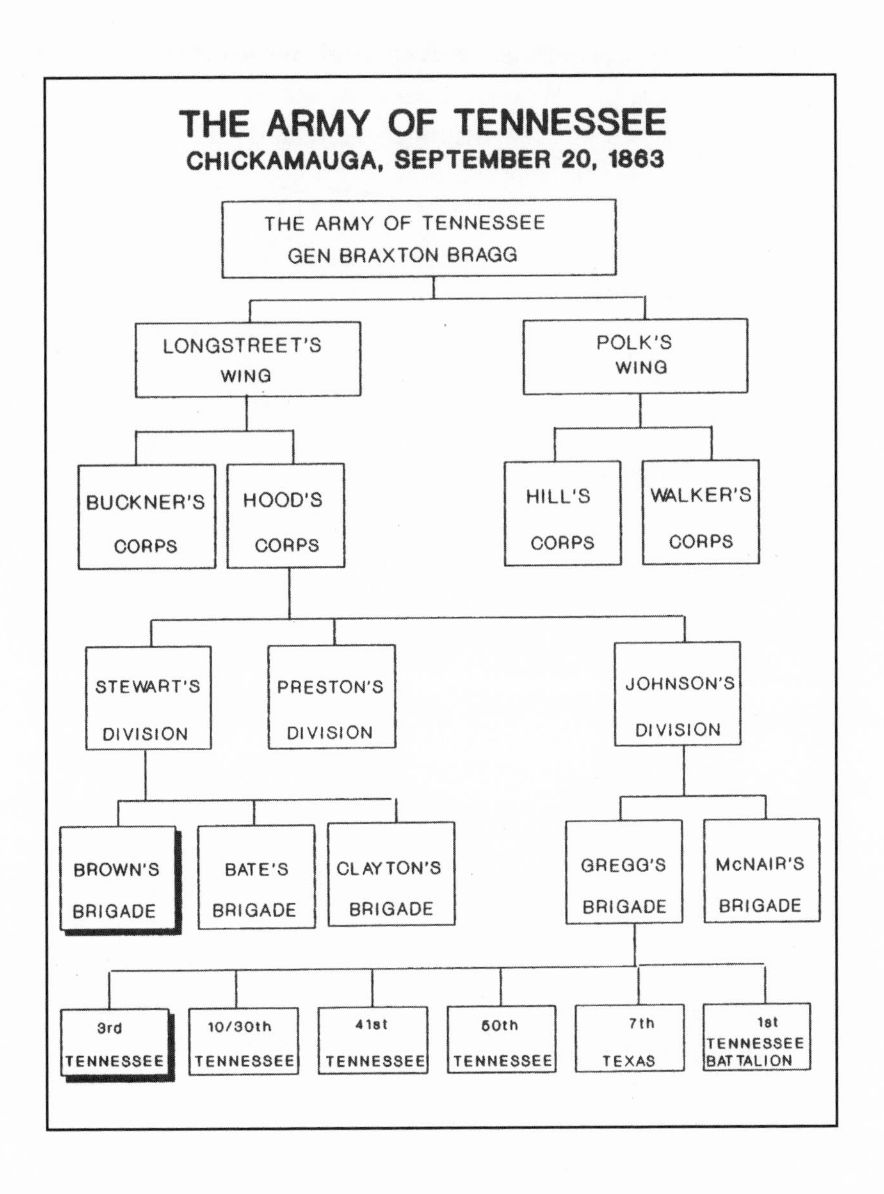
THE ARMY OF TENNESSEE
CHICKAMAUGA, SEPTEMBER 20, 1863
THE ARMY OF TENNESSEE
GEN BRAXTON BRAGG
LONGSTREET'S WING
POLK'S WING
BUCKNER'S CORPS
HOOD'S CORPS
HILL'S CORPS
WALKER'S CORPS
STEWART'S DIVISION
PRESTON'S DIVISION
JOHNSON'S DIVISION
BROWN'S BRIGADE
BATE'S BRIGADE
CLAYTON'S BRIGADE
GREGG'S BRIGADE
McNAIR'S BRIGADE
3rd TENNESSEE
10/30th TENNESSEE
41st TENNESSEE
50th TENNESSEE
7th TEXAS
1st TENNESSEE BATTALION

3rd Tennessee Personnel Strength

Milestone	Strength	Killed	Captured
Organization May 16, 1861	1105	—	—
At Fort Donelson February 9, 1862	743	13	All
Reorganization September 26, 1862	607	—	—
At Battle of Chickasaw Bayou December 27, 1862	549	2	0
At Battles of Raymond/Jackson May 11, 1863	548	35	82
At Battle of Chickamauga September 19, 1863	264	26	7
At Battle of Missionary Ridge November 25, 1863	195	0	1
At Battle of Resaca May 13, 1864	271	9	0

The quotations are from several of the company commanders. The scene hardly coincides with the horrors of combat, or the numbing monotony and drudgery of camp life they were soon to experience.[7]

Actual warfare was a disillusioning experience. Seventeen officers were not up to the task and resigned or were not reelected when the regiment reorganized after captivity. Realism quickly took hold as the soldiers were taught a variety of military skills. The original commander, Colonel John C. Brown, was described as a "strict disciplinarian" who was well regarded by his men because of his consistent devotion to their welfare. Formally a teacher, he entered the legal profession in 1848 becoming one of the state's top jurists and political leaders. Brown was accustomed to being in charge and soon converted an assortment of free-thinking civilians into a military organization with "high proficiency in drill and discipline" according to one company commander. Cool and aloof, Brown was all business, a characteristic his men later came to appreciate in the chaos of combat. Brown taught his men how to maneuver under fire and gave them the capacity to deliver concentrated firepower at the proper time and place. Brown caught the attention of his superiors, and was soon elevated to brigade command. Eventually his aggressiveness on the battlefield and his reliability in rapidly and faithfully executing orders without quibbling earned him the respect of hard fighting (but not always wise thinking) John Bell Hood. During the grinding Atlanta campaign of 1864 he became "a favorite of General Hood's." He became a utility general, filling in for a number of division commanders as they became casualties or were transferred elsewhere.[8]

A major lapse in one area, common to both armies, caused the regiment its first serious casualties. Hygiene was a primitive science in those days and field sanitation was abysmal. While the regiment was still in camp, and before it saw any kind of military action, hundreds of men became sick and eighty-five died.[9]

Despite their limitations, the young and enthusiastic officers of the 3rd Tennessee did their best to insure that the troops were adequately prepared for the field. They learned and improved as they went. There was no lack of courage among them. During the course of the war two regimental commanders were killed, and one badly wounded. One lieutenant colonel was wounded, and two majors were killed. At least five company commanders were killed, and dozens of other officers and NCO's were killed or wounded.

John C. Brown was wounded four times while leading brigade and division-sized attacks. Civil War officers were expected to lead from the front, and that is exactly what the leaders of the 3rd Tennessee did.[10]

Notes For Chapter 1

1 "Rolls of the Third Tennessee Regiment," (hereafter referred to as the Rollbook), p. 120. The Rollbook is divided into two parts: the first "From its Organization at Lynnville, Tennessee, May 16th, 1861, to its Reorganization at Jackson, Mississippi, Sept. 26th, 1862; the second "from its Re-organization at Jackson, Mississippi Sept. 26th 1862 to the End of the War." The Rollbook ceased to be an active document with the beginning of the Atlanta campaign in May, 1864. *The War of the Rebellion: A Compilation of the Official Records of Union and Confederate Armies* (hereafter referred to as *OR*), Vol. XLV, part 1, p. 28. RB, p. 15.

2 For an overview of the western battles and campaign see Stanley Horn's, *The Army of Tennessee*, and Thomas Connelly's, *The Army of the Heartland: The Army of Tennessee, 1861-1862*, and *Autumn of Glory: The Army of Tennessee, 1862-1865.*

3 *The Military Annals of Tennessee, Confederate*, pp. 175-176

4 Rollbook, company records.

5 Studies on soldier motivation include S. L. A. Marshall's, *Men Against Fire*, John Keegan's, *The Face of Battle,* and James M. McPherson's, *For Cause & Comrades: Why Men Fought in the Civil War.* .

6 Paddy Griffith's, *Battle in the Civil War*, provides excellent background information on Civil War unit organization. *Battles and Leaders of the Civil War* (hereafter referred to as *Battles and Leaders.*), Vol.III, pp. 673-676.

7 Rollbook, Company Records

8 Joshua Caldwell, *The Bench and Bar of Tennessee*, pp. 291-297. John Allison, *Notable Men of Tennessee*, pp. 101-103. Margaret I. Phillips, *The Governors of Tennessee*, pp. 90-94. *RB*, pp. 14, 117. Rollbook, Company Records. Arthur M. Manigault, *A Carolinian Goes to War*, p. 195.

9 Rollbook, Company Records.

10 Rollbook. Specifics are contained within each chapter and in the appendices.

John C. Brown, in an early war photo, shows off his new brigadier general's uniform and displays the iron countenance guaranteed to stop a fainthearted skulker in his tracks.

Courtesy: Confederate Veteran

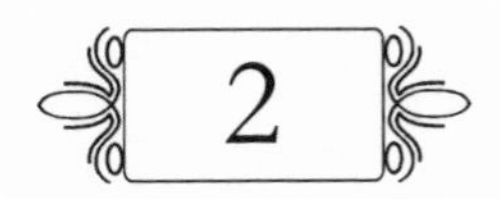

A CALL TO ARMS

The spring of 1861 found Tennessee a state in transition. Though still officially a slave state, large portions of land had few slaves. Much like its neighboring states to the north, industrial enterprises were rapidly increasing, the number of successful family farms was on the rise, and there was a growing middle class. Giles County and its neighbors, situated in the rich agricultural region in central Tennessee, shared these features while still maintaining a few large traditional plantations. The region was enjoying an unprecedented wave of prosperity.

Tennessee had a tradition of pro-Union sentiment. During the 1832-33 Nullification Crises, it was native Tennessean and President of the United States Andrew Jackson that led the opposition to South Carolina and convinced the Palmetto State to back down from a threatened sesession.

Tennessee also played a key role in United States expansion policy. Under James Polk, another President with strong Tennessee connections, the state furnished substantial troops for the

Mexican War which made the United States a continental power. This action earned for Tennessee the sobriquet 'Volunteer State.'

This pro-Union stance was maintained throughout the turbulent days prior to the war until the bombardment of Fort Sumter. Tennessee had not become a 'rebel' state in spite of the efforts of its pro-secession governor, Isham Harris, to join the new Confederacy. In the 1860 presidential election, Tennesseans were solidly pro-Union. John C. Brown, the first commander of the 3rd Tennessee, and his brother Neill were among the conventioneers who took a pro-Union stand. Subsequently, when the states of the deep south began leaving the Union, the Tennessee legislature rejected Governor Harris' proposal that Tennessee do likewise, and called for a public referendum on the issue. John and Neill Brown were among the political leaders urging defeat of the proposal. The people of Tennessee decisively rejected secession by a vote of 91,803 to 24,794. Giles County, home of John and Neill Brown and five of the 3rd Tennessee's companies, voted down secession by a vote of 1831 to 28—a ratio of 65 to 1. Tennesseans of 1860 had a profound regard for the Federal Union and the freedoms and opportunities it provided.[1]

Everything changed after Fort Sumter's fall and Abraham Lincoln's subsequent call for 75,000 troops from all across the country to deal with "combinations too powerful to be suppressed by the ordinary course of judicial proceedings." The people of the 'Volunteer State' saw his action as an attempt to "overthrow ... their institutions and liberties" by the "Abolition States North." The call was deemed a usurpation of the protection guaranteed by the Federal Constitution they revered, and as interference with local and regional political prerogatives. It was perceived by Tennessee's political leaders as a partisan action by northern states to gain domination of the South, and was presented as such to the state's citizens. The use of the term "institutions" was really a code word for slavery. Since the state still contained a substantial slave population, there was a high degree of sensitivity to the anti-slavery rhetoric emanating from the North.[2]

Calvin Clack, later commander of Company A of the 3rd Tennessee, summed it up:

> Many and loud were the appeals she [Tennessee] made to the fanatical and aggressive North, but they were not heeded, and with a reckless determination to disregard the feelings and rights of the Southern People, the President of the United States called for seventy five thousand men to coerce the submission of the South to Federal authority.

He continued:

> The quota of Tennessee troops was called for; but her noble Governor Isham G. Harris, in obedience to the expressed will of her people, indignantly refused to obey this unconstitutional act, and to avert the now-certain danger to our liberties called for thirty thousand soldiers to defend the State against the aggression of the North.[3]

As a result, a Tennessee army was organized to defend the state against anticipated northern aggression. The fact that Lincoln had no intention whatsoever of interfering in Tennessee's internal affairs was somehow lost in the hysteria of the times.

A significant reason Tennessee was led out of the Union while states like Kentucky and Missouri were not was the subtle approach of the state's wily Governor Isham Harris. He led the state down the secession path a step at a time, avoiding precipitate action which might alienate the public, and providing time to build support for his political agenda. First, Harris asked the legislature to declare Tennessee an independent state, breaking off political relations with the federal government. Next, he began raising a state army and formed a 'military league' with the Confederacy. By the time the state got around to another secession referendum the momentum for separation was too great to overcome.[4]

The confusion of the times is evident in the narrative portions of the 3rd Tennessee Rollbook. Four officers indicated that their companies were organized for state defense while two said that their companies were organized to defend the Confederacy.

Neill S. Brown preceded his brother as governor of Tennessee. Neill and John were political partners before and after the war. However, during the war Neill's equivocation toward secession and the South's prosecution of the war earned him the emnity of Tennessee's sesessionist Governor Isham Harris.
Courtesy: Confederate Veteran

Inflammatory oratory was the norm. Men enlisted in the Tennessee Army on the spur of the moment after listening to stirring speeches delivered by prominent citizens. One future officer of the 3rd Tennessee, Nat Cheairs, succeeded in raising his Spring Hill company in only forty-eight hours.[5]

The two men most instrumental in recruiting troops for the 3rd Tennessee were John and Neill Brown, who had a late change of heart from their previous pro-Union sentiments. Both men canvassed Giles County and its neighbors urging the young men of the area to answer the call to the colors. Subsequently the old, ex-governor Neill continued his civilian pursuits including dabbling in Tennessee politics, while the younger John opted for military service.[6]

Many soldiers of the 3rd Tennessee never gave up their affection for the Union. Calvin Clack expressed the basic belief of the people in the Constitution and the Union in his legal justification for the state's actions:

> Tennessee ... did not believe that a state had the constitutional right to withdraw from the Union, but avowed most clearly the doctrine that the Federal government could not coerce a state, and that if this was threatened or attempted it would be the overt act on the part of the Federal government, which would justify any people in a change of allegiance and which a free and independent people should resist by declaring their independence of such government and adopting such other forms of government as suited them.[7]

Of course Clack's statement overlooks the fact that any government's authority is based ultimately upon its ability to 'coerce.' If the states had a constitutional obligation to remain in the Union, they also were obliged to recognize Federal authority in those areas where the Constitution declares Federal authority supreme. To deny the Federal government the power to enforce its laws was to deny it the ability to govern.

Most Union army soldiers enlisted to preserve the Union. It is ironic that when these men faced the 3rd Tennessee they sought to kill men who previously were as pro-Union as themselves. The rub was, who was going to do the enforcing?

Nowhere in the *3rd Tennessee Rollbook* is the issue of slavery raised except indirectly in references to "institutions" and to the "Abolitionist States." Even here the Tennesseans were more similar to their northern counterparts than they might have thought. The men of the 3rd might have been surprised at the viewpoint of one of their frequent battlefield opponents, Ira S. Doty, Private, 26th Iowa:

> I don't think that it is write for me to make my children orphans and my Wife Widow for the niggers and they cant make me believe that it is write I think that they will be worse off if they are set free than they are now and I think that it is wrong for hour army to cokes them from their homes.

Eventually the northern men came to favor abolition, but as a war measure designed to deprive the South of one of its major resources rather than for any esoteric concern for black people.[8]

Once Lincoln had made his call for troops, pro-sesession sentiment held sway in every public debate. Prospective 3rd Tennesseans witnessed harangues by some of the state's more famous personalities including Felix K. Zollicoffer, publisher of the *Nashville Banner.* Zollicoffer was one of the most popular and influential personages in Tennessee. He and his friends toured the state including the 3rd Tennessee home area "advising resistance to the Abolition programme, and making a common cause and common defense with the people of the Confederate States."[9]

Zollicoffer's Civil War involvement is a case history typical of many of the prominent citizens of the Confederacy. During the frantic days of April and May 1861 his enthusiasm for secession impelled him to do everything in his power to stir the passions of the people of Tennessee. On April 20 he was a visitor to Mount Pleasant, a community in Maury County. After speaking to the citizens, he and Mr. D.F. Wade, a prominent local resident, "submitted an enlistment roll for the signatures of such as wished to volunteer in the public service." According to Walter Jennings, recorder of these events, "several of the first young men of the place at once enrolled their names and exerted their influence to enlist a full company of select citizens."[10]

As a reward for this and other successful recruitment efforts, newspaperman Zollicoffer, despite a military background limited to a brief stint chasing Seminole warriors in Florida, was offered command of the entire Tennessee State Army. He refused, but later accepted a commission as brigadier general and commander of the District of East Tennessee. Zollicoffer had barely started acquiring the skills of a seasoned military officer when he was killed at the Battle of Mill Springs, Kentucky.[11]

The "first young men" Walter Jennings mentioned comprised a key element in how small units were organized in the Confederate Army. Recruiting efforts were rewarded universally by election to leadership positions in a company. For example, Jennings mentions D.F. Wade, James D. Moss, Johnston Long, and S.W. Steele as most active in the recruiting for Company C. The first three men were elected to captain, first lieutenant, and junior second lieutenant respectively within the company, while S.W. Steele received an appointment as captain of engineers under the famous Joseph Wheeler. Steele was an interesting character. Originally from Massachusetts, he had resided in Tennessee for only a short time when the crises came to a head. His siding with his adopted home caused him to be singled out for the "greatest commendation."[12]

'Prominent citizens' received more prestigious assignments. John C. Brown canvassed Giles County and beyond, encouraging enlistment in local units and support for the Confederacy. He was subsequently elected captain of Company A and then colonel of the 3rd Tennessee. Calvin Clack accompanied him in his travels and succeeded him as Company A commander. Eventually the 3rd was assigned to Simon Buckner's command. Buckner received his appointment as a result of his recruiting efforts in Kentucky.[13]

'Leading citizens' and the women at home also played an important part in the recruiting process. In order to motivate the young men to risk life and limb in military service, it was necessary for those staying at home to proffer an equivalent sacrifice and show proof of their commitment to the cause. This was done in a variety of ways. The consecration and presentation of the regimental or company flag was foremost. The banner had an aura of righteousness and fervor, and was usually lovingly sewn by the women of the community. It was presented with appropriate remarks and great ceremony by one who best represented the purity, nobility, and beauty attached to the unique symbol. The men from Mount Pleasant were "besought" by Miss Mattie Dobbins "never to abandon the glorious principles it [the flag] represented." In Elkton, Mary Abernathy gave almost the same speech. The flag adopted by the regiment was made by the ladies of Giles and Maury Counties. It was made of silk 5 x 10 feet on a field of blue. On it was sewn a knight in full armor riding a horse "who could never be conquered," and underneath the admonishment "My Life is Devoted." Also spelled out in gilt letters was "THIRD REGT TENN VOL." The flag is now the property of the Tennesse State Museum.[14]

The ladies also busied themselves sewing tents and making uniforms.

The first 3rd Tennessee battle flag as it appeated in 1898. The knight on horseback and part of the motto have been obliterated.

> A splendid gray jeans uniform was presented to each member by their friend, which was made up by the noble and self-sacrificing ladies of the county.
>
> It would be doing violence to the feelings of a gallant company of soldiers not to make especial mention of the noble part taken by the ladies of Mount Pleasant in providing a neat and comfortable outfit of clothing, etc..
>
> The citizens, the ladies taking the most active part, neatly uniformed the company and furnished it with good, substantial tents.[15]

Sometimes the cup overflowed, as in Elkton: "The citizens of the neighborhood subscribed so liberally toward raising funds to equip the company, that it was found necessary to collect only a part of the amount offered."[16]

Wealthier families took on the added responsibility of caring for soldiers' families:

> Among the older citizens too [were those] who were conspicuous for their liberality in donating means to uniform and equip the company, and provide for the support of such as would leave their families in a destitute condition.
>
> Mass meetings were held by the older citizens, and resolutions were adopted for the support of the families of the indigent who might join the company.[17]

Major benefactors for Maury County's Company C were members of the Polk Clan, most famous of whom was the Bishop General, Leonidas, one of the better-known officers in the Confederate Army. The bishop's brother, Lucius J., and another relative, George Polk, were singled out in the *3rd Tennessee Rollbook* for their generosity. Lucius J.'s son, Lucius Junior, compiled an impressive record serving as a brigadier general under the fabulous Patrick R. Cleburne. His other son, William, joined the 3rd Tennessee and served as the regimental sergeant major. He later transferred to the 48th Tennessee, serving as its adjutant, and would later rejoin his 3rd Tennessee comrades for their final battle. The Polk clan had large land holdings near Columbia and throughout Maury County.[18]

William Polk was appointed the 3rd Tennessee's sergeant major on May 17, 1861. He was wounded at Fort Donelson and sent home where he joined the 48th Tennessee as adjutant. He rejoined his old comrades near the end of the war as major of the 4th Consolidated Regiment Tennessee Infantry of which the old 3rd Tennessee comprised Company C. Young Polk was the son of Confederate General Lucius J. Polk, and nephew of the bishop general, Leonidas Polk. *Courtesy: Herb Peck, Jr.*

Other prominent citizens mentioned for their generosity were Monroe Giddens, J. and L. R. Kittrell, and Mrs. L. C. Brown from Spring Hill.[19]

Mrs. Brown made an unusual commitment in that she "proposed to arm it [Company E] with the Minnie rifle," the state-of-the-art British Enfield. In anticipation of being equipped with the latest in infantry small arms, and in honor of their benefactor, Mrs. Brown, Company E adopted the name 'Brown Rifles.' As things turned out, the 'Brown Smoothbore Muskets' would have been more appropriate, the Federal blockading fleet having a say in the matter. "[The rifles] were actually purchased in France, but were captured by the blockaders before reaching a Southern port." Company E did not receive rifled muskets until much later and they were not Enfields.[20]

Men of the 3rd Tennessee were issued U. S. Model 1816, .69 caliber smoothbore muskets, converted from the flintlock to the percussion ignition system. The photograph of 3rd Tennessean W.J. Coker includes this firearm. They were issued from the stocks at the state arsenal at Nashville and were carried until surrendered to the Yankees at Fort Donelson. At the time of issue the men of the 3rd believed that they would only be used for training purposes.[21]

Richmond eventually did provide some four thousand Enfields for the army in Kentucky, but most went to soldiers with no weapons whatsoever; the 3rd Tennessee received none.[22]

Mrs. Brown's failure to follow through on her pledge was not her fault. Some of the people either refused support because of their lack of conviction or they reneged on promises. Walter Jennings, wrote:

> Among those who were loudest in their exclamations and foremost in their zeal are the names of James M. Granberry, Martin L. Stockard, and Col. Webb Ridley, who, though abundantly wealthy and professedly patriotic, are said to have contributed less to the success of our cause, than almost any other three individuals in their community.[23]

Maury County must have had more than its share of backsliders, or else the officers from that particular county maintained stricter accountability on their home folk than did the other companies. "Mr. John McKissack, a wealthy planter of the vicinity, took an active part too, promising himself and all his means; but alas! his promises only were contributed."[24]

The listing of these individuals by name in the official history of the 3rd Tennessee indicates the strong level of betrayal the soldiers felt.

Notes for Chapter 2

1 James M. Patton, *Unionism and Reconstruction in Tennessee*, p. 12. *Nashville Banner*, Feb. 22, 1861. Margaret Butler, *The Life of John C. Brown*, pp. 9-10

2 Bruce Catton, *This Hallowed Ground*, p. 19. According to the *Giles County Census, 1860*, about half the population of Giles County was Negro.

3 Rollbook, p. 13.

4 An excellent description of the state's road to war is presented in Thomas Connelly's *Tennessee in the Civil War.*

5 Nathaniel F. Cheairs Memoir.

6 P.M. Hamer, *Tennessee, A History, 1673-1932*, Vol. I, p. 516. Margaret Butler, *The Life of John C. Brown*, p. 6.

7 Rollbook, p. 13.

8 Ira S. Doty Papers. James M. McPherson, *For Cause & Comrades*, pp. 125-127.

9 Rollbook, p. 37.

10 *Ibid.*

11 Horn, *The Army of Tennessee*, pp. 69, 440.

12 Rollbook, pp. 37-38.

13 *Ibid.*, pp. 15, 116.

14 *Ibid*, pp. 38, 116. C.H. Smart, *Confederate Veteran* (hereafter referred to as *CV*) Vol. IV, p. 117. *Thomas H. Deavenport Diary*, p. 11.

15 Rollbook, pp. 14, 38, 59.

16 *Ibid.*, p. 116.

17 *Ibid.*, pp 38, 59.

18 *Ibid.*, p. 116.

19 *Ibid.*, p. 38.

20 *Ibid.*, p. 59.

21 *Ibid.*, p. 117.

22 Horn, *op. cit.*, p.58.

23 Rollbook, p. 38.

24 *Ibid.* p. 59.

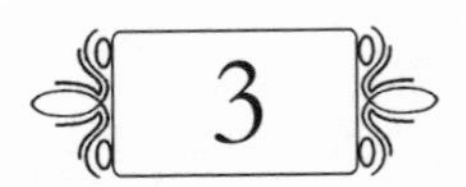

OFF TO WAR

On September 19, 1861, the 3rd Tennessee suffered its first casualty due to enemy action. The 3rd had been dispatched to Bowling Green, Kentucky, in a race against the Yankee forces poised to the north to grab as much of the state as possible. The regiment arrived in Bowling Green by rail. As the train pulled in to the station there were no Union soldiers in sight, but:

> As the cars moved up to the Round House, the Federal flag was seen waving from its top. Our men became much excited and commenced firing at it when Private Thos. Wren, contrary to orders, climbed upon the cupola, and while the firing was still going on, tore down the Stars and Stripes, but on returning, fell and was so severely injured that he has ever since been a cripple.[1]

The unfortunate Private Wren ended up in a hospital in Nashville and was subsequently captured there by Major General Don Carlos Buell's Union forces and imprisoned at Camp Chase, Ohio. Instead of becoming the quintessential hero by capturing an enemy flag, he is remembered today for an ignominious accident. Wren must have been something of a maverick: he had already been demoted from third sergeant back to private for reasons not given. In September of 1862, he was exchanged, traded for a Union prisoner, and immediately mustered out of the Army for disability. Thus ended a brief but colorful military career.[2]

The overwrought reaction of the 3rd Tennessee to the sight of an enemy flag was precipitated by the intense excitement with which the young and unsophisticated men had been dealing over the previous months. Beginning with the organization of the companies in their home towns, they had been the recipients of continuous praise and adulation at every stop. The local belles adored them in Lynnville on May 16 when the 3rd was mustered as a regiment, and a new batch took up the torch in Nashville at their swearing in on May 17. Civil War veterans frequently mentioned this adulation as the high point of their military experience, sometimes of their entire lives.[3]

The desire to live up to the heroic image bestowed upon them by their friends, families, and sweethearts was a strong one. However, before they could meet the "hated foe" the new recruits had to be transported to training camps to learn the myriad skills required for nineteenth century warfare. From exquisite pleasure derived from the adoring sighs of the women, the men plunged into the boring and menial chores necessary to turn them into soldiers. Not everyone was able to deal with it: Lieutenant John Ellett of Company C, "remembering too forcibly 'the girl he left behind him' declined to be mustered into service, and tendered his resignation." Officers, unlike enlisted men, could leave the army simply by resigning.[4]

The first disappointment for the 3rd Tennessee came right after their swearing in when they were marched to the capital to receive their arms. They were "furnished with smoothbore muskets, and the discontent was only quieted by the impression which was spread abroad, that the muskets were to be used only for the purposes of drill, and that so soon as active operations should commence, we should be furnished with minnie [sic] rifles—a promise that was

Private W.J. Coker enlisted in Company B at Lynnville, Tennessee, in April 1861. Coker fought in all of the regiment's major actions during 1862 and 1863 and was wounded at Chickamauga. He went AWOL from the regiment at Missionary Ridge and did not return. Coker's dress exemplifies the typical 3rd Tennessee uniform and equipment issue including an obsolete U.S. smoothbore musket converted from flintlock to percussion.
Courtesy: Herb Peck, Jr.

never fulfilled, until long afterward." Enoch Hancock of Company A wrote,

> We are not verry well prepared for fighting at present as we have nothing but the old fashioned muskets to fight with. We had them boxed up once and sent to Nashville expecting to get improved arms but failed in getting them which came as a great dissatisfaction among the troops.[5]

The 'Minie rifle,' as it is properly spelled, was the armament of choice during the Civil War. It was preferably an Enfield or Springfield rifled musket with three grooves twisting through the length of the barrel to impart a stabilizing spin (much like a football is spun) to a hollow-based cylindrical lead bullet, the 'minie' ball. 'Minie' balls, named for their inventor, French officer Capt. Claude E. Minie, had hollow bases and conical rings, and expanded when fired to engage the rifling of the barrel, making them far more accurate at a much greater range than the smoothbore. A 'minie' ball was slow, heavy and large, 0.58 inches in diameter and one inch long. It could wrench off an arm or a leg, and was deadly to about five hundred yards.

Lack of proper weaponry was only the beginning of obstacles faced by the 3rd Tennessee. Finding qualified drill instructors was another, and the officers scrambled to make themselves proficient. They dug into *Hardee's Tactics* and rapidly achieved considerable success:

> On the evening of May 17th, we pitched our tents at Camp Cheatham [in Robertson County], and the next morning our life in camp commenced in earnest. In a few days we moved our quarters across the railroad, and laid out our first regular camp according to army regulations. We commenced squad drill, immediately, and so soon as the rudiments of tactics were learned, we began company drill, and after five weeks' hard work, we attained the proud position of taking our places in battalion drill.[6]

It was at Camp Cheatham, on May 25th, that the 3rd was joined by its most famous recruit, Jake Donelson. Jake was brought to camp by First Lieutenant Jerome B. McCanless of Company H.

Jake was a 'game rooster' that McCanless fully intended to eat until he discovered that the bird had certain warrior like qualities. Once it was clear he was a "born fighter," the regiment "was glad to offer him enlistment and immunity from every danger, save the enemy's bullets." From that point on Jake accompanied the regiment everywhere while perched on someone's knapsack. As we shall see, Jake was as brave in battle as the best men in the outfit.[7]

Having been elected to their positions of leadership by virtue of popularity or because of their recruiting efforts, the officers of the 3rd Tennessee were not military men, and hardly prepared to train anyone else in the rudiments of drill except for two notable exceptions.

Thomas M. Gordon was an 'Old Army' man. He joined a Tennessee volunteer company when he was only seventeen, and fought with Andrew Jackson in the Creek Wars. He was credited with saving Jackson's command at one point by holding everyone together when they were lost in the Alabama wilderness and on the verge of starvation. He also served in the Mexican War, dropping out of college to serve alongside B.F. Cheatham who was to become famous as one of Tennessee's Civil War fighting generals.

Gordon organized Company B for the 3rd Tennessee in Lynnville. Later the whole regiment mustered on Gordon's lawn. Since the regiment's leadership was selected by election, the popular John C. Brown was elected colonel despite Gordon's credentials. The regiment did elect Gordon to the lieutenant colonel position however, and between Gordon's long time military experience and Brown's penchant for strict discipline it was not long before the 3rd Tennessee began to look like a crack outfit. Gordon soon assumed command of the regiment when Brown was elevated to brigade command.[8]

The other person undoubtedly helpful to the training of the 3rd Tennessee was a young man named Thomas M. Tucker. He was a former student of the Nashville Military School and had some expertise in drill and other technical and disciplinary skills. Tucker was elected Second Lieutenant of Company E and John C. Brown, within a day of his election as colonel, brought Tucker to his side

Thomas M.L. Gordon was elected lieutenant colonel at the regiment's organization. Gordon was the 3rd Tennessee's most experienced officer, having fought in the Creek and Mexican Wars. He was badly wounded in the arm at Fort Donelson and was later captured and severely mistreated. His imprisonment ruined his health and once released he sat out the remainder of the war at home. Gordon is wearing the blue Tennessee militia uniform.

Courtesy: Confederate Veteran

as regimental adjutant. Much of Brown's military success can probably be ascribed to Tucker's influence and skill with a pen since he would author all of Brown's official correspondence. Tucker would be one of only two fatalities suffered by the 3rd Tennessee in their intense fight at Chickasaw Bayou.[9]

The 3rd Tennessee encamped at Camp Cheatham for two months. It was brigaded with the 1st and 32nd Tennessee regiments all under Brown who was appointed acting brigade commander. On July 1 the 1st Tennessee departed for the Virginia theater, and the 3rd Tennessee moved into their old camp.[10]

On July 26, the 3rd took the rails to Camp Trousdale in Sumner County, Tennessee. It was at Camp Trousdale that the 3rd Tennessee was attacked by the biggest killer in the Civil War, disease. The regiment suffered from all the common camp illness, but the most devastating were measles and typhoid fever. In addition to 85 deaths there were 164 men absent sick prior to the battle at Fort Donelson. Camp health was in large part a function of army discipline, and here Brown might have been somewhat lax. He would be chastised in early 1863 for poor camp drainage. Some 264 men, twenty-two percent of the regiment's original strength, were unavailable for combat before the first shots were fired.[11]

Camp life seemed hard to the men of the 3rd Tennessee, but their perspective would change with the horrors of the battlefield and the misery of prison life. As Walter Jennings said later, "At these two camps our soldier life was a continual holiday, but we were then too fresh from the comforts and luxuries of home to realize it." Among other things, the troops were treated to nightly dances.[12]

On August 7 the regiment was transferred from state service to the service of the Confederate States of America. Though the *Rollbook* makes only casual mention of this event, it was of considerable importance in its impact on the future of the 3rd Tennessee. The original commitment made by the men of the 3rd had been to protect Tennessee from Yankee invaders. Now they were expected to pledge their lives and treasure to a broader and much less personal goal. With an aggressive Federal government, and with Isham

Harris constantly fanning the fires of secession, public opinion had at last shifted in favor of joining the Confederacy. A canvass of the troops resulted in a unanimous vote in favor of joining the rapidly growing Southern army.

Military objectives were expanded accordingly. At various times the 3rd Tennessee would spend time "repelling invaders" from Tennessee, Mississippi, Georgia, and North Carolina. Confederate Conscription Acts would soon follow making it almost impossible to get out of the army.[13]

At Camp Trousdale the regiment began losing strength at a troubling rate. It was a problem that the 3rd Tennessee was never able to solve. It was a problem that plagued the rest of the Army of Tennessee, and Lee's army as well. In addition to deaths caused by disease, Southern soldiers tended to simply wander home, especially when ill or hurt. Soldiers were commonly carried on the rolls as absent sick or wounded for a considerable period of time before they were listed as AWOL (absent without leave) or having deserted. Those who left usually did not return. Typically the regiment would be missing 50% to 60% of its strength at any one time.[14]

There was a systemic reason for the Confederate Army's inability to keep these men. No standardized communications were ever established between the Confederate hospitals and medical service detachments, and the combat units operating in the field. When a sick or wounded soldier was released for medical treatment a notation was made in the regimental rollbook, and the regiment had to assume that accountability for the man would be taken over by the medical people. This did not always happen. Once he had recovered and had been released from medical care a soldier was expected to make his way back to his unit on his own, no matter where it might be. The temptation was strong to desert, especially later in the war. Many men did just that, returning to loved ones whom many felt needed them more than did the army. Meanwhile, other soldiers joined nearby Confederate units simply because it was more convenient, and because the army tolerated it.[15]

The other factor accounting for the rapid decrease in size of most Confederate units was the frightful battlefield attrition. Confederate field commanders, especially during the early part of the war, had an affinity for the attack, and paid a heavy price for it. The Confederacy was bled white until trench warfare was employed late in the war during the Atlanta and Petersburg campaigns. However, with the assignment of John Bell Hood to army command during the summer of 1864, the Confederates returned to assault tactics which effectively sounded the death knell for the 3rd Tennessee, and the Army of Tennessee itself.

Most Confederate infantry regiments were fighting units with a high proportion of them participating in at least one major battle. The 3rd Tennessee fought hard in five, in addition to the grinding Atlanta campaign. In two of these battles the 3rd suffered a loss of more than a third of its strength: thirty-six percent at Raymond and thirty-five percent at Chickamauga.[16]

Near the end of the war, at the start of Sherman's Atlanta campaign, the 3rd Tennessee could muster fewer men than the equivalent of three of its ten original companies, less than 20% of its initial strength. By that time the survivors were a tough bunch, however, and acquitted themselves well there.[17]

On September 18, 1861, however, the future still looked bright to the men of the 3rd Tennessee. As the regiment set off for Bowling Green, Kentucky, it had no idea it was about to become a pawn in a deadly game of cat-and-mouse which would start the Confederacy well down the road to defeat.

Notes For Chapter 3

1 Rollbook, p. 117.
2 *Ibid.*, p. 108.
3 *Ibid.*, p. 116.
4 *Ibid.*, p. 38-39.
5 *Ibid.*, p. 117. Enoch Hancock Letters.
6 Enoch Hancock Letters.
7 Buford McKinney, *CV*, Vol. V, p. 419.

8 *CV*, Vol. IX, pp. 417-418.

9 Rollbook, pp. 6, 59, 142.

10 Rollbook, pp. 116-119. While many officers recorded the events of the regiment's early days, the most meticulous record was made by Company K's commander, Flavel C. Barber. He wrote a detailed report for the Rollbook, and maintained his own series of private diaries.

11 Larry Daniel, *Soldiering in the Army of Tennessee*, p. 73. Rollbook, compiled from company records.

12 Rollbook, p. 39. Daniel, *op. Cit.,* p. 84.

13 Rollbook, pp. 13, 15, 117.

14 *Ibid.*, based on analysis of company records.

15 Bell Wiley, *The Life of Johnny Reb*, pp. 142-143. Connelly, *Autumn of Glory*, pp. 6-8.

16 Rollbook, pp. 120, 343-344. Thomas H. Deavenport Diary, pp. 22-23.

17 Tennessee Civil War Centennial Commission, *Tennesseans in the Civil War*, Part I, p. 182.

SOJOURN IN KENTUCKY

For several months prior to the 3rd Tennessee's journey to Bowling Green, large Union and Confederate armies had been glaring at each other from opposite sides of the green hills of Kentucky. The Bluegrass State had declared itself neutral in the forlorn hope that it could somehow keep itself out of the coming conflagration.

The man in charge of the Rebel forces in west Tennessee was the Episcopalian Bishop turned Confederate general Leonidas Polk. After a time he could stand the tension no longer, and lunged across the border without bothering to consult Richmond. He seized the strategic heights along the Mississippi River at Columbus, thereby managing to alienate much of the Kentucky citizenry and placing the Rebel authorities in a dilemma. Unless additional troops were sent forward to protect his rear, his position would be quickly cut off. Thus, the 3rd Tennessee and the rest of their brigade were sent to Bowling Green.[1]

The arrival of the 3rd Tennessee in that city placed it for the first time in 'enemy' territory. The Kentuckians viewed the regiment as anything but liberators. The first sign of trouble was that United States flag flying high above the Bowling Green Roundhouse. This was the one Private Wren, to his great chagrin, had failed to deal with in proper Rebel style. In addition, "A large number of citizens in and around Bowling Green, and among them a majority of the most influential, favored the old government, and were hostile to the movements of the Confederates, and at first expressed much opposition to the company being placed on duty in town."

The men of the regiment eventually earned the respect of the locals because of their "gentlemanly as well as ... soldierly bearing" according to Company A's commander, Calvin Clack. It was a difficult beginning for these young men who saw themselves as liberators.[2]

Four days after their arrival at Bowling Green an expedition of over two-thousand men, including Companies A, D, E, and K of the 3rd Tennessee, was organized by General Simon B. Buckner to "drive back, or if possible, to capture the enemy, who were reported scouring that portion of Kentucky." According to Flavel Barber of Company K the purpose of the expedition was "to break up the Home Guard camps in that region of Kentucky south of the Green River." The Home Guard companies were poorly trained militia units and hardly represented a challenge for the well-trained and well-organized Tennessee troops. Buckner ordered the men to "move with three days' cooked rations," but then kept them in the field for an additional nine days, moving constantly away from their source of supply. The 3rd Tennessee's four companies "made the whole expedition without tents or cooking utensils [and] ate green beef broiled on coals, and frequently without salt, and flour bread without grease or salt, cooked upon ramrods, or upon sticks held over a fire." The march also "caused the loss of many high heeled boots and white shirts."[3]

The expedition marched to Greenville where they destroyed some locks and dams on the Green River which connected with the Ohio River to the north and provided a convenient water route to the Bowling Green area. It then proceeded to Hopkinsville, where the men boarded railway cars for a comfortable ride back to Bowling

Green. At the time, the 3rd Tennesseans felt this march was "little inferior to any march on record in our country."

It probably did not greatly exceed a distance of one hundred miles stretched over a twelve-day period. Later marches undertaken by the regiment would make this one seem like a romp.[4]

While Calvin Clack, claimed "100 muskets captured from the citizens ... which had been furnished them by the enemy," R.B. McCormick of Company E claimed that only a "few arms" were taken. Though Simon Buckner can be blamed for much of the needless suffering during this campaign, it was a harbinger of worse days to come.[5]

One of the 3rd Tennesseans making this march was a new volunteer just off the train from Pulaski. Thomas H. Deavenport, Pulaski's Methodist minister, had spent several months consumed with guilt at having stayed behind as the regiment marched off to war. He finally enlisted and quickly set off for the front by train. Upon his arrival in Bowling Green, he immediately sought Calvin Walker's Company A which was just then preparing to begin the expedition already described. Deavenport:

> Fifty were to go from Capt. C.H. Walker's company. I had gone to join that company and asked to be permitted to be one of that number. He [Walker] hesitated. I was pale, weighed ninety-five pounds. At length he consented and carried me to the surgeon, Dr. Stout. He examined me, said perhaps I would do. Col. Brown was called, looked at me, said I was very delicate but perhaps would make a soldier, mustered me into the service, and gave me a gun, knapsack, haversack and canteen. Thus I was fully equipped for the war. My comrades all laughed at the idea of my going on a tramp.[6]

Deavenport's diary contains some worthwhile impressions of this first ever field campaign of the 3rd Tennessee. First the march:

> About 11 (a.m.) the bugle sounded, we fell in, marched through the town and halted until late in the evening when the order 'Forward march' was given. We marched 11 miles over a very rough hill, the last three or four miles in the rain. I was

very much wearied but said nothing. As we pulled up a long hill through the mud I heard the captain say he was almost broken down, this helped me considerably for I thought I had company. At length the command was given 'Halt, unsling knapsacks and go to bed,' in the rain, no tent, no dinner, no supper. This seemed like soldiering it in earnest, as was rather hard for the first night. It was a considerable change to say the least of it, for I had come out of a comfortable house and bed. I never slept more soundly.

Next the excitement of pending battle:

We built our fires and had commenced preparing supper when the alarm was given, and quickly over the camp was heard 'Fall in.' We were soon at the proper place and in a few minutes the Colonel [Benjamin H. Helm, of the 18th Tennessee] came round, told that we would in all probability be attacked before day by superior numbers, that we must sleep in line, accouterments on, and gun by our side, all lights must be extinguished, thus I lay down dinnerless and supperless and was soon asleep. No enemy came.

The bill of fare:

The next day was Sabbath. The enemy being reported stronger than ourselves, we waited for reinforcements and consequently did not march, but cooked several day's rations. Here was my first experience in the culinary art in camp. It was an art. Cake about six inches in diameter and about one and a half thick, no salt or grease, and made of flour. In addition to all that it was burnt black ... .

We camped in a field of corn in full roasting ears. We had marched all day without eating and the rations were far behind, so we charged the field and ate the last ear. The night was cold and we burnt all the [fence] rails, we also ate a potato patch.

Lastly, the enemy:

> We stopped near Hopkinsville. We had one man killed and one man wounded that day, we killed two, captured a few and some guns. The next day we marched through Hopkinsville and camped near the Fair Grounds. The people, particularly the ladies, seemed delighted to see us. The enemy that disbanded at our coming was raised there.[7]

Deavenport served in the ranks through the Fort Donelson battles and later became chaplain at the regiment's reorganization in September 1862. We shall hear from him frequently.

About the time the 3rd Tennessee began active operations in Kentucky in September 1861, General Albert Sidney Johnston assumed command of the Confederate Western Department. The 3rd Tennessee's fate was now in his hands.

Johnston arrived amidst great celebration and high hopes. He was regarded throughout the South as one of the finest military men in the world. However, his military career up to the Civil War has been described as "undistinguished." Despite intermittent military service since 1828, he had never been tested in the hard arena of real combat. Despite a charasmatic personality and a close friendship with Jefferson Davis, Johnston's ability to handle a large field command was unknown.[8]

Johnston's appointment led to some momentous consequences. During his eight-month stint as a Civil War commander he lost some 25,000 square miles of Confederate territory to Federal control; he lost the South's chief gunpowder works and other critical industrial facilities in Nashville; he lost the vital food and iron production areas of central Tennessee to the Federals; and worst of all, he lost a total of 20,699 of the South's best men, including the entire 3rd Tennessee, killed, wounded, or captured in two mismanaged battles. History has generally been kind to Johnston because of his heroic death at Shiloh. The hard reality is his appointment was an unmitigated disaster for the Confederacy.[9]

For a while Johnston was hugely successful at keeping the Federals at bay. He dispatched contingents into the countryside to cow the locals and to keep William T. Sherman's forces in a state of anxiety. However, the Green River expedition was to be the 3rd Tennessee's sole foray outside the Bowling Green defenses for the next five months. For the duration "the boys learned to perfection the many uses of the axe, pick shovel and spade in the erection of forts, stockades, etc."[10]

Johnston had decided to turn Bowling Green into a strong point on his defensive line. It had some strategic value, lying at the intersection of the rail lines leading to Memphis and Nashville, and it was situated behind the Barren River which provided a natural obstacle to Federal advance. The problem was, it was only one of many important locations on his 400-mile-long defensive line.

Johnston adopted a hands-off approach for most of his area of responsibility except for the Bowling Green defenses. Subordinate commanders were assigned specific geographic areas to defend, but how these areas were to be defended was left to them. Johnston endorsed many decisions of questionable value, never taking firm control.

Leonidas Polk decided to fortify the bluffs at Columbus, Kentucky. He was convinced that the Federals would advance down the Mississippi River and that the area east from Columbus could largely be ignored even though he was responsible for its defense.

Felix Zollicoffer was assigned the defense of the Cumberland Gap area. This was an extremely important position since it protected the Confederacy's main east-west rail line. The terrain was extremely defensible and a competent commander could hold it easily with a relatively small force.

Isham Harris initially was responsible for defending the river routes into central Tennessee, and began construction of Forts Henry and Donelson on the Tennessee and Cumberland Rivers. This was a potential soft spot, but the officers who should have realized this were busy with other things. Johnston was fixated on Bowling Green, while Polk and Tennessee General Gideon Pillow began a feud over whether to take the offense against Federal forces concentrating at nearby Paducah, Kentucky, now being led by U.S. Grant. This petty bickering became a full-time activity for these two men. The opportunity to extend the defenses of the Tennessee and Cumberland Rivers forward into Kentucky in conjunction with Polk's progress into the state was not given serious consideration.[11]

As a result of Confederate inaction, Federal forces continued to accumulate unchallenged for five months of relative inactivity in Johnston's theater. Johnston believed he had insufficient equipment to make an offensive campaign. He also seemed unable or unwilling to make the hard choices required of an outnumbered defender. He felt he owed protection to the entire western Confederacy and was not comfortable economizing forces and sacrificing ground in one sector in order to defeat an enemy in another. In his attempt to defend all, he failed to defend any.

So the 3rd Tennessee continued to improve a line of defense that no intelligent Yankee (there were a few!) would ever attempt to assault. And they continued to drill:

> Col. John C. Brown [was] full of the magnitude of the work ahead, and determined that his regiment, composed of picked material, should not be excelled. Under his instruction, and with the cooperation of his able line officers, the regiment soon became noted for its fine appearance, proficiency in drill, and military bearing. Company, regimental, brigade, and division drill was the order of the day at Bowling Green ... .[12]

The rapidly growing field works and the well-drilled regiments at Bowling Green provided admiring visitors a sense of security. Johnston continued to bask in the limelight, while at Paducah U.S. Grant prepared to smash Johnston's line.

Meanwhile, at Forts Henry and Donelson work proceeded at a leisurely rate. The new man in charge, Lloyd Tilghman, spent most of his time in Nashville where he could enjoy the social life and receive the adulation of the local belles.

Finally, in January 1862, Johnston began to receive indicators that an attack might occur via the Rivers Tennessee or Cumberland and to his utter dismay discovered that the forts were nowhere near ready for defense. He began a last-ditch effort to complete the fortifications and shifted troops in that direction. As part of this force, the 3rd Tennessee moved to Russellville, Kentucky, on January 21.[13]

On February 5th, 1862, terror struck the heart of Albert Sidney Johnston. For the first time he realized how desperate the situation had become. The Federals had built a fierce new fleet of iron-clad gunboats over the previous six months, and the hulking monsters were now approaching Fort Henry on the Tennessee River.

On February 6th the Federal attack was launched by Union Officers U.S. Grant and Andrew Foote, by both land and water. The Confederate soldiers did not flinch. Fighting from a poorly chosen position partially inundated by the rising Tennessee River, they fought valiently from the river batteries while most of the infantry were sent to Fort Donelson to escape capture. After the surrender, Grant immediately sent two gunboats upstream to wreck the railroad bridge connecting Polk's and Johnston's forces, and to spread terror all the way from central Tennessee to the Alabama border.

The Confederates' only hope to retrieve the situation was for Johnston to act decisively. Instead, he equivocated. Rather than concentrating all available resources to defeat Grant and close the breach in his line, he sent only part of his forces to Fort Donelson and evacuated the rest to points further south. Rather than take personal command of the Donelson force, Johnston took himself and his remaining Bowling Green troops to Nashville. The force he sent to Fort Donelson was not sufficient to secure victory; it could only delay the enemy while Johnston established a new defensive line somewhere else.

The entire Tennessee defensive line was evaporating at the first touch of the enemy.

One of the first regiments arriving to reinforce the garrison at Fort Donelson, two days after Fort Henry's fall, was the 3rd Tennessee. Unlike Johnston, the men were anxious for battle, and knew exactly what they wanted to accomplish: to "meet the enemy, who were at that time threatening the fort, and also the Capitol of our native state." They were ready, inured to camp life and anxious for the conflict." Despite the odds against them, the Confederate troops were more than ready to take on Grant's blue horde; and as things turned out it would take some extraordinary bungling by the Confederate command, from Johnston on down, to prevent a successful delaying action, if not an outright Confederate victory.[14]

Notes for Chapter 4

1 Horn, *The Army of Tennessee*, p.44.

2 Rollbook, p.15.

3 *Ibid.*, p.118.

4 *Ibid.*, p.15.

5 *Ibid.*, pp. 15, 60.

6 Thomas H. Deavenport Diary, p.3.

7 *Ibid.*, pp.3-6.

8 Horn, *The Army of Tennessee*, pp.52-54. Charles P. Roland, *Albert Sidney Johnston: Soldier of Three Republics*, pp.132-136. Steven E. Woodworth, *Jefferson Davis and His Generals: The Failure of Confederate Command in the West,* pp.46-49.

9 Thomas L. Connelly, "The Johnston Mystique" in *The Campaigns for Fort Donelson. Battles and Leaders of the Civil War*, Vol. I, pp.429, 537.

10 Rollbook, p.69.

11 Connelly, *op. Cit.* Connelly, *Army of the Heartland*, pp.62-63.

12 Lindsley, *Military Annals of Tennessee*, p.176.

13 Horn, *op. cit.* pp.76-77, 80. *Rollbook*, p.118.

14 Rollbook, p.48. *Military Annals of Tennessee*, p.176.

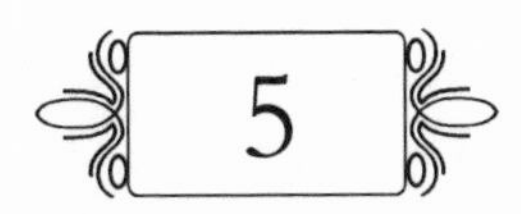

OFF TO SEE THE ELEPHANT

At Fort Donelson the 3rd Tennessee "met for the first time, and on their native soil, the hated foe," wrote Walter Jennings. Captain George Jones of Company F commented:

> It was here for the first time that they were to meet the hated foe in deadly combat; it was here for the first time that they saw the flash of an enemy's gun, or heard the deafening roar of his artillery. And it was here too for the first time they saw that much dreaded monster, a Yankee gunboat, but they saw all and heard all unawed, and I am proud to say that the coolness and courage which they exhibited while engaged with the enemy far surpassed the highest expectations of both officers and friends.[1]

This description applied to all the Confederate regiments participating in the Fort Donelson fight. The river batteries successfully shot Union Flag Officer Foote's gunboat fleet to pieces; the usually superior Federal field artillery was out gunned by its Confederate opponents; and the always superb Confederate infantry completely imposed its will on Grant's midwesterners wherever it chose.

Then the Confederates surrendered!

This incredible outcome had its beginning with Albert Sidney Johnston's indecision and flight south. Johnston's subordinate, Gideon Pillow, led the first relief troops into Fort Donelson, and it was left to him to make all necessary decisions. With reports of the Federal success at Fort Henry rapidly flowing in, Pillow quickly became obsessed with the gunboat threat. He plunged into the construction of river defenses at the exclusion of everything else.

Reinforcements for Pillow began with Buckner's Second Division of the Central Army of Kentucky, including the 3rd Tennessee, rendezvousing with General John Floyd's division at Cumberland City, Tennessee, ten miles upstream from Fort Donelson. Floyd, former Secretary of War in the Buchanan administration, but a novice at commanding troops, proposed "operating from some point on the railroad west of that position [Cumberland City] in the direction of Fort Donelson or Fort Henry, thus maintaining his communications with Nashville by way of Charlotte." This was an excellent plan, not only as a way to conduct a delaying operation while Johnston brought his troops out of Kentucky, which both Floyd and Buckner thought was the operational objective of the expedition, but also for defending Fort Donelson.[2]

On February 11th Buckner arrived by steamer at Dover, the small town adjacent to Fort Donelson, to confer with Pillow. Buckner told Pillow that the military amateur, John Floyd, was considering using his infantry in a flexible defense oriented toward the protection of the strategic prize, Nashville. Pillow, the military 'professional,' rushed upstream for a conference with Floyd and convinced the old politician that the proper course of action was to concentrate all forces at Fort Donelson. According to Buckner, Pillow "did not expect an immediate advance of the enemy, and regarded their approach from the direction of Fort Henry as impracticable." Pillow also instructed his cavalry chief, the indomitable Nathan B. Forrest, "in no event to bring on an engagement should the enemy approach in force." Pillow might as well have instructed the sun not to shine as tell Forrest not to fight.[3]

From a military viewpoint, Pillow's instructions defied explanation. They would have reduced to a minimum the time available to improve the fort's defenses, provided a secure march route to the enemy, and all but eliminated any warning time of an impending attack. Opportunity to attrite and disrupt the enemy force during their march toward Fort Donelson would have been forfeited.

Fortunately for Pillow and the troops, Buckner and Forrest chose to ignore this inane order. As the Confederates conferred, Union General U.S. Grant, despite a barrage of cautionary messages from his boss, General Henry Halleck, was already well underway with Pillow's "impracticable" ten-mile march across the neck of land separating Forts Henry and Donelson. Grant much preferred asking forgiveness to asking permission. He also understood that conducting military operations entails taking a few risks.

Buckner wrote: "During the morning [of February 12th] Forrest reported the enemy advancing in force, with the view of enveloping our line of defense, and for a time he was engaged with his usual gallantry in heavy skirmishing with them, at one time driving one of their battalions back upon their artillery." One is left to contemplate what Forrest might have accomplished had an infantry force been made available to him.[4]

With Pillow absent conferring with Floyd, Buckner was left to deal with Grant. Buckner did not share Pillow's inclination to allow the enemy to advance unopposed. He worked furiously to bring Donelson's land side defenses, almost completely ignored by Pillow, to a proper state of readiness. Floyd and Pillow now had one of those golden opportunities every combat commander dreams about. Spread out before them for ten miles was an enemy column in loose marching order virtually inviting attack. Buckner's and Floyd's forces were squarely on the enemy's flank, and for the time being outnumbered their enemies.

However, Gideon Pillow had it in his mind that the proper way to defend a piece of terrain was to sit on it. He proceeded to convince Floyd of the wisdom that tactic, and they immediately ordered all forces into the Fort Donelson defenses, placing the entire force under siege. The Battle of Fort Donelson became a struggle for survival for the Confederate Army of Kentucky.

Most of Buckner's force, including the 3rd Tennessee, had arrived at Fort Donelson before Buckner. The men of the 3rd underwent an ordeal just getting to the battlefield. First they were crammed into boxcars for the rail portion of the trip. Then they were frozen on the open decks of the steamboat during their ride down the Cumberland River. Many men migrated to the steamer's boiler room for some relief despite the filth and noise.[5]

John C. Brown was placed in command of Buckner's Third Brigade, composed of the 3rd, 18th, and 32nd Tennessee regiments, which began arriving very late in the evening on February 8th. The shock of arriving on a strange field at night was lessened somewhat by the magnanimous reception provided by the 53rd Tennessee.

> [Arriving at Fort Donelson] hungry and without tents, the weather being cold and unpleasant, we were received with many expressions of joy by our countrymen of the 53rd Tenn. And welcomed by their commander, Col. A.H. Abernathy, to the hospitality of their camp. Our fellow soldiers divided with us their provisions and beds, and contributed in every way to our comfort.[6]

On Pillow's arrival Brown also assumed command of half of Buckner's Second Brigade, the 14th Mississippi and the 41st Tennessee. The remainder of the Second Brigade was assigned to Pillow. The army was divided into two wings, Pillow on the left and Buckner on the right. Brown commanded all of Buckner's regiments except for the 2nd Kentucky situated on the far right of the Confederate line.[7]

The 3rd was positioned on a large hill south of the river fort. It was placed second from the left in Brown's line, the 32nd Tennessee on its immediate left and the 18th Tennessee on its right. The Tennessee troops plunged into an effort to make their position as formidable as possible. Brown wrote: I commenced at once the construction of rifle pits and forming abatis by felling timber, but the supply of tools was wholly inadequate, and before the works were scarcely completed the enemy appeared in our front on Wednesday, the 12th, about 12m.[8]

According to the 3rd Tennessee's D.G. Alexander, "We went to work and soon had some pretty fair rifle pits which we improved and strengthened at every opportunity during the siege. We remained in the ditches and near them, cutting away the timber, and preparing for the struggle from Sunday the 8th until Saturday morning the 15th."[9] Flavel Barber added that the fallen trees formed "an abattis which was almost impenetrable."[10]

Despite the lack of time and tools, Buckner was pleased with the result. He said: "The work on my line was prosecuted with energy and was urged forward as rapidly as the limited number of tools would permit."[11]

Brown's line was supported by two batteries of field artillery: Rice E. Graves' battery on the brigade's left flank, and Thomas K. Porter's battery "occupying the advanced salient" in the brigade's center. These batteries, along with Frank Maney's battery on a small hill to the brigade's left, were to bear the brunt of battle for the Confederate center and left for several days.[12]

These Confederate field artillery batteries were elite outfits. They were manned by the best and brightest southern society could offer. Graves' Battery, for example, was recruited and outfitted by a wealthy Mississippi planter Seldon Spencer, who was an 1857 graduate of Yale. Most of the cannoneers filling out the ranks were of similar social status. On entering Confederate service, Spencer requested that Buckner assign a qualified artillery officer to command the battery while he assumed a subordinate position. A field artillery battery was an expensive proposition for the South, in both hardware and horseflesh. The Confederate leadership was careful to place these resources in the best possible hands.[13]

The 3rd Tennessee's benefactors, the 53rd Tennessee, took position along with the 10th Tennessee on the small hill occupied by Maney's Battery. The combined force was under the command of Adolphus Heiman. There were no Confederate forces in the intervening valley between Brown and Heiman, but Maney's and Graves' batteries were sighted to provide raking fire down most of its length.

Graves could also provide flanking fire across Heiman's immediate front while Porter's Battery covered Brown's front.

Porter's men had also cleared enough timber so that the battery could place long-range fire in the far end of the valley, the position from which any potential Federal assault would have to emerge. Buckner's disposition of his heavy weapons could not have been much better. The interlocking fire of his artillery and infantry had created an ideal killing zone for any Federal force foolish enough to attempt to force their way down the valley. Buckner employed one final touch which would make the Confederate position almost impregnable.

From three to five companies of each regiment were deployed as skirmishers in the rifle pits. The other companies of each regiment were massed in columns, sheltered from the enemy's fire behind the irregularities of the ground, and held in convenient positions to re-enforce any portion of the line that might be threatened.[14]

This was a wise move since Floyd and Pillow, by assuming a static defense, had forfeited the initiative to Grant who could now concentrate against any point he chose. Buckner now had a mobile reserve with which he could shore up any point in his defensive line which might be subjected to intense pressure, or counterattack a Federal break through. He was to employ the 3rd Tennessee in both roles before the battle was over.

The 3rd Tennessee adopted a slightly different approach to manning the defensive line, deploying portions of all of its companies in the rifle pits, probably to cover a greater frontage. The companies rotated men in and out of the front line by platoons. Later, the entire regiment was placed in reserve with the 41st Tennessee assuming the 3rd Tennessee's former position.[15]

As it turned out, Buckner's decision to rotate the troops in the front line served another very important purpose. Later in the week the weather turned wet and bitterly cold. Conditions on the front line soon became miserable; men could not build fires nor could they move around due to the ever vigilant Yankee sharpshooters. The rotation policy allowed the men an opportunity to thaw out in sheltered areas, and also gave them a chance to get some much needed rest.

From the Federal viewpoint, the area between Heiman and Brown seemed to invite attack. The only Confederate position easily discernible from the Federal lines was Maney's Battery, easily discernable on top of a small hill. While the art of camouflage was in its infancy in 1862, the Confederate's lack of skill in this area was more than offset by circumstance. Except for Maney, the Confederate batteries were masked by broken terrain and timber. In addition, the Federal sharpshooters kept Rebel infantry from raising their heads, paradoxically preventing the Federals from gaining a clear idea of how the Confederate defensive line was situated.

The Confederate position was a veritable trap with Maney the bait. All the Confederates needed was a Federal commander rash enough to take it. Coincidentally, the North happened to have just such a man on the scene.

Buckner's opposite across the way was John A. McClernand, a political general from Illinois in command of Grant's First Division. McClernand was a war Democrat whose support Lincoln counted on. More than anyone else, McClernand was responsible for rallying thousands of westerners to the Union cause. His efforts won him a brigadier's commission even though his military experience was limited to brief service during the Blackhawk War. McClernand considered warfare a simple craft and detested West Pointers like Grant and Sherman whose abilities he felt were greatly overrated. However it would be another West Pointer, Simon B. Buckner, who would soon teach McClernand a very hard lesson. It was McClernand's troops Brown observed deploying to his left front on February 12th.

The action took place in an area called Indian Creek Valley beginning around 1:00 P.M. with a Federal artillery probe. The broken terrain made finding the Confederate position extremely difficult for McClernand, who had been ordered to invest it as closely as possible, but not to bring on a general engagement. According to Seldon Spencer, the Federals first drove in the Confederate pickets

(Company C of the 18th Tennessee on Brown's front), and continued their advance very cautiously.

> They soon placed a battery in position a little to our left, and sent a few shots to feel our position and provoke a reply. We did not answer. In about an hour they tried us again, sending some six-pound pills over our heads, but still we did not answer. Their battery was hidden from us by the undergrowth, and we did not intend that they should find us out until they were within good range and visible.[16]

It was then that the 3rd Tennessee witnessed one of those dramatic incidents that made the Civil War so colorful.

> In the afternoon [of the 12th], an engineer mounted upon a white horse rode coolly down to the valley to within six hundred yards of our line, and surveyed us with his field glass. A sharpshooter, having obtained permission, crept down the hillside to within three or four hundred yards of him and tried several shots at him without effect. He bowed gracefully, wheeled his horse, and rejoined his escort.[17]

Events later in the day showed the effort at reconnaissance to have been futile, in spite of the gallantry displayed.

The 3rd Tennessee had little time to be concerned with the threat from Indian Creek Valley. A much greater danger was rapidly developing to their immediate front. Brown wrote: "The incessant fire from the enemy's sharpshooters rendered labor upon our works almost impossible during the day, and large fatigue parties were necessary during the entire nights of Wednesday, Thursday, and Friday, although the weather was intensely cold."[18]

Calvin Clack added, "The enemy soon opened upon us with artillery, and filled the woods in our front with sharpshooters who kept up a continual fire, making it dangerous to raise our heads above the breastworks."[19]

On the 13th the 3rd Tennessee played a part in an action which illustrated how an incompetent commander could sacrifice good troops. The affair again started with an artillery exchange. Seldon Spencer:

> The next morning [February 13th] the battle began soon after daylight. The rattle was first heard along the left. A battery which had been placed in position during the night opened on us. Our battery [Graves'] replied and Capt. Porter also opened on it. We soon silenced it, dismounting one of their guns and a caisson.[20]

While this was going on McClernand also in the process of investing the Confederate position. He found the brash Confederate gunners more than he could stand. The open valley, blocked by Heiman and Maney at the far end, invited attack. Despite Grant's order not to bring on a general engagement, McClernand could not refuse the invitation.

This isolated attack by a single brigade against an entrenched army was bound to fail. The Confederates could concentrate all their fire on the threatened point, and they had their entire force available for reinforcement. Many explanations for McClernand's decision have been put forth, but the most likely one is that he was simply in a snit because the Confederate artillery was besting him.[21]

McClernand selected his Third Brigade, the 48th, 17th, and 47th Illinois Regiments, aligned left to right. These were brand new volunteer regiments eager to test their mettle against the vaunted Confederates, and with little battle savy to appreciate the impending danger.[22]

A melodramatic dispute arose between Colonel Isham N. Haynie of the 48th and Colonel William R. Morrison of the 47th over who was senior colonel (the man who received his colonel's commission first) and thus would command this coming fiasco. They agreed that Morrison would command while the column descended the hill to the attack position, and then Haynie would take over. However, when the time arrived for the transfer of command Haynie proposed that they both command the column. This meant that no one was in charge.[23]

The three regiments struggled through the thick black-jack and scrub oak into Indian Creek Valley and into the converging fire of Graves' and Porter's Batteries from their left, and Maney's Battery to their front. Then, to their utter dismay, a fourth battery, Joseph

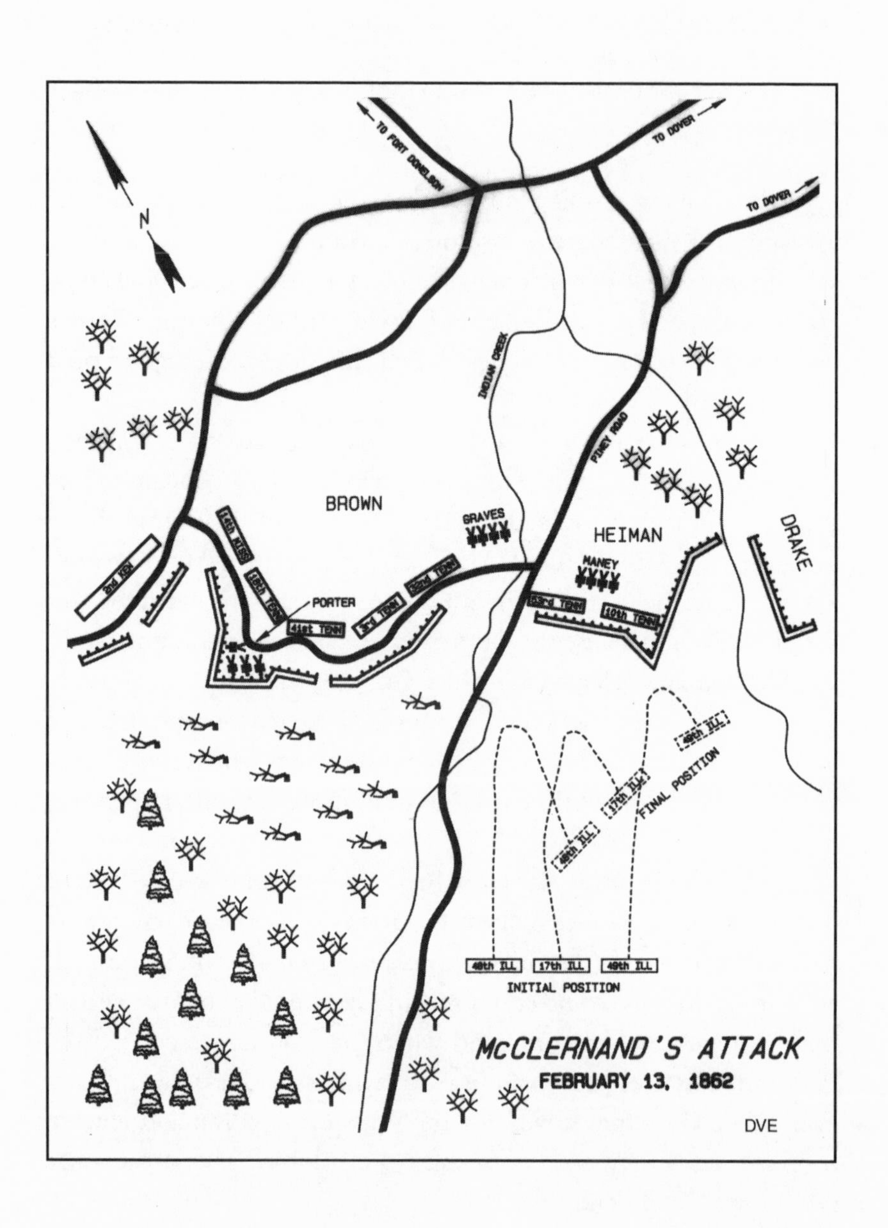
TO FORT DONELSON
TO DOVER
TO DOVER
N
INDIAN CREEK
PINEY ROAD
BROWN
GRAVES
HEIMAN
MANEY
DRAKE
2nd KEN
14th MISS
18th TENN
PORTER
41st TENN
3rd TENN
32nd TENN
53rd TENN
10th TENN
49th ILL
17th ILL
48th ILL
FINAL POSITION
48th ILL
17th ILL
49th ILL
INITIAL POSITION
McCLERNAND'S ATTACK
FEBRUARY 13, 1862
DVE

Drake's, added additional crossfire from their right. The 48th and 17th Illinois found their march route obstructed by undergrowth the entire distance. The 49th entered a cleared field and soon outdistanced the other two regiments. While Porter, Maney, and Drake concentrated a storm of shell, solid shot, and shrapnel on the 49h, the other two regiments marched into Brown's defensive sector, their left flank entirely "in the air."

Brown wrote:

> About 11 o'clock on Thursday I discovered the enemy moving in considerable force upon Colonel Heiman's center, and before the column came within range of Colonel Heiman, and indeed before it could be seen from Colonel Heiman's position, I directed Captain Graves to open fire from all guns, which he did with such spirit and fatal precision that in less than fifteen minutes the whole column staggered and took shelter in confusion and disorder beyond the summit of the hill still farther to our left, when Colonel Heiman opened fire upon it and drove it beyond range of both his and my guns.

The 3rd and 32nd Tennessee Regiments contributed their own "hail of bullets" on the Illinois regiments.[24]

The 47th Illinois was left to deal with Heiman and Maney on its own. Maney kept up a continuous fire of canister. Even so, the 47th advanced to within forty yards of Heiman's line. Then, at point blank range, the 53rd and 10th Tennessee rose as one man and loosed a volley directly into the faces of the Illinois men with devastating effect.

The 47th still managed to muster three desperate assaults against the Heiman line before withdrawing. During the course of the fight, flaming bits of powder bags from Maney's guns started the undergrowth on fire in front of the Confederate line. Some of the Federal wounded were burned to death. The 47th left more than 150 men dead on the field, and accomplished absolutely nothing. Flavel Barber recorded that the Federals departed "leaving their track in mangled corpses."[25]

McClernand's attack infuriated Grant. He issued an immediate order prohibiting any of his commands from changing position without his personal approval. This was to have dire consequences to the Federals later. Grant never did regain his trust for McClernand and little more than a year later sent him packing.

In frustration over the repulse of his infantry assault, McClernand ordered up some artillery to administer retribution to the Confederate batteries and infantry responsible for the horrible devastation of his force. All he got for his efforts was more of the same. Brown wrote:

> Later in the day the enemy planted one section of a battery on a hill almost in front of Captain Graves and opened an enfilading fire upon the left of my line [the 3rd Tennessee], and at the same time a cross-fire upon Colonel Heiman. Captain Graves, handling his favorite rifle piece with the same fearless coolness that characterized his conduct during the entire week, in less than ten minutes knocked one of the enemy's guns from its carriage, and almost at the same moment the gallant Porter disabled and silenced the other, while the supporting infantry retreated precipitately before the storm of grape and canister poured into their ranks from both batteries.[26]

The 3rd Tennessee acquitted itself very well this first day of real battle. Even the fighting rooster, Jake Donelson was impressive. Jake took a position on the breastworks where he

> at frequent intervals gave vent to lusty crows of defiance to the enemy and of encouragement to the besieged. Many of the Company [H] begged that he be removed from so dangerous position, but the lieutenant refused, for he knew how Jake would pine if he could not share the dangers of his comrades. When there was a shriek of a shell Jake sounded that low, guttural warning so common to chickenkind, and would hug close to the breastworks.[27]

The night brought intense cold. The men of the 3rd Tennessee were made more miserable by the weather than they were by the Yankees.

The next day they witnessed the near total destruction of the Federal gunboat fleet: Commodore Foote foolishly closed within

'Jake,' the hero of Fort Donelson.
Courtesy: Gerald Gardner

point blank range of the Confederate battery which were well protected by earthworks. The Confederates wrecked several gunboats and the attack quickly fell apart.

The 3rd Tennessee's rear area, on the reverse side of the hill they were defending, provided a ringside seat for the duel between the shore batteries and the big gunboats. Unfortunately the position also provided a convenient backstop for Federal overshots. The 3rd Tennessee's camp was shredded by the huge Federal shells.[28]

With the failure of the gunboats, Grant tightened his hold on the Confederate position, intending to place it under siege. To avoid starvation the Confederates would have to attempt a breakout. The 3rd Tennessee was about to get its first taste of real offensive combat.

Notes for Chapter 5

1 Rollbook, pp.39, 70.
2 *OR*, Vol VII, part 1, pp.328-329.
3 *Ibid.*, p.329.
4 *Ibid.*
5 Flavel C. Barber Diary, Vol.I, pp.1-2.
6 Rollbook, pp.15-16.
7 *OR*, Vol. VII, part l, p.329.
8 *Ibid*, pp.346-347.
9 Rollbook, p.49.
10 Barber Diary, Vol.I, p.4
11 *OR*, Vol.VII, part 1, p.329.
12 *Ibid.*
13 *CV*, Vol.V, p.282.
14 *OR*, Vol VII, part 1, p.330.
15 Barber Diary, Vol. I, p.8.
16 *CV*, Vol.V, p.282.
17 *Ibid*, p.283.
18 *OR*, Vol.VII, part 1, p.347.
19 Rollbook, p.16.
20 *CV*, Vol.V, p.283.
21 *Battles and Leaders*, Vol.I, p.411.
22 *Ibid.*
23 *Ibid.*, pp.411-412.

24 *OR*, Vol.VII, part 1, pp.347. *Military Annals of Tennessee*, p.857.
25 *Battles and Leaders,* Vol.I, p.412. Barber Diary, Vol.I, p.10.
26 *OR*, Vol.VII, part 1, p.347.
27 Buford McKinney, *CV*, Vol. V, pp. 420-421.
28 Barber Diary, Vol.I, p.10.

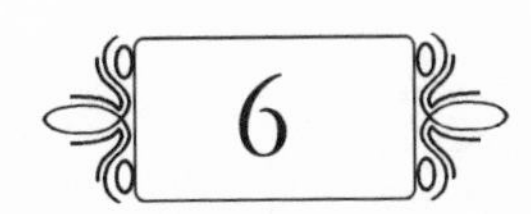

OUT OF THE PITS

With the defeat of Foote's gunboats, the Confederate high command shifted its attention to the land-side threat and the rapidly increasing force opposing them. A steady stream of transports brought more and more reinforcements to Grant while the Confederates were entirely on their own. It was obvious to everyone, that the longer the siege was prolonged, the more difficult would be the task of breaking out. Buckner described the decision to attack:

> The enemy were comparatively quiet in front of my position during the 14th. On the morning of that day I was summoned to a council of general officers, in which it was decided unanimously, in view of the arrival of heavy re-enforcement of the enemy below, to make an immediate attack upon their right ... I proposed, with my division, to cover the retreat of the army should the sortie prove successful. I made the necessary dispositions preparatory to executing the movement, but early in the afternoon the order was countermanded by General Floyd, at the instance [sic], as I afterwards learned, of General Pillow, who,

after drawing out his troops for the attack, thought it too late for the attempt.

> On the night of the 14th it was unanimously decided, in a council of general officers and regimental commanders, to attack the enemy's right at daylight. The object of the attack was to force our way through his lines, recover our communications, and effect our retreat upon Nashville by way of Charlotte, Tennessee ... . The general plan was for General Pillow to attack his extreme right, and for that portion of my division remaining under my command, after being relieved in the rifle pits by Colonel [J.W.] Head's regiment, to make an attack upon the right of the enemy's center, and, if successful, to take up a position in advance of our works on the Wynn's Ferry Road, to cover the retreat of the whole army, after which my division was to act as the rear guard.[1]

The plan almost miscarried right from the start. Buckner wrote: "On Saturday morning, the 15th, a considerable portion of my division was delayed by the non arrival of Head's regiment at the appointed time, and by the slippery condition of the icy road, which forbade a rapid march."[2]

Buckner's inaction, putting the entire Confederate plan in jeopardy, was difficult to excuse. All he needed to do to secure his line was to delay the departure of one of his regiments until Head's arrival, while the rest of his force could deploy to its attack position. This is essentially what John C. Brown did. Exasperated by Buckner's inaction, Brown moved his brigade out on his own hook.

Brown wrote: "[Head] was late in reporting, and without waiting longer, I put the column [led by the 3rd Tennessee] in motion, directing the men in the pits to follow us as soon as relieved, which they did very promptly, but in some disorder."

On their arrival they found Pillow already gone.[3]

Buckner:

> My advance regiment, however, reached its position by daylight in rear of a portion of the entrenchments which had been occupied by General Pillow's troops. As no guards had been left in this position of the line, and even a battery [Maney's] was left

> in position without a cannoneer, I deployed the Third Tennessee in the rifle pits, to cover the formation of my division as it arrived. The regiments were formed partly in line and partly in column, and covered from the enemy's fire by a slight acclivity in front. In the mean time the attack on the enemy's right was made in the most gallant and determined manner by the division of General Pillow.[4]

While Buckner was much too cautious, Pillow, by seemingly leaving a large segment of his line undefended, was probably too careless.

Buckner was assigned an attack zone up a valley formed by another branch of Indian Creek about one-fourth mile further to the Confederate left. The 3rd Tennessee led the brigade into the valley and provided a covering force for the remainder of the regiments as they formed up for the attack force. Pillow also shifted his forces to the left, and for a while the Confederate center was extremely vulnerable to attack.

Brown, not Buckner, led the actual attack. He was ordered to secure the right flank of the army along the Wynn's Ferry road "to allow the retreat of the whole army" as Buckner put it.[5]

Brown elaborated on the purpose of the attack: "My whole command was provided with three day's cooked rations, and marched with their knapsacks, the purpose being to turn the enemy's right wing and march out on the Wynn's Ferry Road to fall back upon Nashville." Statements by Brown's officers all the way down to company commander reiterate this same theme. Nowhere was the capriciousness of Gideon Pillow factored into the plan.[6]

As Brown readied his four regiments for the attack, Buckner strolled along the front line atop the rifle pits, providing a spectacular display of nerve for the troops. The Yankees could see an attack was coming and sent a steady stream of bullets and cannon fire into the Confederate line. The ground around Buckner's feet was churned up by this fire while other rounds zipped past his head. Buckner showed total disdain for it all, eliciting much admiration from the troops. Whatever criticisms might be made of Buckner, he certainly did not lack personal courage.[7]

Buckner's force, including the 3rd Tennessee, was the far right brigade of a seven brigade attack force. While Pillow might have been incautious vacating a portion of his defense line before the arrival of Buckner's troops, he was prompt in delivering his attack, which was well underway shortly after dawn. Around 9:00 a.m. Pillow himself worked his way over to Buckner's position and became extremely excited when he discovered that the latter still had not begun his attack. Buckner immediately turned to Brown and ordered him to move his men forward. Brown first ordered the 14th Mississippi forward as a skirmish line, then the 3rd Tennessee led the main force forward. According to Brown, his attack force was facing "a heavy battery [probably Edward McAllister's] posted on the Wynn's Ferry Road, with another battery [probably Ezra Taylor's] opposite my left -both sustained by a heavy infantry force [W.H.L. Wallace]." This Federal force was already coming under heavy pressure from Pillow's forces on its right. No Federal reinforcements were forthcoming since Grant's commanders were under strict orders not to change position without his personal approval as a result of McClernand's abortive attack the day before. Grant himself was not available to deal with the crises, having gone off for a conference with his river fleet commander, Commodore Andrew Foote.[8]

The 14th Mississippi and 3rd Tennessee advanced on the Yankee battery to their front left, and entered a world gone mad. The Federal fire increased to a steady roar. Powder smoke combined with the dense foliage to reduce visibility to nothing. Within minutes of beginning the advance, Companies H, I, and K, the 3rd Tennessee's left wing, lost sight of the rest of the regiment and became completely lost in the woods. They were out of the fight, and withdrew when they discovered the rest of the regiment returning to the rifle pits.[9]

Meanwhile, Companies A and B, "deployed before the regiment," became isolated as the other five companies also bore off to the left. These two companies conducted a private fight with the Federals. After a few very intense minutes of close combat these two companies broke contact with the enemy and withdrew a short

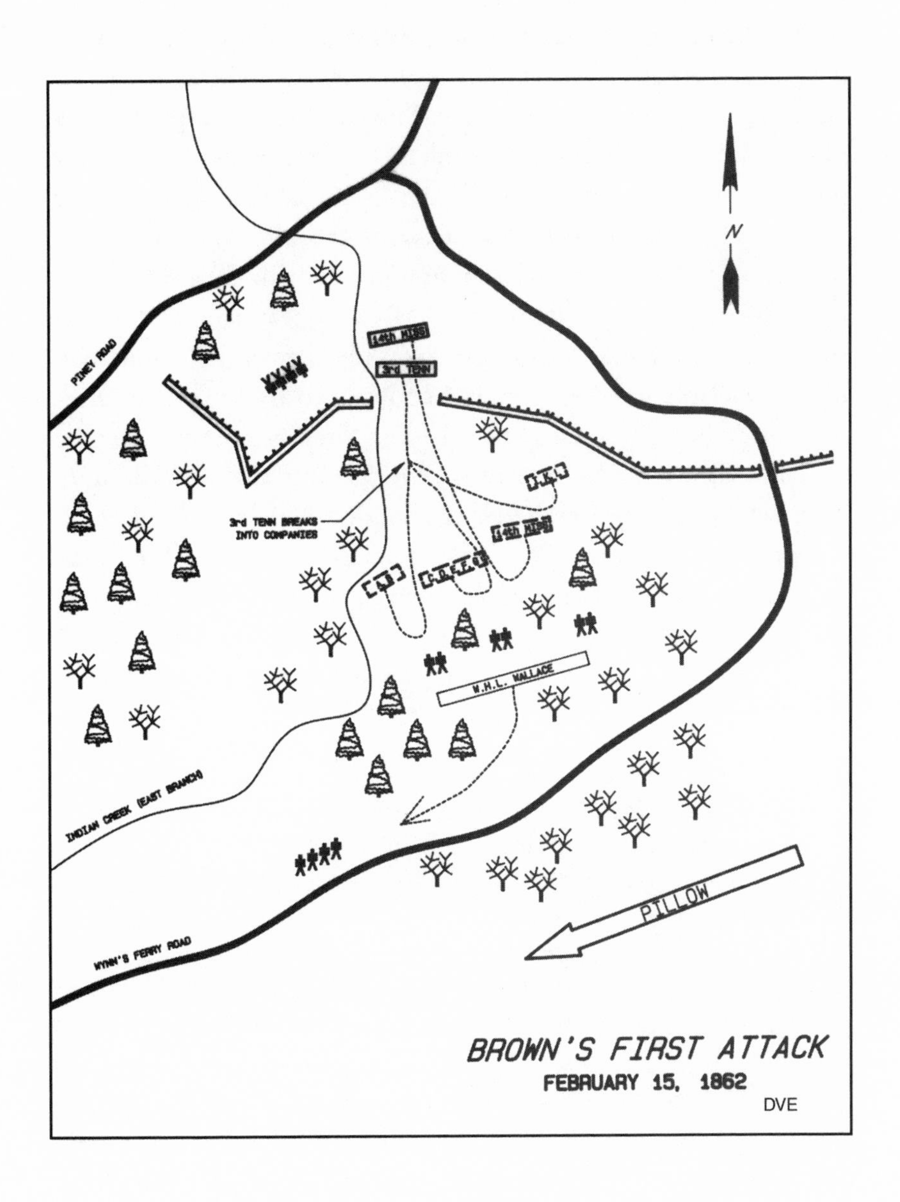
N
PINEY ROAD
14th MISS
3rd TENN
3rd TENN BREAKS
INTO COMPANIES
14th MISS
W.H.L. WALLACE
INDIAN CREEK (EAST BRANCH)
WYNN'S FERRY ROAD
PILLOW
BROWN'S FIRST ATTACK
FEBRUARY 15, 1862
DVE

distance to await support. When no reinforcements were forthcoming they also withdrew to the rifle pits.[10]

On the left flank the remaining five companies of the 3rd Tennessee, along with most of the 14th Mississippi, quickly closed to within musket range. These men exchanged a hot fire at point blank range with the Yankees for a full forty-five minutes. The cover provided by the timber and the broken terrain, and the dense powder smoke hanging in the trees likely prevented their being annihilated.[11]

Exactly which side gave way first in this fight is hard to determine. What is certain is that the 14th Mississippi and the 3rd Tennessee fought the battle on their own. While Brown had four regiments available for the fight, and contrary to his statement afterwards that he committed three of them "in quick succession", he actually did not get around to deploying the third regiment until the issue was already decided. He did not deploy the fourth one at all.

Colonel Joseph B. Palmer, commander of the 18th Tennessee, led the third wave. He described his part in the battle:

> Very soon afterwards the 14th Mississippi and 3rd Tennessee were ordered by Colonel Brown (General Buckner also being present) to attack one of the enemy's batteries just in our front, and about 300 yards beyond the trenches, which from its position was firing heavily upon us. This battery was supported by several regiments of infantry, which, in connection with it, turned a terrible fire on the two regiments just named, against which they fought gallantly and bravely, thus making a severe engagement, which continued for some considerable time, when I was ordered across the trenches to their support, and reached there just about the time the enemy abandoned their position and yielded the ground.[12]

The Confederates also yielded ground. William McKay of the 18th Tennessee described an incident he viewed on the 14th Mississippi's front: "[I] witnessed a sight I have never forgotten a member of the 14 Miss, a young boy looked to be about 15 was calling on his regt for gods sake to reform and charge the Yankees again the tears were rolling down his face and I think he would have gone alone if an officer had not taken him to the rear.[13]

The Federal position soon became untenable and they withdrew, abandoning one section (two guns) of artillery. Though momentum was shifting their way, with the 18th Tennessee closely pursuing the Yankees, surprisingly the Confederates also withdrew. According to Brown, the troops were ordered back to reorganize.

> Further pursuit being impractical in that direction, and companies having become separated and somewhat intermixed, on account of the obstacles over which they had marched, the command retired within the entrenchments, and immediately reformed, to renew the attack still further to the right, whither the enemy were retiring.[14]

A more probable reason for the Confederate retreat was the bungling of one of Buckner's staff officers, Major Alexander Casseday. The major, apparently on his own, began ordering the attacking regiments back to their jump-off point. Buckner had assigned Casseday to guide the attack force to its objective. Casseday apparently "misapprehended" Buckner's instructions and instead "lead" the force back to where it started. Nat Cheairs and several others from the 3rd Tennessee blamed the unfortunate major in their official reports as the cause of the untimely withdrawl. On the other hand, Flavel Barber placed the blame for confusion within the 3rd Tennessee squarely on its acting commander's shoulders, Lieutenant Colonel Thomas Gordon. Miffed at having missed this fight by getting lost, blame for which Barber ascribed to the regiment's field officers, the young captain interpreted the retreat as a blunder by Gordon. "It is said that at the very moment when our men were pouring a destructive fire into the enemy's ranks...our Lt.Col. gave an order to retreat. The inefficiency of our field officers was manifest to our men by this time."[15]

So the opportunity to pursue a retreating enemy was lost. Now the Confederates would have to do it the hard way, again, attacking a reformed enemy in prepared defensive positions.

It did not take long to get the next attack in motion. According to Thomas Deavenport:

> We had scarcely gained the pits when a battery began to shell us at a furious rate. I heard someone behind us, and on turning around saw Col. John C. Brown who was commanding the brigade jump from his horse, wave his sword over his head and cry, 'Men of the 3rd Tennessee, come out of the pits.' The men heard their brave commander (for he was our Col.) and at once obeyed.[16]

The Federals had withdrawn to the southwest and reformed on anotherridge astride the Wynn's Ferry Road. Since the terrain was not as restrictive, this time the Confederates would attack with three regiments abreast: the 3rd Tennessee on the left, the 18th Tennessee in the center, and the 32nd Tennessee on the right. The 14th Mississippi would follow as a reserve. The infantry had masked the artillery during the previous attack, preventing any artillery support until the Federals began their withdrawal, so for this attack Buckner arranged three batteries so that they could fire past the flanks of the attack formation. The converging fire of Porter on the left and Graves on the right was decisive in suppressing the Yankee twenty-four pounders on the Wynn's Ferry Road, and in breaking up the infantry and artillery on the Federal defensive line.[17]

Brown described the attack:

> A charge was ordered [by Brown himself]: "Forward! Storm the enemy!, and the whole command moved forward with spirit and animation; but when within about 100 yards of the enemy, who was upon higher ground, we were met by a fire of grape and musketry that was terrific, but fortunately passing above our heads. We halted and opened a fire of musketry upon them, which, although continuing only a few minutes, killed and wounded not less than 800 of the enemy. Lieutenant-Colonel Gordon, of the Third, having been wounded, ordered the regiment to fall back under cover of the hill. I rallied it at about 100 yards, and placed it in command of Major Cheairs. The Eighteenth and Thirty-second fell back a short distance, and just then, being re-enforced by the Fourteenth Mississippi, we were renewing the attack, when the enemy left the field, leaving his dead and wounded. While we were engaged the gallant Graves came in full speed to our assistance with a part of his battery, and maintained his position until the enemy retired.[18]

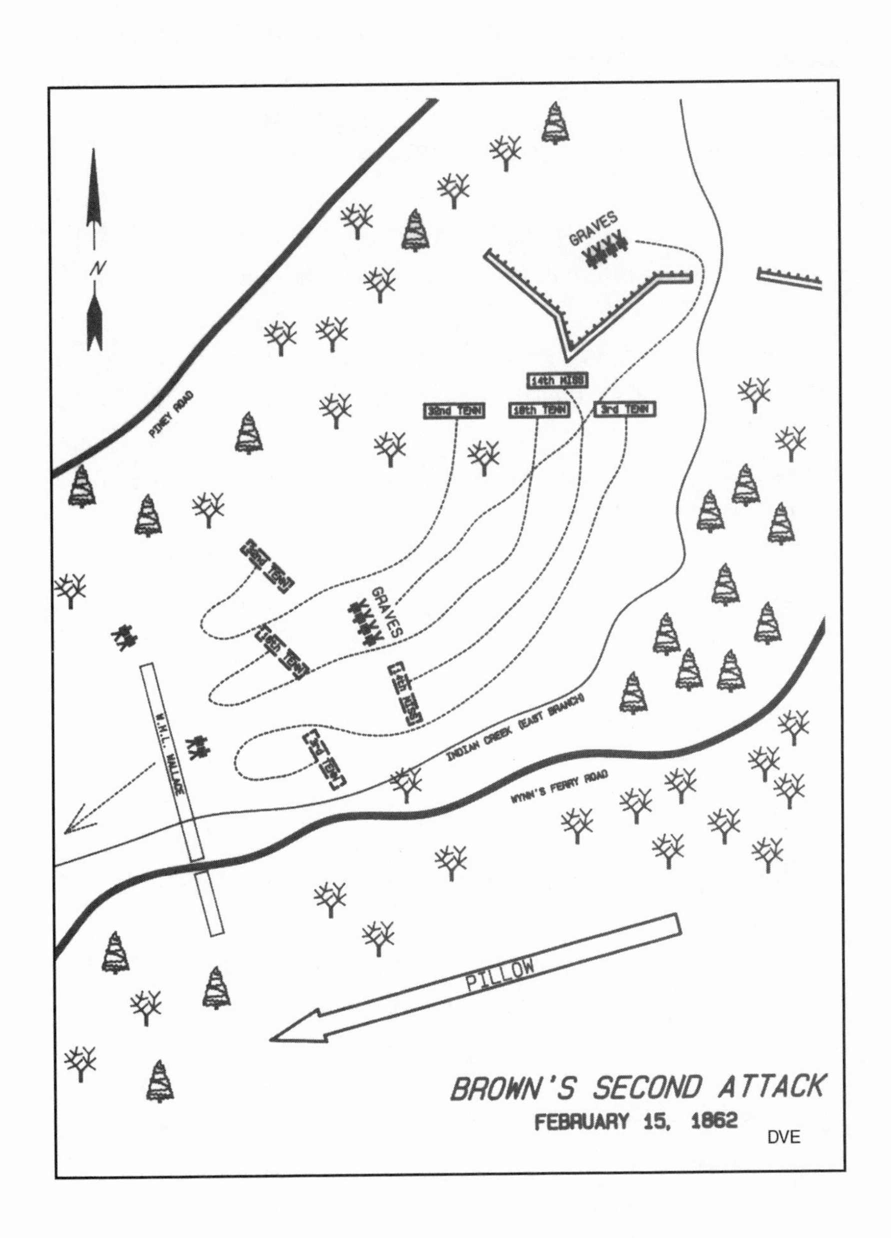
N
GRAVES
14th MISS
32nd TENN
18th TENN
3rd TENN
PINEY ROAD
GRAVES
W.H.L. WALLACE
INDIAN CREEK (EAST BRANCH)
WYNN'S FERRY ROAD
PILLOW
BROWN'S SECOND ATTACK
FEBRUARY 15, 1862
DVE

Brown does not mention that the reason his brigade moved in so close to the enemy was because no one in Brown's command had any idea where the enemy line was situated. The broken terrain, heavy timber, and the large volumes of smoke hanging in the trees made the Federal position impossible to see until the Confederates were almost on top of it. Brown's commanders guided on the creek and the sound of the enemy guns. As the assault force neared the enemy, its skirmish line, provided by the 32nd Tennessee, fell back on the main column without accurately locating the enemy line. Colonels Joseph B. Palmer and Edward C. Cook, commanding the 18th and 32nd Regiments, then conducted a personal reconnaissance and were shocked to find the enemy only 100 yards to their front on the opposite side of a small hill. All three regiments quickly deployed a battle line; at the same time the Yankees opened a "terrific" fire.[19]

Gordon immediately ordered the 3rd Tennessee to lie down while both Palmer and Cook ordered their regiments to kneel down. This maneuver did not quite fit within the guidelines for standard offensive tactics of the day, but it did cause most of the Yankees to overshoot their targets, and kept the casualty lists of all three regiments lower than one would have expected. The three regiments returned fire on the Yankees as fast as humanly possible. Graves quickly joined the fight with a section of artillery adding to a din which Lew Wallace compared to "a million men ... beating barrels with iron hammers."[20]

Brown gained a reputation as a courageous battlefield leader during the course of this fight. He rode up and down the battle line on a white horse seeing to it that the men stuck to the task. Amazingly, he was not shot. His white horse may have actually provided him some protection by blending in with the thick white powder smoke and snow. He rallied the 3rd Tennessee; but according to fellow officer Nat Cheairs, the 3rd had fallen back some two or three hundred yards before he and Brown managed to halt it. In a missive to Brown, Cheairs observed that "[The] unfortunate command to fall back [was] given by someone unknown to you or I."[21]

Cheairs was being kind. There is no doubt that Gordon ordered the retreat. Barber said Gordon issued it immediately after he was shot in the arm. Within seconds of Gordon's wounding the 3rd Tennessee's color bearer, Corporal J.B. Compton, was shot dead. The prognosis for the battle was definitely not favorable. It seems very likely Gordon simply lost his nerve. By the time the regiment reformed its line of battle, the Yankees had withdrawn from their position and there was no need to continue the attack. Buckner then ordered the 3rd Tennessee back to its starting point to retrieve knapsacks and prepare for evacuation of the fort.[22]

The 18th and 32nd Regiments were also having a tough time. Both regiments were using the same 1816 Model U S. Muskets as was the 3rd except that theirs retained the old flintlock ignition system. The two inches of snow the night before had created extremely wet conditions. Large numbers of guns became unserviceable as bits of snow fell into flintlock "pans" and wet the priming powder and sometimes the main charge within the barrel. In the latter event it became necessary for the soldiers to pull the lead ball out through the muzzle and remove the wet powder, a very difficult process.[23]

Despite these problems, those muskets that were firing were wreaking havoc on the Yankee infantry and cannoneers. All three regiments were firing "buck and ball" cartridges which consisted of a large .69 caliber lead ball, and three smaller balls of approximately .44 caliber. This cartridge was almost useless at long range, but in this close-in fight it was the ideal weapon. The Tennesseans filled the air with hundreds of lead balls that, while not always lethal, would produce wounds serious enough to cause the evacuation of the victim. As William McKay of the 18th Tennessee pointed out, it usually required one or two healthy men to carry each wounded man, further depleting the fighting strength of the enemy.[24]

Eventually the other two Tennessee regiments also had to give ground. Colonel Palmer ordered the 18th Tennessee to fall back 150 paces and his men "to put their pieces in order by drying them as rapidly as possible" while he sent back for more ammunition. The 32nd noticed the 18th Tennessee's withdrawal, and began a retreat of its own.[25]

The 32nd Tennessee's commander, Edward C. Cook, seemed unruffled by this unauthorized movement to the rear.

> After a while the left wing of the regiment began to fall back slowly, and then the right wing in good order, and, being satisfied that many of the guns, in good order to do execution, must be wiped and dried, and knowing that the regiment, after falling back a short distance, would be entirely protected from the enemy's shot, I determined to let them fall back. After they fell back about 100 yards I halted the regiment and ordered the men to wipe and dry their guns. Upon inquiry as to why they fell back, the officers informed me they heard an order to fall back, and believed it came from proper authority.[26]

One senses the confusion of the battlefield from the statements of Cheairs and Cook. While Brown invokes a heroic image of himself rallying the 3rd Tennessee on the left, the retreat was hardly a panic. Cook described the withdrawal of the 3rd and 18th Tennessee Regiments as slow and in good order. As they lost their ability to deliver effective battle because of malfunctioning equipment, the soldiers simply withdrew from the fight to avoid the senseless loss of life.[27]

Meanwhile, as a result of pressure from Pillow's forces on the opposite flank, and because of the damage inflicted by Brown's brigade, the Federals also withdrew. After a brief pursuit, theother three regiments joined the 3rd Tennessee in returning to its starting point to prepare for evacuation.

It was at this point that Gideon Pillow forfeited the victory, or "lost his head" as Nat Cheairs put it. Without consulting anyone Pillow rode up and ordered the 3rd back to its original defensive position. Moving on, he located Buckner and ordered him to have his entire division do the same. Puzzled and shaken, Buckner conferred with Floyd, who agreed that this was not the plan. Floyd questioned Pillow, but Pillow was able to convince the war secretary that he knew what he was doing. The victorious Rebels went back to the trenches and Gideon Pillow rushed off to the telegraph office to announce to Richmond that he was the new Napoleon.[28]

Meanwhile, U.S. Grant was organizing counterattacks all along the line.

Thus far the day had produced considerable success for John C. Brown and for the 3rd Tennessee. While these Tennesseans could not claim exclusive credit for the success thus far, they had made a substantial contribution to driving the enemy back. The brigade had captured a section of artillery at each location, and Brown estimated that his men inflicted eight-hundred enemy casualties while suffering only fifty of their own. Brown probably was not too far off. His primary antagonist, W.H.L. Wallace, suffered 547 casualties alone. The battle-wise tactics of taking advantage of the terrain, and of lying down or kneeling in the midst of an assault thereby presenting a smaller target to the enemy, were common-sense innovations by these very green troops. John C. Brown had proven himself a tenacious warrior/leader (in spite of one brief period during the second assault when Barber sighted him standing behind his horse).[29]

The Confederates had learned a hard lesson this day. These Westerners were a tough bunch, and unless the Confederates could find ways to out-general or out-number these men, they would be difficult to beat.

Notes for Chapter 6

1 *OR*, Vol.VII, part 1, pp. 330-331.
2 *Ibid.*, p. 331.
3 *Ibid.*, p. 347.
4 *Ibid.*,p. 331.
5 *Ibid.*
6 *Ibid.*,p. 347.
7 William L. McKay Memoir, pp. 37-38.
8 *OR*, Vol.VII, part 1, p. 331.
9 Rollbook, pp. 16, 119.
10 *Ibid.*
11 *Ibid.*
12 *OR*, Vol VII, part 1, p.352.

13 McKay Memoir, p.38.
14 *OR*, Vol.VII, part 1, p. 348.
15 Flavel C. Barber Diary, Vol.I, p. 17.
16 Thomas H. Deavenport Diary, p. 8.
17 *OR*, Vol.VII, part 1, pp. 332, 350.
18 Barber Diary, Vol.I, p. 19. *OR*, Vol.VII, part 1, p. 348.
19 *OR*, Vol.VII, part 1, pp. 353,356.
20 *Ibid.*, p. 350, 353, 356. *Battles and Leaders*,Vol.I, p. 417.
21 John C. Brown Autograph Book, Cheairs Battle Account.
22 Barber Diary, Vol.I, p.19. *OR*, Vol.VII, part 1, p. 350.
23 *OR*, Vol. VII, part 1, p. 353.
24 McKay Memoir, p. 38.
25 *OR*, Vol.VII, part 1, pp. 353, 356.
26 *Ibid.*
27 *Ibid.*, p. 356.
28 John C. Brown Autograph Book, Cheairs Battle Account.
29 *OR*, Vol.VII, part 1, p. 348. *Battles and Leaders of the Civil War*, Vol.I, p. 429. Barber Diary, Vol. I, p. 19.

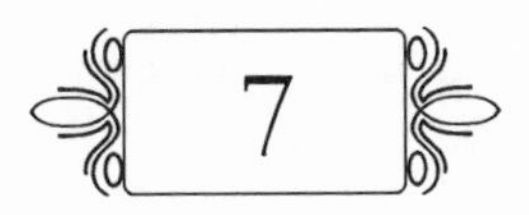

NAT CHEAIRS CALLS GRANT OUT

When the Confederates had concentrated on the left, Buckner had stripped forces from his defensive line so that the far right, the area immediately behind the water batteries, was defended by only three companies from the 30th Tennessee. As soon as the Confederates eased the pressure on the Yankee forces, Grant sought a way to regain the advantage. Since the Confederates attacked from their left, Grant deduced they must have weakened their right and immediately ordered C.F. Smith to the attack. He also began organizing a counter-attack against Pillow, ordering his men to reform, replenish their ammunition, and retake their former positions.

A military unit is about as vulnerable upon completion of a successful attack as it is after a defeat. Organization is disrupted, troops experience an emotional release and let down their guard, and captured defensive positions often provide little or no protection to the rear, the area from which a counterattack would originate. Grant understood this, and set off to hit the Rebels as quickly as possible.

Smith kicked off the counterattack with his rested division and soon overwhelmed the three companies of the 30th Tennessee which was manning the 2nd Kentucky's old position on the far right. Immediately behind the Confederate line was a deep ravine followed by another somewhat higher ridge. According to Nat Cheairs:

> Roger Hanson, Colonel of the 2nd Ky. Regiment and myself, then in command of the 3rd Tennessee Regiment were the first to reach our former positions and found the Federals had possession of our right pits; we being on a high hill and they down in the valley, gave us the advantage of them by having a plunging shot at them.[1]

While the 2nd Kentucky set off to reinforce the companies from the 30th Tennessee on the next ridge to the northeast, the 3rd and 18th Tennessee Regiments, reinforced by a portion of Porter's Battery, opened a "rapid and galling cross-fire" on the exposed Federal right flank.[2]

Porter's Battery had maintained a close association with the 3rd Tennessee since the early days of the Kentucky invasion when both units were brigaded together under John C. Brown. Porter was a former U.S. Navy lieutenant, and brought that special brand of tough Navy discipline to his battery of Tennesseans which perfectly complemented Brown's leadership style.

> Under Capt. Porter, a skillful and most efficient officer, the battery soon became very efficient in drill and discipline—in fact, it was a most excellent training school for officers. Porter and a number of his officers and men subsequently held important commissions in the Confederate service.

This statement was from John Morton, Porter's successor as battery commander. Morton maintained the fighting reputation of the battery after its transfer to Forrest's command under whom it became famous as 'Morton's Battery.' Porter later became division artillery commander under Buckner, and subsequently held that post under Patrick Cleburne.[3]

Thomas K. Porter, field artilleryman extraordinaire and former U.S. Navy officer, Porter's battery created great consternation among the blue forces throughout the Battle of Fort Donelson. During the fierce contests on February 15th, Porter helped clear the way for John C. Brown's successful attacks, then after the unexplainable Confederate withdrawal, raked Union General C.F. Smith's counterattack with devastating flank fire. Several 3rd Tennesseans filled in for some of Porter's fallen gunners.
Courtesy: Military Annals of Tennessee

Porter's Battery had another special relationship with the 3rd Tennessee. In the fall of 1861, and at other times, the battery suffered acute personnel shortages because of disease, and called upon the 3rd and 18th Tennessee Regiments for augmentation in order to maintain full crews for each of the guns. When the 3rd Tennessee and Porter's Battery rushed over to the right to contain C.F. Smith's attack, Porter was provided with a ready-made pool of pretrained men with which to replace his losses and maintain service on his guns.[4]

Porter would need many replacements. While Cheairs and the 3rd Tennessee could make use of whatever cover was available and still deliver a continuous fire on Smith's forces, the artillerymen had to expose themselves to enemy fire in order to service the guns. Since they were now confronting the enemy in an area previously occupied by friendly forces, no provision had been made to defend in that direction.

Porter's Battery contained two six-pounder guns and two twelve-pounder big bore howitzers. The howitzers, while almost useless at long range, were very effective in a close-in fight firing blasts of canister at troops less than five-hundred yards away. Just such a target was now presented to Porter's gunners. The battery's position on the Federal right flank was an artilleryman's dream with long rows of Yankees arrayed in front of the guns just waiting to be bowled over. The blue soldiers recognized the threat and directed a heavy fire toward Porter's positions. Morton provided a good description of the action:

> The horses were shot down, and the guns run into place by hand. Until dark the desperate conflict raged. Lieut. Hutchinson, of Porter's Battery, was severely shot through the neck. Lieut. Culbertson, of the same battery, was hit; and the gallant Capt. Thomas K. Porter, who Hanson said, "always directed his guns at the right time and to the right place," was disabled by a severe and dangerous wound, and was borne from the field. Capt. Porter's marked coolness and dash, and the efficient and intelligent manner in which he handled his guns, elicited the unbounded admiration of all who saw him. While being carried bleeding from the field, he said to me, "Don't let them have the guns, Morton."

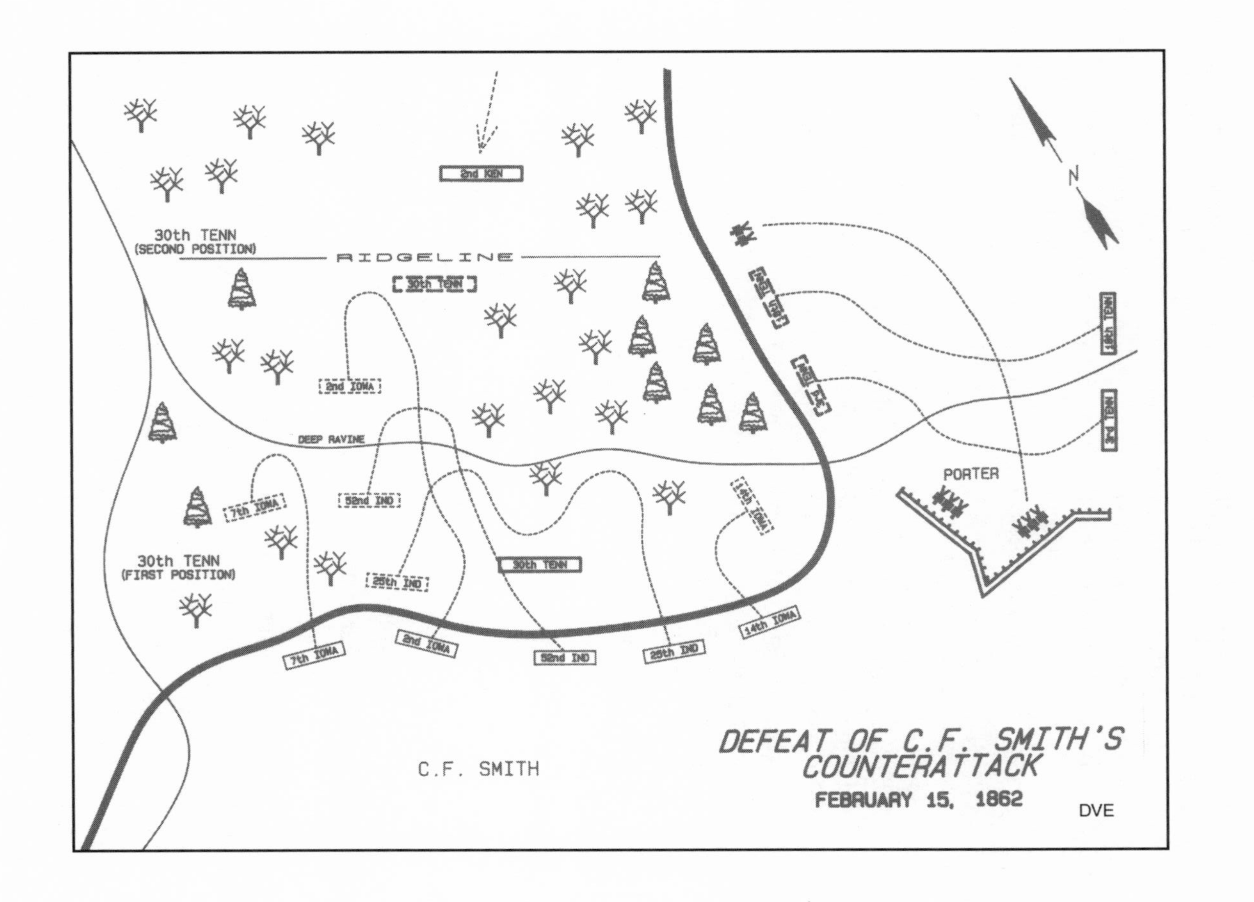
N
2nd KEN
30th TENN
(SECOND POSITION)
RIDGELINE
30th TENN
2nd IOWA
DEEP RAVINE
7th IOWA
52nd IND
25th IND
30th TENN
14th IOWA
30th TENN
(FIRST POSITION)
7th IOWA
2nd IOWA
52nd IND
25th IND
14th IOWA
18th TENN
3rd TENN
PORTER
C.F. SMITH
DEFEAT OF C.F. SMITH'S
COUNTERATTACK
FEBRUARY 15, 1862
DVE

> I replied, "No, Captain; not while I have one man left," little mindful that my apprehensions would be so nearly carried out. The cannoneers had been greatly reduced by frost-bites, wounds, and deaths, until toward the close of the engagement I had only three men left at one gun. One of these was wounded and left where he fell, we being unable to remove him at the moment. Pat Kline, acting number one [the man who rams the charge down the barrel and is most exposed], who was always at his post, seeing the dead and wounded lying thick around us, impelled by that generous and gallant nature and impulsive disposition so characteristic of the Irish race, threw himself in front of me saying: "Lieutenant, Lieutenant, get lower down the hill, or they will kill you;" and actually embraced me, as if to make a shield of himself to the enemy's bullets for my protection. I replied: "No, Pat; let us give them one more round." He promptly seized his ramming-staff, and while in the act of driving the charge home was shot through the heart and dropped underneath his gun. Night soon closed the bloody combat.[5]

Although Porter's men suffered greatly during the engagement, the effect of the combined infantry and artillery fire on the Iowa and Indiana troops was devastating. The regiment on the Federal right flank, the 14th Iowa, made a half wheel right to face the Rebel onslaught, and immediately went to ground to avoid the heavy musket and cannon fire coming down on them. Since these men were in the bottom of the deep ravine with the Confederates directly above them, they were fairly well protected. The Rebels could not fire straight down without exposing themselves.

It was a different story for the next regiment in line. The 25th Indiana's advance took it into perfect range for Porter's cannon and the infantrymen's muskets. These Hoosiers were quickly blanketed by Confederate fire, and began drifting off to the left to escape total destruction. Once they were out of harm's way, they gave up the fight and fell back.

Next in line was the 52nd Indiana. Also hit hard and evading fire by moving to the left, these men managed to continue the advance. The problem was the 52nd slid in behind the next unit in line, the 2nd Iowa, and when the Iowans made contact with the Confederates to their front, the 30th Tennessee and 2nd Kentucky, both Yankee regiments began to fire. Much of the 52nd Indiana's fire fell within the 2nd Iowa's line causing the advance to rapidly fall apart.

The far left Yankee regiment, the 7th Iowa, became lost in the thickets along Hickman's Creek, and failed to make contact with the Confederates at all.[6]

Colonel Palmer of the 18th Tennessee estimated the casualty ratio at seven to one in favor of the Confederates. Total losses in C.F. Smith's Fourth Brigade alone were 357. Though much was made of Smith's attack in the Northern press, it was, in truth, a deadly fiasco.[7]

By nightfall the Confederate position was secure. The Confederates were well satisfied with the result. Nat Cheairs, now acting commander of the 3rd Tennessee, wrote "... we fought them until it was too dark to see them, then we went to our quarters highly elated over the days work. I pulled off my frozen overcoat, drank a hot mug of coffee and tumbled down and was soon sound asleep." The one person who felt otherwise, and it would be fatal for the Rebel army, was Simon Buckner.

Buckner spent the evening of February 15th convincing fellow commanders, Floyd and Pillow, that despite the Confederates complete mastery over Grant the last couple of days, the army was on its last legs. It took much convincing, but finally Floyd and Pillow agreed with him, whereupon the latter two men committed the greatest sin a military leader can possibly imagine short of deserting to the enemy; they abandoned their comrades in the field, an act so onerous to Southern sensibilities that Buckner's role in the debacle was completely overshadowed.

Buckner, because of the peculiar shared leadership arrangement at Fort Donelson, assumed command with the abdication of Floyd and Pillow. His first act as supreme commander of the Fort Donelson forces was to ask for a pencil and paper to request surrender terms from Grant. The Confederates, victorious in every engagement, were to be betrayed by one of the South's professional officers. In connection with his performance on the battlefield, Buckner has been described as a real soldier, a professional who knew his business. In this case, however, he failed utterly in his role as leader. He was the prime instigator of the surrender, and once he assumed command, bore the responsibility for same.

The surrender decision was met with disbelief, and then with rage by John C. Brown, Bushrod Johnson, John Gregg, Nathan Bedford Forrest, and nearly every other field commander in the army. These men had been in the midst of preparing for another breakout attempt the next day, and had not the least intention of quitting. Forrest refused to join the surrender, and led his command, and anyone else who wanted to come along, out of their predicament with little difficulty.

Brown had already begun preparations for another attack and had ordered the 3rd Tennessee to begin moving in the direction of Dover at 11:00 p.m. Cheairs pulled the 3rd Tennessee off the line, arranged the men in marching order, and started them toward the town. The movement was undoubtedly a great relief for the troops since they had spent the last several hours standing or lying in ditches partly filled with ice water. After marching about three-quarters of a mile Cheairs encountered Buckner's adjutant, Colonel George B. Cosby. Cosby asked Cheairs the identity of his command.

> I told him the 3rd Tennessee. He ordered me to halt them and wait for orders—then inquired the way to Colonel Brown's quarters. I directed him how to find them and waited about an hour and receiving no word, and my men about to freeze, for it was bitter cold, the ground covered with snow and sleet. I put the regiment in charge of my senior Captain and rode back to Brown's quarters to find out what the matter was.
>
> I found Brown mad as a hornet, and [he] wanted to know where I had been. I told him, marching in the direction of Dover as he had ordered me to do, when I met Colonel Causby [sic], who ordered me to halt and wait for further orders, after waiting some time and receiving none and my men about to freeze, I had ridden back to see what the friction was. Now tell me so I can relieve the regiment.

Brown then revealed the source of his agitation: "We are going to surrender and I want you to take a flag of truce to Grant with some dispatches from Buckner."

Cheairs was flabbergasted:

Going to surrender after whipping Grant as we had done? I can't believe it. Colonel Causby then spoke up and said it was so, and that General Floyd was then loading his Virginia Brigade upon a transport and that General Pillow had his staff and escort ready to go aboard and would leave at daylight, and that General Forrest refused to be surrendered and has gone with his command.

Realizing the hopelessness of the situation, Cheairs agreed to take the flag of truce out to Grant. Cheairs provided a unique description of the art of surrender.

Brown cut a strip about one and one-half yards long out of his tent and fastened it to a hickory pole for a flag, and selected Lt. Rhea and the leader of our regimental band as bugler to accompany me.

When the question arose what call should we make for a surrender, none of us knew of any particular call to make as it was our first experience of a surrender—Brown told the bugler to blow everything he knew, and if that wouldn't do to blow his d___ brains out.

We reached the Federal lines about daylight and found them all in commotion, evidently preparing to retreat back to Fort Henry, as they were facing in that direction.

Evidently the Federals were not as well prepared to deliver the final blow on the right as Buckner believed they were.

We commenced waving our flag and blowing the bugle and kept it up for an hour or more before they paid any attention to us. Finally General Smith and staff galloped up to where we were and asked what we wanted. I replied saying, I presume I have the honor of speaking to General Grant, if so I have some dispatches from General Buckner.

Smith: "No I am General Smith, hand me the dispatches and I will send them to Grant, he is about four miles down the river."

Cheairs replied:

> "My orders are to deliver these dispatches in person to General Grant—you see I am here afoot—if you will be kind enough to furnish me with a horse and an escort I will take them to him." He complied with my request and I set out to find Grant and didn't go exceeding a mile when we met Grant.
>
> I saluted him and introduced myself to him and handed Buckner's dispatches to him. He opened and read them and we rode back to where General Smith was. He and Grant held a private consultation and wrote out some dispatches for me to take to Buckner (an unconditional surrender message) and asked me how long it would take to deliver them and return with Buckner's answer.

Grant sensed total capitulation and applied as much pressure as he could. Cheairs continued: "I said 'Buckner is at Dover three or four miles away and the country very broken and rough and the roads and paths covered with ice and sleet. I can't tell how long it will take me.'"

Grant responded: "Don't you think you can do it in an hour and thirty minutes?"

Cheairs replied:

> "No that man and horse don't live that can make it in that time, with the country in its present condition."
>
> We then compared our watches and he gave me an hour and fifty minutes and said, "If you are not back in that time I will open my guns upon your army"—I took the dispatches and when I got where my horse was I found Brown with his horse saddled. I told what Grant had said about the time limit and opening his guns. He took the papers and put out in a lope and was three and a half hours making the trip, and Grant didn't open his guns. Buckner accepted his terms, which were unconditional surrender allowing the field officers to retain their private property and side arms.

Cheairs was to have one more encounter with Grant before they went their separate ways. "On [Grant and Cheairs] going to Buckner's headquarters General Grant asked me how many troops we had in this battle the day before. 'General, you have asked me a question I can't answer and if I said any number it would be guess-work.'"

Grant then asked,"Well I would like to know your best idea of the number."

"My best impression is we did not have exceeding 7 or 8 thousand," Cheairs replied

Grant countered, "I didn't ask you for a falsehood sir."

"I then said 'you are the commander in chief of the Federal forces and I suppose I am your prisoner, but sir my father taught me to take the lie from no man,' and off went my coat."

Grant replied, "Oh, I did not mean to insult you sir."

"Under the circumstances I will have to accept your apology, but would like you to be careful of your language in the future," was Cheairs' final response.[8]

Except for this dressing down from Nat Cheairs, U.S. Grant's day went very well indeed.

Once the surrender was completed, both sides relaxed their guard. In fact, they began fraternizing with a vengeance. The Confederates were short on rations and the Federals soon offered to share what they had. With such a relaxed atmosphere, many Confederates took advantage of the poorly organized guard the Federals had in place and simply walked away.

The 3rd Tennessee was ordered to protect the town of Dover. Flavel Barber was placed in charge of one-hundred men from I and K Companies. Rather than protect anything, the irate Barber urged the men to make their escape. In all, twenty-three men eluded captivity in this way. Dover became a scene of chaos.[9]

The Federals offered to parole some of the senior Confederate officers back to their homes, including John C. Brown. Brown declined the offer stating he would share the fate of soldiers. In addition, he pressed the Federals to allow the 3rd Tennessee to board the transports first to spare them any more suffering from the cold. Both of these acts permanently endeared Brown to the men of the 3rd Tennessee.[10]

There was a notable exception to the good treatment the Federals gave their prisoners in this situation. A number of

Yankees had foolishly thrown away their overcoats and blankets during the march from Fort Henry to Fort Donelson. When the Confederates became prisoners these frosty Yankees sought relief from the cold by helping themselves to Confederate stock. Thomas Deavenport reported, "While stacking arms our captors plundered our camp and took all the best of the clothing and blankets. Many a poor fellow was left without a blanket or change of clothes."[11]

No one is certain to this day how many Confederates were surrendered at Fort Donelson. Estimates range anywhere from eight to fifteen thousand men. Casualty rates were fairly even. The Confederates lost four-hundred and fifty men killed and fifteen-hundred wounded while the Federals lost five-hundred men killed and twenty-one hundred wounded.[12]

The 3rd Tennessee entered the battle with 743 men. Losses included thirteen men killed and fifty-six wounded. By the end of battle some sixty-seven 3rd Tennesseans had sought refuge in nearby Dover. Some of these men were ill and some were there because hunger, cold, and wet weather, exacerbated the tension of being under continuous fire for days on end, had become more than they could endure. Included in this latter group were four out of five members of the Deen clan of Company H who were counted as AWOL during the entire fight. Two of the Deens calling it quits were the father-son team M.L. and M.L. Junior. All the Deens were captured and sent to prison, and were exchanged later. Three of the five saw some action later and the older M.L. was badly wounded at Raymond. By the middle of 1863 all five had managed to depart the army alive.[13]

The 3rd Tennessee also left behind a number of sick men in Kentucky and at Nashville, most of whom were rounded up by Don Carlos Buell's forces. In all, some 722 men were carried off to prison.[14]

Then there is the special case of the regiment's lieutenant colonel, Thomas Gordon. His arm shattered in the regiment's second attack, Gordon was helped off the battlefield by his "body servant" (slaves accompanying their masters off to war was very common in the Confederate army) and immediately transported to Columbia, Tennessee, where he was attended for a short time in the home of Gideon Pillow. Thereafter, he was taken to his home in Lynnville. Here he was discovered by invading Yankees.

The Bluecoats took no pity on the wounded Rebel. They ordered him out of his bed and forced him to walk some fifteen miles to Columbia where he was thrown into jail. He was then transferred to another jail in Pulaski. Gordon's health steadily declined until it began to appear that death was imminent. The Federals finally allowed him to return home, but only after they repeatedly forced Gordon's family to pay a huge ransom. The harsh treatment ruined Gordon's health sufficiently to prevent his return to service, but not sufficiently to kill him. Gordon lived another thirty-nine years, until 1901.[15]

The Fort Donelson battle had a profound effect on the course of the War. It launched Grant on his career as the North's premier soldier, and shook the South out of its belief in its own invincibility. Because Fort Donelson was lost, Albert Sydney Johnston abandoned his entire Kentucky defensive line, opening Tennessee to wholesale invasion. Strategically important Nashville and all the war material there that his panicky quartermasters and Bedford Forrest were not able to carry off were lost to the Federals. Thus, what could have been only a moderate setback for the Confederacy became a major strategic victory for the North.

Brown and the 3rd Tennessee had little time to ponder the broader ramifications of their surrender. They were absorbed by grief over their dead compatriots and by the loss of personal freedom, all due to the gross ineptitude of Floyd, Pillow, Buckner, and the person ultimately responsible, Albert Sidney Johnston.

Notes for Chapter 7

1 Nathaniel F. Cheairs Memoir, p. 2.
2 *Military Annals of Tennessee*, p. 859.
3 *Ibid.*, pp. 855-859.
4 *Ibid.*, p. 856.
5 *Ibid.*, p. 859.

6 *OR*, Vol.VII, part 1, pp. 228-232.
7 *Ibid.*, p. 354. *Battles and Leaders*, Vol.I, p. 429.
8 Cheairs Memoir, pp. 2-3.
9 Flavel C. Barber Diary, Vol. I, p. 24.
10 *Military Annals of Tennessee*, p. 180.
11 Thomas H. Deavenport Diary, pp. 9-10.
12 *Battles and Leaders*, Vol.I, p. 429.
13 Rollbook, pp. 87-88.
14 *Ibid.*, p. 120, Company records.
15 *CV*, Vol. IX, pp. 417-418.

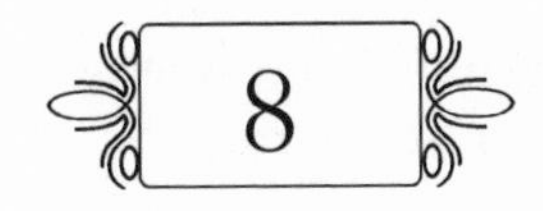

PRISON

The 3rd Tennessee began its march to captivity at 2:00 P.M. on February 18, 1862. The men were placed aboard a steamboat that "should have been consigned to the junk pile years before." The writer, J.T. Lowry of Company B, thought the steamboat ride was at least as dangerous as the Fort Donelson battlefield. The men increased the danger with their cooking method.

> In the engine room was an old-time wood stove, and it was the only place that the thousand men aboard had to broil their meat. The old thing had a depression on the top that would hold at least half a gallon, and it would not be long in filling from the dripping meat. After becoming heated it would get into a blaze, and many who could not even see the stove would have sticks from six to seven feet long with pieces of meat fastened on the ends. When stuck into the blaze, it would increase the flame until it would reach the under side of the upper deck. Had it [caught fire] but few, if any, of us would have survived.[1]

The steamboat first traveled north down the Cumberland to the Ohio River, then on to the Mississippi River. When the steamboat reached the vicinity of Cairo, still on the 18th, it pulled over to the Illinois shore to allow Flavel Barber and a few members of Company K to bury Thomas B. King. King had been laid up sick in Dover. The shock of capture and the misery of the steamboat ride were more than his weakened constitution could tolerate.[2]

Nothing else of note took place during this part of the journey other than the fact that the locals greeted the Confederates with jeers at each landing. At Alton, Illinois, the officers were separated from the rest of the men and sent to Camp Chase, Ohio. Most of the enlisted men continued by rail to Chicago.

The regiment arrived in the cold and gloom around 1:00 P.M. on February 23. Though the railroad ran all the way to the prison, the men were ordered off the cars two miles short, within the city itself, and marched the remaining distance. Three inches of snow were on the ground. The street was muddy and there were armed guards on each side.

Thomas Deavenport described the scene:

> On every hand crowds of men, women and children. Every door, window, fence and every foot of ground was occupied. It seemed that all the great had turned out to give us a grand reception. The [white] haired sire and the little boy, the aged matron and the little misses, the millionaire and the beggar, the fashionable belle and the rough market woman, the soft dandy and the stout dragman, all, all were there and seemed to vie with each other to see who could insult us most.

The Windy City folks viewed these Rebels as some sort of strange beings. Deavenport continued:

> Ear, mouth and eyes were all open. To them it was far better than a menagerie. They seemed at a loss to determine what we were, whether 'spirits of hell or goblins damned.' All were wild with joy. One old woman was so carried away that she shouted "Glory to God, it's the happiest day I ever saw in my life."

The hard-hearted Chicago women shocked the little minister:

> Woman, woman whose mission should be one of mercy, whose tongue should be used only to comfort, yes woman heaped insults on us. The milk of human kindness seemed turned to gall in their breasts. In that vast crowd no friendly, pitying eye was seen. In every hand, at every step all was hatred, deep and fiendlike ... . Women walked through the mud, by our side at least a mile, not to comfort, but laugh at us. They would split through mud holes that I, a rough soldier would shun.[3]

The men showed defiance only once. The incident was initiated by Jake Donelson. As the regiment marched through the streets, Jake "mounted his master's knapsack and gave the old familiar 'cock-a-doodle-doo' as a cheer to the downhearted boys. It was the signal for a regiment to give the old Rebel yell, and gave it they did, as only brave and unconquered hearts could."[4]

Finally, the men entered the high walls of Camp Douglas. The men were assigned to single-story barracks, one-hundred men to a building. Bunks were arranged in three tiers on each side with six men assigned to each tier. Although there was not a "stick of wood or any straw for bedding, blankets, or fire," the men were too tired to care and quickly fell asleep. They were supplied with these necessities the next day. The camp was a few hundred yards from Lake Michigan, and for a while the men could obtain some enjoyment by sitting on the barracks rooftops and watching the sailboats cruise by, that is until the guards were ordered to shoot anyone seen climbing up on the rooftops.[5]

Initially camp authorities allowed local citizens to enter and view the prisoners. This made Thomas Deavenport very uncomfortable since he had not changed clothes for three weeks. One day he was visited by two of the local clergy. Like Deavenport, the men were Methodists and were curious about one of their kind serving in the Rebel ranks. After some introductory remarks, Deavenport recorded the following conversation.

Clergyman: "Do you in the South regard slavery as a bible institution?"

Deavenport: "We do."

Clergyman: "Do you consider the Negro a man? (I suppose he thought we considered him a brute)"

Deavenport: "We do."

Clergyman: "Were you in the fight at Donelson."

Deavenport: "I was."

Clergyman: "Did you fight any?"

Deavenport: "I did."

Clergyman: "Did you take aim?"

Deavenport: "I did."

Clergyman: "Well that is considered murder to take aim in battle, is it not? You should let God direct the ball."

Deavenport: "I do not know. I went out to kill."

Clergyman: "If you were loose again do you think you would fight us any more?"

Deavenport: "Certainly I would, if I were loose without a parole."[6]

Had the two sides adopted the Chicago clergymens' approach to rifle marksmanship the Civil War would undoubtedly have been a far less bloody affair. Despite his desire to get back into the fray, Deavenport's next service would be as regimental chaplain, and he would never take up arms again.

Eventually the in-camp visits stopped, possibly due to incidents between visitors and the prisoners. In one instance, a black youth visiting the camp began making insulting remarks to some of the 3rd Tennesseans. Observing that there was no guard nearby, Felix Martin of Company B, a man "of noted strength and activity ... rushed his tormenter, his right foot striking the rascal in the pit of the stomach." As the man struggled to regain his breath, Martin made off with the man's coonskin coat. Eventually the Federals built a twenty-five foot observation tower outside the walls for visitors use in order to prevent a repeat of such occurrences.[7]

At Camp Douglas the regiment resumed its ongoing battle with its chief enemy, disease. The struggle was exacerbated by the miserable prison conditions. The barracks were drafty, the diet poor, and close confinement facilitated the spread of disease. Death rates in northern prisons closely approximated those of the worst Confederate prisons, including Andersonville: 15.5% Federal versus 12% Confederate. There were forty-one deaths due to disease in the 3rd Tennessee during their six months of captivity.[8]

Meanwhile, company grade officers (captains and lieutenants) were interned at Camp Chase and later at Johnson's Island in Ohio. Conditions for the men at Johnson's Island were little better than those experienced by their comrades in Illinois. It was very crowded and unhealthy, but at least the men could get temporary passes into Columbus on occasion, and the discipline was not as severe.[9]

Contrast the experience of the lower ranks of the regiment to the 'ordeal' of John C. Brown and Nat Cheairs. The field grade officers of the Kentucky army were separated from the rest of the officers at Johnson's Island about three weeks after their arrival, and shipped off to Fort Warren in Boston Harbor. Fort Warren was the antecedent of the modern minimum security prison, a 'country club' jail so to speak. A contingent of political prisoners from Maryland was confined here along with the newly arrived group of distinguished Southern officers. The Marylanders were all pro-secessionists. Casting *habeas corpus* aside, Abraham Lincoln had the Army collect them and lock them in prison to prevent them from taking Maryland out of the Union. This was a completely illegal action, but a very practical one considering the urgency of the situation.

John C. Brown's Autograph Book is full of entries from the Marylanders bemoaning their fate and ranting at the injustice of it all. One must, however, reserve one's tear of sympathy for their fate until after perusal of Nat Cheairs' description of conditions at Fort Warren:

> I was selected to be caterer for 72 officers in the mess. The commander of the prison gave me a casement 100 ft. long and 30 ft. wide with the kitchen attached. Soon after being in prison Henry T. Yaleman of Nashville, Tennessee gave me a letter of introduction and one of credit to the firm of Fisher & Co. of Boston to let me have anything and everything I wanted I

got Mr. Fisher to hire me a first class cook and two assistants. He sent me a Swede, the finest cook I every saw. I furnished my table with the best ware and could imitate any hotel or restaurant in Boston and could seat all at one table.

[We were] furnished the very best rations, but the men concluded we wanted something extra, so we (72 of us) chipped in $2.00 apiece per week and sent over to Boston for the best wines, liquors, beer and cigars that could be bought. About once every two weeks I'd give a dinner and invite Col. Dumich (the commander of the prison), his wife and daughters, and some other officers of the prison to dine with me.

After eating the ladies would retire and we men would smoke fine cigars, drink, etc., and tell tales until about four o'clock in the afternoon when none of us hardly knew the way home.

While in prison about six months—I spent $6,000 in gold—not all for myself, but I had some friends who were cut off from home without money, and I let them have some. They afterwards paid it back in Confederate money.[10]

Prison life seemingly was not much of a hardship for Brown and Cheairs. In fact, the hard-fighting Tennesseans enjoyed a kind of celebrity status.

When they were not in direct conflict, the Yankees and Confederates frequently relaxed with each other. Prisoners were able to escape and make their way back to Dixie relatively easily. Twenty-nine men from the 3rd Tennessee escaped from various northern prisons, and all but two either rejoined their own regiment or picked up other Confederate units.[11]

The men used a variety of means to escape. David Rhea, Brown's surrender assistant at Fort Donelson, managed to procure some civilian clothes and simply walked out, which seemed to be the standard procedure for most of the escapees. In some cases, a successful escape also meant bribing a guard (the going bribe rate ranged from $2.00 to $7.50). Others came up with counterfeit passes or escaped from prison details while outside the prison walls. Once clear of the prison walls, the men would simply book passage on a train or steamboat to return home. There was no passage of lines involved since central Tennessee was occupied by Federal forces by this time.[12]

William G. Kerr of Company B did it the hard way. He and his escape companion, J.J. Montgomery, decided to go over the twelve-foot high wall.

Kerr got near the top, when he fell back, but he tried it again, and on reaching the top said,

> "Didn't I come a climbing?" When over, we were in the commons next to the city. We walked leisurely along until we reached the street car track, and took the first car for the city .... We stopped at the Briggs House, took dinner and supper, and then rode an omnibus to the Air Line depot, where we bought tickets for Louisville, Ky., taking a sleeping car. We missed connection there, and stopped over until the next morning, when we went on to Nashville, arriving there that evening, and stopped for the night at Dr. Hodge's, corner of Broad and Cherry Streets. Taking a walk, we eluded the pickets, and, avoiding all public roads, went unmolested to Giles County.[13]

There was one fatality at Camp Douglas not due to disease. A great deal of mystery surrounds the death of Tom Golden of Company E. T.J. Moore wrote:

> We were allowed to play town ball [baseball], and in a game one day Tom Golden of Company E. was on base when W.H. Kilpatrick, of the same company, accidentally tapped Golden on the head with his pine paddle, and soon Golden got sick. A squad of the guard surrounded us, and took Kilpatrick to the dungeon and Golden to the hospital.

The next day Golden died. Apparently the prison officials viewed this episode as anything but accidental, judging by their initial reaction of throwing Kilpatrick in the "dungeon," and then tying him to a post in front of the prison headquarters for ten days (the men had to pile blankets on him to keep him from freezing to death). The Federals then turned him over to a civilian court which tried and convicted him of murder, and then sentenced him to a year in the Illinois State Penitentiary. Once released Kilpatrick simply disappeared and the 3rd Tennessee was reduced two more soldiers.[14]

In July of 1862 the two sides signed a cartel allowing for prisoner exchange. In August, as the Federal officials began formulating plans for exchanging those Confederates held in midwestern prisons, they also employed an ingenious scheme to reduce the number of Confederates they would be obligated to return. They would assemble each Confederate regiment and offer to immediately release all those who would sign an oath of allegiance to the North. The Yankee officers knew that some of the men accepting this offer would return to Confederate ranks as soon as possible; but they also knew that the majority would simply drift out of the war. This was indeed the case. Many of them went west to scratch out a new life in the great American wilderness.

Twenty-three 3rd Tennesseans took advantage of the offer; none of these men ever returned to the regiment. Six of them drifted back to the South to join other Confederate units, but overall the Federal goal was achieved.[15]

The 3rd Tennessee lost, and then regained, the services of Private Charles Combs of Company H. Apparently Combs' allegiance to the Southern Cause was only luke-warm; he not only took the loyalty oath to the Union shortly after entering captivity, but then proceeded to join up with the Northern Army. However, Combs must have had trouble adjusting to service with the Yankees as he was soon drummed out of the Union Army and returned to captivity with his old 3rd Tennessee comrades at Camp Douglas. Combs was exchanged along with the rest of the Regiment, whereupon he was placed under arrest until he managed a transfer to an artillery company.[16]

Questionable loyalty was not limited to the lowest ranks in the 3rd Tennessee. The top NCO of Company C, First Sergeant John S. Hunter, also took the oath of allegiance to gain his freedom, never to return to the Confederate Army. The same course was followed by Captain William Peaton, commander of Company D.[17]

Soldiers using the oath only as a means to get back into the war faced some unexpected repercussions much later, when it came time to apply for a veteran's pension from their home state. Hard-eyed bureaucrats just could not understand the presence of an oath of allegiance to the Union in a veteran's records. State archives recording the correspondence between men claiming continuous loyalty and faithfulness to the Confederacy and government officials questioning same makes for fascinating and sometimes heartrending reading.[18]

The Union and Confederacy finally got around to exchanging the men of the 3rd Tennessee and the other men held in the mid-western prisons in September of 1862. The junior officers and enlisted men were loaded on rail cars to travel overland to Cairo, Illinois. There they were loaded on six steamboats, one-thousand men per boat, for the next leg of the journey to Vicksburg, Mississippi. In one notable event, the men had a close-up look at one of the feared Federal gunboats. During a stop-over at Helena, Arkansas, the fleet was joined by one of the city-class gunboats, none other than the *Cairo*—currently on display at Vicksburg National Battlefield Park—which provided an escort for the final leg of the journey.[19]

Meanwhile, the senior officers boarded a steamship in Boston Harbor for a sea voyage to Richmond, Virginia. The rail trip took longer than the sea voyage and so the officers were officially exchanged on September 16 and the rest of the regiment was transferred back into Confederate ranks one week later.[20]

John C. Brown was well regarded by his cellmates at Fort Warren, and upon his departure was presented with a beautiful gentleman's walking cane. It was engraved on the head:

Col. John C. Brown
3rd Tenn. Inf
C.S.A
1862
"An Honorable Christian Soldier"[21]

While on his way to Vicksburg to rejoin the regiment, John C. Brown was intercepted by an order promoting him to brigadier general with instructions to report to Braxton Bragg at Chattanooga.

Federal activity in the west was at a standstill at the time. Albert Sidney Johnston had attempted to staunch the Federal tide at Shiloh Church in southern Tennessee, and had lost the battle, and his life in the process. The Federal western commander, Henry Halleck, was unhappy with Grant's performance at Shiloh, and took personal command of the huge army concentrated just north of Corinth, Mississippi. After an excruciatingly slow advance, Halleck captured the rail hub at Corinth, and then scattered his army to occupy various positions that Halleck called strategic points.[22]

Bragg proposed to wrest the initiative from the North by concentrating the Army of Mississippi with all available reinforcements at Chattanooga, and then together with Kirby Smith's small army at Knoxville, Tennessee, make a grand sweep into Kentucky. Bragg's army was nearly ready, but this move into the enemy's rear would be a desperate gamble, and Bragg needed as many experienced brigade commanders (the primary maneuver unit) as he could get. Brown appeared to be just the right man.

The selection of Brown was based on seniority to a degree, but foremost among the factors favoring him was his solid performance at Fort Donelson. He was untainted by the disgraceful conduct of the other officers involved. Despite some awkwardness in both of its assaults, Brown's brigade managed to capture an artillery piece in each advance, a signal indicator of success in Civil War battles. Brown's Tennesseans had also been absolutely stalwart on the defense. Brown's men severely punished McClernand's Illinoisans during the first day of battle, and did likewise to C.F. Smith's Iowans during the last. All in all, John C. Brown's performance at Fort Donelson was very impressive indeed.

Brown possessed another characteristic guaranteed to endear him to a crusty old army regular like Braxton Bragg. The most frequently encountered descriptive phrase Brown's contemporaries applied to him was "strict disciplinarian." The 3rd Tennessee's officers frequently commented on the regiment's widely recognized skill at drill, credit for which, as the regiment's commander, must go to Brown. Brown's strong discipline undoubtedly played a part in the way his brigade was able to sustain itself in the face of some extremely fierce fire at Fort Donelson.[23]

Finally, and most importantly, Brown genuinely cared about his men. They consistently responded by giving him their best. Nat Cheairs expressed the regiment's sentiments in this missive in Brown's autograph book.

> It affords me pleasure to say that no man or officer displayed more true Courage, Skill, and Gallantry than yourself. There upon that bloody field [Fort Donelson] you won never fading laurels, and endeared yourself in the hearts and minds of your entire Command, and your beloved South, that time can never efface or obliterate - your name, Skill and ability as a Commanding Officer will occupy a conspicuous place in the history of the present revolution.[24]

Brown would not see his comrades again for a full year.

Notes for Chapter 8

1 J.T. Lowry, *CV*, Vol. XVIII, p. 334.

2 Deavenport Diary, p. 11. Rollbook, p. 40, 112. Barber Diary, Vol.I, p. 27.

3 Deavenport Diary, pp. 12-13.

4 Buford McKinney, *CV*, Vol. V, p. 420.

5 Lowry, *op. cit.*. T.J. Moore, *CV*, Vol. XV, p. 4.

6 Deavenport Diary, pp. 14-15.

7 Lowry, *op. cit.*.

8 Time-Life, *Civil War: Master Index*, p. 142. Rollbook, Company records.

9 Barber Diary, Vol.I, p. 19.

10 John C. Brown Autograph Book. Several Marylanders wrote tributes to Brown. Cheairs Memoir, p. 4.

11 Rollbook, p.120. Company records.

12 Moore, *op. cit.*. Lowry, Op. Cit.. Barber Diary, p.20.

13 J.J. Montgomery, *CV*, Vol. VII, p. 11.

14 Moore, *op. cit.*. Rollbook, pp. 55-56.

15 Rollbook, Company records.

16 *Ibid.*, pp. 87, 192.

17 *Ibid.*, pp. 29, 41.

18 The author once followed a distant relative's ten-year ordeal in seeking such a pension through records contained in the Tennessee State Archives.

19 Edwin C. Bearss, *Hardluck Ironclad*, pp. 81-82,

20 Rollbook, p.26.

21 Author's Collection

22 Horn, *The Army of Tennessee*, p. 159.

23 John S. Wilkes, "General John C. Brown," *CV*, Vol.III, p. 242.

24 John C. Brown Autograph Book, Cheairs Battle Account.

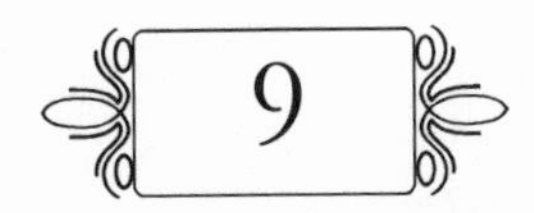

A NEW START

September 23, 1862, was a watershed in the career of the 3rd Tennessee. The exuberant days of 1861 were over; the war had evolved into a grim struggle to the death. When the regiment arrived in Vicksburg, Mississippi, it had left most of its idealism, and all of its delusions about the glory of war, on the hills at Fort Donelson and in the prisons of Illinois and Ohio. The men were well on their way toward becoming professional soldiers, and were about to prove themselves a dangerous force on the battlefield in the days ahead.

Arrival in Vicksburg was cause for considerable rejoicing. Captain George Jones of Company F was moved to poetry:

> Where with gladdened hearts they leaped on shore,
> To meet with friends they'd met before;
> Where with rapturous joy they looked to see
> Their country's flag still floating free.[1]

The Southerners were happy to be home, and were not daunted by the depths to which the fortunes of the Confederacy had sunk in the west in the days following Fort Donelson.

Since the battle at Fort Donelson and the 3rd Tennessee's imprisonment much had transpired. The Confederacy fought and lost major battles at Shiloh and Corinth, and Bragg was just beginning his aborted Kentucky invasion in which the 3rd Tennessee's old commander, John C. Brown, would play a prominent part.

As the Confederate forces steadily retreated, more and more of the strategic Mississippi River waterway was lost to the enemy leaving only a short strip between Vicksburg and Port Hudson under Confederate control. Most of the Confederate military in the west had been given over to Braxton Bragg, who was eventually made army commander after A.S. Johnston's death at Shiloh. This left the Department of Mississippi and Eastern Louisiana short on manpower and in a somewhat vulnerable position should the Federals decide to seize the initiative in that quarter again. As men began arriving in Vicksburg to be exchanged, including the 3rd Tennessee, many were immediately assigned to this very weak department.

The fate of the regiment was now in the hands of John C. Pemberton. He was a Pennsylvanian who had opted to serve the Confederacy largely because of his spouse's Virginia background. He had recently been assigned to the Charleston, South Carolina, defenses where he was shunned by polite society because of his Yankee roots. He was having no better success at acceptance in Mississippi. He was, however, regarded as a capable officer and respected by Jefferson Davis.[2]

The 3rd Tennessee now experienced wholesale changes internally as well as in brigade affiliations and command. John C. Brown, promoted to brigadier general, had been diverted to Chattanooga, Tennessee. The regiment's lieutenant colonel, Thomas Gordon, his health ruined, resigned. Nat Cheairs, the regiment's major, was left to "reorganize the regiment, which I did and then [I] came home to raise a cavalry command, which I failed to do." He also resigned from the 3rd, apparently having had his fill of life in the infantry. He was later employed by Nathan B. Forrest as a commissary

Twin brothers Calvin and James Walker were stalwart leaders of the 3rd Tennessee. Calvin (l.) began the war as commander of Company G and later commanded the regiment in its toughest battles. He was killed by a stray shot from the 123rd New York at the Battle of Kolb's Farm during the Atlanta campaign. James, in his colorful Confederate battle shirt, began the war as regimental ordnance sergeant before succeeding his brother as commander of Company G. Wounded at Raymond and Chickamauga, James served through to the surrender.

Courtesy: Herb Peck, Jr.

officer. He made frequent forays into his home area to purchase provisions for the army from the agricultural abundance there. Cheairs was captured twice more. During one of these episodes he was nearly hanged as a spy, and would have been had he not been a shrewd negotiator. The fact that he and his captor were both Masons also helped.[3]

With the top three officers now gone, and with the experience of a full scale battle under its belt, the regiment now needed to select new leaders to replace those who departed for one reason or another, and also to replace those who obviously were not up to the task (massive change overs in leadership was typical in most front line regiments as true fighting men came to the fore). Selections were again made from within the regiment.

Calvin Harvey Walker, former physician and commander of Company G, was elected colonel, and Calvin J. Clack, former lawyer and commander of Company A, was elected lieutenant colonel. Both Walker and Clack proved to be excellent combat leaders and were officially commended by several of the top officers of the Army of Tennessee, including Pemberton and John B. Hood. Command of the regiment shifted back and forth between these two men because Walker was often too ill to command.[4]

Ironically, both Walker and Clack would be killed within days of each other, one north and the other south of Atlanta.

Thomas Tucker replaced Nat Cheairs as the regiment's major. Five companies elected new company commanders, presumably the most capable lieutenants. All but one were to prove equal to the task.[5]

All companies except Company B received new letter designations according to the seniority of their commanders. The changes were: A to G, C to D, D to I, E to F, F to E, G to H, H to C, I to K, and K to A. To avoid confusion, this narrative will continue to refer to each company by its original letter.[6]

What the 3rd Tennessee needed most was a complete reissue of all the required paraphernalia of war, especially new weapons with their appropriate accouterments. Two companies, I and K, finally received the latest issue rifled muskets, the long coveted 'minie' rifles the men had been promised what seemed a lifetime ago. However they were not the top of the line Enfields they had hoped for, but Richmond manufactured rifles for Company K and Belgian made rifles for Company I. Company K also received sword bayonets for their new weapons.[7]

The Yankees had employed some unfair exchange practices that fall. Some of the men returning to the ranks should have been classified as damaged goods. Private Sam McCoy of Company K was minus one arm, removed because of a wound sustained at Fort Donelson, and had to be discharged. Privates B.F. McGaugh and S.H. McCanless of Company G were also each missing one arm, but these men voluntarily returned to the regiment. They were retained in the ranks for three months and discharged only when battle was imminent. Their dedication was probably in large part due to the fine leadership of Calvin Walker, who was much loved as commander of Company G before he became the regiment's new colonel.[8]

While 607 men were exchanged at Vicksburg, the 3rd Tennessee received further accessions during the months ahead. Some twenty-seven escapees from the encirclement at Fort Donelson and from various northern prisons returned to the ranks, as did some men who were home sick at the time of the battle. Many of the 3rd Tennessee's officers were granted furloughs to return home for the purpose of recruiting replacements for the regiment. These new men, plus a few transfers from other units, brought in an additional one-hundred forty men to the ranks. Most of the new men were from Giles County and were assigned to the Giles County companies (A, B, D, G, & K).[9]

That fall also ended the service of the 3rd Tennessee's most famous recruit, Jake Donelson. Lieutenant McCanless took Jake along when he returned home on furlough. Jake was not the only member of the feathered community ending his service with the Confederate Army. While serving his time at Camp Douglas Jake took a mate, and the union produced three sturdy sons. The first, General Morgan, returned home with McCanless's brother; the second, Jeff Davis, accompanied Will Everly to Pulaski; and the third, Stonewall Jackson, accompanied Calvin Walker to Lynnville. Jake was officially mustered out and settled in Cornersville. Jake died suddenly in 1864 and was buried there with much ceremony.[10]

The recruits added to the ranks that fall would be the only significant influx of new blood into the regiment during the course of the war; from December 1862 to the end the 3rd Tennessee had to fight with whoever was left. The regiment's battlefield strength peaked at five-hundred and forty at Chickasaw Bayou, declined to less than three-hundred for the start of the Atlanta campaign, and continued to drop from that point onward until by late 1864 it was no longer recognizable as a regiment.[11]

The most significant event that fall for the six-hundred and seven men of the 3rd Tennessee was the assignment of the regiment on November 10 to a new brigade under the command of former Texas mathematics instructor, lawyer, pro-secessionist politician, and former commander of the fierce 7th Texas Regiment, John Gregg.[12]

Gregg was described by Flavel Barber as "somewhat particular and exacting, and a little awkward." To the good (or ill) of the 3rd Tennessee, Gregg was also to prove one of the South's most aggressive combat leaders. In addition to the 3rd Tennessee, the new brigade included the 10th, 30th, 41st, and 50th Tennessee Regiments, and the 1st Tennessee Infantry Battalion. It was immediately assigned to the defense of Vicksburg.[13]

The 3rd Tennessee enjoyed a period of relative quiet with U.S. Grant temporarily on the shelf, and Federal attention firmly fixed on Braxton Bragg's romp through Kentucky. General Halleck's penchant for garrisoning strategic points had robbed the Federals of their offensive capability in Mississippi, and Pemberton's force was not strong enough to take the initiative on its own. There was nothing for Gregg and his men to do but wait.

Meanwhile, "Old Brains' Halleck had become the new Federal Commander in Chief of the Union Army. Lincoln very shortly realized that Halleck was an admirable administrator, but no general, and was almost incapable of making a decision. Lincoln and Secretary of War Edwin Stanton were forced to make operational decisions that should have been left in the hands of the military professionals. Eventually, Lincoln became so desperate for some sort of positive military action that when political General John McClernand of Fort Donelson fame totally ignored military protocol by leapfrogging several layers of command and proposed to Lincoln that he, McClernand, raise an army of midwesterners expressly for the purpose of capturing Vicksburg (with McClernand at its head, ofcourse). Lincoln immediately approved the plan since Halleck was not forthcoming with any alternatives, and Lincoln needed more troops anyway. The plan was better than nothing even though Lincoln knew relying on McClernand entailed great risk.[14]

While he may have been completely erratic on the battlefield, John McClernand was a world-class recruiter. Soon steamboat loads of new Union regiments came streaming down the Ohio and Mississippi Rivers, and a new army accumulated at Memphis.

In the meantime, Grant, at Lincoln's insistance, had been reinstated in command of the Union Army of the Tennessee. Grant devised a plan to use these new troops as soon as possible, before McClernand could arrive to take command of the force. Grant felt no obligation to honor any agreements Lincoln and McClelland might have arrived at "outside of channels."

Grant placed William T. Sherman in command of McClernand's troops at Memphis and ordered him to advance down the river by steamboat, find a suitable debarkation point along the Yazoo River north of Vicksburg, and attack the city from the northeast. Meanwhile, Grant would lead a second force down through the heart of Mississippi, and attack the city from the east. Grant snatched McClernand's army just like a fox sneaking a chicken out of a hen house.[15]

In mid-November, 1862, Grant made the first move, seizing Holly Springs, Mississippi. He then sent a force of twenty-thousand men under General Alvin Hovey forward to seize the Confederate rail center at Grenada. Among the forces opposing this advance was Gregg's Brigade, including the 3rd Tennessee.

The Tennesseans did their best to slow the Federals, making a stand first at Oxford, and then suffering some embarrassing losses, including Private Thomas McCarter of Company B killed, and nine men captured when they were ambushed at Springdale. Eventually numbers prevailed, and Hovey seized some fifteen locomotives and one-hundred railroad cars the Confederates were unable to evacuate.[16]

At this point Pemberton made the best move of his military career. He ordered Earl Van Dorn to take a cavalry force and attack Grant's supply lines. Van Dorn was wildly successful, decimating the advance depot Grant had established at Holly Springs.

His supply line severed, and not yet aware of the ability of his soldiers to sustain themselves with whatever the countryside had to offer, Grant ordered his forces to return to their starting point. Sherman knew nothing of all this, and was well down the Mississippi River as Grant began his retreat.

Pemberton received word of Sherman's advance not a moment too soon. He immediately dispatched forces to meet it: Gregg's Brigade was on its way to Vicksburg.[17]

Sherman entered the Yazoo River on December 23 and began looking for a way through the dismal swamps and bayous to Vicksburg, about fifteen miles away. He had thirty-thousand troops with him, more than enough to overwhelm Pemberton if he could just find a way to get at him. Pemberton had no idea of Sherman's whereabouts until December 24. For three days, until December 27th when Confederate reinforcements began arriving, Sherman, had he known the pathetic condition of the Rebel defenses, could have walked into Vicksburg almost at will. Only five regiments totaling barely three-thousand men were on hand to defend the city. Luckily for the Confederates, the terrain, spiced with a handful of dead-eye Mississippi sharpshooters, kept Sherman in the muck and in befuddlement. The Confederates had plenty of time to get ready.[18]

Once Pemberton was sure of Sherman's plan, he dispatched three brigades of reinforcements to the Yazoo line north of Vicksburg including Gregg's.

For a while Sherman convoyed his force up and down the Yazoo River, testing the strength of the Confederate defenses with cannon fire from his big ironclad gunboats and with occasional probes with his infantry. He could not find an attack route that suited him. Eventually he approved a full scale assault in the Chickasaw Bayou, Chickasaw Bluffs area opposite McNutt Lake.

This area was almost undefended because of the forbidding terrain. An attack force would be constricted to such a narrow frontage that a small defense force could probably hold it.

The Federal commander on the scene, Brigadier General George W. Morgan, believed that if the narrow part of McNutt Lake could be bridged surreptitiously, an attack column might be rushed across up onto the bluffs beyond before the Confederates could react. The Yankees could then insert their entire force through the breach and roll up the Confederate positions further south. The gateway to Vicksburg would then be wide open.[19]

The operation kicked off with Morgan conducting his engineer officer, Captain W. F. Patterson, down to the lake for a personal reconnaissance of the portion to be bridged. Morgan instructed Patterson to begin construction of the bridge before daylight the next day, December 29th. Two Federal brigades would then launch an assault across the bridge at daylight.

Morgan discovered the first difficulty with his plan when he went to check on Patterson's progress before dawn on the 29th. A bridge was under construction, but it was not on McNutt Lake. Instead, it was on a slough parallel to the lake along its north side, a position completely useless to the Federals. Patterson was building a bridge to nowhere. Morgan pointed out the error and ordered Patterson, "an intelligent and efficient officer," to haul up his equipment and begin construction at the proper point.[20]

Patterson had a sufficient number of pontoons for the job (eight), but he somehow had not included stringers, the planks used to hook the pontoons together and upon which the bridge flooring is laid. Morgan and Patterson puzzled over this new predicament before lashing the pontoons together side by side, and then attempting to bridge the remaining thirty-two feet of lake with surrounding timber.[21]

Several dozen engineer troops set to work chopping timber and producing a prodigious racket in the quiet dawn which soon drew the attention of the Confederates. In short order the unfortunate men were subjected to a murderous artillery barrage by J.L. Wofford's Mississippi Battery assisted by a two-gun section under Lieutenant J.A. Tarleton, another Mississippi contingent. The Federal pontoons were shot to pieces along with a fair number of engineers. What had been a bad situation for the Federals soon degenerated into outright catastrophe.[22]

Morgan now felt that an assault on this part of the Confederate line was hopeless, and reported as much to Sherman. Sherman arrived on the scene in person. After some profound contemplation, he ordered the attack to proceed. An assault column was organized along the causeway bordering Chickasaw Bayou. It would have to rely on an old corduroy bridge spanning the branch of the bayou fronting the Confederate defensive positions to gain access to the Confederate position on the bluffs beyond. The whole thing would be conducted in broad daylight down a narrow road, across a primitive, narrow bridge. The men would then debauch into a relatively open area directly below a steep bluff upon which were perched an unknown number of heavily armed Confederates. To Morgan and Colonel John F. DeCorcy, the man who would lead the attack, it looked as if they would be walking into a gigantic trap. It was.[23]

The man assigned responsibility for preventing Sherman from breaking out of the swamps and bayous was South Carolinian Stephen D. Lee. Lee was a veteran of Robert E. Lee's army and had an impressive reputation. At Second Bull Run he commanded the field artillery force that unhinged the Federal left and paved the way for James Longstreet's assault that swept the Federal army from the field. Lee was young and energetic, a West Point graduate, and well seasoned by a variety of assignments in the east. He was about to prove himself more than a match for William T. Sherman.[24]

With all his heart, Lee wanted Sherman to attack his positions at Chickasaw Bayou. He purposely let the corduroy bridge remain intact in the hope that the Federals would be foolish enough to try an attack there. The bridge was in plain sight of the Confederate position, and was only wide enough to allow the passage of three or four men abreast. This meant that initially the Federals would have virtually no firepower to their front while at the same time offering a dense column of blue targets to their enemies. Once across the bridge the attackers would have to re-form directly under the guns of some of the toughest Confederate infantry in the west. Lee made his final preparations by simply withdrawing his infantry screen from along the bayou to increase the likelihood that the Federals would attempt the assault. Lee: "Before daylight on the 29th Colonel Hall's Regiment [26th Louisiana] was withdrawn from its rifle pits and the dry crossing left open to the enemy, as it was desired he should attack my position in front." Sherman could not have obliged Lee more.[25]

The Confederate reinforcements Morgan had hoped to avoid by attacking early were in place. Lee decided he only needed to use two regiments from Gregg's Brigade. These two, the 3rd and 30th Tennessee, were placed in the middle of his defensive line under the direct command of Lee.

As one of Lee's biggest regiments, the 3rd Tennessee was positioned as Lee's front line with the 30th Tennessee and 28th Louisiana placed in a second line a short distance behind. Calvin Clack, commanding in Colonel Walker's absence, placed Companies I and K with their rifled muskets, reinforced by Company B, on the forward edge of the bluff. These men looked directly down on the attack area, and would be in position to deliver a lethal flanking fire on the Federal assault column once it stormed across the bridge. The rifled muskets would quickly show their worth. The ensuing battle was to be the most lopsided contest the 3rd Tennessee would participate in during the entire war.[26]

Notes for Chapter 9

1 Rollbook, p. 71.

2 Woodworth, *Jefferson Davis and His Generals*, pp. 170-172.

3 Cheairs Memoir.

4 Rollbook, p. 141.

5 *Ibid.*, Company records.

6 *Military Annals of Tennessee*, p.178.

7 Barber Diary, Vol.II, p.5.

8 Rollbook, pp. 77, 156, 290.

9 *Ibid.*, p.120, Company records.

10 Buford McKinney, *CV*, Vol. V, p. 420.

11 Rollbook, p.343.

12 Patricia L. Faust et. al., *Historical Times Illustrated Encyclopedia of the Civil War* (hereafter referred to as the *Encyclopedia of the Civil War)*, p. 325.

13 Barber Diary, Vol.II, p. 4. *Battles and Leaders*, Vol.III, p. 471.

14 McPherson, *Battle Cry of Freedom*, pp. 488, 577. Richard Wheeler, *The Siege of Vicksburg*, p. 76.

15 McPherson, *op. cit.*, pp. 577-578. Wheeler, *op. cit.*, p. 80.

16 Barber Diary, Vol.II, p. 5. Rollbook, p. 178.

17 *OR*, Vol.XVII, part 1, pp. 666-667.

18 *Battles and Leaders*, Vol.III, pp. 462-464.

19 *Ibid.*

20 *Ibid.*, p. 465.

21 *Ibid.*, p. 466.

22 *Ibid. OR*, Vol.XVII, part 1, p. 682.

23 *Battles and Leaders*, Vol.III, pp. 466-477.

24 *Encyclopedia of the Civil War*, p.431.

25 *OR*, Vol.XVII, part 1, p. 682.

26 Barber Diary, Vol.II, p. 11.

10

BATTLE AT THE BAYOU

The 3rd Tennessee deployed 549 men to the bluffs above Chickasaw Bayou. This was about two-hundred fewer men than at Fort Donelson, but it was a leaner, tougher group than it was ten months before, and the regiment had a chip on its shoulder. The men were eager to erase the stigma of the Fort Donelson surrender from their record.[1]

The regiment was without the ten men lost at Springdale the month before, but sickness continued to take the greatest toll during the months preceding the battle—nine men had died from various illnesses while another one-hundred and fourteen were absent, too sick to fight. Of these, thirty became permanently disabled, and six more died. While the mortality rate from disease had slowed, the continual diminishing of the 3rd Tennessee's ranks was inexorable. Among the missing men too ill to fight was Colonel Calvin H. Walker, the 3rd Tennessee's new commander. Lieutenant Colonel Calvin Clack would command the regiment at Chickasaw Bayou.[2]

'Absent without leave' (AWOL) was a serious problem during this Christmas season of 1862. Fifty-six men were listed as AWOL at the time of the battle; sixteen of these were later reclassified as deserters. Eleven more men 'deserted' to the cavalry. The Confederate Army had a policy allowing the cavalry to recruit from the ranks of the infantry and this was an irritant.[3]

The regiment was also without the services of Sergeant John Jackson of Company C, Privates J. M. Abernathy and T.L. Jackson of Company A, and Private I.M. Park of Company G. With the Christmas season upon them, these men were unable to resist the temptation of holiday cheer as all four men were classified as "drunk" or "inebriated at the time of the battle." This was not to be the only instance Private Park would have problems with 'John Barleycorn.'[4]

Then there is the intriguing case of Private J.P. Caldwell of Company E. Private Caldwell missed the battle because he had been "excused for cowardice." Caldwell's commander, Lieutenant D.G. Stevenson, must have found some convincing evidence of faint-heartedness in Caldwell's behavior to provide him this unique favor. As we shall see, Caldwell never did seem to muster the courage to perform his duties as a fighting man.[5]

Though the 3rd Tennessee was now partially equipped with rifled muskets, there was still a shortage of armament for the troops. Privates J. McCarroll and R.W. Owen of Company E arrived at the field of battle unarmed, and were excused from the fight for that reason. The Battle of Chickasaw Bayou was to provide a ready made solution to Confederate equipment shortages.[6]

Private Charles Combs of Company H, still under arrest for having joined the Yankee army while in prison, also missed the battle.[7]

A recapitulation of the 3rd Tennessee's strength at the time of the battle is as follows:

Exchanged at Vicksburg	607
Rejoined on their own	80
Replacements	140
Total	827

Men lost from September 26 to December 28, 1862:

Killed in battle	1	
Captured	9	
Wounded	1	
Died	9	
Absent sick	114	
AWOL/deserted	56	
Transferred	12	
'Deserted' to cavalry	11	
Detached	47	
All other reasons	18	
Total	279	(34%)

Men deployed to Chickasaw Bayou: 549 (66%) [8]

While this number (549) is about half the authorized strength of a standard infantry regiment, by late 1862 a regiment of more than five-hundred men was considered a very strong unit, and was sometimes mistaken for a brigade.

As mentioned before, the 3rd and 30th Tennessee regiments were detached from Gregg's Brigade to thicken the center of Lee's line. In addition, a regiment from John C. Vaughn's Tennessee brigade was dispatched at the last minute by Pemberton. Vaughn was the former commander of the other '3rd Tennessee,' the 3rd Confederate. It was the 80th Tennessee that Vaughn deployed to the battlefield, however (on the right side of line, not shown on map).[9]

The 3rd and 30th had all night the 28th and until 11:00 a.m. the morning of the 29th to prepare their positions, and were ready for anything the Federals had to offer. The fight that followed was very similar to the first day's fight at Fort Donelson ten months earlier. Coincidentally, the 3rd was again fighting troops that technically belonged to John McClernand. This time, however, part of the 3rd Tennessee had muskets with several times the effective range of its old smooth bore weapons. This greater range plus the regiment's excellent field position gave it the capability to lay fire over most of the battlefield.

Just prior to the attack the Federal commander, George Morgan, sensing disaster, made one last appeal to common sense and

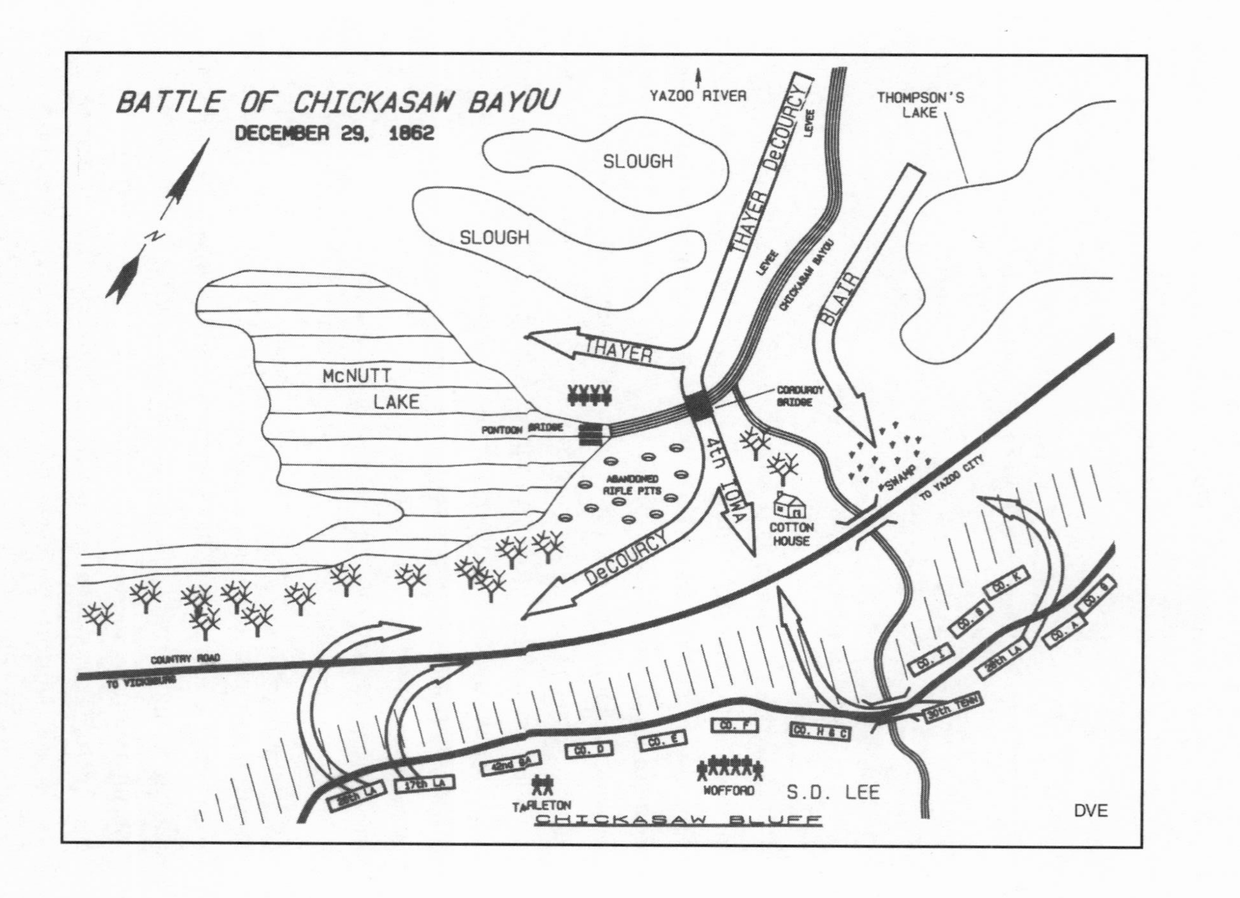

BATTLE OF CHICKASAW BAYOU
DECEMBER 29, 1862
N
YAZOO RIVER
THOMPSON'S LAKE
SLOUGH
SLOUGH
THAYER DeCOURCY
LEVEE
LEVEE
CHICKASAW BAYOU
BLAIR
THAYER
McNUTT LAKE
CORDUROY BRIDGE
PONTOON BRIDGE
4th IOWA
ABANDONED RIFLE PITS
SWAMP
TO YAZOO CITY
COTTON HOUSE
DeCOURCY
COUNTRY ROAD
TO VICKSBURG
CO. K
CO. B
CO. I
28th LA
CO. A
CO. G
30th TENN
CO. F
CO. H & C
CO. E
CO. D
42nd GA
17th LA
28th LA
TARLETON
WOFFORD
S.D. LEE
CHICKASAW BLUFF
DVE

begged Sherman to call off the assault. Sherman responded with the unsettling message: "Tell Morgan to give the signal for the assault, that we will lose 5000 men before we take Vicksburg, and we might as well lose them here as anywhere else."[10]

The Federals began the attack with a fierce but ineffective artillery bombardment, and then three brigades, some six-thousand men, sprang to the assault. After several wet and miserable days of endless tramping around in the Mississippi swamps the Yankee troops were relieved that they were finally doing something to get them out of their predicament. They had no idea that Sherman had committed them to a suicidal attack.

The men of John F. DeCourcy's and John M. Thayer's brigades followed each other across the corduroy bridge spanning the bayou, while Frank P. Blair's brigade attacked down the levee on the opposite side of the bayou. From the moment the assault began the Confederate infantry and artillery responded with a roar. According to Morgan, men were "mowed down by a storm of shells, grape and canister, and minie-balls which swept our front like a hurricane of fire." DeCourcy's brigade veered to the right and immediately went to ground, taking refuge in the abandoned Confederate rifle pits. When Thayer's brigade arrived at the bridge, the lead regiment, the 4th Iowa, crossed over and took off at a run directly for the base of the bluff. These men were quickly pinned down by the 3rd Tennessee and could neither advance nor retreat without exposing themselves to deadly fire.[11]

In desperation, the 4th Iowa, supported by individuals and groups from other regiments, made repeated assaults, and each time were met by a "sheet of flame" from the 3rd Tennessee rifles. According to Flavel Barber "the dead and dying lay in heaps." During the heaviest of the fighting Stephen Lee rode along the 3rd Tennessee's line advising the men to "keep cool," which the men, caught up in the throes of battle, found quite humorous.[12]

Meanwhile, Thayer's other four regiments became confused and turned off to the right before they reached the bridge. These men ended up in the woods on the north side of McNutt Lake, and missed out on the fight completely, an event George Morgan thought fortunate. One of these fortunate Bluecoats was Ira Doty, the man whose qualms about freeing the blacks was quoted earlier.

Blair's brigade, moving down the east side of the levee, immediately bogged down as soon as they entered the left branch of the bayou and its surrounding swamp.

With the Federal attack in total collapse, the Confederates pounced upon the survivors to make the victory complete. The 28th Louisiana and 30th Tennessee stormed directly through the 3rd Tennessee's line straight into the demoralized Yankees, while the 26th and 17th Louisiana Regiments moved forward from the Confederate left. The Tennesseans, Georgians, and other troops on the main defensive line scooped up twenty-one officers, three-hundred and eleven soldiers of other ranks, four stands of colors, and more than five-hundred rifles. Those Yankees not captured quickly fled the battlefield, abandoning their dead and wounded.[13]

Soon after the Federal retreat, Yankee sharpshooters opened up a hot fire to prevent any further Confederate pursuit. However, since the Southerners had too few troops for an offensive, the only real effect was to delay the treatment of the large numbers of Federal wounded. Morgan asked Sherman for permission to offer a flag of truce to the Confederates so that these men could be helped. Initially Sherman refused, not wanting to admit by such a gesture that he had been whipped. By the time the red-haired commander finally relented it had gotten dark, and when the flag of truce was brought forward, the Confederates, not knowing the reason for the Yankee movement, fired on the flag bearers. Meanwhile, the Confederates were able to collect only eighty of the Yankee wounded for treatment in Rebel hospitals.[14]

The Battle of Chickasaw Bayou was one of the most lopsided Confederate victories during the Civil War. Sherman licked his wounds for a short while, and groped around in the swamp fog looking for another place to attack. Then on January 2, 1863, he loaded his army (actually McClernand's army) back on the transports.

As the Federals retreated, they were dogged by the 3rd Tennessee joined by the 2nd Texas. The pursuing Confederates helped themselves to the plentiful food rations abandoned by the blue forces in their entrenchments, a godsend to men on a near starvation diet for several days. They also captured twenty more Yankee stragglers. When the two regiments came in sight of the Federal fleet, the Tennesseans impetuously rushed to the shoreline and opened fire. The Federals replied with huge exploding shells from the gunboats, whereupon the panic stricken 3rd Tennesseans quickly and unceremoniously dove into a nearby ravine. The 3rd ended the adventure by detaching Companies B and G as rearguard, and returned to the bluffs.[15]

Sherman withdrew to his supply base at Milliken's Bend on the Louisiana side of the river. Two days later, an irate John McClernand arrived and assumed command of the army. The two generals decided that another assault on Vicksburg was not feasible and moved off to the north into Arkansas, where there were easier targets, and launched a successful attack against a remote Confederate garrison called Arkansas Post.

The casualty figures for Chickasaw Bayou show just how lopsided the Confederate victory was. The Federals suffered 208 killed, 1005 wounded, and 563 missing (nearly all captured) for a total of 1776. In contrast, the Confederates had 63 men killed, 134 wounded, and 10 missing for a total of 207.[16]

Despite its position at the center of the Confederate line, the 3rd Tennessee suffered only two casualties. However, both were fatalities (James Osborne of Company K was struck in the foot but apparently was not wounded badly enough to qualify as a casualty). One of the features of men fighting from entrenched positions is that while casualties were usually very light, those men who were hit were often hit fatally as the only portion of the body constantly exposed was the head. In addition, officers had a bad habit of climbing up onto the breastworks to bolster the men's courage by showing contempt for the enemy's fire. This was inspirational up to the moment the officer was hit by an enemy bullet.[17]

This was the case with the two 3rd Tennesseans killed at Chickasaw Bayou. With the regimental commander gone, Major Tom Tucker was the regiment's acting lieutenant colonel. He was killed while commanding a portion of the regiment's defensive line.

Flavel Barber recorded that "Major Tucker when the enemy commenced their final flight, sprang upon the breastwork, waving his sword and cheering. He instantly fell dead, pierced by three balls, one through his heart."[18]

The other soldier killed was Second Lieutenant James P. Bass of Company K, Barber's company. "James Bass of my company was standing erect behind our low breastworks, when he received a ball in his stomach which passed through his body and lodged in his back." After a night of horrible agony, Bass died the next day.[19]

The 3rd Tennessee was cited for gallantry by both John C. Pemberton and Stephen Lee. According to Lee, "the Third, Thirtieth, and Eightieth Tennessee Regiments, occupying the pits where the enemy made their most formidable attack ... displayed coolness and gallantry and their fire was terrific." Calvin Clack was personally commended by Lee.[20]

While the 3rd Tennessee had no one officially missing at the end of the battle, two men present at the start of the battle were definitely not there at its end. Privates J.M. Harwell and G.B. Smith, both from Company I, established a pattern each man would follow until both deserted the regiment in November of 1863. Harwell "ran in every engagement," and Smith was "present at the commencement of every engagement, but always missing at the end."[21]

If the 3rd Tennessee had any doubts about the value of entrenchments, they evaporated with their experience at Chickasaw Bayou. The casualty rate of eight to one favoring the Confederates was a clear indicator of the futility of head-on assaults against entrenched infantry. Unfortunately, it took most Civil War commanders quite a while before they got this message, if ever.

Once Sherman finished his foray at Arkansas Post, attention again shifted back to the Mississippi Valley, where U.S. Grant and his Navy counterparts, David Farragut and David Porter, were looking for some way to pry the Confederates loose from the river. With Sherman's withdrawal from the north of Vicksburg, the emphasis shifted downstream one-hundred and fifty miles to the Rebel bastion at Port Hudson. As the Federals built up their forces for combined land/river assault, the Confederates also shored up their defenses. Among the reinforcements was John Gregg 's brigade, including the 3rd Tennessee.

While a Yankee land force under the inept Nathaniel Banks bogged down in the swamps, and never did pose a serious threat to the Confederates, Farragut's naval task force of seven vessels, supported by the ironclad *Essex* and six mortar barges, ran the Rebel batteries at Port Hudson the night of March 14, 1863. The 3rd Tennessee's position on the Confederate left, the furthermost position downstream, was the first one the Federals encountered.

Starting around 11:00 p.m., the 3rd was subjected to a barrage of huge mortar shells which either burst in the air, or buried themselves deep in the ground before exploding and creating a huge fountain of dirt. Flavel Barber was very impressed: "I can compare it to nothing less than that great day when the stars of heaven shall fall from their places." One of the regiment's soldiers, John T. Goodrich of Company F, found the trajectory of the huge mortar rounds a little deceptive. "While standing on the large embankment of one of the forts [I] saw one of those large mortar shells coming right toward me, when I jumped about twenty feet to get out of the way, to learn later that the old screeching shell fell something like a fourth of a mile from me." Amazingly, no one in the 3rd Tennessee was seriously hurt.[22]

Despite the heavy firepower the Yankee warships employed, this was a lopsided victory for the Confederate shore batteries. In short order the Confederates heavily damaged four vessels, which retreated down the river. The two lead vessels, Farragut's flagship *The Hartford* and its escort the gunboat *Albatross*, were lashed together to provide the flagship extra protection. They ran aground under the Confederate guns but managed to pull themselves free and proceed up the river. The last vessel in the Federal force, the side-wheeler *Mississippi*, was badly hit and also run aground, then blown up by her crew.

This action was a spectacular sight for the men of the 3rd Tennessee. The Confederates lit fires along the shoreline to illuminate the Yankee vessels. This light reflected off the billowing clouds of white powder smoke from the big guns. Bright red flashes of hundreds of shells bursting in the air added to the spectacle, creating a scene the Tennesseans would never see again.

Casualties were equally lopsided. Eighty-four Federals died versus one Confederate, hardly justification for the meager accomplishment of moving two ships to the north of Port Hudson. However, the Federals learned from the experience.[23]

The 3rd Tennessee came through the action completely unscathed. It was not long, however, before another crisis developed on the Vicksburg front. This time the Tennesseans would not be so lucky.

Notes for Chapter 10

1 Rollbook, p. 343.
2 *Ibid.*, Company records.
3 *Ibid.* p.178, Company records.
4 *Ibid.*, pp. 204, 262, 267, 291.
5 *Ibid.*, p.254.
6 *Ibid.*, pp. 248, 250.
7 *Ibid.*, p. 192.
8 *Ibid.*, compiled from Company records.
9 *OR*, Vol.XVII, part 1, pp. 666-667.
10 *Battles and Leaders*, Vol.III, p. 467.
11 *Ibid.*, p.468.
12 Barber Diary, Vol.II, pp. 14-16.
13 *Ibid.*, p. 18. OR, Vol. XVII, part 1, p. 682.
14 *Ibid.*, p. 683.
15 Barber Diary, Vol.II, p. 25.
16 *Battles and Leaders*, Vol.III, p.471.
17 Barber Diary, Vol.II, p. 9.
18 *Ibid.*, p. 19.
19 *Ibid.*, p. 20.
20 *OR*, Vol.XVII, part 1, p. 683.
21 Rollbook, pp. 329, 334.
22 Barber Diary, Vol.II, p. 46. John T. Goodrich, *CV*, Vol. XVI, p.126.
23 Time-Life, *War on the Mississippi*, p. 162.

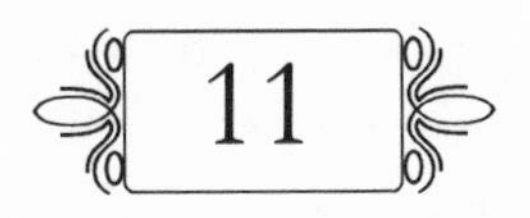

RAYMOND

May 12, 1863, seemed a day of opportunity for Brigadier General John Gregg. He was wrong.

After months of groping around in the swamps north of Vicksburg looking for a way into the city, U.S. Grant finally hit on an idea. He would take everyone south of the fortress along the Louisiana side of the Mississippi River, then cross his troops to the Mississippi side and attack the city from the south where the terrain was more open and the defenses less mature. Grant's spearhead units would march along a line which would take them directly to Jackson, the Mississippi state capital. John C. Pemberton, commanding all the southern troops in Eastern Mississippi, expected Grant to swing west at any moment for a direct thrust at Vicksburg.

On May 11 General Gregg, located in Raymond, just southeast of Vicksburg, sent out a reconnaissance unit. The only men available were forty Mississippi State Troops, mostly farm boys and gray-beard old men. They set out southwest, down the Utica Road, in search of Grant's elusive army which was known to be moving in Gregg's general direction, toward the northeast, roughly parallel to the Big Black River.[1]

Captain J. M. Hall, the militia company commander, surprised Gregg by locating the Yankee march column. Not only that, Captain Hall's men then managed to drive in the feeble blue cavalry screen which in turn caused the following infantry to deploy. This slowed the Federal advance, allowing Gregg more time to position his forces south of Raymond.

Gregg was not confident of Hall's ability to accurately estimate the size of the approaching Federal force, so the Texan dispatched his own scouts. These men reported a force of only twenty-five hundred to three-thousand men. This report, plus the success his irregular troops had in disrupting the Federals' progress, confirmed Gregg's theory that he was facing nothing more than "a brigade on a marauding excursion" on their way to destroy Confederate stores at nearby Edward's Depot.[2]

Gregg made ready to pounce. Since the enemy's force was estimated to be about the same size as his own, and since the Confederates were accustomed to fighting and winning outnumbered, Gregg set out to 'capture' the Yankee brigade.[3]

What really was approaching Gregg and his men was the vanguard of James B. McPherson's XVII Army Corps, three divisions strong. Because of a severe drought that spring of 1863, marching columns created huge dust clouds that made all but the front portions of the column invisible. Another problem was Gregg had arrived on the field only the day before so his reconnaissance time was extremely limited. Gregg took a great risk by initiating battle when a more prudent course would have been to harass and delay the Yankees until a larger Rebel force could be concentrated.[4]

However, reinforcements would not be forthcoming. No one was sure of what Grant's intentions were, so dispatching replacements to the right place was extremely difficult for the senior Confederate commanders. Contrary to Pemberton's expectations, Grant had no intention of swinging west toward Vicksburg just yet. Pemberton had to hold the mighty city, true, but he also could not afford to lose the key rail hub and logistics center at Jackson, Mississippi. Yet he did not have sufficient forces to defend both. The wily Grant placed his army squarely between these two targets, thus placing Pemberton on the proverbial 'horns of a dilemma.'

Pemberton had done what he could, partially stripping his Port Hudson defenses to shore up those at Jackson by ordering John Gregg to move his brigade there as quickly as possible.

Gregg's Brigade first traveled on foot to Magnolia, Mississippi, and then to Jackson via the New Orleans and Jackson Railroad. While a few odd Confederate units would continue to arrive at Jackson, Gregg was essentially on his own. Pemberton maintained his primary forces along Big Black River protecting Vicksburg.[5]

There was little the high command in Richmond could do for Pemberton. William Rosecrans was expected to begin another offensive in central Tennessee against Braxton Bragg at any moment. Robert E. Lee was fully occupied with Joseph Hooker's advance in Virginia. Richmond sent the Virginian, Joseph E. Johnston, to do what he could, but Johnston was ill and immediately took to his bed.

Gregg would have to fight with what he had. His brigade at this time consisted of five regiments: the 3rd, 41st, and 50th Tennessee; the 10th and 30th Tennessee Regiments Consolidated; and the 7th Texas, Gregg's first regimental command. Also included were the 1st Tennessee battalion, and Captain H.M. Bledsoe's three gun battery of Mississippi artillery. The most powerful element in Gregg's command was the 3rd Tennessee with 548 men.[6]

The 3rd Tennessee's strength was only one man fewer than the number the regiment had deployed at Chickasaw Bayou, despite the fact that the regiment had seventy-seven fewer men on the rolls than it had four months earlier. The greatest number of these losses were due to discharges; thirty-eight men completing their enlistments were allowed to return home. Of interest here is the fact that on April 16 of the previous year the Confederacy passed its first Conscription Act extending the terms of enlistment for all one-year soldiers to three years. Apparently these men did not fall within the 18 to 35 (amended to age 45 in September 1862) age group specified by the new law and were allowed to return home.

As usual, disease continued to take its toll, killing fourteen.

Permanent losses since Chickasaw Bayou were:

Died	14
Discharged	34
Disabled	10
Deserted	7
Transferred	12
Total	77

The bulk of these losses was offset by men returning to the ranks from AWOL status. Only seven men were AWOL at Raymond versus fifty-six at Chickasaw Bayou. There were also ten fewer men sick. Among the men returning was the commander, Calvin H. Walker. The personnel status of the 3rd Tennessee as the Battle of Raymond opened was:

Present for duty	548
Absent sick	74
Detached	38
AWOL	7
Absent other reasons	9
Total	676

This was a significant gain in the percentage of men available for combat: 81% at Raymond vs 69% at Chickasaw Bayou.[7]

By now the regiment was beginning to feel the effects of the atrocious supply system. Four men missed the battle because they were "footsore" or "absent barefoot." However, the Yankee troops suffered as much or more for lack of uniform and equipment items during the Vicksburg campaign. When Grant made his move south of Vicksburg along the west side of the Mississippi River, and then crossed over the river into the Confederate rear, his supply line to the north was effectively severed. What transport he did have was almost exclusively devoted to moving ammunition.[8]

Brigadier General John E. Smith, Gregg's primary antagonist at Raymond, described his soldiers' condition at the time of the battle:

> Nearly one-third of the command at this time had no shoes, having worn them out on the march, and in consequence were very foot-sore. This, together with their want of supplies, which at times were very short, were subjects of pleasantries with the men who consoled themselves with the prospect of a fight every other day to make amends for their privations.[9]

The Federals found that sustenance was not a problem. On his initial lunge into Mississippi, Smith was unable to locate any Rebels, but he did come across a huge store of seven-thousand to eight-thousand pounds of bacon which kept his brigade well fed for some time.[10]

It was the Rebel Army, not supply problems, that concerned Smith on May 16th. On reaching Fourteen Mile Creek he encountered a serious Rebel presence to his front, and deployed his brigade to find out just what he was up against. Smith fanned out his regiments and ordered them forward into the thick jungle along the creek.

Gregg's plan was to use his two strongest regiments, the 3rd Tennessee and the 7th Texas, to hold Smith's brigade in place, and then swing two of his remaining regiments, the 10th/30th Tennessee Consolidated and the 50th Tennessee, around the enemy's right and rear using Fourteen Mile Creek as a screen. The two wings would crush Smith between them. Gregg told Calvin Walker that once the 3rd Tennessee's attack was well underway the 10th/30th would connect with Walker's left as it reached the open space at the far (south) side of the creek. The 3rd Tennessee and 7th Texas would be supported by Bledsoe's Battery which, in turn, would be supported by the 1st Tennessee Battalion. The 41st Tennessee would occupy the 3rd Tennessee's jump off position once the 3rd began its advance, and would remain there as the brigade reserve throughout the battle. The attack would commence with the advance of the 7th Texas on the 3rd Tennessee's right.[11]

The men of these two veteran Rebel outfits were hot and dusty in the springtime Mississippi drought, and they were annoyed by the Federal artillery battery which was pecking away at them from long range. On the other hand, the prospect of pouncing on an

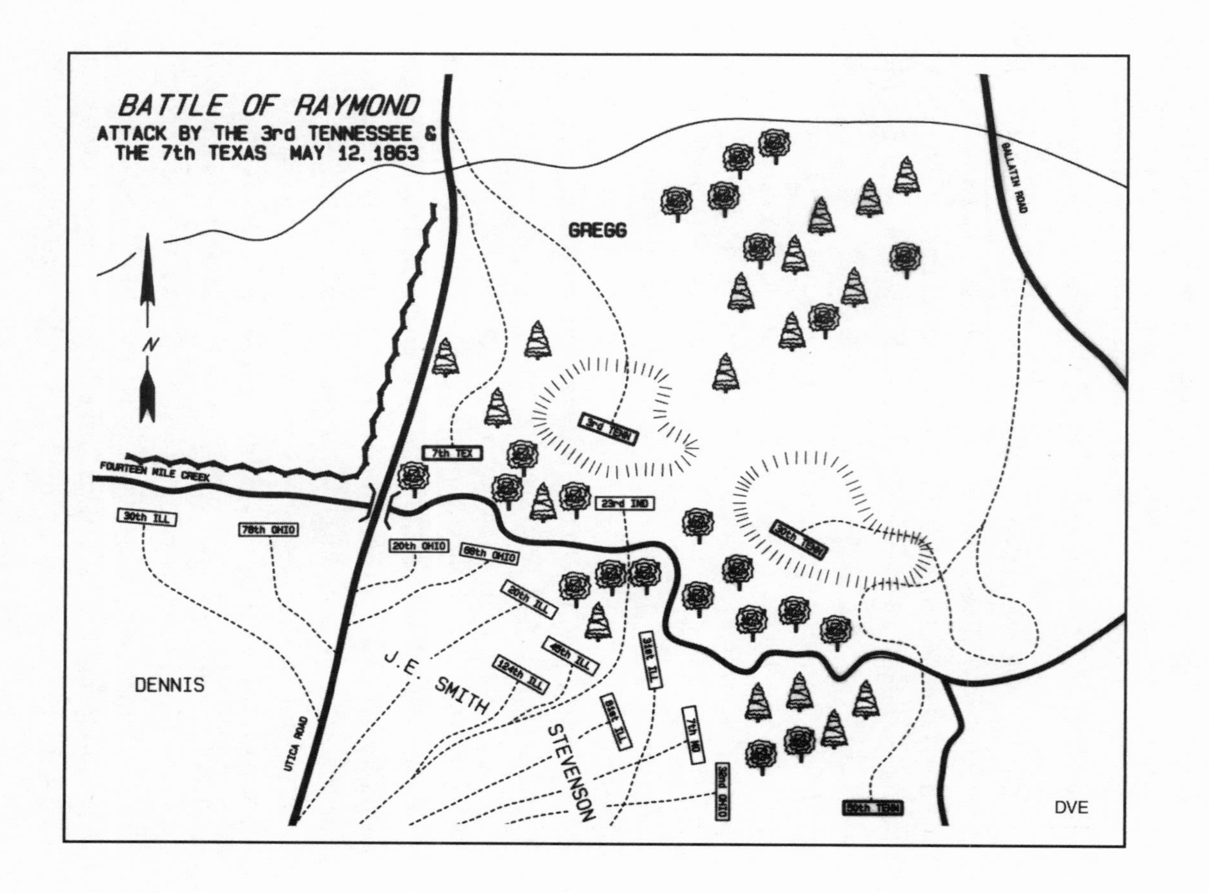
BATTLE OF RAYMOND
ATTACK BY THE 3rd TENNESSEE &
THE 7th TEXAS MAY 12, 1863
GREGG
GALLATIN ROAD
N
FOURTEEN MILE CREEK
7th TEX
3rd TENN
30th TENN
23rd IND
30th ILL
78th OHIO
20th OHIO
68th OHIO
20th ILL
45th ILL
124th ILL
31st ILL
81st ILL
7th MO
32nd OHIO
50th TENN
DENNIS
J.E. SMITH
STEVENSON
UTICA ROAD
DVE

isolated Federal brigade gave the men some extra energy. Walker moved the 3rd Tennessee out of its staging area, appropriately a graveyard, to its jump-off point situated in a ravine behind a steep hill. This position was only two-hundred yards from the closest advancing Federal regiment.[12]

This regiment, about to come face to face with the 3rd Tennessee, was the 23rd Indiana. It was on the right end of Smith's line and was far out in advance of the rest of the brigade, having worked its way through the dense undergrowth along Fourteen Mile Creek much more quickly than the other blue regiments. When the 23rd reached a clearing on the far side of the creek, it found itself uncomfortably alone. It was at this moment that the Confederates struck.[13]

The Texans began the attack on the Confederate right and were quickly joined by the 3rd Tennessee. The Tennesseans, "yelling like demons," bounded down the steep hill covering the two-hundred yards between themselves and the 23rd Indiana so quickly that the Indianans were only able to deliver a single ragged volley before the Tennesseans were literally on top of them.[14]

The fight quickly turned into a melee. Soldiers brained each other with clubbed muskets, tree branches, rocks, or anything else that came to hand. Very few bayonets were used—the Indianans did not have time to fix them to their muskets—and only one company of 3rd Tennesseans was equipped with them. It was war at the primal level, soldier against soldier, each trying to smash each other. The contest swayed back and forth for a few moments, but then the superior numbers of Tennesseans and their advantage of position on the 23rd Indiana's right flank began to tell, and the Indianans had to give ground. The retreat became a rout, the Tennesseans driving the Federals back to the creek.

Calvin Walker recorded:

> They [the Indianans] attempted to rally behind a deep ravine, with almost perpendicular banks, but our advance was so rapid (the men jumping into the ravine and climbing up the opposite side) that the enemy again gave way and fled out of the woods into the open field. There they planted their colors in the

ground, and made another effort to rally around them, but a sharp volley from our side speedily dispersed them.[15]

Meanwhile, to the right of the 3rd Tennessee, the 7th Texas was having its own success. The Texans were initially opposed by a line of skirmishers, and chose to deal with these pesky Federals by sending forward their one company equipped with Enfield rifles. These troops quickly disposed of the blue skirmish line, and the entire 7th Texas advanced into the undergrowth along Fourteen Mile Creek where it soon encountered the 20th and 68th Ohio regiments.[16]

Except for the deployment of some skirmishers, neither of these Federal units had gone beyond the ravine containing the creek. By the time the 7th Texas bumped into them, the 68th Ohio had already come under pressure from the 3rd Tennessee as it was moving past the Ohioans' right flank. The sight of the Texans bearing down on them like a pack of hungry wolves was more than the Ohioans could bear and they deserted the field en mass. Taking the cue from the 68th, the 20th Ohio followed suit.

However, the retreat came to an abrupt halt. Confronting the two fleeing Ohio regiments was a sight even more frightening than the charging Texans. Bearing down on them from the opposite direction was former Illinois politician turned battlefield commander, Brigadier General John A. 'Blackjack' Logan, mustachios flying, dashing to and fro on a big black horse, and screeching "like an eagle" for the men to turn back. The two regiments re-formed a short distance behind their original position and stayed put. Logan then began moving reinforcements forward as fast as he could.[17]

Gregg still thought he was fighting a single Federal brigade. The entire valley was filled with dust and smoke, and Gregg could see nothing of the sixteen fresh Yankee regiments rapidly deploying against his front. Gregg's first clue that he was in trouble came when his two flanking regiments, the 10th/30th and the 50th Tennessee, reached the jump-off points for the attack. At the edge of the timber south of Fourteen Mile Creek they encountered lines and lines of blue infantry already arrayed in battle formation. Instead of the flank and rear of an exposed Federal brigade, the Tennesseans were face to face with masses of fresh Yankee units.

In the face of this predicament, the two Tennessee regiments carried out some curious maneuvers. The 10th/30th moved about six-hundred yards to the left, probing for the flank and rear of the line facing them. However, once the 3rd Tennessee and the 7th Texas became engaged, the 10th/30th moved back to its right to support the 3rd on its left flank, in accordance with Gregg's battle plan.

Meanwhile, the 50th Tennessee, already close to the 3rd Tennessee's left flank, moved in the opposite direction. According to its commander, Lieutenant Colonel T.W. Beaumont, the object was "to prevent the force I had seen in that direction [to his left] from outflanking us." This was the about same position the 10th/30th had just occupied. The two regiments simply exchanged positions.[18]

While this game of musical chairs was played on the Confederate left, the 7th Texas and the 3rd Tennessee were coming under extreme pressure. The 3rd received a vicious and unexpected attack on its left and rear. Calvin Walker's description:

> Upon reaching the edge of the woods, I received a heavy volley into the rear of my left flank. Not being able to see, on account of the thick brush, and supposing that the Tenth and Thirtieth Tennessee were there for my support, and General Gregg had assured me [this] would be the case, I did not order a change of position, but directed the whole line to be held firm, until I went to the left and became satisfied that the enemy was in the rear, and at the same time a new column made its appearance in front.[19]

Walker was shocked to find the blue-clad 31st Illinois on his left instead of the 10th/30th Tennessee as Gregg had promised. The 31st had been detached to the Federal right by General Smith as flank guard and was inadvertently in perfect position to launch a surprise attack on the Tennesseans. Then, to make a bad situation worse, while Walker was off checking on his left, another attack slammed into the regiment's front. As a final stroke of bad luck, the regiment's lieutenant colonel, Calvin Clack, was off aligning

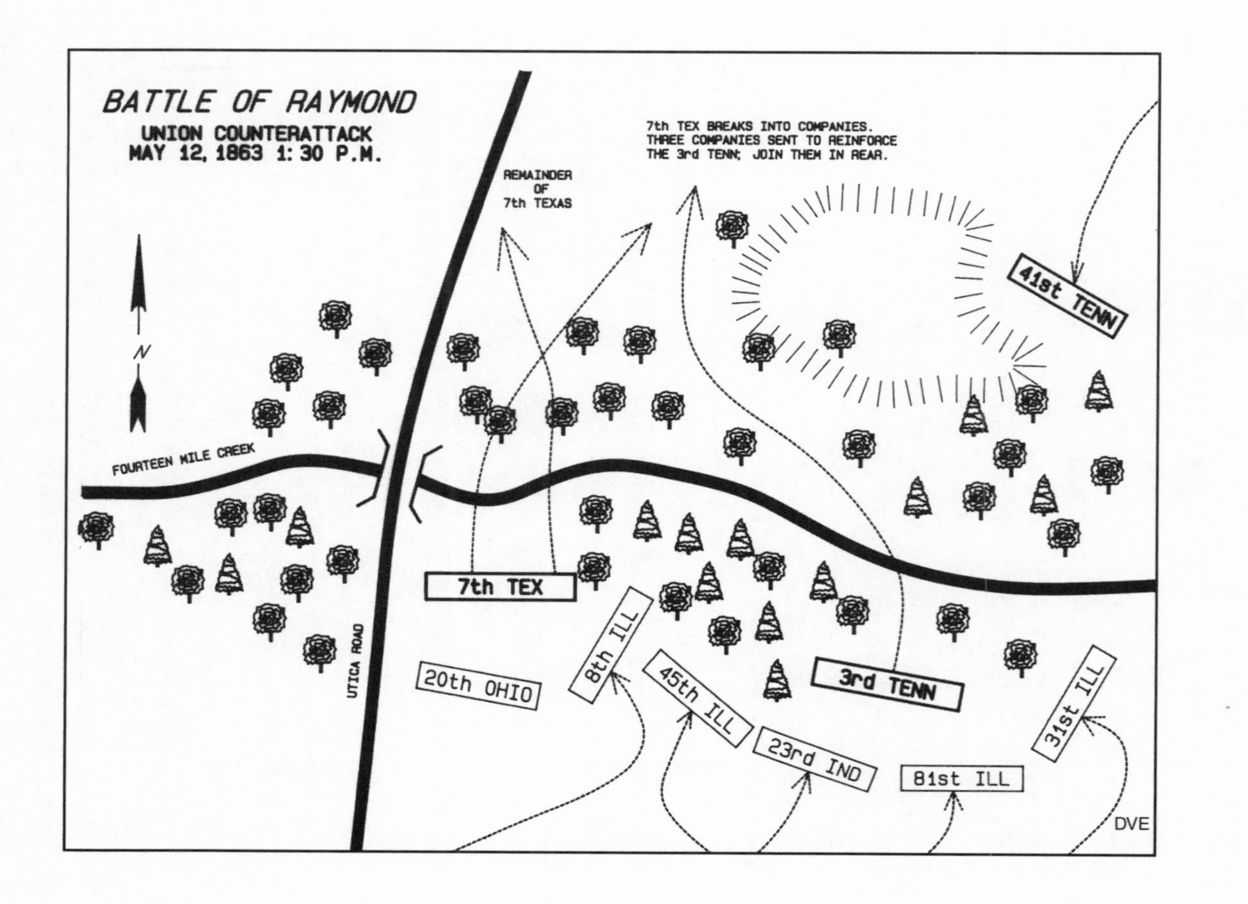
BATTLE OF RAYMOND
UNION COUNTERATTACK
MAY 12, 1863 1:30 P.M.
N
FOURTEEN MILE CREEK
UTICA ROAD
REMAINDER OF 7th TEXAS
7th TEX BREAKS INTO COMPANIES.
THREE COMPANIES SENT TO REINFORCE
THE 3rd TENN; JOIN THEM IN REAR.
41st TENN
3rd TENN
7th TEX
20th OHIO
8th ILL
45th ILL
23rd IND
81st ILL
31st ILL
DVE

the 3rd Tennessee's right flank with the 7th Texas' left. Both senior commanders were absent at the critical moment of the battle.

The new attack came from the regiment's first adversary, the 23rd Indiana, reinforced by two additional blue regiments, the 45th Illinois from Smith's brigade, and the 81st Illinois from John D. Stevenson's brigade. This was the same brigade disrupting the movements of Gregg's flanking regiments.

Walker came rushing back and tried to regain some control. He ordered his men to lie down, and for an hour the Tennesseans fought the four Federal regiments to a standstill. The air seemed alive with the thousands of minie balls fired at the Tennesseans from all directions. As Flavel Barber put it, the regiment was "severely galled by the enemy on both flanks." Added to the din were the salvos of canister fired by the 1st Illinois Light Artillery, brought in close to fire point blank at the Tennesseans.[20]

Although the 7th Texas was also under heavy attack, Calvin Clack requested assistance from them in shoring up the 3rd Tennessee's rapidly disintegrating line. Hiram Granbury, the commander of the Texans, responded with supreme unselfishness by detaching three companies from the right of his line and sending them to the Tennesseans' assistance. However, these men had barely begun their march to the left and rear when the Tennesseans' line disintegrated completely.[21]

The collapse of the 3rd Tennessee's line was not sudden. The men slowly ran out of ammunition. As they lost the ability to fight, individuals and small groups began to make their way to the rear. The men probably expended in excess of thirty-thousand rounds of small arms ammunition in this fight. Many were captured because they were not aware of the retreat or were cut off by the enveloping Federals.

The 7th Texas held on with the seven companies that remained in the expectation that the reinforced Tennesseans would retake the lost ground. The Texans soon were in desperate shape themselves. The 8th and 20th Ohio regiments assaulted them on their front and left flank almost as soon as the three companies departed to help the 3rd Tennessee. Numbers prevailed, and the Texans also were forced to withdraw.

The 3rd Tennessee did not stop its retreat until it reached the same ravine from which the attack had begun earlier that day. The regiment was a wreck. When Gregg saw the dazed condition of the men, he ordered Walker to march them back to Raymond as quickly as possible even though Gregg's line was disintegrating everywhere.

The 3rd Tennessee's withdrawal was covered by the 41st Tennessee assisted by the three companies detached from the 7th Texas. These men occupied the high ground overlooking Fourteen Mile Creek and were able to hold this position for the remainder of the day beating off several Federal attacks in the process. The Federals were vulnerable because they could not maintain an organized attack formation through the tangles along the creek.

The Yankees were also knocked off balance by a supporting attack conducted against their right flank by the 10th/30th Tennessee. The commander of this regiment, Colonel R.W. MacGavock, ordered his men to attack just as a lull occurred in the battle. The Federal corps commander now on the scene, James B. McPherson, then directed all of his artillery to concentrate their fire on that part of the battlefield. MacGavock, in a dramatic gesture, threw open his cloak to expose its bright red velvet liner, drawing even more enemy fire, and then led his men in a violent charge which checked the Federal advance once and for all.[22]

Gregg finally realized he was in serious trouble and began to extricate his force as fast as he could. Bledsoe's Battery and the 1st Tennessee protected what was left of the 7th Texas as they withdrew, while the 41st Tennessee and the three detached 7th Texas companies continued to provide cover for the rest of Gregg's units.

The 3rd Tennessee had one more humiliation to deal with later that night. According to John Goodrich of Company F:

> We had bivouacked for the night on each side of the road to Jackson and paralleling the same. About 11 P.M. an awful commotion was caused by a terrible noise as if a thousand Federal cavalry had dashed into our camp with their sabers clanking and their horses at full speed. To our great relief as well as our chagrin, we discovered that the unearthly noise was occasioned by a

yoke of oxen, with a big chain dangling after them, coming down the road at a long trot. Many were the 'cuss words,' expressions, and ludicrous remarks of the worn out veterans … .[23]

The 3rd Tennessee and 7th Texas never fully recovered from this battle. Of the 514 casualties suffered by Gregg's Brigade, 345, or 67% of the total, were inflicted on the 3rd Tennessee and the 7th Texas. In total numbers the 3rd was hardest hit with thirty-two men dead, seventy-six wounded, and sixty-eight captured for a total loss of 176 men, 32% of its deployed strength. The 7th Texas lost twenty-two men dead, sixty-six wounded, and seventy captured for a total of 158. This was a lower number, but it was more than half of that regiment's strength.[24]

Of greater importance impacting the effectiveness of the regiment was the loss of key leaders. For example, the 3rd Tennessee's Company F lost:

First Lieutenant J.B. Murphy	Captured
Second Lieutenant B.G. Darden	Wounded
First Sergeant N.G. Walker	Killed
Fifth Sergeant H.A. Martin	Captured
Third Corporal J.R. Taylor	Killed
Fourth Corporal G.D. Matthews	Captured

Company D was left without any officers:

Captain D.G. Alexander	Captured
First Lieutenant J.P. Lock	Absent sick
Second Lieutenant J.B. Farley	Captured
Jr. Second Lieutenant N.B. Rittenbury	Killed [25]

Colonel Hiram Granbury, the 7th Texas commander, lost four captains—two killed and two wounded, and seven lieutenants—three killed, two wounded, and two missing.[26]

The worst humiliation of the day was the fact that for the first time in the war the 3rd Tennessee and 7th Texas were forced to abandon their wounded on the battlefield.

At the end of the day Gregg asked General Smith for permission to remove his wounded men, which Smith denied. Having to ask for consideration from an enemy was a new experience for Gregg, and was undoubtedly deeply humiliating. Smith's refusal to allow Gregg to retrieve his wounded resulted in a positive payback for the Federals: almost none of the wounded cared for by the Yankees ever returned to their regiments.[27]

U.S. Grant used a very wise expedient in the handling of prisoners during this drive through Mississippi. Since his move south of Vicksburg cut him off from his 'rear,' he had nowhere to collect and hold prisoners; so the practical Illinoisan simply paroled them on the spot. These men were supposed to return to their units and wait for proper exchange, but Grant had discovered that Confederates left on their own to decide where to wait out their paroles almost invariably returned home. This is precisely where most of the sixty-eight men captured from the 3rd Tennessee went.[28]

Most of these men were eventually classified as deserters, while in other cases notations made on individual service records simply cease indicating failure to return to duty. Some 3rd Tennesseans were captured more than once. T.Y. English was wounded and captured at Raymond on May 12. He apparently wandered away and was re-captured in the same area on the 1st of June. He managed to slip away a second time and made it home to Tennessee before he was captured a third time two months later.[29]

Most of the regiment fought well at Raymond, but a few individuals received less than complimentary notations in the Rollbook. John Goodloe and O.W. Williams of Company C, W.P. Renfrow of Company F, and J.W.F. Wilson of Company I all "left the field without leave," while Noah Roberts of Company G "ran from the field," as did F.L. McAllister of Company I. Some of the men, already in bad graces for previous poor performance, were beginning to show a consistent pattern. G.W. Taylor of Company G was cited as "always AWOL," J.M. Harwell "ran in every engagement," and G.G. Smith of Company I was "always missing at the end" of each fight . Private I.M. Park of Company G, absent from Chickasaw Bayou drunk, was also absent from this battle—drunk. J.P. Caldwell, the man excused for cowardice at Chickasaw Bayou, summoned up the courage to show up for this fight, but not enough to stay around for the finish. Caldwell "left the field without leave."[30]

At Raymond the 3rd Tennessee had a rare experience: a company commander deserted his troops during the course of the battle. The death of Captain Robert Cooper, and the resignation of the first and second lieutenants of Company H before the battle left Junior Second Lieutenant James A. Doyel in command. Doyel "left the field at Raymond during the battle without leave." Despite this failure, Company H elected Doyel captain the following month. In August, shortly before the Chickamauga campaign, Doyel went on furlough and disappeared from the rolls.[31]

The only positive result of this battle from the Confederate viewpoint was the realization that the big Yankee army rampaging in their rear was aimed at Jackson, not Vicksburg. Gregg continued to delay the Federal column as much as he could, but the effort was futile. Grant drove Gregg out of Jackson, and then directed his fast moving columns toward Vicksburg. Joseph E. Johnston, sensing disaster in the making, advised Pemberton to move his army north and east on the premise that it is better to lose a city than to lose the army. The problem was, Pemberton had peremptory orders from Davis to hold Vicksburg, so he stayed put. Grant soon had him surrounded.

The 3rd Tennessee could do little more than watch; they were still nursing their wounds. Events were unfolding quickly that year of 1863, and it would not be long before the regiment would be back in battle. It was to be one of an intensity probably never equaled before or since on the American continent—Chickamauga.

Notes for Chapter 11

1 *OR*, Vol.XXIV, part 1, pp. 736-737.
2 *Ibid.*, p.737.
3 *Ibid.*
4 *Ibid.*, p. 707.
5 Barber Diary, Vol.III, May 7-8, 1863.

6 *OR*, Vol.XXIV, part 1, p.737.

7 Rollbook, p. 343. Statistics compiled from Company Records.

8 *Ibid.*

9 *OR*, Vol.XXIV, part 1, p. 707.

10 *Ibid.*, p. 706.

11 *Ibid.*

12 Barber Diary, Vol.III, May 12, 1863.

13 *OR*, Vol.XXIV, part 1, p. 708.

14 Barber, op. cit. *OR*, Vol.XXIV, part 1, pp. 739-740.

15 *OR*, Vol.XXIV, part 1, pp. 711-712, 740.

16 *Ibid.*, p.747.

17 Stephen E. Ambrose, Thomas L. Connelly, et. al.. "Struggle for Vicksburg," *Civil War Times Illustrated*, 1967, p. 19.

18 *OR*, Vol.XXIV, part 1, pp. 741, 744.

19 *Ibid.*, p. 740.

20 Barber Diary, Vol.III, May 12, 1863.

21 OR, Vol.XXIV, part 1, pp. 747-748.

22 "Struggle for Vicksburg," pp. 20-21.

23 John T. Goodrich, *CV*, Vol. XVI, p. 126.

24 *OR*, Vol.XXIV, part 1, p. 739.

25 Rollbook, pp. 223-225, 303.

26 *OR*, Vol.XXIV, part 1, p.748.

27 *Ibid.*, p. 708. Rollbook, Company Records.

28 Rollbook, based on analysis of company records.

29 *Ibid.*, p.308.

30 *Ibid.*, pp. 211, 216, 232, 254, 291, 294, 299, 332, 334.

31 *Ibid.*, p. 189.

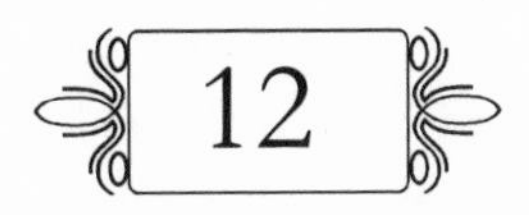

INTO THE INFERNO

For most of May and June of 1863, General Joseph E. Johnston built up his forces and looked for a way to break U.S. Grant's bulldog grip on Vicksburg. Pemberton's thirty-thousand men trapped in the city, combined with the twenty-thousand or so men under Johnston's command outside, could have opened an escape route. However, such a plan would have required the two generals to go against the wishes of their government which was loath to give up the Mississippi fortress.

Pemberton and Johnston sent a steady stream of messengers back and forth through the Union lines in a futile attempt to agree on a plan, but the only real actions were a few cautious probes by Johnston. Johnston wanted Pemberton to break out, while Pemberton wanted Johnston to break in. Johnston's main force moved west toward the Big Black River, while another force led by John Gregg took up position northeast of Vicksburg near Yazoo City. Fortunately for the 3rd Tennessee and 7th Texas, still healing from the pounding received at Raymond, contact with the enemy was limited to a few brushes with the Yankee gunboats on the Yazoo River.[1]

Eventually starvation took its toll on the trapped men at Vicksburg, and on July 4th, Pemberton capitulated. The huge haul of prisoners could have created a logistical nightmare for the Yankee army, but Grant had his usual solution. Rather than tie up nearly all of his river transport and a large part of his infantry force moving the Confederates north, Grant paroled most of the twenty-nine thousand soldiers surrendered at Vicksburg.[2]

With the surrender, the Confederate position further downstream at Port Hudson became untenable, and its surrender soon followed. The Mississippi was a Union waterway once and for all. No longer would the Confederacy enjoy an uninterrupted flow of tough Texas frontiersmen to refill its ranks, nor would new supplies of longhorn beef on the hoof be arriving to nourish the soldiers' bodies. The Confederacy was now two separate and distinct parts each incapable of helping the other.

Individual 3rd Tennesseans were caught in the surrenders at both Vicksburg and Port Hudson. At Vicksburg, Private E.S. Galloway of Company F had been detailed as a butcher for the previous eight months to Lloyd Tilghman's command that included the city's big shore batteries. During the last few weeks of the siege Galloway probably gained considerable expertise on the various ways to fricassee a mule, since that quadruped became the army's sole meat source (no mention will be made of the use of rodents as an alternative). Galloway, to his credit, returned to the regiment after receiving his parole with the Vicksburg garrison, but was too weakened by the siege to continue service. He was furloughed home where he died the following October. The soldier captured at Port Hudson was Private W.J. Wilsford of Company D. Wilsford had remained behind as a teamster when the regiment departed in May. He immediately deserted upon receiving his parole.[3]

With Vicksburg secured, the one piece of unfinished business remaining for Grant was Johnston's force threatening his rear along the Big Black River. Grant turned with a vengeance; he sent Sherman and thirty-thousand men to deal with him.

Johnston retreated to the fortifications at Jackson where, had Sherman acted quickly enough, there was the potential for another siege. The short stay at Jackson was a bleak one for the 3rd Tennessee. The regiment reached Jackson on July 6th and was posted at the fairgrounds. On the 8th, they were moved into the trench line northwest of town between the Canton and Clinton Roads. They were cannonaded on the 10th, and on the 11th part of the regiment was ambushed while marching toward the outpost line. Three men were killed and eleven wounded.

It was on this day that an incident occurred illustrating the personal nature of skirmisher duty. While manning an outpost, Private John Goodrich had the misfortune of being singled out as the victim of a tenacious Yankee sharpshooter positioned at the top of a tree. While Goodrich attempted to shield himself behind a six inch post, the sharpshooter blazed away with his long-range rifle, firing ten times before finally creasing Goodrich on the arm. Goodrich's Enfield did not have the range to place effective fire on his tormentor, so he was absolutely helpless. The Tennessean could see the smoke from the man's rifle each time he fired, and then had to wait a second or so in gut-wrenching anticipation to find out whether he had any time left on this earth. Luckily for Goodrich the wound was only superficial, and he soon returned to duty.[4]

The 3rd Tennessee suffered more losses on the 15th when the Federals launched a surprise raid on the Tennessean's line and hauled off a dozen more men as prisoners.[5]

Sherman avoided a direct assault on Jackson, and sent his columns swinging around the city. Though Sherman had a reputation as the 'total war' general of the Civil War, he lacked Grant's capacity to go for the jugular. He had a way of leaving his adversary an escape route, thus avoiding a decisive battle. So it was here. Johnston and his army, including the 3rd Tennessee, escaped to the east on the 16th.

To paraphrase Jefferson Davis, those were dark and cloudy times for the Confederacy, that summer of 1863. The loss of Vicksburg combined with Lee's disastrous invasion of the north culminating in his defeat at Gettysburg, threw the South into a frenzy. Something had to be done, and quickly.

When the high command in Richmond pondered their limited options, it became evident that only one army still possessed any capability of achieving a decisive battlefield victory and reversing the Confederacy's fortunes. Braxton Bragg's Army of Tennessee had been stampeded out of central Tennessee by the skillful maneuvering of William Rosecrans, but it was still intact and ready to fight. It only needed some extra muscle.

Up to this time, Davis had maintained the policy that each military department was responsible for the defense of its own territory, on the theory that each was sufficient on its own regardless of how large a force the Federals threw against it. Usually whenever cross-boundary cooperation was needed, Davis asked the respective commanders to work it out. This worked poorly at best, since Confederate commanders were loath to give up what limited forces they had. Jefferson Davis now took firm charge and the Confederacy began to transfer forces across departmental lines with a vengeance. Bragg received all the help he needed.[6]

Most readily available were Joseph Johnston's forces. They were presently standing idle east of Jackson watching Grant's big army, which had now become inactive after the Vicksburg surrender. Among the troops dispatched to Bragg in early September was Gregg's Brigade, including the 3rd Tennessee.

The regiment was down to 264 available men, a drop of 102 since their escape from Jackson. It was a shadow of the powerful force which had taken on James B. McPherson's corps less than three months before. Death and sickness took their usual toll, but more alarming was the marked increase in two categories—desertions and absent wounded. A recapitulation:

Total Number on Rolls	583
Died	23
Deserted	65
AWOL	45
Sick	79
Wounded	40
Detached	34
Disabled	8
Captured	7
Barefoot	12
All other reasons	6
Total Absent	319
Present for Duty	264 (48%)[7]

Many of the deserters were men captured at Raymond who had not rejoined the ranks.

There were three primary factors for this severe degeneration of the strength of the regiment. The most obvious was the combativeness of the brigade commander. Gregg's assault tactics, plus his miscalculations at Raymond, caused frightful losses the regiment was never able to make good.

Second was the general demoralization throughout the South in the summer of 1863. With the strategic setbacks at Vicksburg and Gettysburg, the South no longer seemed invincible. The more likely defeat became a possibility, the more likely it became that the less dedicated soldier would give up the fight and return home.

However, the most important factor in the demoralization of the regiment was the loss of of its key leaders. By this time, the 3rd Tennessee had only twelve out of forty (30%) of its company officers present for duty, and only one of these was a captain. Two companies had no officers at all of their own, only those borrowed from other companies. It was usually the most courageous and inspirational leaders who were the first to become casualties. Without the close ties, and without the positive influence of a good leader, the men were less likely to stay around. After Raymond, the present for duty percentile dropped from 81% to 45%, and it continued to stay low until the end of the war.[8]

Gregg's Brigade was assigned to a provisional (temporary) division under the command of the extremely competent Tennessean, Bush-rod Johnson. He was a West Point graduate, a veteran of the Seminole and Mexican Wars, and most recently a college teacher at the University of Nashville. He managed to sneak off after the Fort Donelson surrender, and had since fought at Shiloh, Perryville, and Stones River. Johnson would display outstanding skills in the coming battle.[9]

Meanwhile, the original commander of the 3rd Tennessee, John C. Brown, had sufficiently recovered from his Perryville wound to resume brigade command. Brown was assigned four Tennessee regiments, the 18th, 26th, 32nd, and 45th, plus the 23rd Tennessee Battalion. Brown's Brigade was assigned to a division under the command of another Tennessean, Alexander P. Stewart.[10]

As luck would have it, although they were serving in different divisions, Brown and the 3rd Tennessee were to fight nearly side by side in the coming battle.

On September 4, 1863, Bragg retreated into Georgia while at the same time reinforcements began arriving. The prickly general looked for an opportunity to strike at a portion of Rosecrans' army. The Yankee march columns were isolated from each other as they moved south and east across the long spine comprising Lookout Mountain. Bragg had several opportunities to bag part of the Yankee army, but was always thwarted by the difficult north Georgia terrain and a balky chain of command.[11]

Having failed in his effort to pounce on Rosecrans' scattered units during the first half of September, Bragg fell into a funk for several days. By September 17th Rosecrans was able to concentrate his army along Chicamauga Creek, well within hailing distance of his reserve at Chattanooga. Bragg then revived himself and announced a plan designed to bag the entire Federal army.

The Yankees were positioned a little to the northeast of a natural mountainous cul-de-sac called McLemore's Cove. If Bragg could swing his army around the Federal left flank, he would cut them off from Chattanooga and drive them into this natural trap. From there they would find no escape and the Federals would have no choice but to surrender.

The plan was a good one, but try as he might, Bragg could never get his army moving where and how he intended. Bragg eventually came within a whisker of wiping out the Federal army, but it in no way resembled Bragg's plan. By the time Bragg realized that he had Rosecrans in a serious predicament, it was too late to do anything about it. Following the progress of the 3rd Tennessee illustrates just how out of control the Chickamauga battle was.

Bushrod Johnson's provisional division, including John Gregg's brigade and the 3rd Tennessee, was selected by Bragg to lead the attack on the Federal left. Bragg did not issue his order for an attack on September 18th until early that morning. At 5:00 a.m. Johnson had already begun his march from Ringold and Catoosa Station toward Chickamauga Creek. His march route was not in the direction Bragg wanted. One of Bragg's staff arrived and told Johnson to reverse his march and begin all over again, which delayed his movement across the creek by several hours.[12]

Bragg ordered Johnson to march to Reed's Bridge and expected him to make an unopposed crossing. However, the Federals were already at Reed's Bridge and were not inclined to get out of Johnson's way. Bragg's time table was upset even more.

As Johnson approached Reed's Bridge, another courier arrived from Bragg with a copy of the battle order for the day. Johnson finally knew what Bragg expected him to accomplish. He was to move across Chickamauga Creek at Reed's Bridge and "turn to the left by the most practicable route and sweep up the Chickamauga toward Lee and Gordon's Mill [the position supposedly held by the Federal left]." As Johnson did this he was to be joined in the attack by units crossing the Chickamauga further south: W.H.T. Walker's corps of two divisions at Alexander's Bridge and Buckner's Corps with another two divisions at Thedford's Ford. If the Confederates moved promptly they would have five veteran divisions squarely on Rosecrans' flank, separating his army from his support base at Chattanooga.[14]

As he approached the bridge, Johnson's skirmishers reported Yankee cavalry ahead, so Johnson deployed three brigades on line to drive them away. Gregg's Brigade with the 3rd Tennessee was aligned on the right. About this time Johnson was joined by Bedford Forrest and his escort. Forrest had been holding several crossings open further north. The always aggressive Forrest happily joined in the fray.

The Confederates were facing the cavalry brigade of Colonel Robert Minty, a tough Irishman and former British Army officer lately from Michigan. Minty's brigade was further stiffened by one regiment of U.S. Army Regulars. Minty had his men well posted in the hills east of Chickamauga Creek and they opened fire with their quick firing breech loading carbines. On average, a breechloader could be fired three to four times faster than the infantryman's muzzleloader, and it could be easily reloaded while its handler was lying down.[14]

The Confederate weight of numbers began to tell, and Minty was forced to give ground. He moved his force to the opposite side of the stream while calling for reinforcements.

The men responding were from John T. Wilder's 'Lightning Brigade,' mounted Indiana and Illinois infantry equipped with the latest in military hardware, the Spencer repeating rifle, and they spelled trouble for the Confederates.

Before the war, Wilder was one of the new breed of entrepreneurs rapidly turning the United States into the world's leading industrial power. When military duty beckoned he sought the best equipment, which at the time happended to be the Spencer. The U.S. Army Chief of Ordnance, James Ripley, denied Wilder's request for repeaters. The crusty old Regular felt that the traditional smoothbore muzzle loaders the Army used were sufficient firepower for anybody, plus they consumed less ammunition. So Wilder and his men purchased the Spencers with their own money. Later, an embarrassed Lincoln Administration reimbursed them.[15]

The Spencer rifle/carbine was the most dominant firearm to appear on Civil War battlefields (the Henry rifle could fire more rounds faster, but sufficient numbers of this rifle were never available to have a significant impact). This repeating-rifle held seven self-contained .56 caliber cartridges in a tubular magazine through the stock and could be fired as fast as the soldier could actuate a loading lever located under the trigger. Wilder estimated that one of his regiments armed with the Spencer rifle was equal to a brigade of Confederate infantry.[16]

Wilder's artillery battery was commanded by none other than Eli Lilly of pharmaceutical fame. Wilder sent the 72nd Indiana and seven companies from the 123rd Illinois, plus one section of artillery from Lilly's Battery, to Minty's aid. They poured torrents of fire on Johnson's men, delaying the Rebel advance, and completely disrupting Bragg's timetable.

Finally, around 4:00 p.m., Johnson pryed the Federal horsemen from their position by using Gregg's Brigade to flank them out of position. The crossing was his. As he marched his men across the partially destroyed bridge, Major General John B. Hood, lately of Robert E. Lee's Army of Northern Virginia, appeared along the column and announced that he was now in command.[18]

Despite the fact that Johnson's Division was part of Buckner's Corps, that it was the only organized force at Reed's Bridge, and that Hood had just arrived on the scene and knew nothing about the situation or the disposition of the opposing armies, Bragg placed Hood in charge. This further complicated his already hopelessly complicated chain of command.

In his war memoir, Hood claimed that he orchestrated the entire action at Reed's Bridge. Reports submitted immediately after the action refute this.[17]

Hood's first order was for Johnson to take the most direct road toward Alexander's Bridge to open that crossing for the passage of Walker's Corps. The order was superfluous since Johnson was now in Wilder's rear, and the Indianan would have to abandon his position anyway. The movement placed Johnson's Division between the Confederate forces along the Chickamauga and the Federal forces along the Lafayette Road further to the west. This meant Johnson would turn short of the Yankee flank. Had he gone forward as he had planned and reached Lafayette Road, he would have created great consternation for Rosecrans, who was not ready for an attack from this direction on the 18th.

The Yankees abandoned Alexander's Bridge when Johnson approached, but not without first stinging the leading Rebel brigade which happened to be Gregg's. Johnson halted his brigades in the woods and aligned them to hold their position for the night. Two brigades faced mostly south while Gregg's Brigade was swung back along the right flank facing west.

When Wilder arrived back at the main Yankee line he reported to the division commander there, Brigadier General Thomas Wood, that large concentrations of aggressive Rebels were rapidly converging on the Federals from the north and east. Wood refused to believe that so many Confederates could have gotten so close so fast, and reported same to his corps commander, Thomas Crittenden. The Yankee commanders finally ordered a brigade forward at twilight to feel for the Rebel positions; in a few minutes these men bumped into Gregg.[19]

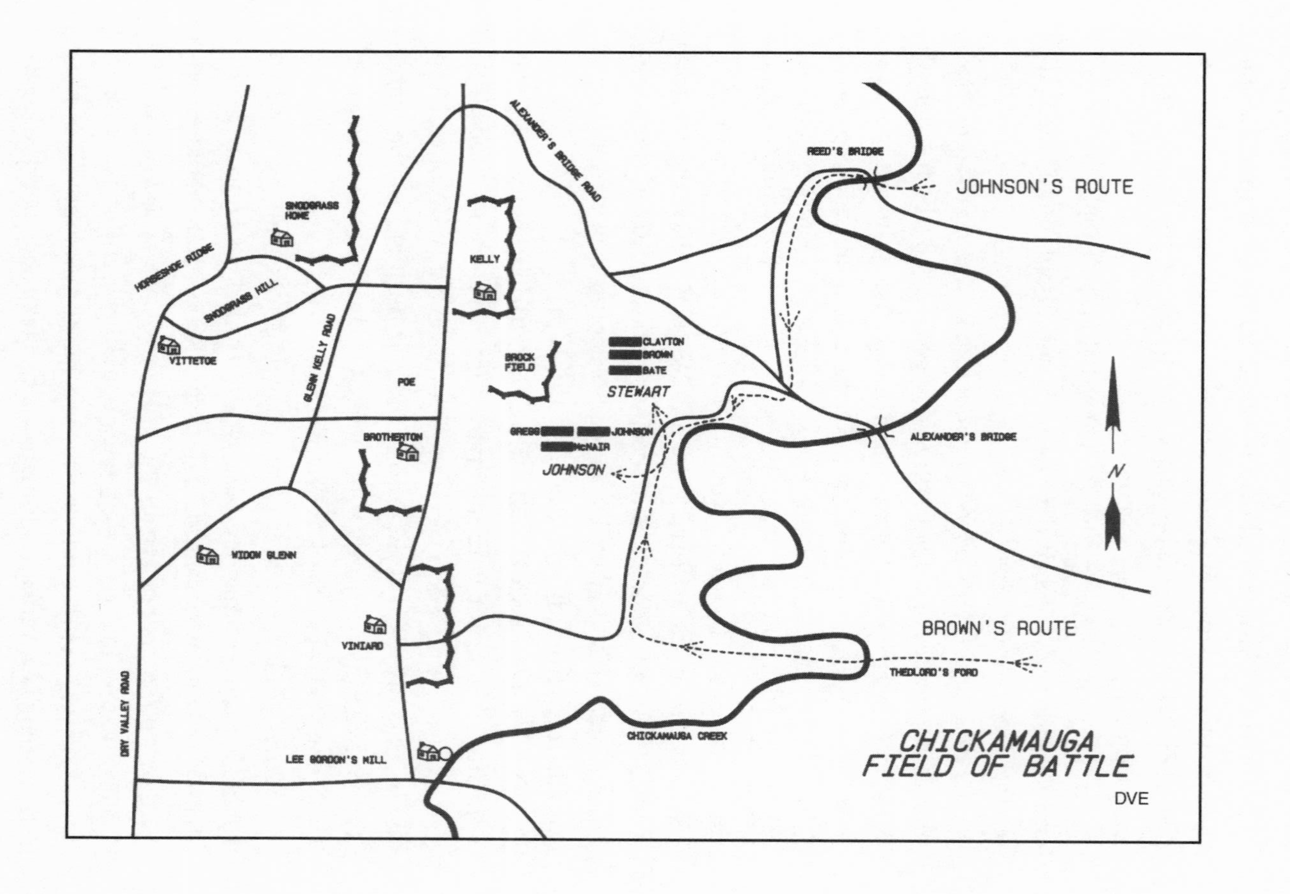

REED'S BRIDGE
JOHNSON'S ROUTE
ALEXANDER'S BRIDGE ROAD
SNODGRASS HOME
HORSESHOE RIDGE
SNODGRASS HILL
KELLY
VITTETOE
GLENN KELLY ROAD
POE
BROCK FIELD
CLAYTON
BROWN
BATE
STEWART
GREGG
JOHNSON
McNAIR
JOHNSON
ALEXANDER'S BRIDGE
N
BROTHERTON
WIDOW GLENN
VINIARD
BROWN'S ROUTE
THEDLORD'S FORD
CHICKAMAUGA CREEK
DRY VALLEY ROAD
LEE GORDON'S MILL
CHICKAMAUGA
FIELD OF BATTLE
DVE

In the glooming forest the advancing Federals could see little, and none of the ragged butternut Confederates arrayed among the trees. At point blank range Gregg's men let loose a volley that tore into the Federal ranks and sent them running. Wood and Crittenden suddenly realized they were in serious trouble.[20]

Because of Johnson's actions, John C. Brown and the rest of A.P. Stewart's Division made an unopposed crossing of Chickamauga Creek upstream at Thedford's Ford. Stewart aligned his division facing west; directly to his front was Johnson's Division facing south. Neither division was in a position to support the other, and both were in poor position to kick off operations the next morning. Brown ended up within a few hundred yards of his old comrades of the 3rd Tennessee.

Thus far, the 3rd Tennessee had been lucky. Although they had been under fire most of the day they had suffered no casualties. They had, however, done the enemy some serious damage. The Army of Tennessee, frustrated in its attempts to corner Rosecrans, was ready for a fight; and there was no doubt in anyone's mind that as soon as the sun rose, Braxton Bragg was going to do his best to eradicate the Yankees. The question was: at what cost in southern blood.

Notes for Chapter 12

1 Horn, *The Army of Tennessee*, pp. 217-218. Connelly, *Autumn of Glory*, pp. 96-107.

2 Wiley, *The Life of Johnny Reb*," pp. 143-144.

3 Rollbook, p. 228, 314.

4 Barber Diary, Vol.III, July 6-16, 1863.

5 Bragg provided Johnston two divisions despite the large force accumulating against him in Nashville. See McPherson, *Battle Cry of Freedom*, pp. 633-634.

6 Rollbook, compiled from company records, p. 264.

7 Wiley, *The life of Johnny Reb*, pp. 144-145.

8 Rollbook, compiled from company records.

9 *Encyclopedia of the Civil War*, p.397.

10 *OR*, Vol.XXX, part 2, p. 370.

11 Horn, *op. cit.*, pp. 112-114. Connelly, *op. cit.*, pp. 70-92. Woodworth, *Jefferson Davis and His Generals*, pp. 90-94. Grady McWhiney, *Braxton Bragg and Confederate Defeat*, pp. 1-119.

12 *OR*, Vol.XXX, part 2, p. 451.

13 *Ibid.*

14 Glenn W. Sunderland, *Wilder's Lightning Brigade*, pp. 70-74.

15 *Ibid.*, pp. 25-35.

16 Roy Marcot, *Spencer Repeating Firearms*, p. 53.

17 Peter Cozzens, *This Terrible Sound: The Battle of Chickamauga*, p. 105.

18 *OR*, Vol.XXX, part 2, p. 452. John B. Hood, *Advance and Retreat*, pp. 61-62.

19 Sunderland, *op. cit.*, p. 75.

20 *Ibid.* *OR*, Vol.XXX, part 2, p. 452.

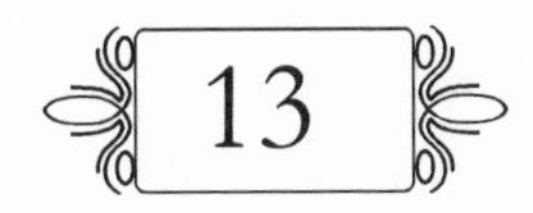

CHICKAMAUGA: DAY 1

By the fall of 1863, all pretenses that the Civil War might be conducted in a "civilized" manner were falling by the wayside. Armies of both the North and the South were conducting spectacular and brilliant campaigns which inflicted staggering losses on each other. For example, the battle of Gettysburg alone accounted for fifty-thousand casualties. There was to be one more great bloodletting that year. After a long period of inactivity, the great armies of William Rosecrans and Braxton Bragg were like coiled snakes poised to strike each other. When they finally did, it would be the second greatest battle of the Civil War—Chickamauga.

This was a battle of professionals. The wide-eyed excitement the soldiers experienced in 1861 had evolved into a colder, more calculated desire to see the job through. The fear and horror of the early days had been alleviated somewhat by the realization that men do survive battle, and that with a little luck, and some common sense, one could manage to stay alive. By the fall of 1863, a core group of true fighters had evolved in each regiment possessed with a cold apathy toward death and mutilation. This was necessary for the preservation of sanity, and kept the men fighting despite the odds. These men would continue to deal destruction to their enemies as long as they had to, with little remorse—simply waiting for the war to end and a chance to return home.

The 3rd Tennessee had become a first class military organization. Given anything like equal numbers, the Tennesseans had learned they could handle their blue enemies. The commanders also had developed some battlefield savvy. The regiment would be on guard for predicaments like occurred at Raymond, would tend to flank and rear, and would withdraw when the situation called for it.

Braxton Bragg's battle plan guaranteed a desperate fight. Bragg aimed to drive the Yankee army into the cul-de-sac known as McLemore's Cove, trap it, and annihilate it. An ancient principle of war is to allow an enemy a means of escape lest he fight all the more desperately. That was the case in this battle. The Union soldiers, from generals to privates, quickly discerned Bragg's intentions and fought all the harder because of it.

Bragg's plan, issued on September 18th, called for the Confederate right, now held by the Georgian W.H.T. Walker, to roll up the Federal left supposedly anchored at Lee and Gordon's Mill. The problem was, the Yankees had already shifted their lines well to their left in anticipation of just that move by the Rebels. In fact, Bragg himself was now outflanked on his right. To upset Bragg's plan even further, the men in blue struck first.

The battle opened early next morning near Reed's Bridge. A Federal infantry brigade caught Forrest's cavalry moving toward the Union left as a screen for W.H.T. Walker's Corps. Walker quickly reinforced Forrest, and the battle began in earnest. Each side fed in more and more brigades with the momentum swinging back and forth as one side and then the other gained the advantage. Because events unfolded so rapidly, and because of the difficulty both Rosecrans and Bragg had communicating with their subordinates, the battle on the 19th belonged to the soldiers, with minimal influence by anyone higher than brigade or division commander.

Despite his position behind and to the left of his old comrades, John C. Brown entered the fray ahead of the 3rd Tennessee, around 11:00 a.m.. By that time both of W.H.T. Walker's two divisions, and the oversize division of hard drinking, hard swearing Tennessean B.F. Cheatham, had all worn themselves out assaulting the Yankees. It was at this point that Brown's division commander, A.P. Stewart, after a brief consultation with an already frustrated Braxton Bragg, committed his three brigades.

Brown and his brigade launched several attacks and at one point managed to punch through the Lafayette Road, cutting the Yankee army in half. His attack was not supported however, and eventually he was obliged to assume a position a few hundred yards to the east to allow his men time to recuperate. The other two brigades of Stewart's division met the same fate.[1]

Now it was the 3rd Tennessee's turn. Not long after Stewart ordered his first attack, John Bell Hood, beside himself at having to stand idle because of a lack of orders, finally could stand the tension no longer and ordered his divisions to the attack, starting with Bushrod Johnson on the right. Bragg's string of uncoordinated attacks would continue.

Ready to attack since early morning, Johnson had Gregg's Brigade on the left, Johnson's Brigade (under J.S. Fulton) on the right, and Evander McNair's brigade in reserve behind Gregg. The only action Johnson had seen all day was a Federal probe against his far left regiment, the 50th Tennessee, about 2:00 p.m..[2]

No doubt the men of the 3rd Tennessee viewed the impending action with trepidation. By now every man in Confederate gray was familiar with John B. Hood's reputation as a head-on attacker. Hood had an unfortunate propensity for equating the amount of blood spilled by his own soldiers as the true measure of Southern courage.[3]

All fighting units were finding that an organized battle line was next to impossible to maintain in the dense timber along the Chickamauga. Now it was the 3rd Tennessee's turn to find itself cast adrift in a sea of uncontrolled jungle fighting. Sometime after 2:30, Hood ordered Johnson to "wheel to the right," northwest, to bring his division into proximity with Stewart who was by this time heavily engaged. Hood's own division, posted to Johnson's right and rear, was directed to move due west. As the two divisions advanced, a gap slowly opened between them, exposing the flanks of both, and dissipating the force of the attack over too wide a front.[4]

Gregg started losing control of his brigade at the outset due to some extremely thick undergrowth. He then bumped into a line of Federal skirmishers who had ventured far out into the woods.

For the 3rd Tennessee, this fighting more resembled a gigantic bushwack than a pitched battle. The units lost their cohesion in the woods and the fighting degenerated into thousands of individual confrontations. Former 3rd Tennessean Sam Watkins, fighting with B.F. Cheatham on the right, provided a flavor of what fighting in the woods was like: "Double quick, close up in the rear! siz, siz, double quick, boom, hurry up, bang, bang, a rattle de bang, bang, siz, boom, boom, boom, hurry up, double quick, boom, bang, halt, front, right dress, boom, boom, and three soldiers are killed and twenty wounded."[5]

Johnson's brigade got further and further ahead while Gregg's split apart. Gregg's two right flank regiments, the 3rd and 41st Tennessee, managed to keep pace with Johnson. Eventually they lost sight of their own brigade and were forced to attach themselves to Johnson's Brigade.[6]

Then what was left of Gregg's brigade also split apart. The 50th Tennessee had extended to the left to maintain connection with William Preston's Division. Somehow the Federals located this seam between the two Confederate attack forces, and attacked it before Gregg's advance was fairly underway. The 50th became involved in a fight for its own survival and was lost to the attack. The 50th eventually linked up with Jerome B. Robertson's Brigade of Hood's Division, and participated in the bitter fight between Hood and Federal General Jefferson Davis's Division, as did three regiments from McNair's Brigade.[7]

Gregg's remaining regiments reached the Lafayette Road, but with no support available on either flank, the combative Gregg for once chose discretion over valor. He had his regiments hold on in the woods while he tried to piece his brigade back together.

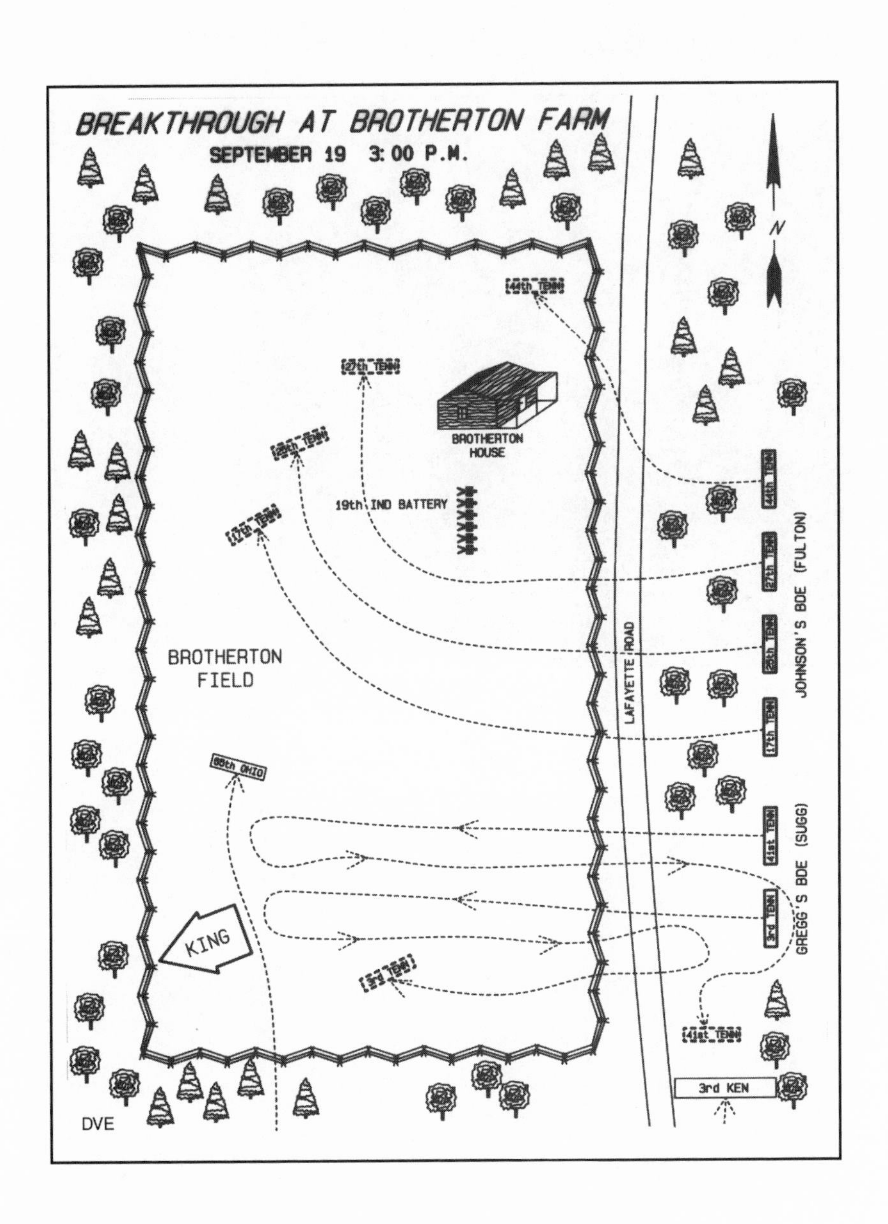
BREAKTHROUGH AT BROTHERTON FARM
SEPTEMBER 19 3:00 P.M.
N
44th TENN
27th TENN
BROTHERTON HOUSE
25th TENN
19th IND BATTERY
17th TENN
BROTHERTON FIELD
LAFAYETTE ROAD
44th TENN
27th TENN
25th TENN
17th TENN
JOHNSON'S BDE (FULTON)
41st TENN
3rd TENN
GREGG'S BDE (SUGG)
88th OHIO
KING
3rd TENN
41st TENN
3rd KEN
DVE

Brotherton farm at Chickamauga—it was here, in the far distance, that the 3rd Tennessee and its sister regiments broke the Federal line on the first day of battle. On the second day, in the near distance, they broke it again, this time for good.

Courtesy: Author

When he finally did attack, he was grievously wounded in the neck and was assumed dead by both sides. In fact, a Yankee robbed him of his fancy Mexican spurs and beautiful presentation sword. He recovered, however, and would later join Robert E. Lee's army to die later fighting in Virginia.

Johnson's Brigade, now a powerful force six regiments strong, met no substantial resistance until they reached the Lafayette Road. There they slammed into Edward King's brigade in position along the east side of the road. The two brigades traded intense rifle and artillery fire until the 3rd and 41st Tennessee regiments managed to turn the right flank of King's far right regiment, the 101st Indiana. King's whole line then began to fall back from right to left. As the bluecoats fell back across the road they fully exposed themselves to Confederate fire, and the retreat quickly turned into a rout. The Rebels stormed across the road, scooped up the 19th Indiana Artillery Battery, and suddenly found themselves with no Yankees to fight. The Federal position was theirs; but for how long?[8]

Once King's men were driven off there were no Federal troops readily available to replace them. Johnson's Brigade happened to pierce the seam between the two halves of the blue army, with George Thomas commanding the northern half, and Rosecrans himself commanding the southern half. What reserves that were available had already been committed to the north in the effort to contain Stewart's penetration, and south to contain Hood. The Confederates had a golden opportunity to drive a deep wedge between the two halves had they only known how vulnerable the Yankees were. The problem was Johnson's Brigade was all by itself. Two full divisions, Preston's and Thomas Hindman's, were still uncommitted, but they were in the wrong place. More than a mile of dense forest separated these units from Johnson's Brigade, and the Confederate high command was in a state of utter confusion.

As the charging Rebel infantry crossed the Lafayette Road they diverged in two directions. The 3rd and 41st Tennessee continued on straight ahead in pursuit of King's harried brigade. Then the 25th and 17th Tennessee wheeled to the right, taking possession of King's field artillery battery, the 19th Indiana. The rest of the brigade joined them in a right wheel orienting the brigade battle line to the north and northwest.[9]

Up to now Johnson's Rebels were having their own way; but their fortunes were about to take a radical change for the worse.

Rosecrans had been frantically shifting units to contain Confederate penetrations, first by Stewart's Division, then by Hood's, now by Johnson's. Three divisions had been brought over from the Federal far right: Davis's, Wood's, and Philip Sheridan's. However, it was a single brigade in Wood's division, Charles Harker's, that would be the ruination of Bushrod Johnson's brigade.

Harker was one of the true battlefield masters the Union produced during the course of the war. He possessed Phil Sheridan's aggressiveness, but deployed and maneuvered his regiments with greater finesse. Harker's career was cut short when he was killed during the Atlanta campaign. On this day, it was the misfortune of the 3rd Tennessee to experience Harker's military skills at their best.

Harker was brought up to reinforce the left of Davis's line, which was being hard pressed by repeated attacks from Hood's Division. Hood launched a furious attack just as Johnson's Brigade was breaking through several hundred yards to the north. Harker resorted to the extraordinary expedient of attacking in two directions at once. He ordered two of his regiments to move forward and swing to the right to attack the right flank of Hood's force. Meanwhile, Harker, himself, led the 65th Ohio and 3rd Kentucky in the opposite direction to deal with the penetration by Bushrod Johnson.[10]

The first Confederate to detect this dangerous threat to the Rebel flank and rear was Calvin Walker, now acting as a defacto brigade commander, having assumed command of the 41st Tennessee in addition to his own regiment. Confronted by a whipped but still dangerous Federal brigade to their front, and the two blue regiments rapidly advancing up both sides of the Lafayette Road directly toward his rear, Walker sensed impending catastrophe. He ordered both the 3rd and 41st Tennessee to about face and promptly marched them back into the woods from whence they came. He also ordered the 41st Tennessee's commander, Lieutenant Colonel James D. Tillman, to alert Colonel Fulton, commanding Johnson's

Brigade, about the approaching threat. Walker's withdrawl did not bode well for the rest of Johnson's Brigade.[11]

Just as Tillman began to deliver his warning, the 65th Ohio moved through the trees to within thirty yards of the 17th Tennessee's rear and delivered a terrible volley directly into the unsuspecting Tennesseans' backs. According to Bushrod Johnson, "[The] brigade now moved by one impulse to the right, and fell back to the east of the road ... leaving 11 officers, 60 men, and the captured battery in the hands of the enemy."[12]

The brigade was now in danger of complete destruction. Organization was disintegrating, there was no established position to fall back on, and Charles Harker was close behind. Something had to be done quickly. Bushrod Johnson called on the only troops available, the 3rd and 41st Tennessee regiments, still out of breath from their own exertions, to do what they could to stabilize the situation.

Harker's advance on Fulton had left him vulnerable to an attack on his own flank from the woods to the east, where the 3rd and 41st Tennessee were now safely ensconced. Walker ordered his men forward again, and this time it was Harker's turn to give ground. The 3rd Tennessee caught the 65th Ohio in flank and inflicted some devastating casualties on the Ohioans, taking a particularly harsh toll on the regiment's officers. The two Tennessee regiments drove the Ohioans and Kentuckians back, and then established a defensive line on both sides of the road blocking any further Yankee advances from the south. Fulton was now able to safely extract the remainder of his brigade and reform them in the good defensive position Johnson had chosen for them six-hundred yards back in the woods east of the Lafayette Road. Once everyone was safely posted, the 3rd and 41st withdrew and took up an adjoining position.[13]

Bragg made one more desperate attempt to break the Federal line that day, ordering an assault by Cleburne's Division on the Federal left, an attack which did not get underway until well after dark. Except for increasing the casualty lists on both sides, it accomplished nothing.

The first day's battle at Chickamauga was a draw. William Rosecrans managed to strike Braxton Bragg first, and all day long Bragg tried to gain control over the battle, to no avail. However, while Rosecrans committed his entire army to a fight for its life on the 19th, for most of the day the Confederates allowed four veteran divisions to stand idle.

Although most accounts of the battle blame Bragg for this first day's failure, culpability for the misfortune suffered by the 3rd Tennessee can be directly ascribed to Daniel Harvey Hill.

Hill was a newcomer to the Army of Tennessee, having spent the previous two years serving creditably under Robert E. Lee. Like his old friend Braxton Bragg, Hill had an abrasive personality, and had won the enmity of Jefferson Davis by openly criticizing Lee. Shortly after arriving, he managed to alienate Bragg as well. Though he is often credited with being a key player in the Confederate victory at Chickamauga, hundreds of needless casualties this first day, including many suffered by the 3rd Tennessee, were the direct result of Hill's inaction. The troops who marched unmolested away from Hill's front were the very ones that sealed the penetration made by the 3rd Tennessee, as well as other penetrations made by Hood's troops further south.

Hill was in command of the far left corps of the army and had under his direct control the divisions of Patrick Cleburne and John C. Breckenridge. Also, as senior officer on that part of the field Hill could also call on Hindman's and Preston's divisions if needed. Hill's job that day was to hold the Union forces opposite him in place to prevent their being used for a Federal counter-attack. If he determined that the Yankees on his front were being used to reinforce other parts of the Federal line, he was to launch an attack of his own. Paragraph 5 of Bragg's written order is very explicit on both of these points.

> 5. Hill will cover our left flank from an advance of the enemy from the cove, and, by pressing the cavalry in his front, ascertain if the enemy is reinforcing at Lee and Gordon's Mills [Bragg's attack objective], in which event he will attack them in flank.[14]

In other words, Hill was to pin down the right portion of the Federal army to prevent it from reinforcing its left. Hill did "ascertain" that the enemy was "reinforcing," but did absolutely nothing about it. In his own words:

> The clouds of dust rolling down the valley revealed the precipitate retirement of the foe, not on account of our pressure upon him [Hill would have had to be the one applying any such pressure], but on account of the urgency of the order to hurry to their left. This was the time to have relieved the strain upon our right by attacking the Federal right at Lee and Gordon's.

Hill then attempts to pass the blame to Bragg contending he had no order to do so. Among the troops marching away from Hill's front was Thomas J. Wood's division whose Third Brigade belonged to Charles Harker.[15]

Had Hill taken decisive action on the 19th, there is little doubt that the dramatic results obtained on the 20th could have been achieved a day sooner. As it was, Hood's and Johnson's Divisions had to bear the cost of Hill's malfeasance.

That cost was very personal for the 3rd Tennessee. Of 264 men engaged, the 3rd Tennessee had fourteen men killed, twenty-eight wounded, and two captured in this fight. They also lost their brigade commander, John Gregg. In light of the intensity of this combat, these numbers are not surprising. Compared to the horrendous casualties suffered by some of their sister regiments, these numbers might be considered low. However, another day of battle even more intense than that of the 19th still lay ahead.[16]

Prospects for the second day were good. Much of the Confederate Army was still fresh, and during the night James Longstreet arrived with his second division.

Meanwhile, instead of establishing a potentially impregnable position among the precipitous hills immediately to his rear, Rosecrans stayed where he was and waited for Bragg's next move. The initiative was given over to the Confederates.

Bragg then did an incredible thing. In spite of being in the midst of the biggest battle of his life, he reorganized his army again. He divided the army into two wings giving Longstreet command of the left and Leonidas Polk command of the right. Longstreet was not familiar with the field of battle nor with the Army of Tennessee. However, as things turned out, he arranged for some interesting troop dispositions that set the stage for a spectacular Confederate victory. Bragg's selection of the pettish Polk, however, was an unmitigated disaster.

The night of September 19 was one of misery and horror for the men of the 3rd Tennessee. Sharpshooters constantly fired at any movement or sound, and hundreds of wounded men scattered throughout the woods kept up a continuous chorus of moaning and pleas for help. No fires were allowed, so the men were forced to get what sleep they could in clammy, sweat-soaked clothes. Brown's men, close to the 3rd Tennessee's right, decided that orders to the contrary or not, they were going to get themselves some warmth. According to a soldier of the 32nd Tennessee:

By midnight the temperature had fallen low enough to bring a light frost; and some of the men getting very chilly, stirred up some smoldering logs. The flames shot out suddenly and showed the enemy our position and brought on us an alarming fire of artillery and small arms knocking limbs from the trees about us and causing a little excitement. General Brown rushed to the front and gave us a reprimand severe enough to the settle the matter of having a fire for the rest of the night.[17]

The Rebels at least had Chickamauga Creek. Water was scarce on the drought stricken fields, and the Federals suffered.

Meanwhile, the generals on both sides planned new miseries for the morrow.

Notes for Chapter 13

1 Cozzens, *This Terrible Sound*, p. 235. *OR*, Vol.XXX, part 2, pp. 361-362.

2 *OR*, Vol.XXX, part 1, pps. 371,453.

3 Richard M. McMurry's *John Bell Hood and the War for Southern Independence* provides excellent examples of Hood's attitude toward battle. See pp. 98-99.

4 *OR*, Vol.XXX, part 2, pp. 453-454.

5 Sam Watkins, *Co. Aytch.*, p. 104.

6 *OR*, Vol.XXX, part 1, pp. 454-455.

7 *Ibid.*, p. 455.

8 Cozzens, *op. cit.*, p. 233. *OR*, Vol.XXX, part 1, p. 455.
9 *OR*, Vol. XXX, Part 1, pp. 691-692.
10 *OR*, Vol. XXX, Part 2, p. 455.
11 *Ibid.*
12 *Ibid.*, pp. 455-456. Cozzens, *op. cit.*, p. 261.
13 *Ibid.*
14 *Battles and Leaders*, Vol.III, p. 647.
15 *Ibid.* p. 651.
16 Rollbook, compiled from company records.
17 T.I. Corn, *CV*, Vol. XXI, P. 124.

CHICKAMAUGA: DAY 2

At the beginning of the day on September 20, 1863, Braxton Bragg had a war and nobody came. The attack he had ordered for early morning failed to happen. Hour after hour Bragg waited while the man he had ordered to start the attack, Leonidas Polk, was sitting on the front porch of the house he had commandeered as headquarters, reading a newspaper. Polk was to have Hill's Corps, now posted on the Rebel far right, begin the Rebel attack against the Federal left flank at dawn, spearheaded by John C. Breckenridge's division. Bragg's chain of command had failed him again and he had to take personal control to get things moving.

For the soldiers, the delay was a welcome respite. The time was well spent untangling units, having a little breakfast if it could be found, and doing their best to clean themselves and their equipment. Meanwhile they exchanged opinions on how well they had done and tried to figure out who was winning this god-awful battle.

Bushrod Johnson had his division efficiently realigned and ready to resume the offense by 7:00 a.m., even though his division had broken into several widely separated pieces the day before. Johnson moved his own brigade, along with McNair's, still augmented by the 7th Texas and the 50th Tennessee regiments, into the front line, with McNair on the right and Johnson (Fulton) on the left. The rest of Gregg's Brigade, the 3rd, 10th/30th and the 41st Tennessee Regiments, formed a second line. With Gregg wounded, command of his brigade passed to the senior colonel, Cyrus A. Sugg of the 50th Tennessee. Hindman's Division was moved up on Johnson's left and Stewart's Division closed up on his right.[1]

The most interesting troop dispositions in Johnson's vicinity that morning, however, were the forces lined up behind him by James Longstreet, Johnson's new wing commander. Directly behind Johnson was Hood's Division under Evander Law, bloodied but not broken by the tough fighting on the 19th. Then behind Johnson and Law, Longstreet stacked a third division, Lafayette McLaw's, under the command of Joseph Kershaw, fresh off the rickety rails from Virginia. In all, Longstreet had arranged an assault column six brigades deep, one of the most powerful strike forces in terms of depth and raw combat power ever assembled by the Confederates.[2]

The Federals opposite Longstreet organized a formidable defense of their own some three lines deep. These were some of the best troops in the Union army. Included was Charles Harker's excellent brigade. It is possible that the Yankees still might have held, as at Gettysburg, if it had avoided a terrible blunder brought on by George Thomas's incessant calls for reinforcements.

A short distance from the right of the 3rd Tennessee, John C. Brown was also busy preparing to renew the attack. Bragg had again planned for an echelon attack progressing from right to left. Brown's attack would be the signal for the 3rd Tennessee to begin its own advance.

The long delay caused by the confusion within the Confederate high command allowed the Yankees to again strike first. The aggressive Harker was never one to stand idle when there were Rebels in the neighborhood. Assisted by George P. Buell's brigade, he began probing Johnson's front. Johnson had all he could handle for a while, but the bluecoats eventually returned to their original positions.

As the sun rose higher Braxton Bragg became desperate. He took the extraordinary step of ordering everyone he could find to attack at once. His aides flew everywhere, sometimes issuing orders directly to captains. Just about then the battle finally got underway on Johnson's right as the Rebel flank attack began.

One of Bragg's aides found Stewart and ordered him to attack at once. "Old Straight" was puzzled by this breach of protocol; the order bypassed both his corps commander, Hood, and his wing commander, Longstreet. Stewart did not tarry long immediately passing the order to John C. Brown.[3]

Brown delivered a smashing attack that struck precisely at the boundary between Brannon's and Reynold's divisions, and the Tennessean managed to advance some six-hundred yards into the Federal rear, again splitting the Federal line in two. While bluecoat counterattacks again forced him back as they did the day before, what Brown did accomplish was to convince the Yankees, and in particular George Thomas, that reinforcements were needed. Rosecrans began a general shift of his army to the left.

Shifting troops in the face of a powerful enemy like this was always a dangerous practice. Eventually a critical error did occur, and it happened directly in front of the powereful attack force Longstreet had organized, with the 3rd Tennessee in the second line.

The sequence of events leading to the Confederate breakthrough began with a young Federal staff officer reporting to Rosecrans that a gap existed between Joseph J. Reynold's and Thomas Wood's divisions. In reality, this space was occupied by John M. Brannon's division, the same blue troops so roughly handled by John C. Brown's brigade a short time before. Brannon's men were hidden from the staff officer's view by the thick timber. Wood assured himself that Federal reserves would move into the space he was vacating and started his division to the left. At that precise moment, 11:10 a.m. by Bushrod Johnson's watch, John Bell Hood started his attack.[4]

Johnson's and McNair's brigades stepped out quickly with Gregg's men (now under Sugg) close behind. They were under heavy fire immediately, most of it emanating from the right. The division had to advance about six-hundred yards before it reached the Lafayette Road a few hundred yards north of the position it had occupied briefly the day before.

Johnson had no idea how weak his enemy had become. He paused to give his artillery time to soften up the Yankee line posted at the far side of Brotherton Field, and to allow his infantry a few minutes to catch their breath. Resistance was weak from their immediate front, but they continued to receive a tremendous fire from George P. Buell's brigade of Wood's division on their far right. This affected McNair's men most, and they started to give ground. However, some words of "encouragement" from the brigade officers and the sight of Hood's tough veterans deploying out of the woods in support behind them re-stabilized the line.[5]

Johnson ordered everyone forward in a simultaneous rush. The Yankee line to the front and left, now occupied by only a few left-overs from Wood's division, quickly disintegrated, but McNair's brigade on the right continued to receive a pounding from Brannon. After advancing a few hundred yards, the Confederates paused in a forest of small pines west of the Brotherton farm to figure out what to do next.

Johnson's men were now solidly in the rear of the Federal position, but unlike the day before, this time they had Hood's tough division pouring in behind them. Johnson, sensing that the Confederates were at the brink of achieving a great victory, did not pause long. Sugg asked that his brigade be allowed to pass to the front to spearhead the advance, to which Johnson assented. Johnson then ordered Fulton to angle his brigade (Johnson's) to the left in the general direction toward which most of the Yankees were retreating. McNair was ordered to angle to the right to confront the Federals tormenting his right flank.[6]

Once everything was ready Johnson's Brigade started forward again, this time with the 3rd, 41st, and 10th/30th Tennessee Regiments leading the way. These three veteran Tennessee regiments were now the spearhead for Bragg's entire army.

As Johnson got underway, Hood rode up and issued his final order of the battle. It was simple: "Go ahead, and keep ahead of everything." When Hood charged off to check on the right, the Yankees promptly shot him off his horse. Hood would lose a leg.[7]

The Tennesseans broke out of the forest into some open fields where they enjoyed their first clear view of thousands of Union soldiers fleeing in raw panic. Johnson waxed eloquent.

> The resolute and impetuous charge, the rush of our heavy columns sweeping out from the shadow and gloom of the forest into the open fields flooded with sunlight, the glitter of arms, the onward dash of artillery and mounted men, the retreat of the foe, the shouts of the hosts of our army, the dust, the smoke, the noise of fire-arms—of whistling balls and grape-shot and of bursting shell—made up a battle scene of unsurpassed grandeur.[8]

For the battle-hardened veterans of the 3rd Tennessee, and the equally tough men of the regiments beside them, this undoubtedly was their supreme moment of combat. Rarely were private soldiers so situated that they could view more than just a tiny portion of a battlefield. Arrayed before the 3rd Tennessee was a major part of a Union field army in utter rout. The Tennesseans charged ahead with new vigor.

As Gregg's Brigade moved into the open, they began receiving fire from nine assorted Federal cannon which had collected on a slight elevation to the Confederates' right front. Johnson had Sugg wheel the brigade to the right to take these cannoneers in flank. The Tennesseans moved out at the double-quick and charged among the artillerymen before they could remove themselves or their guns. The Confederates forced the captured Yankee teamsters to limber up the nine guns and drive them at gun point to the Confederate rear. In a touch of irony, later, when the guns were later distributed to Rebel artillery units, several of the guns belonging to the 1st Missouri Battery (Union) were issued to the 1st Missouri Battery (Confederate).[9]

Once the Federal artillery was captured, Gregg's Brigade continued its advance unopposed for another six-hundred yards toward a ridge to the west. Upon reaching it, the Confederates were able to look down upon rows of Yankee rear elements lined up along the Crawfish Springs Road. Johnson wrote:

> Along this road a line of telegraph wires extended from Chattanooga to General Rosecran's Headquarters, and at the gorge of the gap a train of wagons filled the road, while a number of caissons and a battery of artillery for defense of the train occupied the grounds near Vidito's house. The ridge on the east of the cove was taken without resistance, though the enemy had there constructed a breastwork of rails, and had piled up a large number of their knapsacks, secure, as they doubtless thought, from the danger of the battlefield.[10]

The telegraph wire Johnson referred to actually extended all the way to Washington. Lincoln's personal representative, Charles Dana, was sending a running account of the battle directly to the president.

The appearance of Johnson's infantry did not elicit much response from the Yankees, but when the Rebels opened on them with a battery of artillery, the tranquil valley instantly turned into a scene of complete bedlam. Teamsters frantically tried to escape the Rebel guns any way they could. Wagons were overturned or smashed into trees as the drivers tried to take their teams and wagons up the steep sides of the gorge, or, as Bushrod Johnson described them, the "precipitous acclivities adjacent." A Federal battery began firing on Johnson's men from the high ground to the right, but Johnson's artillery quickly drove off these Yankee gunners.[11]

Johnson's and Gregg's brigades moved up to take possession of their vast haul of booty—four field guns, seven caissons, and about thirty wagons filled with various types of ammunition. Most of the Yankees had vanished having fled to the north along the Crawford Springs Road.

The pivotal moment of the Battle of Chickamauga was now at hand for the Confederates. Bushrod Johnson's division was squarely in the rear of what was left of the Army of the Cumberland under George Thomas. Rosecrans had skedaddled to Chattanooga along with the other fugitives from the right wing of his army. What was needed now was an attack force of a division or two to circle to the right, up the sides of Horseshoe Ridge, and then move directly east into Thomas's rear. At that particular moment, about 12 noon, the only Yankees available to contest such a movement were a few disorganized remnants from Brannon's division which offered only token resistance. Johnson knew such an attack might well result in the annihilation of the remainder of the Federal army, and immediately set about making it happen.

The Battle of Chickamauga was a showcase of missed opportunities for the Army of Tennessee, and the events that followed were a continuation of more of the same. The first mistake was made by Johnson himself. Before his men could continue the attack they would have to replenish their ammunition. Though there were tons of captured Federal ammunition in wagons all around him, perfectly usable in Confederate arms, Johnson ordered a supply brought up from the rear. Then he sent aides in every direction looking for supporting units to continue the advance, and finally galloped off himself looking for help and guidance from higher commanders who were nowhere to be found.[12]

Leonidas Polk and Daniel Harvey Hill had squandered the early hours of the day; now it was Longstreet's turn to miss an opportunity. With Hood out of commission, the Dutchman would have to take direct control of the battle; but where was he?

While Johnson's Tennesseans were breaking through to the Yankee rear, and laying the Federal army wide open for destruction, Longstreet was busy elsewhere. In his own words, he "rode along the line to observe the enemy and find relations with our right wing." Then he "rode away to enjoy my spread of Nassau bacon and Georgia sweet potatoes." Finally, he was called to the rear by Bragg.[13]

Longstreet sought the commanding general's permission to move into the Federal rear, in particular to block the Federal escape route by moving blocking forces into the Dry Valley (Crawford Springs) Road, the exact position Johnson's men had already occupied. By this time Bragg was an emotional wreck from the frustration of dealing with his subordinates and had no advice to offer Longstreet.[14]

The delay in the attack resulting from Johnson's search for supporting units provided a welcome breather for the 3rd Tennessee after the hard fighting of the morning. No doubt they were elated by their success, but they knew there was tough fighting ahead. Bushrod Johnson would not be content while there were still live Yankees on the battlefield.

After two hours of frustrated hunting for a senior commander, Johnson finally organized his own assault force. He sent an aide to search for his own detached brigade, McNair's, while he personally acquired two brigades from Thomas Hindman's division. These were commanded by Zachariah Deas and Patton Anderson. As these two brigades moved into attack position, Johnson took his own three brigades and resumed the advance, this time up the slopes of Horseshoe Ridge.

Johnson oriented the two brigades already at hand to the north, Johnson's on the left and Gregg's on the right. They were accompanied by W.S. Everett's and S.H. Dent's batteries of field artillery, the latter detached from Hindman's Division. Advancing around 2:00 p.m., the two brigades reached the top of the first spur without opposition. Here Johnson paused to allow his supporting units to catch up.[15]

At this point the two regiments detached from Gregg's brigade earlier that day caught up with their comrades. The 50th Tennessee had been roughly handled and could only muster about fifty men. These men were added to the ranks of the 3rd Tennessee. The other regiment was the 7th Texas, the same unit that fought along side the 3rd Tennessee at the bloody battle of Raymond. The Texans took position on the 3rd Tennessee's left. Most of the division's field artillery, seven guns, were assigned to Johnson's Brigade advancing on the left of Gregg's Brigade.[16]

Support began arriving from other divisions. Coming up on the right of Gregg's Brigade was Patton Anderson's brigade from Hindman's Division. Deas' Brigade, also from Hindman, conducted a wide wheeling movement to the left and came up on Johnson's left, extending the advance to the next hill to the west. Once these units were in position, Johnson ordered the advance to continue.[17]

Within minutes, Johnson's Brigade came under heavy fire from the adjacent ridge to the left. Fulton had his men take cover and began pouring artillery and rifle fire across the valley on this new threat. This made it possible for the remaining brigades to continue the advance, but eliminated Johnson's Brigade from the attack force. As the two remaining brigades neared the crest, Anderson's Brigade was blistered by a sudden volley of rifle fire from Brannon's battered, but still dangerous units. The unexpected volley threw Anderson's men back. Gregg's Brigade was left to continue the advance on its own.[18]

For the 3rd Tennessee and the 7th Texas what followed was a nightmare revisited.

Coming directly at them from across the ridge to the north were ten fresh regiments of Yankee infantry, advancing in battle order as fast as their legs could carry them. The delays caused by the Confederate high command were about to be paid for with the blood of Johnson's Tennesseans and Texans.

The blue soldiers approaching were two large brigades belonging to Gordon Granger's Reserve Corps. Granger had spent the day guarding the ground immediately south of Chattanooga, and had grown impatient at the realization that a major battle was raging within earshot and he was not part of it. Finally, on his own initiative, Granger took two of his three brigades, James Steedman's division, straight down the Lafayette Road toward the battle.

The two brigades were entirely on their own during the march, and should have been easy prey for the tough Confederates on Polk's line. Had anyone else been in command on that part of the battlefield, Granger would never have reached Horseshoe Ridge. But Polk it was, and except for a little harassment fire from Bedford Forrest's cavalry, Granger was able to join George Thomas and the Federal main force essentially unscathed.

Thomas ordered Granger to march to his unprotected right rear. Granger had also brought 95,000 rounds of ammunition, much

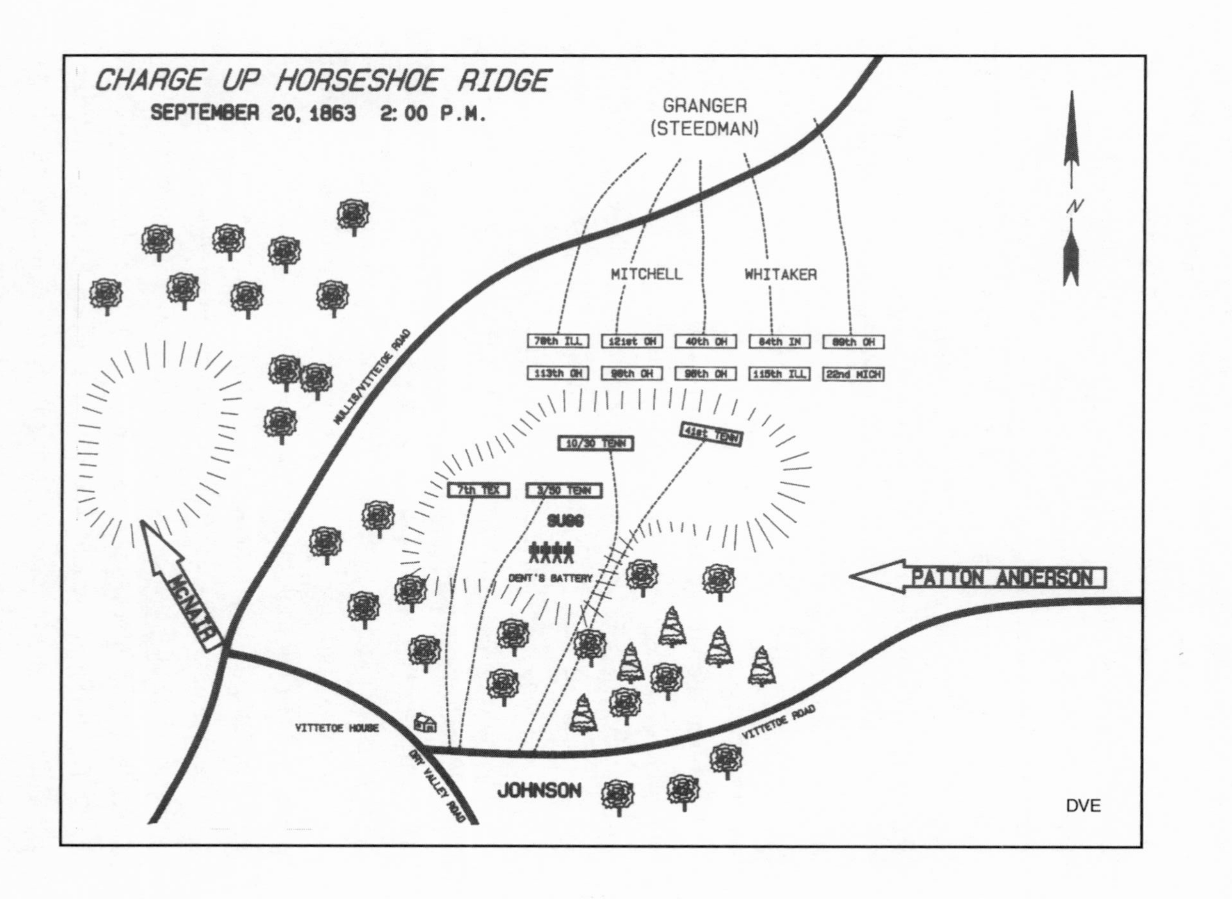
CHARGE UP HORSESHOE RIDGE
SEPTEMBER 20, 1863 2:00 P.M.
GRANGER
(STEEDMAN)
N
MITCHELL
WHITAKER
78th ILL
121st OH
40th OH
84th IN
89th OH
113th OH
98th OH
96th OH
115th ILL
22nd MICH
MULLIS/VITTETOE ROAD
10/30 TENN
41st TENN
7th TEX
3/50 TENN
SUGG
DENT'S BATTERY
PATTON ANDERSON
McNAIR
VITTETOE HOUSE
DRY VALLEY ROAD
VITTETOE ROAD
JOHNSON
DVE

needed by Thomas's men. Granger's men arrived at the north side of the crest just as Johnson's men reached the south side.[19]

For a while, until they realized they were fighting by themselves, Gregg's men were the attackers, about eight-hundred and fifty Tennesseans and Texans versus ten Yankee regiments with four-thousand men. The 41st Tennessee led the Rebel attack along the hogback to the right and took the brunt of the Federal assault, the Tennesseans' chief antagonist being the 115th Illinois. The 41st was pushed off the ridge, regained it, and in the process lost its commander, Lieutenant Colonel James D. Tillman.

Meanwhile, the 3rd Tennessee was engaged by the 89th Ohio while the 7th Texas squared off with the 96th Illinois. The Confederate regiments began falling back from right to left until there was no one left on the hilltop except the 3rd Tennessee and the 7th Texas, plus the two guns from Dent's Battery. All the Federal fire was now directed at these few men.[20]

Being attacked from several directions at once was nothing new for the tough veterans of the 3rd Tennessee and 7th Texas. They extracted a terrible price from the Yankees before yielding the hilltop. The two field guns greatly extended their range of fire and provided the men time to throw up breastworks and brace themselves. They yielded ground grudgingly without losing their organization and taking everything with them. Control of the field guns was maintained by withdrawing them by hand over short distances and reforming them into battery at appropriate intervals to fire blasts of cannister at the blue infantry. The little two-regiment force, supported by Dent's guns, prevented a Confederate rout and allowed Bushrod Johnson time to bring up more reinforcements.

Eventually the Confederates retook the ridge the hard way, lining up Deas', Arthur Manigault's, Johnson's, Gregg's, and Anderson's brigades from left to right, and marching them into the face of the Yankee fire. The Confederates successfully drove Granger's men off, but at a cost in soldiers' lives the Confederacy could not afford. The 3rd Tennessee and the rest of the men of Gregg's Brigade expended their second issue of ammunition of the day in this fight. About sundown they were finally relieved by Robert C. Trigg's brigade from William Preston's division. The 3rd Tennessee took up a supporting position in Johnson's second line.[21]

The battle on the 20th was a costly one for the 3rd Tennessee. The regiment lost another fourteen men killed, seventeen wounded, and three captured. Losses for both days amounted to twenty-eight killed, forty-five wounded, and five captured, almost a third of the regiment's strength. Losses were about the same in the rest of Bragg's army. They gave much worse than they got, combining with the 7th Texas to inflict most of the eighteen-hundred casualties on Granger's two brigades. In addition, the 3rd Tennessee played the key role in capturing the nine pieces of artillery on the 20th.[22]

That night Thomas managed to extract most of his troops. If the Confederates had moved quickly in the pursuit, they might have achieved decisive victory. Then the horrible cost in blood might have been justified.

The brief period of good luck the Army of Tennessee enjoyed on September 20th was not to last. Braxton Bragg would see to that.

Notes for Chapter 14

1 *OR*, Vol.XXX, part 2, pp. 456-457.

2 *Ibid.*, p. 457. Glenn Tucker, *Chickamauga: Bloody Battle in the West*, p. 260.

3 *Ibid.*, pp. 363-364.

4 *Ibid.*, p. 457.

5 *Ibid.* Cozzens, *This Terrible Sound*, p. 370.

6 *Ibid.*, pp. 457, 495.

7 *Ibid.*, p. 458.

8 *Ibid.*, pp. 457-458.

9 *Ibid.* p. 458.

10 *Ibid.* p. 459.

11 *Ibid.*

12 *Ibid.*, p. 460.

13 Longstreet, *From Manassas to Appomattox*, pp. 450-451.

14 *Ibid.* p. 452.

15 *OR*, Vol.XXX, part 2, p. 461.

16 *Ibid.*

17 *Ibid.*

18 *Ibid.*

19 *OR*, Vol.XXX, part 1, pp. 854-855, 860.

20 *OR*, VolXXX, part 2, pp. 462, 495-496. Cozzens, *op. cit.*, pp. 447-448.

21 *Ibid*, p. 496.

22 Rollbook, compiled from company records. *Battles and Leaders*, Vol.III, pp. 673, 675-676.

15

THE CHATTANOOGA BATTLES

For two and one-half days Bragg's army crept toward Chattanooga harassing the rear of William Rosecrans's battered Army of the Cumberland. Almost everyone in the Army of Tennessee, from private to general, knew that the Yankee army was on its last legs. Unfortunately, Braxton Bragg was physically and mentally incapable of finishing the job begun by the victory at Chickamauga. He was in a state of shock at the Confederate losses of eighteen-thousand men. He was exhausted, worn down by ill health and balky generals, and his bad temperament was out of control. Bragg was not capable of the improvisation such a pursuit required.[1]

Bragg made no effort to force his way into Chattanooga. John C. Brown and his brigade, as well as the 3rd Tennessee with the rest of its brigade, assumed advanced positions side by side in the Chattanooga Valley a short way south of the town. Other parts of the army occupied the heights of Lookout Mountain to their left and Missionary Ridge behind them and to their right. The Confederates brought Rosecrans under siege.[2]

Bragg then set about punishing those officers whom he felt performed in a substandard manner during the campaign just ended, which might be viewed as strange behavior coming off such a spectacular victory for anyone but Bragg. Polk and Hill were sacked which led to an effort by Bragg's other subordinates including James Longstreet, Simon Buckner, Patrick Cleburne, and B. F. Cheatham, to get rid of Bragg. These men dispatched a petition directly to the Confederate War Department asking that Bragg be removed. John C. Brown was a participant in this conspiracy which seems a little less than generous since it was while serving under Bragg that Brown received the wreath to his three colonel's stars denoting his promotion to brigadier general.[3]

Since it was impractical to fire everyone with stars on his collar, Bragg's response to all this was to reorganize the army from top to bottom. He broke apart the state affiliation of several of his divisions on the excuse that it would prevent excessive casualties from any one state. The Tennessee troops were especially hard hit since their commanders were considered by Bragg to be his worst enemies. The divisions of B.F. Cheatham, A. P. Stewart, and Bushrod Johnson were all broken up. However, state integrity within brigades was maintained.[4]

Though he was among Bragg's detractors that fall of 1863, John C. Brown continued to receive about the same level of confidence from the North Carolinian that he had before. He retained his original command of four Tennessee regiments and one Tennessee battalion and enjoyed the addition of one more: his original command, the 3rd Tennessee, was reassigned to his brigade.[5]

The 3rd Tennessee was familiar with Brown's style as a stern taskmaster from the old days, and now he was also viewed as a fierce fighter. While the regiment was undoubtedly happy to have its old chief back, it is also likely that it had some qualms about what to expect from the hard-fighting Brown on the battlefield.

No doubt a big regret for the 3rd Tennessee was the departure of its old battle companion, the 7th Texas. The 7th was assigned to an all new Texas brigade commanded by its own Hiram Granbury, and assigned to Patrick Cleburne's division. Granbury was the second officer from the 7th Texas to make general officer (John Gregg was the first). The Texans were destined to achieve spectacular results and immortal fame under Cleburne's and Granbury's leadership.

Brown and his Tennesseans were assigned to a new division composed mostly of former Vicksburg defenders under a new commander, Major General Carter Stevenson. Stevenson was a career army man with experience fighting Mexicans, Indians, and Mormons. A West Point graduate, Stevenson started out the war commanding a Virginia regiment, then was sent west to Bragg's army after he was promoted to brigadier general. He participated in Bragg's Kentucky invasion, so he and Brown were already well acquainted. As one of the Old Army regulars, however, he apparently possessed a common characteristic which straight-laced Flavel Barber found disturbing. Barber commented that "Stevenson has not gained the confidence and affection of our brigade [due to his] intemperance."[6]

Stevenson and a few others managed to piece together tough and cohesive units, but the turbulence at the top created structural weaknesses in many parts of the army as the upcoming battle would amply demonstrate.

In addition to his dissatisfaction with his top commanders, Bragg was very unhappy about his lack of supplies and transport. He blamed his failure to finish off Rosecrans's army on it. The army had to sustain itself from the surrounding countryside and that fall of 1863, with armys constantly criss-crossing the Chattanooga area, did not bode well for finding food stuffs. If Bragg could have side-stepped to the left a little and taken his army across the Tennessee River he might have done better. The central basin of Tennessee, the 3rd Tennessee's home area, was still one of the South's best granaries. When the army finally did return to central Tennessee during Hood's invasion the following year, they found themselves surrounded by a "superabundance of rations" as William Bate described it then.[7]

While Bragg dithered, the Union forces took action. Abraham Lincoln sent every available soldier he could find from throughout Yankeedom to the aid of William Rosecrans. With the victory at Chickamauga, the Confederacy was back in the ascendancy in the war. Bragg's inaction allowed momentum to shift back in favor of the North. John C. Brown and his 3rd Tennessee comrades watched with trepidation as U.S. Grant, Lincoln's best general, gathered masses of blue in front of them.

Grant immediately opened a supply line to the beleaguered Union men and prepared for action. He had under his command portions of four armies — the Army of the Cumberland, the Army of the Ohio, the Army of the Tennessee, and the Army of the Potomac. His objective was very clear: to attack the Confederate Army of Tennessee, and if possible, destroy it.

Bragg, on the other hand, never firmly established exactly what it was he wanted to accomplish beyond attempting to starve out the beleaguered Rosecrans. With a massive Federal force concentrating in his front, he took the extraordinary step of sending a major portion of his army away; James Longstreet was sent to Knoxville in an effort to divert Grant's attention in that direction. Grant would not take the bait. The only thing Bragg accomplished was to deplete his strength even further, and demoralize his men. The victorious spirit gained at such enormous cost from the Chickamauga victory evaporated. The only advantage retained by the Confederates at Chattanooga was their position—they held the high ground.[8]

With Longstreet gone, overall defense of Lookout Mountain was assigned to Carter Stevenson. Since Stevenson now commanded a corps sized force, he assigned command of his own division to John C. Brown. Brown was to defend the summit and western approaches to the mountain extending for a distance of ten miles to the south. This was a difficult assignment since his force would be spread extremely thin and the Yankees could pick out a weak point and concentrate against it. Brown's own brigade, including the 3rd Tennessee, was placed near the left end of the line which turned out to be far away from the action on the first day of the battle.[9]

As the battle began, most of the Confederate regiments were still recovering from the devastation of Chickamauga. The 3rd Tennessee still had fifty-nine men absent from wounds and ninety absent sick due to the miserable weather and lack of food. The regiment was able to deploy only 195 men.

Total strength	442
Absent sick	90
Absent wounded	59
AWOL	24
Deserters	12
Detached	31
Absent barefoot	13
Absent other reasons	18
Number present	195 [10]

Stevenson was reinforced by two brigades from Cheatham's Division, both commanded by John K. Jackson, who would earn the nickname 'Mudwall,' a parody of his more famous namesake in Virginia, 'Stonewall,' because of his less than sterling performance in the coming battle. B.F. Cheatham was absent. He had tried to resign when Jefferson Davis sustained Bragg during the command upheaval. When his resignation was refused by Richmond, he furloughed himself. Jackson's troops were assigned to the defense of the northern slope of the mountain, the most direct access into the Chattanooga Valley.[11]

Grant's plan, scheduled to commence on November 24, was to envelop both ends of Bragg's line, attacking Lookout Mountain first and Missionary Ridge second. He sent three full divisions against Jackson's two brigades. The Alabamans and Mississippians holding the northern slopes of the mountain were quickly overwhelmed.

During the battle, John C. Brown, perched high above the action on the summit of Lookout Mountain, peered down into a dense fog listening to the two sides flail away at each other, and trying to make some sense out of the racket. Jackson begged for reinforcements so Brown sent Pettus's Alabama brigade down to the lower slopes. Then he took his strongest regiment, the 32nd Tennessee, to the point of the mountain directly above the battle to anchor that part of the line.

Once his infantry was in place, Brown took personal charge of a two-gun section of Napoleons belonging to Captain Max Van Den Corpet's Cherokee Battery. These were large smoothbore cannon with about four and one-half inch diameter barrels and were

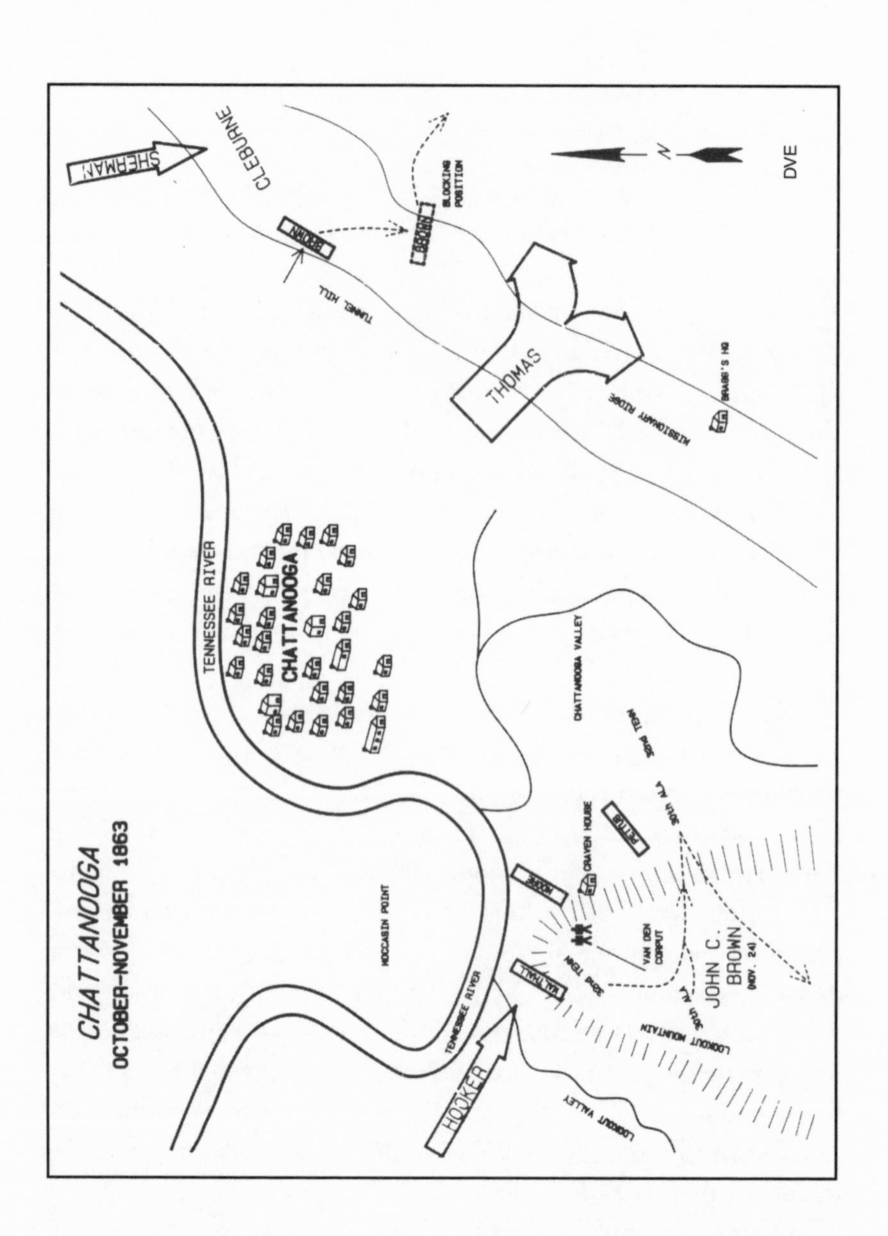
CHATTANOOGA
OCTOBER-NOVEMBER 1863
SHERMAN
CLEBURNE
BLOCKING POSITION
TUNNEL HILL
THOMAS
BRAGG'S HQ
MISSIONARY RIDGE
TENNESSEE RIVER
CHATTANOOGA
CHATTANOOGA VALLEY
CRAVEN HOUSE
PETTUS
MOORE
MOCCASIN POINT
VAN DEN CORPUT
JOHN C. BROWN
(NOV. 24)
WALTHALL
TENNESSEE RIVER
LOOKOUT MOUNTAIN
HOOKER
LOOKOUT VALLEY
N
DVE

extremely good close-range weapons. Brown's most difficult problem was determining where to fire since he could not make out friend or foe through the fog.[12]

Finally the Tennessean was able to locate the Yankee line near the Cravin House by sound alone. A detachment of Confederate signal corps troops then helped him establish a direction of fire. Brown described the action:

> At 1 p.m. the two Napoleon guns on the point opened fire upon the enemy, then passing near the Craven house, and continued it incessantly for two hours. At the same time I deployed sharpshooters from the Thirty-second Tennessee and the Thirtieth Alabama down the sides of the mountain, and directed a fire upon the enemy's flank. I ordered rocks rolled down the mountain also. The fog was so dense that we could not see the enemy, although we could hear his march, and guided by this and the report of his musketry ours was directed. His advance was quickly checked and his fire materially abated, and doubtless the effect of the shells from the fire from our sharpshooters contributed largely to this end.[13]

Bragg decided he could not hold both Lookout Mountain and Missionary Ridge, so later that afternoon Brown was ordered to evacuate his division which he did in good order. This was no small achievement considering the awkward position from which he had to fight and the size of the force opposing him.

Meanwhile, an attack by William T. Sherman was expected at any moment against Bragg's far right flank on Missionary Ridge. That night Bragg moved Stevenson's Division, including Brown's Brigade and the 3rd Tennessee, to that end of the battle line. Not everyone in the 3rd Tennessee was eager to join their comrades on Missionary Ridge. With no Yankees in front of them, the temptation to desert was too much for fourteen of the men. These deserters comprised the bulk of losses for the regiment for both days of battle at Chattanooga.[14]

The right flank on Missionary Ridge was commanded by reliable old William Hardee, author of the tactics which the 3rd

Tennesseans had learned two years before. Hardee replaced Polk. Patrick Cleburne secured Hardee's far right flank.

Almost as soon as he opened his attack on November 25th, Sherman discovered that he was outmatched even though he had a big advantage in numbers. Cleburne constructed a defensive position in depth with Stevenson's Division, Brown and the 3rd Tennessee included, comprising his second echelon. Eventually Stevenson shifted to a front line position on Cleburne's left as the Irishman concentrated his own division on the right. John C. Brown, back in command of his own brigade, placed the 3rd Tennessee directly over the railroad tunnel which adjoined Cleburne's left. The two commanders joined in repelling charge after charge of Yankee bluecoats at almost no cost to themselves. For the 3rd Tennessee it, was repeat of Chickasaw Bayou.

During the course of the battle, a disagreement arose between Brown and Cleburne. As various Federal assault units were repulsed by Brown and Cleburne's men, portions of these Yankee units were sometimes left behind on the battlefield as their companions withdrew. Cleburne liked to sortie units out on the flanks of these unfortunate troops to administer a final coup de grace and scoop up bunches of prisoners. When Cleburne asked Brown to conduct one of these movements Brown refused, saying, "I would be exposed to a terrible fire on my flank from the enemy who was lying under the hill not more than 300 yards in my front." Cleburne went along with Brown's refusal since this was a defensive battle and there was little impact on the final outcome. Undoubtedly an unintended outcome of this decision was the low casualty count in this fight for the 3rd Tennessee.[15]

In spite of the masterful defensive fight waged by Patrick Cleburne and John C. Brown on the right end of Missionary Ridge, the entire Confederate position suddenly came unhinged. The precipitate cause of this disaster was a sudden forward lunge against the Confederate center by the Army of the Cumberland, the same troops Bragg had ravaged two months before at Chickamauga. Grant had ordered this movement for the purpose of easing the pressure on Sherman, but it quickly escalated into a full-scale assault mostly on the initiative of the men themselves.

The first indication John C. Brown had that all was not well was the receipt of an order "to move rapidly toward the center and report to Major-General Cheatham." Cheatham had just returned from furlough and was able to take part in the second day's battle, but in command of a new division. Part of Cheatham's Division was caught in the general stampede, while the remainder attempted to contain the breakthrough as well as protect the forces further north up the ridge.

Brown's Brigade fell in alongside Edward C.Walthall's Brigade of Cheatham's Division, which was showing obvious signs of stress. Ahead of them an "irregular" line was still contesting the Yankee advance as Brown approached, but quickly gave way just as Brown was arranging his line behind it.

Brown's and Walthall's brigades had barely assumed the front line position when suddenly Walthall's line also collapsed. Brown managed to hold his position as Walthall's men were reformed a short distance to the rear. Finally, once the right wing had safely withdrawn, Brown was allowed to move by the left flank across Chickamauga Creek to relative safety. Brown's line never cracked.[16]

The army's rear was a sight to behold. Former 3rd Tennessean Sam Watkins, fighting with Cheatham's Division, found whole regiments "gunless, cartridge-boxless, knapsackless, canteenless, and all other military accoutermentless ... ." In other words, it was an army in utter rout.[17]

Volumes have been written on the Confederate failure at Missionary Ridge, but the root cause for the collapse of the Rebel position was probably the lack of a solid cohesive line. There were too many defensive lines (three) for the manpower available, thinning troop density to the breaking point. The man in the ranks was isolated by the necessity of separating him from his companions by four or five yards. Instead of standing shoulder to shoulder with his comrades, he often could not even see them. His isolation grew in direct proportion to the advance of the massive blue line until he could stand the tension no longer, and broke for the rear.

Unit cohesion above regimental level was also badly shaken by Bragg's reorganization just before the battle. The men were no longer serving under familiar commanders. They had not had time to learn to trust their new leaders, and confidence was replaced by fear.

The Confederates retreated to Dalton, Georgia, saved from annihilation by the rear guard actions first by Brown and then by Cleburne. Once the Confederates were safely ensconced behind Rocky Face Ridge, Grant gave up the pursuit and returned north to reap the rewards of success. In a few months he was promoted to lieutenant general and given command of all Union land forces. In the meantime, Bragg asked to be relieved of command. He was, but was kicked upstairs to become Jefferson Davis's personal military advisor.

Considering the scope of the disaster, battle losses in the 3rd Tennessee were remarkably light: one killed, one wounded, one captured, and three more captured during the retreat to Dalton. However, the regiment was humiliated, worn out, and ready for a prolonged period of rest and recuperation.

John C. Brown's star was in the ascendancy despite the decline of the army in which he was serving. He assured his own future in the army with a one-sentence paragraph contained in his official report on the battle: "My entire command without exception behaved well."[18]

Well not quite the entire command. There were at least two instances of less than exemplary behavior within the ranks of the 3rd Tennessee. The first was I.M. Park of Company G, who, for the third time in his term of military service showed up for a major battle drunk. This time, however, before his comrades could move him out of harm's way, he was swept up and captured by the Yankees who were probing Lookout Mountain.[19]

The second was J.P. Caldwell of Company E. Caldwell lengthened his string of consecutive battles missed to five, this time because of a lack of shoes. Caldwell was "absent barefoot."[20]

With these two exceptions the performance of the 3rd Tennessee and the rest of Brown's Brigade must be judged as excellent, especially in light of the chaos swirling around them during much of the battle.

The war in the west entered a pause, and the regiment's officers concentrated on refilling its ranks. Most of the effort was directed toward returning sick or wounded men back to the army. The winter of 1863-64 would be the last respite for the 3rd Tennessee before the final cataclysmic struggle for control of the Confederate heartland.

Notes for Chapter 15

1 Horn, *The Army of Tennessee*, pp. 272-273.

2 Tucker, *The Battles for Chattanooga*, p. 20.

3 Horn, *op. cit.*, p. 286.

4 Connelly, *Autumn of Glory*, pp. 250-252.

5 *OR*, Vol.XXXI, part 2, p. 724.

6 Barber Diary, Vol. IV, April 1, 1864.

7 Connelly, *op. cit.*, p. 157. *OR*, Vol. XLV, Part 1, p. 747.

8 *Ibid.*, pp. 262-263.

9 *OR*, Vol.XXXI, part 2, pp. 725-726.

10 Rollbook, compiled from company records. RB, p.344.

11 Christopher Losson, *Tennessee's Forgotten Warriors: Frank Cheatham and His Confederate Division*, pp. 124-125.

12 *OR*, Vol.XXXI, part 2, pp. 725-726.

13 *Ibid.*

14 Rollbook, company records.

15 *OR*, Vol. XXXI, part 2, p. 727.

16 *OR*, Vol. XXXI, part 2, p. 272.

17 Watkins, *Co. Aytch*, p 119.

18 *OR*, Vol. XXXI, part 2, p. 727. Rollbook, company records, p. 344.

19 Rollbook, p. 291.

20 *Ibid.*, p 254.

16

INTERLUDE AT DALTON

Confederate hopes for victory in the great War Between the States were fading in the closing days of 1863. Bragg's disaster at Chattanooga took the spirit out of the Army of Tennessee. The men were on the edge of mutiny at Dalton, deserting in droves, and reprovisioning themselves any way they could, even hijacking their own supply trains.

Davis and company in Richmond agonized over who to select to replace Braxton Bragg, someone who could restore discipline and esprit-de-corps to the Army of Tennessee, and get it back to fighting form. The Confederate high command was coming to realize that if they lost the war in the west all would be lost, and that critical repairs would have to be made in the Army of Tennessee if the Confederacy was to have even a prayer for survival.

It had taken several disasters to teach the Richmond government this lesson—the loss at Fort Donelson depriving the South of the Tennessee breadbasket; the loss of Vicksburg depriving the South of the vital Mississippi River waterway; and most recently the loss of the rail hub at Chattanooga effectively cutting the Confederacy in half again. With the Federals poised to strike even further south, Robert E. Lee commented, "If Georgia is lost Virginia is lost."[1]

The first candidate for Bragg's job was Robert E. Lee himself. But Lee was so closely tied to the Virginia army that Davis concluded that he had best remain there to avoid demoralizing the eastern army too. The consensus among Lee, Bragg, and Davis's cabinet was that the best choice was Joseph E. Johnston.[2]

Johnston and Davis had detested each other since the war began, so appointing Johnston commander was a bitter pill for Jefferson Davis to swallow. Johnston was the ideal man for rebuilding and reorganizing a demoralized army, however. It is significant that Flavel Barber resumed his diary, suspended since the previous summer, when Johnston assumed command of the army.[3]

Johnston is often described as a good administrator and a stern disciplinarian. This is accurate, but not complete. Johnston was attentive to detail, able to assign responsibility, and rarely failed to personally follow up to make sure his intentions had been carried out. His discipline worked from the top down. He made sure that his officers, support staff, and service troops were doing their jobs. Only then did he concern himself with the troops on the line. He understood that his soldiers would cheerfully accept discipline as long as it was applied on an equal basis to everyone. Johnston disciplined fairly, and ruthlessly.

His presence was felt immediately by the 3rd Tennesseans, now settled into camp several miles southwest of Dalton. Suddenly food was available, and it was good. Men stopped looking like "tatterdemalions" and started looking like soldiers again. Johnston was everywhere, seeing to it that supplies were going where they were supposed to go, and were not being skimmed off by greedy quartermasters along the way. When he inspected the combat troops it was to find out what he could do to help them, not to condemn them. He checked on the presence of weapons; the Army of Tennessee was short six-thousand muskets when Johnston took command. Military accouterments, uniform items, and other materiel required to make war began to appear in significant quantities. Barefoot 3rd Tennesseans suddenly found themselves re-shod with brand new army brogans, probably from the blockade runner *Giraffe*, just in from Nassau.[4]

The despair brought on by the disaster of Chattanooga was replaced by a grim determination to see the thing through. Flavel Barber expressed the prevailing attitude: "Submission has been made impossible by the conduct of our insolent foe; and the only tolerable alternative left to us is resistance to the bitter end. We must fight, we can do nothing else if necessary forever."[5]

Despite the new optimism, Johnston had one major flaw. The little Virginian did not like to initiate military action until he was satisfied that sufficient men and material were on hand to make a successful outcome certain. In the 1864 resource starved Confederacy, this was not possible. As a result, Johnston constantly deferred taking action until finally his boss, Jefferson Davis, reached a frenzy of impatience.[6]

Five full months elapsed before Sherman and his hordes did anything. The Confederates settled down for a long winter respite. Oddly, the camp positions selected by each regiment were exactly the same as they had been the day after the general retreat from Chattanooga, as though they expected the Federal pursuit might be resumed at any minute. The army seemed frozen in time and place.

The men constructed semi-permanent huts made of split rail walls chinked with Georgia red clay which hardens like brick when dry. They also built mud and stick fireplaces with chimneys which often caught fire. The roofs were canvass from their tents. Each hut was about ten by fourteen feet, and about seven feet high at the sides. A hut could shelter four men with their four-poster straw beds, a small table, and several three-legged camp stools.[7]

These huts were quite adequate for a normal Georgia winter, but during the first seventeen days of January 1864, north Georgia experienced one of the worst cold snaps in the state's recorded history. Many days the temperature dropped below zero, accompanied by high wind, snow and rain. Military drill was suspended, and the men spent most of their time standing or sitting near warm fires in their huts. They had to rise from their bunks during the nights to warm themselves near the fire.

Young men who fight wars can find fun anywhere, and the troops in the Army of Tennessee staged battle royal snowball fights every time it snowed. During one of these, in March, Brown's men took on Edmund Pettus's brigade and succeeded in 'capturing' the 10th South Carolina's colors.[8]

For much of January 1864, the regiment and the rest of Brown's Brigade were detailed repairing the road between Dalton and Resaca, Johnston's supply line and prospective line of retreat. In the evenings, John C. Brown would often invite his old 3rd Tennessee comrades to his quarters to discuss prospects for the coming campaign and to share a little eggnog. As the winter progressed into spring, Brown's despondency changed to optimism. He was convinced the spring campaign would begin on the Dalton front with an advance by the Federal Army, which was exactly what happened. Flavel Barber speculated that Johnston's army would be used to reinforce Lee in Virginia.[9]

There was some discontent in the 3rd Tennessee's ranks related to the issue of reenlistment. Although the Confederate conscription laws obligated all soldiers currently in the ranks for the duration of the war, the army, as a morale booster, proceeded to reenlist each regiment anyway. The 3rd Tennessee balked at this. On January 20th, the men finally agreed to reenlist, but only on condition that they be allowed to reorganize, i.e., elect new officers and NCOs. Obviously the men were not satisfied with the way they were being led. Eventually John C. Brown, Flavel Barber, the Alabaman Zachariah Deas, and others, delivered some stirring speeches to the boys who received this extra attention with "good humor and with much enthusiasm." The regiment then reenlisted en masse, without conditions.[10]

Another interesting phenomena that winter of 1864 was the mammoth religious movement that swept the entire Confederate Army including the Army of Tennessee. Revival meetings became the rage with praying and hymn singing often extending into the wee hours of the evening. Thomas Deavenport, now the regimental chaplain, never found himself so busy as during this period. He preached often, and to standing room only audiences. The chapel for Brown's Brigade, built by the 26th Tennessee, was soon inadequate, and by adding an arbor was soon expanded to hold more than a thousand soldiers.[11]

Once discipline and morale were restored, Johnston's next big challenge was reconstitution of the manpower of the army. When Johnston arrived the Army of Tennessee mustered barely thirty-six thousand men of all arms. Word of the change in command, improved conditions, and a general amnesty for deserters combined to entice men back to the ranks. By early May overall strength had increased to fifty-three thousand, a forty-seven percent increase.[12]

Even after the new campaign kicked off in the spring, the army continued to grow. Fourteen thousand men arrived from Polk's department increasing the total to seventy thousand. Johnston amassed a formidable force to contest Sherman's advance.[13]

The 3rd Tennessee mirrored the army as a whole. The regiment increased by seventy-six, from the 195 men who fought at Missionary Ridge, to 271 men at the beginning of the spring campaign of 1863, a thirty-nine percent increase.[14]

The Achilles' heel in Johnston's new strength was the cavalry. The number of troops in this service ranged from eight to thirteen thousand during the course of the campaign, but Southern lack of horse flesh caused as many as three-quarters of these men to be dismounted at any one time. The Southern Army failed to utilize the foot-bound cavalry in any other capacity, making them useless to anyone. In addition, cavalry regiments were allowed to recruit from the infantry. The net effect was the cavalry created a drain on Johnston's deployable combat power. The large number of transfers of 3rd Tennesseans to the cavalry reflect this problem.[15]

One policy instituted by Johnston to boost morale which failed was the furlough program. One enlisted man out of thirty, and one officer out of three was to be given thirty days off. The problem was the soldiers had a tendency to stay on furlough. The men of the 3rd Tennessee treated it as a joke. The Yankees were posted literally in their own back yards. In fact, one of Sherman's corps commanders, Grenville Dodge, had located his headquarters in Pulaski where he could keep an eye on the rail link between Nashville and Huntsville.

The furlough program was a variation on a Yankee idea which worked very well. The Union army had instituted the program to promote re-enlistments in the three-year regiments scheduled to muster out the coming summer. The Union soldiers were enticed into trading three more years of service for an early visit home. Since Confederate soldiers were in for the duration, such enticements were wasted on them.

Some ranking officers took advantage of the lull in campaigning to cultivate romantic interests. William Hardee had time to 'rob the cradle,' tieing the knot with a Mobile, Alabama, beauty about half his age. John C. Brown departed the army in March bound for Griffin,Georgia, where he finally wed the beautiful Murfreesboro belle, Elizabeth 'Bettie' Childress.

Brown arrived in Griffin the day before the wedding, the social event of the season for that quiet little town. Before he could shake the dust from his uniform, he received a telegram from army headquarters ordering him to immediately depart for duty at Rome, Georgia, to help counter a Federal threat emanating out of Alabama. What to do about the wedding? Like a scene from a romantic novel, Brown requested that the ceremony be moved up from afternoon to morning. The minute the ceremony was completed, Brown leaped aboard a train and heroically started off toward Rome to confront the enemy.[16]

The Federal threat evaporated before Brown arrived and he soon returned to his bride. The newlyweds set off for a delayed honeymoon and toured several cities in Georgia and South Carolina, spending the majority of their time together in Charleston. Apparently their joy was unaffected by the black hulking Yankee gunboats lurking just outside Charleston harbor.[17]

When Brown arrived back in Dalton, he found the army making intensive preparations to give Sherman a hot reception when

Elizabeth 'Bettie' Childress Brown
Courtesy: Confederate Veteran

he began his soon expected move south. The Confederacy was again on the defense; Johnston had successfully resisted all attempts to prod him into taking offensive action.

The Confederates now hoped that they could at least prolong the war until the Yankees tired of it and went home. The plan was to hold the Northerners back and to deny them the conquest of such strategic targets as Atlanta, Savannah, Mobile, Richmond, and Charleston. Eventually, the Yankees might become frustrated and quit the war.

For the 1864 campaign, the dependable Hardee was retained as corps commander.

The army also regained the services of John Bell Hood, fresh from convalescent leave in Richmond. In the spring of 1864, Hood was still one of the heroes of the Confederacy. He was a key player in the victory at Chickamauga, and since he was not present for the disaster at Chattanooga, none of the stigma from that defeat was attached to him. He had a reputation as a hard fighter, but a poor administrator, and his experience as a corps commander was limited to two days at Chickamauga. He was still an unknown quantity in a high level position.

John C. Brown and the 3rd Tennessee, part of Stevenson's Division, were assigned to Hood along with Thomas Hindman's and A.P. Stewart's divisions. All the men in Hood's new corps knew Hood won victories, but they also knew those victories often were the result of head-on attacks with high casualty rates. Still, Joe Johnston was in overall charge, and confidence in him was unbounded.

At the end of April, Sherman began assembling his huge army at Chattanooga for the last grand offensive of the war. According to Sherman the objective was Johnston's army. Like most American commanders throughout history, he also had a ground objective. His goal was Atlanta, by way of Resaca.

Since Johnston would not take offensive action, Davis ordered him to hold his position at Dalton at all costs. The little Virginian established a formidable defensive line pinned on Rocky Face Ridge. Brown and the 3rd Tennessee were first assigned to the valley east of Rocky Face and north of Dalton. Sherman's plan was to fix

Johnston in his position at Dalton by deploying the bulk of his army against the Rebel army's impregnable position on Rocky Face Ridge. In the mean time, he would slip the 3rd Tennessee's old antagonist from Raymond, James B. McPherson, with his Army of the Tennessee, around Johnston's left flank and rear at Resaca.

The diversionary attack provided Johnston all he could handle, and went a long way to convince the Rebel commander that the attack on Rocky Face was the main effort. One of the reasons the Federals were so convincing is that most of the men making the attack on Rocky Face Ridge had no idea they were there only as a diversion, and did their very best to accomplish the impossible.

The bluecoats created an impressive spectacle as they fanned out across the broad valley between Rocky Face to the east and Taylor's Ridge to the west. The Rebels manhandled artillery to the top of the ridge, but when the Yankees were within range, the Southerners encountered a problem they had also faced on Missionary Ridge: they could not depress the guns low enough to deliver an effective fire. The Rebel cannoneers contented themselves with firing airbursts over the heads of the Yankees. The angry overhead blasts looked and sounded impressive to inexperienced bluecoats, but the veterans knew the crude Rebel shells normally produced only a few fragments and posed little danger to the men below.[18]

Yankee artillery quickly responded, and the big Federal rifled guns quickly smothered their feeble Rebel counterparts. The Federal guns created a continuous din in the valley by firing impact detonating shells at the Rebel positions, many of which burst on the sheer western face of Rocky Face Ridge. The acoustic effect of artillery exploding against a flat surface like this was very impressive.

Brown's sister brigade, the Alabamans under E.W. Pettus, anchored the northwest corner of Johnston's line, a local landmark appropriately occupied by buzzards in normal times (and still is today). Pettus came under heavy pressure by elements from the Federal IVth and XXth corps. Included was Charles Harker's brigade, the 3rd Tennessee's nemesis at Chickamauga. Brown shifted his men to the left on Rocky Face Ridge to shore up this critical angle.[19]

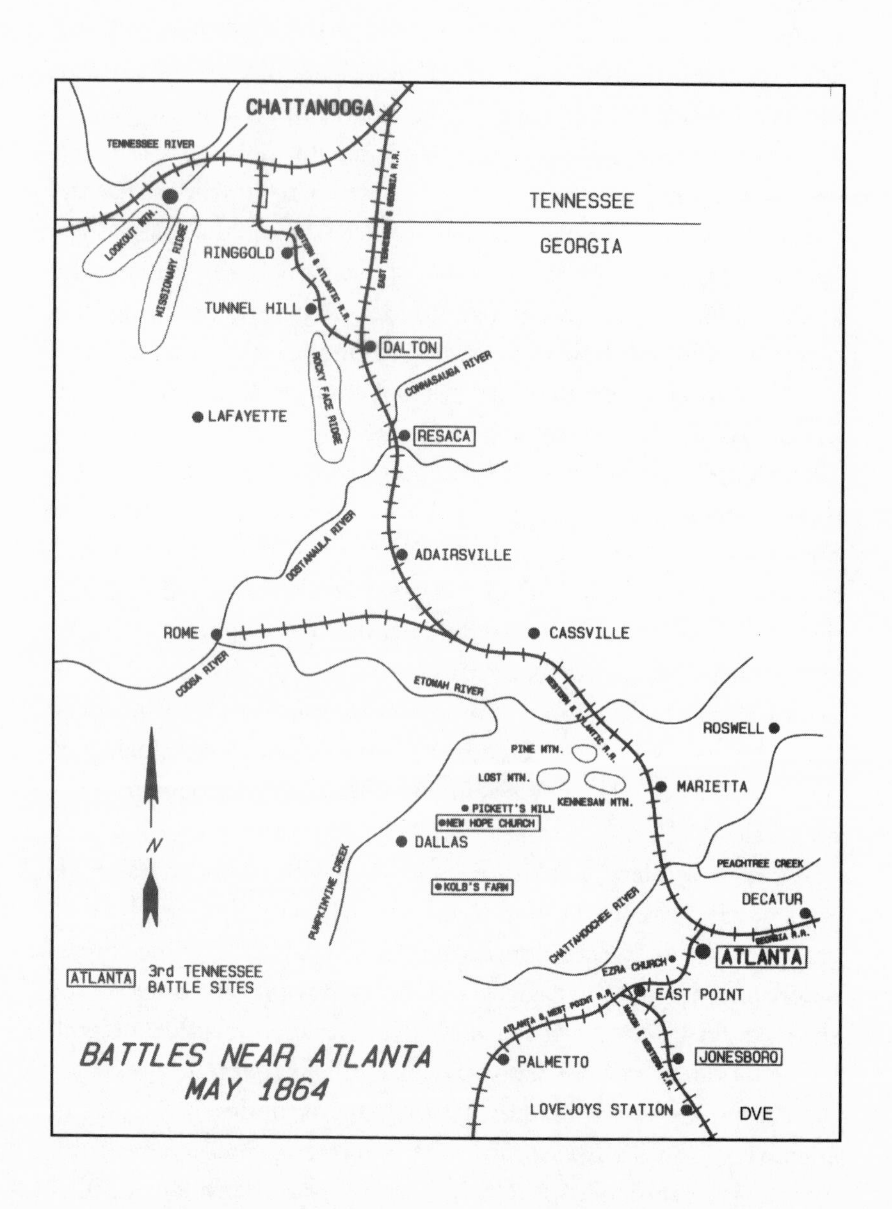
CHATTANOOGA
TENNESSEE RIVER
TENNESSEE
GEORGIA
LOOKOUT MTN.
MISSIONARY RIDGE
RINGGOLD
WESTERN & ATLANTIC R.R.
EAST TENNESSEE & GEORGIA R.R.
TUNNEL HILL
DALTON
ROCKY FACE RIDGE
CONNASAUGA RIVER
LAFAYETTE
RESACA
OOSTANAULA RIVER
ADAIRSVILLE
ROME
COOSA RIVER
CASSVILLE
ETOWAH RIVER
WESTERN & ATLANTIC R.R.
ROSWELL
PINE MTN.
LOST MTN.
KENNESAW MTN.
MARIETTA
PICKETT'S MILL
NEW HOPE CHURCH
DALLAS
PUMPKINVINE CREEK
KOLB'S FARM
PEACHTREE CREEK
DECATUR
CHATTAHOOCHEE RIVER
GEORGIA R.R.
ATLANTA
EZRA CHURCH
EAST POINT
ATLANTA & WEST POINT R.R.
MACON & WESTERN R.R.
PALMETTO
JONESBORO
LOVEJOYS STATION
DVE
N
ATLANTA 3rd TENNESSEE BATTLE SITES
BATTLES NEAR ATLANTA
MAY 1864

The 3rd Tennesseans were soon embroiled in another "turkey shoot" similar to the fights at Fort Donelson, Chickasaw Bayou, and Missionary Ridge. Something new for the 3rd Tennesseans in this fight was the discovery of their old commander's penchant to use rocks as a defensive weapon. Just as he had done five months before on Lookout Mountain, John C. Brown soon had his men rolling boulders down the side of the ridge in an attempt to flatten his bluecoat enemies. It was not all one sided. Thomas Deavenport recorded that the Tennesseans also had to contend with rocks rolled down the mountain by friendly units posted higher up.[20]

The Federal assault soon ground to a halt, and the battle seemed to favor the Confederates. What the Rebel commanders did not realize was that every hour spent holding Rocky Face Ridge was plunging them deeper and deeper into trouble. McPherson was rapidly moving on Resaca well to their rear, and if that position were to be occupied by the Yankees, escape to the south would be next to impossible. In a stroke of good luck, Johnston had requested reinforcements be sent from Polk's command in Mississippi and Alabama, and the vanguard of this force had just arrived in the little town. It was in time to prevent the encirclement of the Confederate army at Dalton.[21]

Johnston began shifting his men to the south. Brown and the 3rd Tennessee were some of the last forces out. As the Federals crossed Rocky Face Ridge behind the Tennesseans, they made a discovery that shocked them and revealed an unknown side of Joe Johnston. In a neat row were fourteen execution posts where Johnston had had a like number of deserters shot by firing squad.

Thomas Deavenport had ministered to these men, some of whom had deserted in a desperate attempt to care for their loved ones back home. Deavenport described the scene:

> Most of them met death manfully. Some, poor fellows, I fear were unprepared. I saw them wash and dress themselves for the grave. It was a solumn scene, they were tied to the stake, there was the coffin, there the open grave ready to receive them. I have seen man die at home surrounded by loved ones, I have

seen him die on the battlefield among the noble and brave, I have seen him die in prison in an enemy land, but the saddest of all was the death of a deserter, but even there Christ was sufficient. 'Tell my wife,' said one but a few minutes before the leaden messengers pierced his breast, 'not to grieve for me, I have no doubt of reaching a better world.' ... I think they were objects of pity, they were ignorant, poor, and had families dependent on them. War is a cruel thing, it heeds not the widow's tear, the orphan's moan, or the lover's anguish.[22]

Providing the men good food was not the only way Johnston maintained discipline in his army.

Notes for Chapter 16

1 Horn, *The Army of Tennessee*, p. 307.
2 *Ibid.*, pp. 305-308.
3 Barber Diary, Vol. IV, begins Dec. 28, 1863.
4 Horn, *op. cit.*, pp. 311-312.
5 Barber Diary, Vol.IV, Dec. 31, 1863.
6 Horn, *op. cit.*, p. 308.
7 *Echoes of Battle: The Atlanta Campaign*, pp. 16-17.
8 Barber's Diary, Vol.IV, March 22, 1864.
9 *Ibid.*, Jan. 3 - April 24, 1864.
10 *Ibid.*, Jan. 20, Feb. 2, 1864.
11 Daniel, *Soldiering in the Army of Tennessee*, p. 120.
12 *Battles and Leaders*, Vol.IV, pp. 281-282.
13 *Ibid.*
14 *Tennesseans in the Civil War*, p. 182.
15 *Battles and Leaders*, Vol. IV, pp. 281-282,
16 Butler, *The Life of John C. Brown*, p. 21.
17 *Ibid.*
18 *Echoes of Battle*, pp. 65-68.
19 *OR*, Vol.XXXVIII, part 3, p. 811.
20 Deavenport Diary, p. 21.
21 Richard M. McMurry, "Atlanta Campaign: Sherman Plunges Into a North Georgia Hell Hole," *Blue and Gray Magazine*, April 1989, p.18.
22 Deavenport Diary, pp. 19-20.

RESACA

It was essential to Joe Johnston that, regardless of whatever else happened on the battlefield, he protect his lifeline to the rear, the Atlantic and Western Railroad. When word arrived that James B. McPherson had appeared well to his rear, just outside Resaca, all thoughts of holding the Dalton line evaporated. Luckily for Johnston, McPherson chose this particular time to be over-cautious and paused outside the village.

Once Johnston recognized Sherman's plan, he ordered his entire army to march for Resaca as quickly as possible. Brown was given responsibility for providing the rear guard and he assigned the mission to the 3rd Tennessee. This was an extremely important assignment since Johnston still had to move his huge wagon train out of harm's way. The 3rd Tennessee skirmished with Federal cavalry off and on, and was even outraced by fast moving Federal infantry columns moving along both flanks. As the Tennesseans marched into the night their progress was punctuated by sudden bursts of gunfire along both flanks, the nearby hills and trees periodically lit up with orange flashes from angry Yankee muskets. The 3rd Tennessee reached shelter among the hills bordering the north side of Resaca around midnight on May 14th. The regiment suffered only a few men wounded.[1]

Johnston held his combat formations at Resaca in order to give his trains time to cross the Oostanaula River south of town. Hood's Corps again constituted the right wing of the army, forming a defensive arc in the hills about three miles north of town, its right anchored on the Connasauga River. The remainder of the army occupied the ridges running south along the west side of town. The army's left was anchored on the Oostanaula River.

The position was temporary. Johnston's intention was to make his real stand on the south side of the Oostanaula, but the Yankee pursuit was so rapid and aggressive that the Confederates were thrust into a fight for their lives.[2]

Johnston was now in serious difficulty. With the Connasauga and Oostanaula in his rear, rapid retreat in case his lines were broken would be impossible. If the Yankees were to cross the Oostanaula first, and occupy a position opposite the Confederates (which McPherson might have accomplished had he not been so cautious), the Confederates would be trapped.

The priority was to establish a solid defensive line. Hood, facing generally to the north, aligned his three divisions with Stewart's on the right, Stevenson's in the center, and Hindman's on the left. Stevenson placed Alfred Cumming's and Brown's brigades in his first line with Brown on the right. A small portion of Cumming's Brigade extended just across the Dalton road where it made connection with Hindman. Pettus's Brigade lined up behind Cumming while Alexander W. Reynolds' Brigade supported Brown.[3]

Reynolds' Brigade was the one brigade in the Army of Tennessee composed entirely of eastern troops, mostly Virginians and North Carolinians. Brown's Tennesseans would not find their eastern counterparts lacking as fighting partners.

Within hours after the Confederates assumed their new position, elements from Joseph Hooker's XXth Corps began probing Brown's position from the north and west. Hooker, though remembered today for his disastrous stint as commander of the Army of the Potomac during its terrible defeat at Chancellorsville, was an aggressive commander when in a subordinate role, and was eager for a fight. He did not waste time at Resaca.

Hooker first had David Stanley's division begin pummeling Cumming's line on Brown's left with his artillery. The Confederates on Hood's front line discovered the position selected for them by Johnston and company, though sited on hills, was dominated by higher terrain to the front.

The situation became intolerable. The Confederate artillery, more exposed than the infantry, started taking terrible casualties, while the infantry could do little more than hunker down in their holes. Fortunately, these Federals were part of an isolated division. Finally, to the great relief of these harried Confederates, Johnston ordered Stevenson and Stewart to organize an attack and clean out those troublesome Yankees.[4]

Six days of battle after the spring campaign began, at 5:00 p.m. on May 14th, Johnston's Confederates made their first offensive move. Stevenson ordered John C. Brown to spearhead the assault. Brown's position was to the right of the Yankee occupied ridge, and slightly forward of the rest of the division's line. Stevenson ordered Brown to move his brigade forward and then swing to the left, taking the Yankee position in flank. Reynold's Brigade would support him from behind, while Cumming would also advance to apply pressure on the Federal front. Stewart would protect the brigade's right flank.

Brown executed the movement flawlessly. The Tennessean formed his brigade in an attack column behind the Rebel fortifications, placing the 3rd Tennessee in the lead. When everything was ready, the brigade advanced into the open fields leading to the Yankee occupied ridge.

This was an old-style Rebel attack with all the enthusiasm of the early days of '61. Brown's skirmisher unit (the 32nd Tennessee) brushed away their Yankee counterparts. Then the brigade lunged into the left end of the blue line. The 3rd, 18th, and 45th Tennessee Regiments delivered a crushing attack against the Yankee flank, inflicting a "most disastrous defeat" to the bluecoats, and "driving them in utter confusion from their breastworks, killing, wounding, and capturing many." It was a marvelous assault. Carter Stevenson, Brown's division commander, commented: "Too much praise cannot be awarded Brown's gallant brigade."[5]

In addition to administering an unqualified defeat to the enemy Brown's men gained some useful plunder, including knapsacks, haversacks, and guns. The Federal artillerymen also left in a hurry, leaving most of their rammers behind. According to Thomas Deavenport, "The ditches were lined with them."[6]

The attack force did not stop until it reached the next Federal position, and then it was stopped abruptly, and at considerable cost to the Rebels. The Yankee troops responsible for halting the Rebel attack were Alpheas William's brigade from Hooker's Corps and the 5th Indiana Battery.[7]

The regiment certainly felt great pride in its success. While Deavenport described the 3rd Tennessee's losses as light, they were losses the regiment could ill afford. As was the case with most successful attacks, it was purchased with the blood of some of the regiment's best men. The regiment lost six enlisted men and Lieutenant W.C. Dunham of Company C. All were buried in the little Confederate cemetery at Resaca.

The regiment came close to losing one of its best captains. The Indianan shell that killed several of the men also sent a fragment through David Rhea's blanket and clothing grazing his chest. Rhea was a fighter and frequently employed a musket himself during the regiment's battles, an unusual practice for a Civil War officer. In fact, Rhea was considered the best marksman in Company A.[8]

The greatest pain was caused by the death of the regiment's major, Flavel C. Barber. Barber was highly regarded throughout the regiment, and his loss portended darker days ahead for the 3rd Tennessee's top commanders. Barber formerly commanded Company K and was appointed regimental major with the death of Tom Tucker at Chickasaw Bayou. His death was also lamented outside the regiment. A soldier of the 32nd Tennessee commented: "The loss of no one of our brigade, perhaps during the whole war,

Flavel Barber
Courtesy: Anna Jane Hill Andrews, Elizabeth Hill Dinsmore, Margaret Hill Pruitt, the late Nat. U. Hill, and The Lilly LIbrary, Indiana University.

was more deplored ... ." Among Barber's personal affects at the Lilly Library at Indiana University is Barber's blood-stained pocket Bible. In the back, Calvin Clack inscribed the following:

> May 16. Maj F. C. Barber 3rd Regt. Tenn was mortally wounded while gallantly charging the enemy on the 14 of May, 1864 in the fight near Resaca. His last and only words spoken after being shot were 'I know the Third will do its duty.' He died next morning of Sunday 15th. Officers and men of the 3rd Tenn without exception deeply mourn his loss .... By his old messmates of the Third Tennessee.
>
> Signed: Calvin J. Clack, Lt. Col., 3rd Tenn; Col. C. H. Walker; Adj. D. S. Martin.

Thomas Deavenport recorded that the 3rd Tennessee had three color bearers shot down, one of whom was killed and the other two severely wounded. When the regiment's thirty-two wounded are included, the attack at Resaca was costly indeed.[9]

That night, Johnston ordered the brigade back to their original position. The little Virginian received a report that the Yankees had crossed the Oostanaula in his rear, and he immediately ordered the army to pull back and make preparations for a retreat. As darkness set in, Brown's, Cumming's, and Reynold's brigades silently withdrew to their starting points. Just before dawn, Johnston discovered the threat to his rear had evaporated, so he ordered everyone back to their former positions on the captured enemy line.

That morning, May 15th, the same three brigades again moved forward (Edmund Pettus's brigade remained in its original position as a division reserve on the left throughout the action at Resaca). The Yankees were delinquent in monitoring their front that night and left the ridge unoccupied. The Confederates again took possession, this time unopposed, and frantically began digging in. Thomas Deavenport remarked, "Never did I see fortifications built so fast ... ."[10]

The Yankees were coming in force, two full divisions of Hooker's XXth Corps. It was here that Hood committed one of his less than brilliant tactical moves, an episode which Joe Johnston would frequently mention to support his contention that Hood was a greater incompetent than he.

Hindman was receiving a terrible pounding on the left end of Hood's defensive line. Hood decided that a part of the ridge extending forward toward the Federal line would provide an excellent position for a field artillery battery to deliver flanking fires on the Yankee guns tormenting Hindman. Max Van Den Corpet's battery, the same unit John C. Brown used to batter the Yankees from the top of Lookout Mountain, was again teamed with its old comrades and ordered to occupy the selected position located about seventy-five yards directly to Brown's front. Hood ordered Brown to move part of his brigade to the front edge of the point as an infantry support.[11]

Brown's and Van Den Corpet's men had barely begun digging in when Hood ordered the battery to commence firing. Instantly, eighteen Federal guns fired in reply. Van Den Corpet's four new Atlanta made guns (one named 'Minnie, the Belle of Alabama') were only partially protected and were almost helpless before the combined fire of the three Federal batteries firing at them from front and both flanks. In short order, those gunners still alive were forced to take refuge under the gun carriages and any other cover they could find.[12]

The Federal artillery attack was followed with a massive infantry assault by Hooker's Second Division. It became obvious that the battery might be lost if not withdrawn quickly, so Stevenson galloped off to find Hood and request his permission to do so. He found Hood standing next to the railroad near Stewart's position. Hood, exhibiting an incredible lack of compassion for soldiers he personally had placed in mortal danger, told Stevenson that the artillerymen would remain where they were "until killed."[13]

Van Den Corpet's big smoothbores were generally useless since the forward slope of the ridge dropped off so abruptly that most of the approaching blue infantry were safe from cannon fire as soon as they reached the base of the ridge. The heavy columns of Federal infantry were more than Brown's weak forward line could handle and the men quickly retreated to the main defensive line

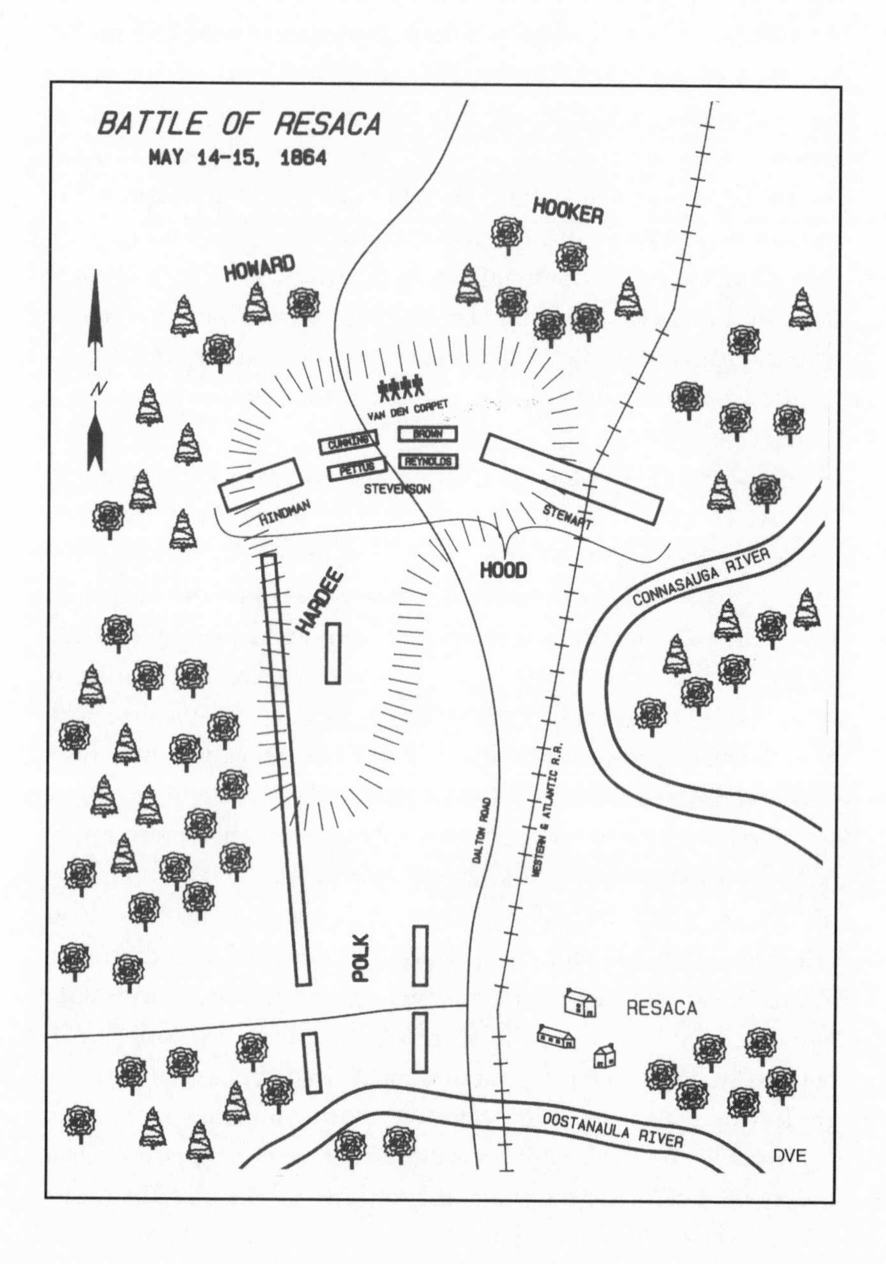

BATTLE OF RESACA
MAY 14-15, 1864
HOOKER
HOWARD
N
VAN DEN CORPET
CUMMINGS
BROWN
PETTUS
REYNOLDS
STEVENSON
HINDMAN
STEWART
HOOD
HARDEE
CONNASAUGA RIVER
DALTON ROAD
WESTERN & ATLANTIC R.R.
POLK
RESACA
OOSTANAULA RIVER
DVE

behind the guns. On the Yankees came, and once the blue forces reached the top edge of the ridge a tremendous fire fight broke out between the opposing lines of infantry, with Van Den Corpet's guns and a few surviving gunners caught in the middle. Starting about 1:00 p.m., and not ending until after sunset, Brown's line was subjected to almost continuous heavy assaults, at times advancing to bayonet range. The line of Tennesseans never faltered.[14]

While the placement of Van Den Corpet's guns was an unmitigated disaster for the poor artillerymen, it was a good tactical move by the Confederates, albeit an accidental one. The abandoned guns proved an irresistible magnet for the Federal infantry, always eager to grab a few specimens of the ultimate battle trophy. Though well protected by the lip of the ridge as they approached the guns, in order to assault the butternut infantry the Federals had to crest the ridge and face the dug-in Confederates only thirty yards away. They were within point blank range.

The 3rd Tennessee was conducting what soldiers today would call a reverse slope defense which, when executed correctly, is deadly. In this type of defense the attacker cannot see his dug-in enemy until the very moment he is exposed to the defender's fire. He has no idea which way to shoot (or which way to duck) until he is subjected to the defender's most lethal fire.

Each time the blue column charged over the forward lip of the hill, the men were slaughtered. Thomas Deavenport provided this description: "Never did I hear such a heavy fire from small arms, but firm and resolute our boys stood pouring volley after volley into the lines of the enemy, driving them back and covering them with the dead and wounded." The 3rd Tennessee and its sister regiments were on the line during the entire fight except for "a few minutes" when they were relieved by Reynolds' Brigade while the Tennesseans replenished their ammunition.[15]

The 3rd Tennessee had barely returned to their rifle pits when the brigade received an order to attack. Johnston, unaware of the immense pressure being applied to his right, sought a repeat of the previous day in order to ease the pressure being applied by James B. McPherson on his left.

Before the attack could begin, Johnston again received word that McPherson had crossed the Oostanaula River (it was one regiment). Then he received word that one of McPherson's skirmish lines had seized a hill on the Confederate side overlooking Johnston's river crossings and was rapidly being reinforced. Either threat posed a mortal danger to the army.

All thoughts of offensive action quickly evaporated from Johnston's mind, and an order canceling the attack on the right was dispatched to Hood. However, before the order could arrive, Stewart's Division, supported by Reynold's Brigade, launched an attack that was quickly smothered by Hooker's huge force. Had Brown's Brigade been a little slow returning to the rifle pits, there is little doubt that it would have had the misfortune of taking Reynold's place in this forlorn attack.

As night fell and the Confederates prepared to retreat, a problem remained: what to do about Van Den Corpet's four guns still standing between the two battle lines in Brown's front. Stevenson began preparations for an attack and sought Hood's permission to do so. Hood discounted the importance of the guns; it was his meddling in small unit tactics that lost them in the first place. With Johnston's concurrence, Hood told Stevenson to leave them where they were, that the cost in lives it would take to recapture them far outweighed their value.[16]

Meanwhile, the Federals, having been thoroughly battered trying to carry off the guns in a conventional way, began digging a hole through the front of the battery position in an attempt to sneak them out in the dark. While everyone in the blue line held their breath, an Ohio regiment was ordered forward to dig the hole, which they somehow managed to do without once drawing Confederate fire (the hole is still there). Then a detachment of New Jersey troops was brought up to carry out the actual theft of the big guns.[17]

If nothing else, Johnston was a master of the tactical withdrawal, and his escape from the cul-de-sac at Resaca was one of his best. As at Dalton, Brown's Brigade, with the 3rd Tennessee again the last unit to pull out, was the rear guard for the entire army.

Gravestone in 3rd Tennessee section of the picturesque Resaca Confederate Cemetery marked:
LIEUTENANT
3 TENN
probably belongs to Lt. J.F. Matthews of Company F.
Courtesy: Author

A skirmish line of 3rd Tennesseans under the command of the regiment's lieutenant colonel, Calvin Clack, protected the rear of Brown's brigade, and these were the last troops to safely cross the river. According to Thomas Deavenport, the withdrawal was conducted flawlessly with not even a picket being lost.[18]

The defense of Resaca cost the 3rd Tennessee another three men killed and "eight or ten" wounded. Lieutenant J.F. Matthews of Company F and Captain D.G. Alexander of Company D were both killed. The depletion of the regiment's leadership would continue nonstop. The 3rd Tennessee performed courageously and well at Resaca, but the total casualties for the regiment of eleven killed and forty some wounded placed the casualty rate at around twenty percent, a serious loss for the already undersized regiment. Thomas Deavenport noted that the regiment's spirits remained high, however. Baseball had become a popular pastime during inactive periods of the war: a stalwart lad with one leg torn off by an artillery shell managed to joke, "Well boys, I'm done playing ball with you."[19]

Worse was yet to come.

Notes for Chapter 17

1 Deavenport Diary, p. 21.

2 Albert Castel, in *Decision in the West*, p. 157, contends that Johnston deliberately selected Resaca to make a defensive stand.

3 *OR*, Vol.XXXVIII, part 3, pp. 811-812.

4 *Ibid.*, p. 812. *Battles and Leaders*, Vol.IV, p. 265.

5 *Military Annals of Tennessee*, p. 475. *OR*, Vol.XXXVIII, part 3, p. 812.

6 Deavenport Diary, p.22.

7 Castel, *op. cit.*, pp. 164-166.

8 Deavenport Diary, p. 22. *CV*, Vol. XXII, p. 71.

9 *Military Annals of Tennessee*, p. 479. Deavenport Diary, p. 22.

10 *Ibid.*

11 *OR*, Vol.XXXVIII, part 3, p. 812.

12 Castel, *op. cit.*, p. 180.

13 *Echoes of Battle*, p. 89.

14 *OR*, Vol.XXXVIII, part 3, p. 812.

15 Deavenport Diary, p. 23. *OR*, Vol. XXXVIII, part 3, p. 812.

16 Hood, *Advance and Retreat*, p. 96.

17 *Echoes of Battle*, pp. 89-95.

18 Deavenport Diary, p. 23.

19 *Ibid.*

DISASTER AT KOLB'S FARM

The men in the Army of Tennessee had great faith in Joe Johnston's ability, but the Virginian could not retain the confidence of his troops if all he did was retreat. The debacle at Chattanooga still smarted, and with stable leadership in place the men expected some positive results. The army longed for the day it would again be able to dictate its will to its Yankee adversaries. It definitely did not want to be viewed as a second string outfit to Lee's Army in Virginia. Captain W.E. Colville, an officer who served under Calvin Walker for a time at Dalton, put it this way: "I believe we are as certain to whip them as we fight, and if we once get them started back like we did at Chickamauga, Johnston will follow them up and drive them out of Tenn." Colville's statement reflected the general hope of the army and most of the Confederacy.[1]

Johnston had to find a way to "get them started back," both to live up to his soldiers' expectations and to keep his job. Jefferson Davis had emphasized over and over that if Johnston expected to continue as commander of the army, he would have to strike an offensive blow and make some substantial progress in recouping the losses of 1863.

As Johnston retreated from Resaca, he finally began preparations for what everyone was waiting: an offensive strike against Sherman. As he retreated south, Johnston divided his army between two widely separated roads which merged north of Cassville. Johnston expected Sherman also to split his army and follow both columns. Johnston would then concentrate his force for a gigantic ambush against whichever force followed him along the eastern route. Once Johnston had made his dispositions for the ambush, he issued an order to be read to all the troops "declaring the retreat over and his intention to fight." Thomas Deavenport recorded that the 3rd Tennessee received the order with "loud shouts."[2]

The ambush was a bust.

Johnston ordered Hood to move his corps along a path about a mile east of the road upon which the Federals were approaching. Once Hood's men were in position, they were to face west and strike the Federals on the flank and rear, while Polk's Corps attacked them in front. This was a good plan but for one problem. While Hood was getting into position, some stray Federals, it is disputed whether they were infantry or cavalry, approached his right flank and rear. This threat Hood could have handled with a fraction of his force, certainly with no more than one of his infantry brigades. Instead he overreacted, ordering his entire corps into a defensive posture. Thomas Deavenport observed that the 3rd Tennessee, instead of keeping to their feet and staying in readiness for an offensive move, "was soon in line and began to fortify ... by 5 P.M. they had good works ... " The 3rd Tennesseans obviously intended to defend.[3]

Seeing his plan disrupted, Johnston called off the attack even though the Federals to the west continued to march blithely into the trap. Hood could have approached the Federal flank in a matter of minutes since the entire route was controlled by Rebel cavalry. It was not to be. Johnston was not a risk taker, so it is not surprising that when things started going awry he quickly scuttled the plan. Meanwhile, the other Federal marching column was in the process of turning Johnston's left flank. At midnight the 3rd Tennessee was ordered out of its newly prepared positions and joined the rest of the army in its march south.

Johnston made a brief stand south of Cassville, decided the position could not be held, and resumed his retreat, not making a stand again until he was fully sixty miles further south.

The reason for this dramatic loss of real estate was a superlative operational move on the part of Sherman. Instead of cautiously poking around the edges of Johnston's flanks and keeping close to the railroad lifeline, Sherman set off cross-country to the west, taking a wide sweep around Johnston's army. The area he entered would soon be dubbed the Georgia 'Hell Hole' by both sides.[4]

Sherman's move into the Georgia hinterland yielded him great quantities of Confederate territory, but it subjected 170,000 soldiers of both armies to one of the worst ordeals ever experienced by American troops. The wild terrain consisted of endless ravines between abrupt hills, bottomless swamps interspersed with impenetrable thickets filled with vicious brambles, and dense forests broken here and there by small, hard scrabble farms. Then there was the weather.

As the two armies began their descent into the 'Hell Hole,' they were beset by seventeen straight days of some of the most spectacular (and sometimes deadly) thunderstorms anyone there had ever experienced. Roads turned to quagmires, and men were constantly soaked to the skin regardless of what rain wear they might employ. At times, the aerial displays in the heavens made the savage combat occurring on the ground seem almost insignificant.

Johnston tried to establish a line along the Etowah River, and the 3rd Tennessee for a short while was employed in guarding crossings. Sherman quickly skirted this line, taking a direct route toward Pumpkin Vine Creek. Johnston rushed his army west: first sending Hardee on the 23rd of May to block Sherman at a village called Dallas, and then sending Hood the next day to prolong Hardee's line to the east. Hood's Corps extended on either side of another tiny settlement on the road with a somewhat incongruous name for the events soon to follow: New Hope Church. Polk's Corps lagged behind constituting the army's reserve.

Brown and the 3rd Tennessee exerted enormous effort just to get to the battlefield. The men conducted a forced march of over twenty miles beginning at 12:30 a.m. on May 25th, arriving on the battlefield just before noon. Hood's Corps fell in next to Hardee with Hindman's Division on the left, Stewart's Division in the center, and Stevenson's Division (including Brown's Brigade and the 3rd Tennessee) on the right. Sherman's advance was expected at any second, so the Confederates quickly dug in.[5]

This was no easy task, exhausted as they were by the twenty-mile march through the extraordinarily rough Georgia countryside. Undaunted, after ninety minutes or so, the regiment had some "pretty good works of timber" built. Then they were ordered to move![6]

One can imagine the consternation of the Tennesseans. With the Yankee advance already audible, they were ordered to march a short distance forward and construct completely new defensive works. According to Thomas Deavenport, they did so without a murmur, and "cheerfully" built a second fortification.[7]

The new field works were barely far enough along to stop a rifle bullet when Sherman's men came crashing through the thickets. The Yankee commander was convinced that Johnston was too slow and too tied to his railroad supply line to seriously interfere with his march to the Chattahoochee River and thence into Atlanta; but Johnston could maneuver his army with the best of them, providing it was not in a forward direction. The men bumping into Stewart's and John C. Brown's front were, ironically, the same troops they had faced at Dalton and at Resaca: 'Fighting' Joe Hooker's XXth Corps. His lead troops, John Geary's division, immediately suspected trouble and sent word back that Confederates were ahead— lots of them. Geary personally verified this fact, and set off to confer with Hooker and Sherman.

Sherman could not believe his well-executed flank movement had been brought to an ignoble halt. He declared that what his men were seeing was not what it seemed. According to the red-headed Ohioan, there was nothing more than a thin line of Rebel cavalry in front of Geary, and he should push on through.[8]

Geary protested, but to no avail, and the advance was on. Geary's Division immediately bumped into Stewart's front, then Butterfield followed, hitting the 3rd Tennessee's line on the left of Stevenson's front. Geary's men were blistered by the gray infantry and sixteen Rebel field guns. Sherman then compounded his blunder by committing Hooker's entire corps to the attack.

These men were also riddled with bullets and cannon fire. Adding to the pandemonium, one of the wildest thunderstorms anyone had ever experienced broke out in the midst of the battle. A few men fortunate enough to escape enemy bullets were killed by some of the dozens of lightning strikes on the battlefield.[9]

By now the 3rd Tennessee was accustomed to this type of fighting. The men fired as fast as they could for two hours and the Confederates repulsed three major Federal assaults. Very few shots were wasted. Brown's Brigade and the three brigades of Stewart's Division fought this Battle of New Hope Church essentially by themselves. In the end, one Confederate division, reinforced by Brown's Brigade, defeated an entire Federal corps.[10]

The next day the battlefield presented a pitiful sight. The debris of battle included broken weapons, shredded uniform pieces, leather accouterments and haversacks, and assorted personal items belonging to Union soldiers such as letters, testaments, and cookware. Confederate casualties were negligible, including the 3rd Tennessee's.

Sherman was not through.

The Yankee commander immediately sought a way around the obstinate Confederates and perceived an opening to his left. Johnston had deployed a thin cavalry screen to protect Hood's right flank. If Sherman could brush these Rebel horsemen aside and slip around Johnston's flank, he could take Johnston's line in reverse. If that failed, he could at least interpose his force between the Rebel army and Atlanta.

Johnston suspected this move and readied Cleburne's Division for a possible blocking action on the right. At the same time, Hood's skirmish line started picking up indications of a Federal movement, and Hood likewise prepared to defend on his right.

Hood ordered the butternut cavalrymen guarding his flank to offer only feeble resistance to Yankee probes along that line to convince Sherman that the way was open. Then, once the Yankee attack force was committed, he would move Cleburne's men into position, taking the bluecoats in ambush. The plan worked to perfection.

Spearheading Cleburne's Division was the 3rd Tennessee's old friend, Hiram Granbury along with his Texas Brigade. These were some of the toughest soldiers ever to put on an American uniform. The 7th Texas was part of this division. Also included were a number of dismounted cavalry, now reduced to the level of common foot soldier. These men were more than willing to take out their frustrations on Sherman's unsuspecting column. On their way to the front, these hard-bitten Texans stopped off at Hood's far right formation, Cumming's Georgia brigade, and reminded them that they were responsible for protecting the Texan's left flank. If they failed in this responsibility by withdrawing, the Texans would most assuredly shoot them if the Yankees did not![11]

Cleburne's men were barely in position when Thomas J. Wood's division of O.O. Howard's corps appeared. Although the Confederates had little time to prepare, their position, on high ground with lots of natural cover, was an ideal one for defense, and another slaughter ensued. Again, Sherman persisted in the attack well past the point where there was any hope of success.

Meanwhile, back at New Hope Church, John C. Brown and his Tennesseans were engaged in some skirmishing which, at times, approached the intensity of a general battle.

The Pickett's Mill battle, along with the New Hope Church fight, would have been strong contenders as Sherman's most poorly conducted battles had anyone bothered to notice; but John Bell Hood was present, and it was not long before the one-legged Kentuckian took measures to even things out with a huge blunder of his own.

For the next month, the two armies clawed and scratched at each other in the tangled woods. Sherman constantly probed for a way around or through the Confederate defenses. Johnston blocked each attempt, but gave up a little ground with each attempt. Hood's Corps was assigned the role of mobile blocking force, constantly moving from one end of the line to the other. For the 3rd Tennessee, the last week of May and first three weeks of June were a maze of random skirmishes with the Yankees, and spectacular thunderstorms almost daily. Thomas Deavenport's diary for the first two weeks of June provides a glimpse of life "on the line" that summer of 1864:

> June 1st. - Again moved to the left and fortified.
> June 2nd - Again to the right and fortified. Hard rain of which I have had full benefit.
> June 3rd - More rain, but little fighting.
> June 4th - Still it rains.
> June 5th - Marched six miles before daylight, through mud often knee deep yet the boys bore it very cheerfully. They laugh and fast passed around [the mud] as though nothing was the matter. When halted they washed their socks and pants and all was right. Preached in the evening. We remained two days, fortified, rained hard.[12]

And so it went until June 22nd when the 3rd Tennessee's beloved colonel, Calvin H. Walker, was killed.

As Johnston consolided his army along the Kennesaw Mountain line, Sherman made one last lunge around the Rebel flank in an attempt to beat the Confederates to the Chattahoochee River. He assigned this task to Hooker with John Schofield's corps in support. Johnston again used Hood's Corps as a mobile reaction force and moved them from the army's extreme right to the far left to counter this latest Yankee flank march. What transpired next was almost a repeat of the disaster at Pickett's Mill in reverse.

Hood never explained what he intended to accomplish at the affair known as the Battle of Kolb's Farm. Hood's official report is a classic example of military dissembling and obfuscation. Though Johnston had ordered Hood to simply block Hooker's advance, Hood attacked. His reasoning for this deviation from orders is as follows: "General Ferguson's cavalry being driven back to-day while establishing my line, I was attacked. I moved forward and drove the enemy back, taking one entire line of his breast-works and a portion of his second on the right."[13]

The 'attack' referred to was nothing more than a reconnaissance probe by the 123rd New York, augmented by some artillery. It certainly did not constitute a significant threat to Hood's line.

A more likely reason Hood opted to attack is he knew a large enemy force was on the march in his front, and with his combat blood boiling, he could not resist the temptation to pitch into what he thought was an exposed Yankee flank.

Hood deployed two of his divisions for the attack, Hindman's on the right and Stevenson's on the left. Stevenson organized his force into two attack columns. Brown's Brigade, under the command of Colonel Edward Cook of the 32nd Tennessee (Brown was temporarily absent) would lead the attack on the division right supported by Cumming's Georgians in a second line. Pettus's Brigade would lead the left attack column supported by Rey-nold's Brigade.[14]

Things started going wrong immediately.

Calvin Walker had barely begun shaking the 3rd Tennessee out into an attack line when he was killed by a stray shot from the 123rd New York posted in the woods to the regiment's front. This was a devastating blow for the Tennesseans.

"The brave, warm-hearted, noble Col. Walker," wrote Thomas Deavenport, "who had led the 3rd Tenn. on so many well contested fields was killed just before starting on the charge. Never did I see soldiers weep so over a man. He had been like a father to them."[15]

Other 3rd Tennesseans continued paying tribute to the gallant and kind Walker long after the war ended. Civil War soldiers tended to view competent commanders as father figures, and Walker certainly fit this mold. The downside was Walker might have been a little too kind-hearted. W.E. Colville complained in one of his letters just prior to the Atlanta campaign about Walker's failure to take stern action against some of the 3rd Tennessee's many deserters.[16]

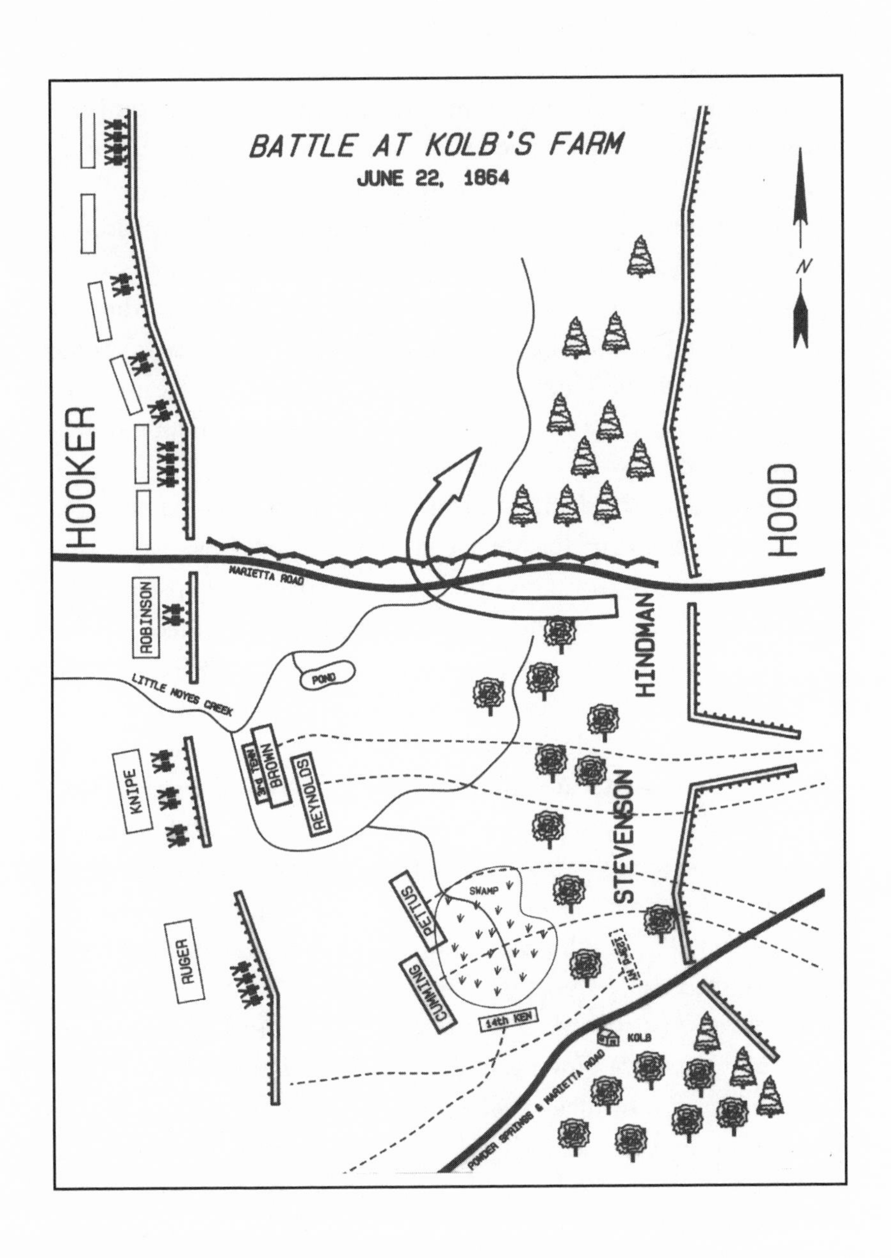
BATTLE AT KOLB'S FARM
JUNE 22, 1864
N
HOOKER
HOOD
MARIETTA ROAD
ROBINSON
HINDMAN
POND
LITTLE NOYES CREEK
KNIPE
BROWN
REYNOLDS
STEVENSON
SWAMP
PETTUS
RUGER
CUMMING
14th KEN
KOLB
POWDER SPRINGS & MARIETTA ROAD

Walker's death portended worse things to come. About 5:00 p.m., the main attack began and the butternuts were in trouble right from the start.

While the Confederates were forming for the attack, the New Yorkers had been reinforced, and these men, supported by large volumes of long-range artillery fire, caused great havoc in the gray ranks even before they reached Hooker's advanced line.

This artillery fire was unique. The Federal gunners could not see the Tennesseans because their vision was blocked by the same hill occupied by the 123rd New York. The New Yorkers adjusted the artillery fire by sending hand signals back to the gunners on the ridge behind them. This is one of the rare cases where indirect cannon fire was used in the Civil War. All other artillery strikes except area fire by mortars were line-of-sight.[17]

Finally, the Confederates were able to drive the New Yorkers off and took possession of the Yankee first line which "consisted of one line of logs and rail works complete, and one partially constructed," according to Stevenson. This is the line Hood mentioned.[18]

The 3rd Tennessee and the rest of Brown's Brigade then entered a broad, open field half a mile across, ending at a small ridge, with a cotton gin between. This was the actual Kolb farm area. The 3rd Tennesseans must have looked upon the scene with trepidation. They knew the Yankees were posted in some force on the far side of the field. An advance against any number would be difficult, but, if it was Hooker's main army, the open terrain would spell disaster. The result was as bad as the Southerners could ever have imagined.

The time it took the Confederates to organize their line of battle, plus the extra time the 123rd New York bought for the blue forces, gave the advantage to the Yankees. Hooker's men were taking position on the ridge while Hood was organizing his attack at the far side of the woods.

The bluecoats, crusty old veterans, dug in quickly. Breastworks constructed of nearby trees and rail fences were quickly thrown up, and even worse for the exposed Confederates, several dozen field guns were interposed in the gaps between the Federal brigades.[19]

The moment the 3rd Tennessee and the rest of the Confederate attack force broke into cleared fields of Kolb's farm, it was subjected to one of the most intense artillery bombardments these men had ever experienced. The attack rapidly fell apart.

Hindman's Division on the right maintained its attack formation across the open fields only to find an impassable swamp blocking its way at the far side. Hindman's men immediately sought whatever cover was available and hugged the ground until darkness allowed them to make a safe exit.

On the left, Stevenson's two left flank brigades, Reynold's and Pettus's, had their own problems. These brigades had to cross a part of the field that had been left to nature, and they bogged down in the thick undergrowth. The struggling Confederates presented an excellent target for the Yankee cannoneers. To make matters worse, they were ambushed by a regiment of Kentuckians hiding in the fringe of this same thicket. They were squarely on the Rebel flank, and held their fire until the Confederates were at point-blank range. The left brigades, occupied in the running fight with these pesky Kentuckians, continued to dodge salvos from the Federal artillery. Pettus's and Reynold's attack rapidly disintegrated.[20]

The Tennesseans and Georgians of Brown's and Cumming's brigades were left to carry on the attack by themselves. With the Tennesseans in the lead, the two remaining brigades continued their advance into the teeth of the Yankee rifle and artillery fire. Upon reaching the foot of the hill on which the Federal main line was situated, the butternuts encountered a deep ravine through which flowed the same stream feeding the bog in Hindman's front. The momentum of the attack was quickly lost in crossing this ravine, and though the attackers were only thirty-five yards from the Yankee breastworks, their opportunity to breach the Federal line rapidly evaporated.

Try they did. Though assailed by rifle fire from above, and blasts of canister from enemy batteries on both flanks, the Tennessee brigade launched three assaults up the steep creek bank. Each attack was beaten back with only more and more dead and wounded Confederates to show for the effort. Finally, the exhausted Rebels hunkered down, like their comrades on the flanks, and waited for the safety of darkness before attempting to withdraw.[21]

At this point, the 3rd Tennesseans found a modicum of safety by simply hugging the wall of the ravine nearest the Yankee infantry line. Soldiers refer to this as 'dead space,' an area that could not be reached by any of the Union weapons. The blue infantry could not fire at Rebel targets directly below them without rising and exposing themselves to lethal return fire, and the irregularities in the course of the creek bed provided sufficient cover from the field batteries on the flanks.

As night arrived, Stevenson extracted his harried brigades and took stock of the extent of the disaster. His division was a wreck. He estimated that more than 807 men were lost in this pointless attack. Thomas Deavenport reported that 270 of the killed and wounded were from Brown's Brigade. Stevenson's guess was probably conservative: the Federals reported 400 Confederate captives. The battle savvy of Brown's Tennesseans prevented even more casualties. By "hugging their enemy's belts" and by waiting for dark to withdraw, the loss rate was held to twenty percent.[22]

Hindman's cancellation of the attack at the first sign of trouble saved his command from serious damage. His total loss was estimated at about 200. Yankee losses were disproportionately low at 350. Rarely in the Civil War were battle losses so lopsidedly in favor of the Federals—nearly four to one.[23]

It was the Confederacy's misfortune that no one in the Army of Tennessee informed the Confederate War Department about Hood's part in this monumental battlefield disaster. Considerable time elapsed before Johnston knew about it. By the time the facts were known, Hood had already assumed command of the Army of Tennessee, and Richmond was not able to consider the Kolb's Farm debacle in their apprasal of Hood's fitness for high command. John Bell Hood was as skilled at concealing his blunders with his pen as he was at ordering suicidal attacks. His report was only one paragraph long because, he explained, it was written late at night and he was busy arranging his lines. He gave no indication of the extent of his losses, mentioning only the death of Calvin

Walker and the wounding of Colonel Cook and "two or three other field officers." Hood completely misrepresented the tone of the battle by claiming that Federal artillery had simply stopped his "pursuit." Hood's war biography, *Advance and Retreat*, makes no mention of Kolb's Farm.[24]

After the battle, both Brown and the 3rd Tennessee received a brief respite.

Meanwhile, Sherman was making a classic blunder of his own. Thinking the Confederates had thinned the middle of their line to counter Hooker's and Schofield's thrusts to the right, Sherman ordered an all-out attack against the Rebel middle. This was the most impregnable Rebel position of the entire campaign. The result was a Federal disaster known as the Battle of Kennesaw Mountain. Wave after wave of Sherman's best men were sent to certain slaughter against the stout Rebel fortifications. Fortunately for the North, this was the red-haired commander's last attempt at such flawed tactics.

One result of the Kennesaw Mountain battle was the wounding of Thomas Hindman. John C. Brown was assigned as temporary replacement in command of Hindman's Division, and in the future would only rejoin his 3rd Tennessee comrades for brief periods in between major battles. Thereafter, Johnston, and later Hood, habitually picked him to command divisions as commanders were wounded or were otherwise unavailable. According to Brown, he became Hood's 'Military Convenience.'

Sherman went back to his flanking tactics and forced the Confederates back to the Chattahoochee River. The 3rd Tennessee fought most of its final actions north of the Chattahoochee along the left of the Confederate line, and during the last days of June and early July was subjected to several intense Federal artillery bombardments. Although these artillery attacks were frightening, they generally produced few casualties. During the first week in July, the regiment retreated behind the Chattahoochee line with the rest of the army. The men now braced for what they knew would be a final defense of one of the South's most strategically important cities: the much fabled Atlanta.

Notes for Chapter 18

1 W. E. Colville Letter, April 29, 1864.

2 Deavenport Diary, p. 24.

3 Govan and Livingood, *A Different Kind of Valor*, p.275. Deavenport Diary, p. 23.

4 See Richard M. McMurray's "Atlanta Campaign: Sherman Plunges into a North Georgia Hell Hole," *Blue and Gray Magazine*, April, 1989.

5 Deavenport Diary, p. 24. McMurry, op. cit. p. 57.

6 Deavenport Diary, p.24.

7 *Ibid.*, p. 25.

8 Albert Castel, *Decision in the West*, pp. 221-226.

9 *Echoes of Battle*, pp. 100-109.

10 Deavenport Diary, p. 25.

11 *Echoes of Battle*, pp. 120-121.

12 Deavenport Diary, p.26.

13 *OR*, Vol.XXXVIII, part 3, p. 760.

14 *Ibid.*, p. 814-815. Stevenson indicates in his official report that all four brigades attacked on the north side of the Powder Springs road. The attack is also illustrated this way in the *Official Military Atlas of the Civil War*, Plate CI, No.19, drafted by Maj. R. M. McDowell, Chief Topical Engineer of the Federal 20th Corps. Castel, in *Decision in the West*, p. 294, contends that Stevenson attacked with two brigades on each side of the road.

15 Deavenport Diary, p. 27-28.

16 McPherson, *For Cause & Comrades*, pp.53-56. Colville, op. cit.

17 *Echoes of Battle*, pp. 154-156.

18 *OR*, Vol.XXXVIII, part 3, pp. 814-815.

19 *Echoes of Battle*, 154-156.

20 Dennis Kelly, "Atlanta Campaign: The Battle for Kennesaw Mountain," *Blue and Gray Magazine*, June 1989, p. 24.

21 *Ibid.*

22 *OR*, Vol.XXXVIII, part 3, p. 815. Deavenport Diary, p. 28. Echoes of Battle, p. 156.

23 Kelly, *op. cit.*, p.24.

24 *OR*, Vol.XXXVIII, part 3, p. 760.

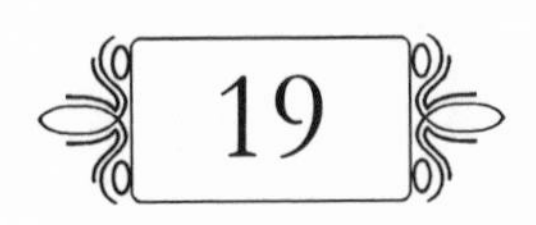

ATLANTA

Despite Hood's recklessness with the lives of his men, Joseph Johnston's conservative strategy and the regiment's well-honed fighting skills had prevented the 3rd Tennessee from disintegrating completely. Johnston's emphasis on preservation of his army over all other considerations had been remarkably successful in maintaining the army's integrity. In fact, with the addition of some new regiments from other parts of the Confederacy, Johnston's army in July 1864, on the eve of the climactic Atlanta battles, was about as strong as it was when the campaign started.[1]

The problem with Johnston's strategy was that it lacked any objectives beyond maintaining the welfare of the army itself and getting in Sherman's way whenever he could. Unfortunately for Johnston, Richmond expected much more.

Sherman's penetration to the gates of Atlanta provided the Confederates a golden opportunity. Sherman was now more than one-hundred miles from his nearest supply depot at Chattanooga, or any form of safe sanctuary. That tenuous Yankee supply line was Sherman's 'Achilles' heel.' However, Johnston habitually cringed at the thought of venturing into the perilous world of offensive operations. In addition, the Confederacy's long-range strike master, the always dangerous Nathan Bedford Forrest, was tied down in Mississippi guarding against raids. Davis's failure to use Forrest properly was considered one of his greatest strategic failures.[2]

The period between the Kennesaw Mountain battle and Sherman's thrust across the Chattahoochee provided a short lull in the campaign. However, crossing to the south side of the Chattahoochee did not provide the 3rd Tennessee much of a respite. The regiment constantly fought—and continued to bleed. This from Deavenport's diary:

> July 5th - 1 A. M. again fell back, stopped at the Chattahoochee, heavy cannonading.
> July 6th - Cannonading heavier.
> July 8th - Moved to the right and back.
> July 9th - Crossed the Chattahoochee.
> July 10th - Moved to the left a few miles, started about 1 A.M., preached.
> July 11th - Rested, ate blackberries etc..
> July 12th, 13th, 14th - On picket at the river, lost several men.[3]

A few days later, on July 17, John Bell Hood replaced Joe Johnston as commander of the army. This event portended the doom of the 3rd Tennessee as a viable regiment. Many feel it was the death knell of the Confederacy itself.

Johnston's failure to stop the Yankees, or at least to finesse them out of Georgia, cost him his job. Many top Confederate commanders, including Robert E. Lee, had reservations about Hood's ability to command an army, but Jefferson Davis wanted a fighter to save Atlanta. Hood knew how to conduct violent attacks and might be just the right man tohalt Sherman's inexorable progress.[4]

To wrest the initiative away from Sherman, Hood would have to attack. The question was how and where. The easiest solution was to attack isolated or weakened portions of Sherman's army along his front forcing them onto the defensive. This involved the least risk, but yielded the smallest gains. The Confederate breakout at Fort Donelson was a successful example.

A riskier option was to swing a major portion of the army around Sherman and attack him in flank and rear destroying a major portion of his army. The danger here was the Yankees might concentrate and attack one of the separated wings. Robert E. Lee launched a successful attack like this at Chancellorsville.

Hood's third option was to gamble and swing his entire army deep into the enemy's rear to attack his communications. If successful, this would upset the enemy's plans and reverse whatever gains he had made. The risks were possible isolation and exposure to enemy attack from all sides, and loss of lines of retreat. A prerequisite is a strong, capable, and very mobile army. To some extent, Bragg's Kentucky invasion of 1862 was an operation like this.

Hood had no plan of his own, so he visited army headquarters and inquired about any plans Johnston might have under consideration. Johnston's plan was the most conservative one possible. Since time was critical, Hood decided to try it. He then tried the other options in the order given.[5]

His first attack on July 20 was known as the Battle of Peachtree Creek. The object was to hit George Thomas's force as it straddled the creek on its way to Atlanta. Fortunately for the 3rd Tennessee, it was not involved in this fight which ended very badly for the Confederates. It was to be an echelon attack, each brigade advancing sequentially after the brigade to its immediate right. Because of confusion in getting into position, the wild terrain, and the fact that Thomas had most of his force across the creek and in position before the attack began, the Confederates were decisively beaten, suffering five-thousand casualties. Federal losses were less than half that.

Meanwhile, the 3rd Tennessee, now part of Tennessean Benjamin Franklin Cheatham's corps, was absorbed with preventing James B. McPherson's Army of the Tennessee from sneaking into Atlanta from the east. Cheatham and the 3rd Tennessee would get a chance to try their luck in an offensive move several days later.[6]

Determining that Thomas's force was too large and too well prepared to be successfully attacked, Hood next took aim at McPherson's army, which was somewhat isolated on the Yankee far left flank. McPherson wrecked the Georgia Railroad running east through Decatur, and then turned west, probing the Atlanta defenses. The Ohioan appeared to be too far from the rest of the blue army to receive rapid reinforcement should Hood hit him with full force. This is what Hood intended to do.

On July 22nd, Hood tried the second alternative. His plan called for Hardee's Corps to disengage from Thomas's front to the north, march some sixteen miles south completely through the city and beyond, and then circle to the east and fall on McPherson's left flank and rear. Once these Confederates were fully engaged, Cheatham's Corps would join the attack from the west. In the meantime, to complete the destruction of McPherson's army, Wheeler's cavalry would attack the Federal supply trains near Decatur.

Hood's plan was good in concept, but was seriously flawed. He had not properly reconnoitered the attack area and Hardee met a serious obstacle, a dam with a half-mile long reservoir of water behind it sitting squarely in the middle of his attack route.[7]

After much fumbling, Hardee's troops were in attack position around noon, about four hours late, and McPherson had placed a division directly in Hardee's path. Between negotiating his way around the terrain obstacles and battling the unexpected Yankee division in his front, Hardee's attack bogged down.

The one thing the Confederates had in their favor was that McPherson had left a mile-long gap between his main line facing west and Grenville Dodge's line facing south. Into this gap plunged the division of Patrick Cleburne.

While Walker's and Bate's Divisions to Cleburne's right were bogged down in the tangled terrain fronting the Yankee brigades from Dodge's division, Cleburne quickly rolled up two brigades belonging to G.A. Smith's division, and had a fair start at unhinging the entire blue line. As the Yankees fled Cleburne's hard-charging troops, they fell in with units further to the north, strengthening the Federal defenses. Cleburne was forced to stop. He needed help to keep the advance rolling. At this moment, about 3:00 p.m., Hood ordered Cheatham's Corps forward.

Cheatham had arranged his divisions with Carter Stevenson's division and the 3rd Tennessee on the right. Stevenson's troops pitched into the Federal position blocking Cleburne, but could not move it. Mortimer D. Leggett's Yankee division conducted one of the most stubborn defenses of the war. The men shifted back and forth to beat off repeated attacks, first from Cleburne, then from Stevenson, then again from Cleburne, at times resorting to fighting from both sides of their barricades.[8]

The 3rd Tennessee participated in several assaults along this front with the rest of Stevenson's Division, and suffered terribly. Stevenson and Cleburne were stopped with nothing to show for their efforts but some very grim casualty lists.

The most spectacular success of the day was made by John C. Brown, in temporary command of Thomas Hindman's division. His spearhead of South Carolina and Alabama troops accidentally plunged into a sunken road and rail line and found themselves well protected from Yankee fire. The rail line led directly to a weakly held segment in the Yankee front line where Brown was able to pry open a half-mile breech. This breakthrough, at the Troup Hurt house, is the centerpiece illustration in the Cyclorama of Atlanta. However, when no relief materialized, he ordered his men to withdraw.[9]

The Battle of Atlanta, as this particular fight was designated, was a disaster for the Army of Tennessee. Hood lost in excess of 5000 men versus 3722 for the Federals—losses he absolutely could not afford without the compensation of some sort of dramatic strategic gain. The Federals lost McPherson, but the Confederates lost W.H.T. Walker, a cantankerous but extremely aggressive and effective division commander.[10]

The two sides paused for about a week to catch their breath and prepare for the next round.

During the pause, Hood replaced the very competent Benjamin F. Cheatham, who temporarily commanded Hood's old corps, with Stephen D. Lee, the same officer who had so competently commanded the 3rd Tennessee's defensive line at Chickasaw Bayou. Lee's appointment broke the army's back. Soon Lee would lead a series of disjointed attacks in a fight west of Atlanta known as Ezra Church. He nearly destroyed Hood's old corps in a single battle. The 3rd Tennessee missed this battle, but John C. Brown played a prominent role, ending the battle before it became a greater disaster than it was.

The line was stabilized where the battle ended, and the next day Brown returned to his old brigade. For a while Brown and the 3rd Tennessee helped fend off Sherman's probes along Atlanta's western defenses, and ducked 'camp kettles,' the huge shells constantly lobbed at the city by Sherman's big siege guns. The Army of Tennessee was now like a punch-drunk boxer doing little else than waiting for the climactic blow to be struck.

Despite the pounding Brown took at Ezra Church, his aggressiveness was greatly appreciated by John Bell Hood. According to Arthur Manigault, a brigade commander who served under Brown, "Brigadier General J.C. Brown, of Tennessee [was a] favorite of General Hood's, and an officer whose promotion as a Major General was daily expected." The promotion arrived one week after the Ezra Church fight. [11]

Sherman initiated the next phase of the campaign on August 25th, executing the precise move his Confederate counterparts probably should have attempted a couple of months earlier. Sherman took almost his entire army, six full corps, on a wide sweep west and south of Atlanta, too far out for interference from Rebel probes. He then turned east, aiming directly for Jonesboro, Hood's final life line. Sherman kept one corps at the north side of Atlanta to protect his own supply line. [12]

If Sherman could place his army solidly astride the Macon and Western rail line, he would completely isolate Hood from his final source of sustenance and from the rest of the Confederacy. If he could get there first, he would force Hood into more of the costly attacks that had already bled the Rebel army. Even if Hood chose not to fight, Sherman's position deep in Hood's rear made evacuation of Atlanta inevitable since the Confederates must either come out of the city or starve.

Hood was dumbfounded by Sherman's movement. For a while he entertained the idea that one of Joseph Wheeler's feeble raids on Sherman's supply line was precipitating a withdrawal. Then ominous intelligence reports from his cavalry screen indicated all was not right. When word came that Yankee troops were at the outskirts of Jonesboro, he decided it was nothing more than a raid by two or three Federal corps. Hood could not believe Sherman would separate himself so far from his supply line. He dispatched Hardee's and Lee's corps to deal with this new threat. Hardee was placed in command with orders to drive the blue forces away.[13]

The 3rd Tennessee was among the group with the greatest distance to travel, and the forced march of twenty-two miles on the night of August 30th was hard on the men after several sedentary weeks in the trenches. Hardee did not begin aligning his six divisions for an attack until well after noon on the 31st.[14]

The Confederates aimed their attack at the Federal XVth Corps, posted in advance of the rest of the army on a hill directly west of Jonesboro. Hardee placed Cleburne in charge of his own corps and ordered him to lead off the attack on the left. Cleburne placed his own division on the Confederate far left, and William Bate's division, now commanded by John C. Brown, Bate having been wounded, was positioned on Cleburne's right. They were to conduct a right wheel to come up on the right of the Federal position.

Meanwhile, at the other end of the line, the 3rd Tennessee was placed in Stevenson's first assault line facing west. These men were to come at the Federals head on.[15]

Cleburne's Division started the attack, and it immediately encountered trouble. Federal cavalryman Judson Kilpatrick, posted along the Flint River to the right of the Federal main line, discovered a long line of Rebel infantry making a sweep directly across his front. Kilpatrick opened with everything he had, including artillery and Spencer repeating rifles. Mark Lowrey shifted his direction of attack to the left to deal with these cavalrymen, causing a gap to open between his division and Brown's. Meanwhile, Brown's men advanced through a corn field, and for a while managed to brave the concentrated Yankee artillery fire. The brigades moved into musket range delivering one ineffective volley against the Yankee line. Resuming the advance, the men suddenly encountered a deep ravine that traversed most of Brown's front and part of the division tumbled in. The men discovered they were safe from enemy fire in the ravine, and remained there despite the exhortations of Brown and his officers to continue ahead. The Confederate attack rapidly fell apart.[16]

Stephen Lee ordered his troops forward as soon as he heard Cleburne's guns. Lee's men met a fire as hot as Brown had faced, and the attack quickly ground to a halt. Lacking cover, most of the men simply hugged the ground. Whenever a group of Confederates signaled an intention to surrender, the Federals ordered a temporary cease-fire on that part of the line and the surrendering Johnnies scurried across no-man's land to safety on the other side.

The first day's battle of Jonesboro was another disaster for the Confederates. Casualty rates were exceptionally disproportionate, nearly ten to one in favor of the Federals. In Lee's Corps 1300 men were lost. The 3rd Tennessee suffered heavily, the exact number of losses unknown. The regiment's greatest loss was its very able lieutenant colonel, Calvin J. Clack, who replaced Calvin Walker as commander at Kolb's Farm. Cleburne's loss was 400 or so, mostly from Brown's Division.[17]

Still unaware of what Sherman intended, and fearing a direct assault on Atlanta, Hood ordered Hardee to return Lee's Corps to the city later that night. These men had to swing well to the east to avoid the swarms of Yankees tearing up the railroad north of Jonesboro. They were fortunate in one respect; they would avoid the second day's blood bath at Jonesboro. What Hood hoped to gain by leaving Hardee behind is a mystery. Sherman already had a firm grip on the Macon and Western Line north of Jonesboro, so Hood's communications with the rest of the Confederacy were already cut. Jonesboro itself had no value, so Hardee's men were left to face Sherman's wrath on their own—six Federal corps versus one Confederate. Defeat was inevitable.

The next day Hardee fought a gallant but hopeless battle, but by nightfall was obliged to withdraw his worn-out corps to the south. Back in Atlanta, Hood finally realized his army was about to be hopelessly trapped unless he managed a quick exit. He ordered everyone out to the southeast, toward McDonough. All supplies that could not be carried by the army were to be distributed to the local population or destroyed. Hood lost a huge amount of munitions, but extracted his army in good order. He soon rendezvoused with Hardee at Lovejoy Station southeast of Jonesboro.[18]

Sherman's XXth Corps, posted north of Atlanta, was the first into Atlanta. The prize the Ohioan had pursued for the past four months was finally his. The entire North celebrated. Grant, stalled in front of Lee at Petersburg, ordered his cannoneers to fire a salute to Sherman's army. Naturally, so as not to waste ammunition, all shots were aimed toward Lee's army.

Though he had the Army of Tennessee on the run, Sherman suddenly lost interest. Offensive operations abruptly stopped, and the red-haired commander returned to Atlanta to inspect his hard won prize, and to relish the adulation from the folks back home.

Hood shifted his army west, to the little town of Palmetto, and pondered his next move. The Army of Tennessee was in despair. With the loss of Atlanta morale hit its nadir and desertions soared.

Because of the continuous fighting and disintegration within the Army of Tennesssee, the Army's reporting systems were rapidly breaking down and regimental reports became extremely rare. Fortunately, Thomas Deavenport took time out to recount the events of the campaign and record his impressions, probably a fair representation of the feelings of the entire 3rd Tennessee.

> Two months have passed since I wrote any in my journal. During that time much has been done and suffered. We remained near Atlanta till 31st Aug.. Around that city we lost many brave men. It was a dreadful time and yet our boys held up bravely. At last we had to leave, marched down to Jones Borough,

twenty-two miles, and fought a battle the same day. There we lost Lt. Col. C. J. Clack, and many more. We gained nothing. Early next morning we started back, bivouacked for the night in a few miles of Atlanta. It became necessary to evacuate the place and at daylight we began the march, and on the 3rd Sept. bivouacked near Lovejoy. Hardee's Corps in the meantime had another desperate engagement which resulted in a drawn battle though the enemy's loss was much heavier than ours. On the night of the 4th the enemy began to fall back, which they continued till they reached Atlanta. Thus ended the Summer Campaign. An Armistice of ten days was agreed upon, that the citizens of Atlanta might be sent through the lines. Here was a piece of Heartless cruelty. There seems to be no deed too base or cruel for a Yankee. Gen. Sherman had without warning shelled the city more than a month destroying a vast amount of property and many lives and when he gained possession of it immediately ordered every man woman and child to leave, and also all living in five miles of the R. R. in the rear, thus several thousand women and children were turned out of their homes, driven away from all they possessed and cast upon the charities of the world. How shall that base man answer for all his dark deeds. The campaign just closed has been the most arduous of the war. For four months we listened daily to the roar of cannon and rattle of musketry. All day, all night the leaden messengers were flying round us. It seems incredible that men could endure so much. Cheerfully each labor was performed, each danger met. True many looked worn and haggard but still their spirit was unbroken. We rested a few days and again took up the line of march and are now fortifying near Palmetto on the W.P.R.R. [West Point Railroad].

A new campaign has been inaugurated, how it will end God only knows. We have been compelled to give up much of our country at this point. It has cost the enemy much. At other points we have been successful. I am not discouraged, though there is some discontent in the Army. Oh God, how long will this cruel war last? My heart yearns for the society of home. I count each day and ask when will the last come? Poor weak human nature is ready to complain and say my burden is too heavy. Cease thy murmuring, God is wise and good. He doeth all things well. Health is yet mine. Through many dangers I have been led, have just escaped death time and again. It seems that I have led a charmed life. God be praised for his goodness. I see around me much distress and my heart sickens at the destruction of life and property on every hand, in the army and out of it. I see grey hairs and helpless infancy driven from home, penniless almost friendless. I see the strong men cut down without a moment's warning, or left a cripple for life. I see the poor soldier as he toils on, sustained by the hope of better days and by the love he bears for those far away. I saw but yesterday the Captain commanding his regiment barefoot. Such men will not be conquered. I cannot give the history of this campaign language to describe its suffering. It has been long and bloody, many of our noblest have fallen. 'Requiescant in pace.' They live in our hearts.[19]

The "Captain commanding his regiment barefoot" was Walter S. Jennings of Company C, the last official commander of the 3rd Tennessee. In the campaign that followed, the 3rd was combined with the 18th Tennessee, the consolidated regiment commanded by the colonel of the 18th, W.R. Butler.[20]

It was not long before Jefferson Davis made a brief visit to the army at Palmetto to raise its spirits. His grand review turned into an embarrassment when the troops shouted at Davis to return Joe Johnston to them. Davis sustained Hood.

Hood made the troops pay for their indiscretions. Even worse, he slandered the army's fighting ability, and continued to do so for many years afterward.

Hood finally exercised the third offensive option, that of conducting a grand sweep into Sherman's rear. This was the move that probably should have been made by Joe Johnston four months earlier when the Confederates still had sufficient combat power to create real havoc. It was three more months before Hood was ready to strike. He first had to find Walter Jennings some shoes.

Notes for Chapter 19

1 Horn, *The Army of Tennessee*, pp. 341-345.
2 Robert Selph Henry, *First With the Most: Forrest*, pp. 308-309.
3 Deavenport Diary, p. 28.
4 Horn, *op.cit.*, pp. 343-344.

5 *Ibid.*, pp. 346-348.

6 Stephen Davis, "Atlanta Campaign: Hood Fights Desperately," *Blue and Gray Magazine*, August 1989, pp.12-17. Castel, *Decision in the West*, pp. 365-383. Horn, *op.cit.*, pp. 350-354. Connelly, *Army of the Heartland*, pp. 439-444.

7 Davis, *op.cit.*, p. 20.

8 Davis, *op.cit.*, pp. 20-22. Castel, *op.cit.*, p. 405.

9 A.L. Johnson and Brook Jones Reports, B.F. Cheatham, Papers. Castel, *op.cit.*, pp. 407-408.

10 Davis, *op. cit.*, p. 25.

11 Manigault, *A Carolinian Goes to War*, p. 195.

12 Davis, *op.cit.*, p. 49.

13 *OR*,Vol.XXXVIII, Part 3, pp. 700-701. Davis, *op. cit.,* p. 49.

14 Deavenport Diary, p. 29.

15 Davis, *op. cit.*, p. 53.

16 *Ibid.*, p. 52.

17 *OR*,Vol.XXXVIII, Part 3, p.708. Davis, *op. cit.*, p. 52. Deavenport Diary, p. 29.

18 Davis, *op. cit.,* p. 60. Castel, *op. cit.*, pp. 510-520.

19 Deavenport Diary, p. 29-31.

20 *Battles and Leaders*, Vol. IV, p. 291.

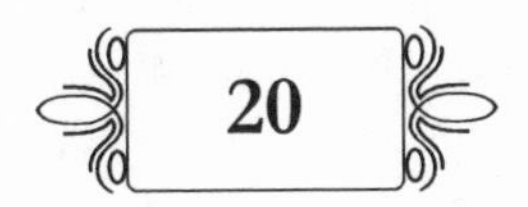

SORTIE INTO TENNESSEE

It was Hood's opinion that his front line commanders, especially Hardee, were lacking in the proper zest for combat. William Hardee, for his part, was fed up with John Hood and wanted out. Hardee and a scratch force was sent to Savannah to stop Sherman's sixty-thousand men from reaching the Atlantic Ocean.

To replace Hardee, Hood again elevated B.F. Cheatham to corps command. William Bate had healed sufficiently to resume command of his old division, so John C. Brown moved over to assume command of Cheatham's Division.

Hood spent about a week at Palmetto. He began his move north on September 28th, crossing the Chattahoochie the same day. His march took him over the same ground covered the previous months. Sherman followed him with most of his army until finally, in frustration over his failure to bring the Confederates to bay, he detached two of his corps to watch Hood, and set off with the rest of his army on his famous march to the sea. Hood retired into Alabama to recoup and refit his army for further action.[1]

The last entry in Thomas Deavenport's diary summed up the army's march to the Tennessee border.

> Nov. 8th. - Bivouac near Florence, Ala. Many supposed when we sat down at Lovejoy that the work for the year was over, but our General saw otherwise and inaugurated a new campaign taking the offensive. We rested only eight days and again took up the line of march, recrossed the Chattahoochee, struck the [railroad] in Sherman's rear at Big Shanty tore it up for thirty-five miles capturing several important stations with garrisons, at one place nine hundred Negroes. We turned westward through Somerville, Ga., Gadsden, Ala., Courtland to Florence where we crossed the river and have remained till now. It has been a long weary march of nearly five hundred miles, still the soldiers have stood it nobly. Many of them marched barefoot, both officers and men. Where we will go next is uncertain, and great is the anxiety. Every eye is turned toward Tennessee. Oh, may she soon be free. God of hosts be with us and give us success.[2]

The little parson's prayer was not to be answered. In fact, the worst fears of Deavenport and the rest of the army were realized.

Hood's presence along the Tennessee line created considerable consternation for the Federal high command. Weakened though it was by constant fighting, the Army of Tennessee was still a dangerous foe as the garrison forces tending the Yankee rear were finding out. The two corps detached by Sherman could delay Hood, but it would take a full-sized army to defeat him. The Federals ordered all available forces to concentrate at Nashville, the most threatened strategic point, for just that purpose. It required considerable time for these men to arrive and to get ready. As it turned out, Hood provided most of the time they needed.

It took Hood a month to reach the Tennessee River in Alabama, and the better part of another month before he was ready to strike. Hood found the railroad to Decatur was not repaired, and no supplies stockpiled at Tuscumbia, so he delayed. Had Hood been able to march directly to Nashville ahead of Sherman's veterans, he might have created real problems for Grant, Sherman, and company.

When Hood finally advanced, he had two objectives in mind. The first was to destroy the two Federal corps arrayed in his front and seize the huge Federal depot at Nashville. Once that was achieved, the second more grandioise objective was to then move across the Appalachian Mountains and attack Grant's rear, thus providing relief to Lee's army pinned down at Petersburg. Both objectives presented great hazards, but Hood had to do something if the Confederacy was to have any chance of survival.[3]

Hood first had to deal with John Schofield.

The Federals under Schofield were positioned on in the 3rd Tennessee's home turf, in and around Pulaski. On November 21st, by multiple march routes, Hood moved rapidly to Schofield's rear. The Federal commander realized his danger and quickly retreated to Columbia and the Duck River where he intended to make a stand. Hood then devised a masterful plan—use one corps to hold Schofield in place while the other two enveloped the Yankee left and destroyed Schofield's army from behind.

First Hood sent Forrest to the right to clear the way for his infantry which the cavalryman accomplished handsomely by driving the Yankee horsemen off to the north. Despite having Forrest outnumbered and outgunned, the Federal cavalry commander, James Wilson, decided that Hood was driving straight for Nashville, and took his force entirely off the field. Before abandoning the field, he messaged Schofield that Hood was moving most of his army around the Federal flank. Schofield was not convinced. With his 'eyes' gone, since James Wilson's cavalry screen was no longer on the field, he was hard pressed to find out.[4]

Hood chose Cheatham's Corps, his strongest, to lead his infantry column across the Duck River, followed by Stewart's. Lee's Corps was to demonstrate in front of Columbia to hold Schofield in place. Lee was eminently successful.

The actions of the 3rd/41st Tennessee Regiment were notable in this success. The consolidated regiment was deployed as a skirmish line to press Schofield's rear as the Yankee commander was in the process of shifting from the south to the north side of the Duck River at Columbia. This it did with great elan. The

Tennesseans literally stampeded the Yankee rear guard across the Central Alabama Railroad bridge spanning the Duck, and in the process secured a bridgehead opposite Schofield's right flank. Lee quickly sent Pettus's Brigade across. This threat, combined with the heavy artillery fire emanating from the Rebel side of the river, caused Schofield to ponder exactly what Hood's intentions were. He ordered his supply trains and two of his divisions to withdraw, but held the remainder of his army in Columbia to await developments. His objective was to delay Hood as long as he could, and he certainly could not accomplish this by running to Nashville at Hood's first touch.[5]

As Schofield equivocated, the Confederates were making slow progress in their march toward the little town of Spring Hill. Since Hood's march would expose his army to a possible flank attack, he had his divisions march in parallel columns. Taking the lead on the Davis Ford Road on the left was Cleburne's Division, now back under the command of the Irishman, with William Bate next in line. John C. Brown was ordered to march parallel to Cleburne's right across open fields, thus providing Hood a second line if the Confederates were attacked.

Ambrose Bierce, with the Federal left flank at Columbia, observed the crossing of Brown and company across the Duck River: "We formed a line of battle at a distance perhaps a half-mile from the bridgehead, but that unending column of gray and steel gave us no more attention than if we had been a crowd of farmer-folk. Why should it? It had only to turn to the left to be itself a line of battle." The battered Army of Tennessee was still an intimidating sight to the men in blue. To the Confederates' misfortune, Brown's march up and down the rolling hills and through the frequent brush thickets and steep little creeks slowed the army dramatically, and fatally.[6]

After several disjointed attacks at Spring Hill, nightime closed in, and Schofield managed to sneak his entire army past the Confederates and take up a new position further north at Franklin.

The next morning, November 30, 1864, the Rebels found the Yankees completely gone. Hood breakfasted with his commanders at the mansion of former 3rd Tennessean Nat Cheairs, and

Nat Cheairs home at Spring Hill was the scene of the bitter breakfast confrontation between John Bell Hood and his errant generals the morning of November 30th after John Schofield had escaped the Confederate's clutches the night before. According to John C. Brown, Hood was "wrathy as a rattle-snake." Cheairs, serving with Forrest, was the 3rd Tennessee's major during the first year of the war.

Courtesy: Author

apparently it was not a pleasant occasion. Brown observed: "General Hood is mad about the enemy getting away last night, and he is going to charge the blame of it on somebody. He is wrathy as a rattlesnake this morning, striking at everything."[7]

Hood was in a rage and most certainly was emotionally unfit to command an army. The Kentuckian had allowed the Yankee army to slip past him, a military setback, but not necessarily a fatal one. Schofield halted his army at Franklin while he repaired the bridges over the Harpeth River. When Forrest suggested a move around the Yankee flank, much like the one which had worked so well the day before, Hood rejected it out of hand. He stated later that he wanted to teach the army (his own) a lesson; he would come at the Yankees head on.

Later that day, November 30, 1864, Hood threw his army against the Yankee fortifications at Franklin.

Hood, still in a snit, had given up attempting any flanking maneuver. He advanced immediately to the attack, deploying Stewart's Corps on the right and Cheatham on the left. Lee's Corps, along with most of Hood's artillery, advanced from Columbia and was too far behind to influence the battle. Luckily for the 3rd Tennessee, they were among this group.

Brown and Cleburne's Divisions comprised the middle of the attack force, Brown advancing along the left of the Columbia and Franklin Pike, Cleburne along the right. They marched into the teeth of the Federal defenses.

They had two things going for them that beautiful autumn day. There was a break in the Federal line where the Columbia Pike passed through the middle of the Federal position. The Yankees had also posted two brigades in advance of their main line, apparently to delay Hood's approach. This force was too small for a forward defensive line, and too big for a skirmish line. It was almost a fatal error.

The Confederates overran the forward position easily, and the whole mass, Rebels and Yankees intermixed, came toward Franklin in a rush. The Yankees on the main line were afraid to fire lest they hit their own men, and the center of the blue line cracked wide open. Rebels came streaming up the pike past the Fountain Carter house and through the center of the Union line onward into Schofield's rear.

Brown accompanied his troops through the center of the Federal line, advancing with them all the way to the Carter house. Then disaster struck. As Brown's men charged past both sides of the house, they suddenly met a surprise: a Federal brigade, arranged in a gigantic wedge formation, was coming at them at a run not two-hundred yards away.[8]

This was Emmerson Opdycke's brigade of tough mid-westerners. As Opdycke's men closed the gap, fugitives from the main line joined them and the wedge increased in combat power as it advanced. The disorganized Confederates, forced back to the original Yankee line, took cover on the reverse side.

Brown himself was shot off his horse near a locust grove below the Carter house while guiding John C. Carter's brigade into position. Ironically, the bullet hit him in the same leg and in nearly the same spot where he was struck at Perryville two years earlier.[9]

For the next five hours, well into the night, the two sides shot, and jabbed, and clubbed each other sufficiently to even satisfy the blood lust of John Hood.

The Army of Tennessee was destroyed. Of the approximately eighteen-thousand men attacking at Franklin, over six-thousand became casualties. The army's leadership was devastated. Brown was badly wounded and out of action for the next six months. Patrick Cleburne was dead. Three of Brown's brigadiers were killed and one was captured. Many regiments, like the 3rd Tennessee, had no one higher than a captain left to command. Hood was unscathed, having observed the fight from Winstead Hill over a mile to the rear.[10]

The next morning Schofield was gone. Hood proclaimed the battle a victory, and again concealed the scope of the disaster until much later. He followed Schofield to Nashville, where George Thomas was assembling a huge army to settle accounts with Hood once and for all. Hood dug in south of the city and waited, apparently for reinforcements from the Trans-Mississippi Department, but that was only wishful thinking.

The Fountain Carter home at Franklin was the hub of the action during the bloody confrontation there on November 30th. It was here John C. Brown was grievously wounded for the fourth time. The house and outbuildings were riddled with bullet holes during the intense five-hour fire fight.

Courtesy: Author

Hood had trapped himself. He had created the impression in Richmond of leading a victorious army when in reality it was only a hollow shell.

Then he did an amazing thing. With Thomas's huge force assembled and coiled to strike directly at his front, he sent Forrest, with most of the cavalry, on a railroad wrecking expedition. When Forrest discovered a large concentration of Yankees assembled at Murfreesboro, Hood sent Bate's Division and two additional brigades, to either "watch" these isolated Yankees or to assist in wrecking the railroad, depending on whose version is believed, Bate or Forrest. [11]

The latter two brigades were Joseph B. Palmer's and Claudius Sears', detached from Lee's and Stewart's Corps respectively. Palmer's force included the 3rd/41st Tennessee Consolidated Regiment.

With Sherman embarked on his march to the sea, the rail line from Nashville to Chattanooga was of absolutely no importance to the Union effort. Cutting it was an exercise in futility. Regardless, the combined force, now under Forrest's command, tore up the rails anyway until, to Bate's chagrin, Forrest decided to move against Murfreesboro. Forrest marched his combined force a mile and a half to the west of town, threatening the Federal redoubt on Stones River called Fort Rosecrans.

The ensuing fight took place on the very ground fought over by Bragg and Rosecrans two years before.

The affair at Murfreesboro on December 7th was only a side show to the big event soon to occur at Nashville, but it set the tone for that disaster. It also marked an eclipse in Bedford Forrest's otherwise sterling career. He probably intended one of his famous bluffs. The scenario called for Forrest to align his forces in preparation for an assault. Once ready, he would call for a parley with the Federal in charge and issue dire threats of impending doom to the defenders, and strongly emphasize that all the blood about to be shed would be on the hands of the Yankee for having failed to surrender. At this point, the Federal commander was supposed to lose his nerve and raise the white flag, thus giving Forrest an easy victory.

This time, however, Federal commander Lovell Rousseau refused to play by the script.

Before Forrest could do anything, Rousseau ordered Robert Milroy to take seven regiments of infantry, a battery of artillery, and a few cavalry (among this group was the 5th Tennessee Cavalry Vols. [Union]) and probe Forrest's position. Milroy took his force west and then swung north toward Forrest's position. Forrest observed this movement and readjusted his line toward Milroy's approach. Palmer's Brigade, including the 3rd/41st Tennessee, held the middle.[12]

As the Federals approached, Forrest opened with his artillery, to which Milroy's battery replied. For half an hour the cannoneers on both sides had a lively little fight until Milroy's men ran out of ammunition. The cannoneers had only brought a small supply in their limbers. Milroy withdrew his force, sent his cannon back to Murfreesboro, and pondered his next move.[13]

An attack against Forrest's right would place Forrest between his force and the Federal main force at Murfreesboro. He opted to attempt to roll up at Forrest's left.

Before he began, however, he decided to deal with the matter of the sixty fat hogs discovered on the farm of a Mr. Spence. Milroy was determined that these porkers not end up as part of the Confederate larder and detailed a company to herd them back to Murfreesboro.[14]

Once the hogs were disposed of, Milroy dropped back into the thick woods and began a long swing past Forrest's front and around the Tennessean's left. Milroy then arranged his two brigades into two battle lines and ordered them forward.

Milroy was right on target. Forrest had ordered Abraham Buford's cavalry division to attack Murfreesboro, thus vacating the very area being attacked. Forrest assumed that when Milroy vacated his front he was heading back into town. Buford swung into Murfreesboro from the rear, where he took possession of the courthouse whose sole occupants were a large community of rats. He did not accomplish much else.[15]

Meanwhile, Milroy's men stumbled through the brush, rocks, and cedar thickets, on their way to Forrest's position. Forrest could

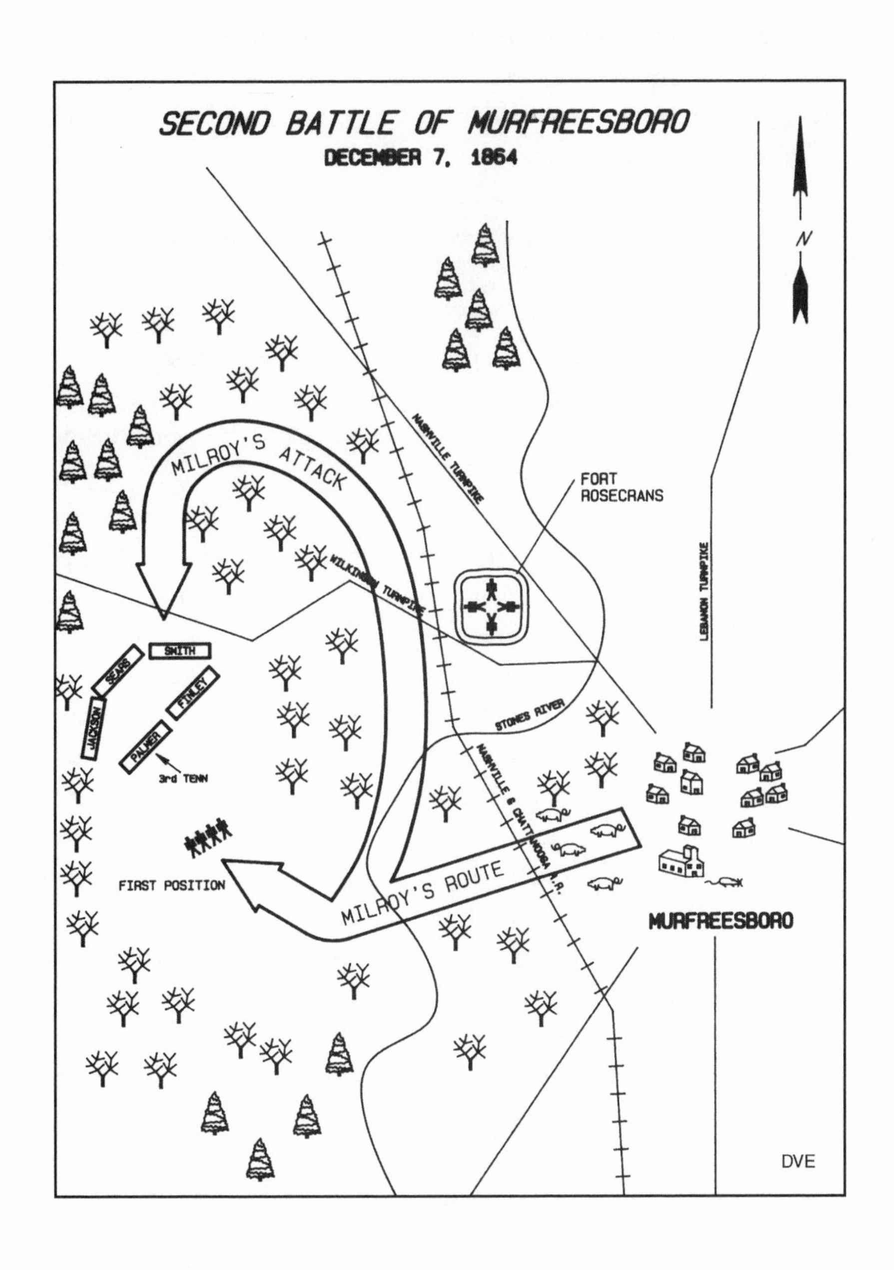
SECOND BATTLE OF MURFREESBORO
DECEMBER 7, 1864
N
MILROY'S ATTACK
NASHVILLE TURNPIKE
FORT ROSECRANS
LEBANON TURNPIKE
WILKINSON TURNPIKE
SMITH
SEARS
FINLEY
JACKSON
PALMER
3rd TENN
STONES RIVER
NASHVILLE & CHATTANOOGA R.R.
FIRST POSITION
MILROY'S ROUTE
MURFREESBORO
DVE

hear Milroy coming and shifted his brigades from right to left to meet him, but not quickly enough. Forrest had one brigade barely in position to protect his left when Milroy's men came charging across an open field. Though the Yankees had no artillery support, they employed the innovative expedient of opening a rolling fire of musketry as they advanced. Usually troops advanced at right shoulder arms until they were within effective musketry range, and then conducted volley fire. When they were about half way across the field the Yankees halted, and for ten minutes the two sides exchanged fire that sounded like "thunder." Finally, just as Milroy started deploying his second line, the Confederates broke.[16]

Milroy swept over two of Forrest's brigades, including Palmer's, which was still in position facing southeast. Federal fire was so heavy that most of the hard-pressed Rebel infantry could not run without receiving one or more minie-balls in the back. Milroy captured over two-hundred Confederates, no doubt some of them 3rd Tennesseans. Forrest's tough cavalry, brought up in support, did not fare much better. Forrest frantically tried to rally his line even going so far as to shoot down a fleeing color bearer with his revolver. Seizing the flag himself, he attempted to use it as a rallying point. However, his efforts were all in vain. According to Rousseau, "Forrest's cavalry [made] the finest time ... down the Nashville road, I have seen in many a day."[17]

Thus, Forrest, for once with superior numbers, suffered the embarrassment of being bested by a couple of obscure Federal commanders. The Confederates regrouped about a mile behind their original line, while Milroy marched back into the Murfreesboro defenses.

To add to the Confederates' misery, the next day the weather turned bitterly cold and began to sleet. The 3rd Tennessee was not adequately clothed for this weather, and probably a fourth or more of the men were still without shoes. Shortly after the fight on the seventh, Bate's Division was ordered back to Nashville where an attack by Thomas was expected any day. The two brigades detached from the other two divisions remained with Forrest. When Forrest was ordered to hurry back, to save time, he left his two infantry brigades behind.

Sear's and Palmer's Brigades were cast adrift in a sea of Confederate misfortune. The infantrymen became cattle and hog drovers for the large herd of livestock the Confederates had gathered from throughout the area. Then, when Hood's army was routed at Nashville on December 15th and 16th, they were left to their own devices to find their way back to the army as it retreated south.[18]

The cattle and hog herd provided food and an additional benefit. As the animals were butchered, those men lacking shoes divided up the hide and improvised footware. One of Hood's staff officers observed, "Some would have a pretty good shoe on one foot and on the other a piece of rawhide or a part of a shoe made strong with a string made from a strip of rawhide tied around it, some of them would have all rawhide, some were entirely barefooted, and some would have on old shoe tops with the bottoms of their feet on the ground."[19]

As Palmer's Brigade made its way through Maury and Giles Counties through the cold and wet, the temptation for the 3rd Tennesseans who had escaped the rout at Murfreesboro to visit their homes became overwhelming. When Palmer's Brigade was added to Edward Walthall's division at Columbia on December 20th, the regiment reported only seventeen men present, of which, twelve were "effectives," plus three colored servants. However, the missing men did not stay gone for long. For example: "A private soldier got permission ... to visit his mother. When he got in sight of his home and saw the Yankees were there, he turned around, came back, and fell in line." These Yankees were probably Wilson's cavalry who dogged Hood's heels all the way into Mississippi.[20]

Mack Dabney was one of the 'colored servants' that marched off to war with the 3rd Tennessee. He faithfully served John C. Brown, Calvin H. Walker, and other officers until the war's end. He applied for a Confederate pension in 1890.

Courtesy: Confederate Veteran

The Battle of Nashville completed the destruction of the Army of Tennessee. With the army's destruction, the South knew that the Confederacy was finished. However, Jefferson Davis and company apparently felt compelled to fight to the last Confederate soldier. As the survivors of the 3rd Tennessee straggled back to the colors they found one more task to perform.

Notes for Chapter 20

1 Horn, *The Army of Tennessee*, pp. 381-382.

2 Deavenport Diary, p. 31.

3 Hood, *Advance and Retreat*, pp. 258-263. Connelly, *Army of the Heartland*, pp. 484-485.

4 *OR*, Vol. XLV, Part 1, p. 550.

5 *Ibid.*, p. 693. Wiley Sword, *Embrace an Angry Wind - The Confederacy's Last Hurrah: Spring Hill, Franklin, and Nashville*, p. 116.

6 *Ambrose Bierce's Civil War*, p. 63.

7 *Louisville Courier-Journal*, Dec. 4, 1881.

8 Faust, *Encyclopedia of the Civil War*, p. 83.

9 Sword, *op. cit.*, pp. 237-238. Robert H. White, *Messages of the Governors of Tennessee*, p. 114.

10 Horn, *op. cit.*, pp. 403-404. James L McDonough and Thomas L. Connelly, *Five Tragic Hours: The Battle of Franklin*, p.157.

11 *OR*, Vol.XLV, Part 1, pp. 744-746, 751-756.

12 *Ibid.*, p.746.

13 *Ibid.*, p. 617.

14 *Ibid.*

15 *Ibid.*, p. 756. Rice Bull, *Soldiering: The Civil War Diary of Rice Bull*, p. 94. Bull provides a very humorous account of rats as tame as cats encountered during an overnight stay at the courthouse the previous fall.

16 *OR*, Vol. XLV, part 1, pp. 617-618.

17 *Ibid.*, p. 613. Sword, *op. cit.*, pp. 297-298.

18 *OR*, Vol. XLV, Part 1, p. 756.

19 James D. Porter, *CV*, Vol. XVII, p. 20.

20 *Ibid. OR*, Vol. XLV, Part 1, p. 728.

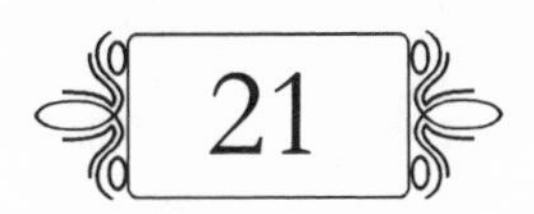

COMPANY C: THE LAST BATTLE

While John C. Brown mended, the remnants of the 3rd Tennessee suffered through the sleet and cold in Corinth, Mississippi. For more than a month, John Bell Hood sat silent while his men shivered because of inadequate clothing, insufficient blankets, and the usual lack of footwear. When the disasters of November and December could no longer be hidden, Hood had no choice but to resign.

Jefferson Davis had been pressing him to provide substantial reinforcements to the Carolinas to resist Sherman's advance, something Hood could no longer do. The once mighty Army of Tennessee was now no more than the equivalent of an average size brigade in the early days of the war.

The 4000 men who finally made the trip east, including at least eighty 3rd Tennesseans still present, did so either because of a profound sense of duty, or because they could not think of anything else to do. Never have men embarked on such a hopeless venture as this handful who marched off to face Sherman's sixty-thousand.[1]

Extensive reorganization was required to come up with units resembling regiments and brigades. The 3rd Tennessee's experience illustrates how conditions had degenerated. It took the remnants of eleven regiments, plus what was left of a battalion, to come up with one good sized field regiment. A new regiment, designated the 4th Consolidated Tennessee, was made up of the old 2nd, 3rd,10th, 15th, 18th, 20th, 26th, 30th, 32nd, 37th, and 45th Tennessee regiments, and the 23rd Tennessee Battalion. Together these outfits were only to seven-hundred plus men. The new commander was Colonel Anderson Searcy, former commander of the 45th Tennessee. The new regiment was assigned to Joseph Palmer's brigade of Cheatham's Division.[2]

Except for Thomas Deavenport, who became the new regiment's chaplain, the former 3rd Tennesseans were all assigned to Company C. The eighty or so men present were about the same number that participated in the Murfreesboro fight in November. To continue the fight at this stage of the war required tough and dedicated men indeed.

A noticeable characteristic of this thrown together army was its top-heaviness in rank. Among the notables present to oppose Sherman were Joseph Johnston, P.G.T. Beauregard, Braxton Bragg, William Hardee, B.F. Cheatham, A.P. Stewart, S.D. Lee, Carter Stevenson, D.H. Hill, and from the east, Jeb Stuart's replacement as commander of Robert E. Lee's cavalry, South Carolinian Wade Hampton. John C. Brown eventually arrived there, but not until the worst of the fighting was over.

This top-heaviness was also evident in the ranks. Company C boasted not less than six captains. Just who commanded the company is not certain, but most likely it was Robert Mitchell, former commander of Company B, who would have been senior to everyone else because of his low-numbered company. Also present was David Rhea, the man who bore the surrender flag for John C. Brown at Fort Donelson. Calvin Walker's twin brother James was also present. Unlike his brother, he survived the war. Among the notables in the ranks was J.P. Caldwell, the man who never seemed up to a fight, but stuck with his comrades to the bitter end. Besides the six captains, the company contained five lieutenants, eleven sergeants, and eight corporals. In other words, the company had thirty leaders for just under fifty private soldiers.

An addition to the new regiment was its major. The 3rd Tennessee's old sergeant-major and lately adjutant of the 48th Tennessee, William Polk, was reunited with his former comrades.[3]

The new regiment moved east sometime in February, but it was delayed several weeks in Augusta while the Confederate high command sorted out who would be in charge of this last ditch defense, and determine which way Sherman was likely to march. Finally, because of intense political pressure, and because Robert E. Lee supported the idea, Joe Johnston was put in charge, again.

By the time the Confederates were organized, Sherman had marched through South Carolina, isolating Charleston and burning Columbia in the process. Johnston decided to try to ambush one of Sherman's two wings as it marched on Goldsboro, North Carolina.

To execute the attack, Johnston pulled together three separate forces: Hardee's force of Georgia and South Carolina troops, Braxton Bragg's collection of North Carolina state troops, and the survivors from the Army of Tennessee under A.P. Stewart.

Johnston's plan was to trap a portion of Henry Slocum's march column in a heavily wooded area south of Bentonville, forcing both Henry Slocum's wing and another wing further east to halt. This, in turn, would give Johnston and Lee time to concentrate their armies against either Sherman or Grant. It was an ambitious goal, but to Johnston, it was better than nothing.

Johnston planned to post Bragg's troops across and to the left of the road to Bentonville. Hardee would be echeloned behind Bragg's right and angled forward to face the road, and Stewart was placed on Hardee's right. Stewart's men were to deliver the main blow against the Yankee flank and rear once Bragg and Hardee forced them to deploy.[4]

This plan had one major flaw. As the Yankees approached the ambush area on March 19th, Johnston did not have all of his troops on hand. While the Federal XIVth Corps marched blithely into the trap, Hardee's troops were just arriving at Bentonville.

As Hardee rushed his men south, Bragg, without too much difficulty, held the line on his own. The first contact was only a reconnaissance-in-force and posed no real threat to Bragg's line. However, it scared Bragg enough so that he asked Johnston for reinforcements. Johnston posted Hardee's first division directly behind Bragg, but this completely disrupted the plan of battle. Instead of positioning his assault force in such a way as to envelop the enemy, Johnston needlessly wasted his strength thickening his blocking force. By mid-afternoon, the rest of Hardee's men arrived. With the center of his line now secure, Johnston ordered Stewart, along with only one of Hardee's divisions, to attack the Federal left. The problem was that more and more Yankees accumulated in their front, and the attack would now be directed against two divisions rather than one.[5]

The 3rd Tennessee survivors were about to embark on their last attempt at an old-style Rebel charge. The bluecoats had established several temporary defensive lines facing Stewart and had sent skirmishers forward to probe Stewart's position. These men advanced through the thick woods to within fifty yards of Stewart's position before being driven off. Shortly afterward, the attack was ordered. W.H. Ogilvie, a private in the 3rd Tennessee's new regiment, described what happened.

> The order being given immediately to [move] forward (with confidence that we would take the works or 'Old Joe' would not order it) we advanced with a yell and double quick, checked only a moment by a volley from the enemy. On we went, driving them from their works, and about one mile beyond, when Gen. Clayton, temporarily commanding the Division, ordered us to halt, saying that we had done enough for one day. Then he sent forward an Alabama brigade, which did not advance far before it retreated.

The Tennesseans again picked up the attack tempo.

> Again we advanced, the color bearer of the 26th Tenn. leading—his name I have forgotten. Then wheeling to the left, we

> soon reached the rear or third line of the enemies works. They still occupied the front on their extreme right.[6]

That last line is critical.

Johnston had intended that once Stewart had started rolling up the Yankee line, Bragg would launch a supporting attack crushing the Federals in a pincer. However, because these Yankees had built some substantial breastworks, and because of a black-jack oak thicket blocking the way, or maybe because the North Carolina state troops lacked the starch it took to capture the enemy position, Bragg's attack ground to a halt.[7]

This left the Tennesseans in a precarious position. Federal reinforcements were rapidly moving up the road in their rear, and escape to the front was blocked by the force facing Bragg. Ogilvie continued:

> After fighting from it [the third line] an hour...a force of the enemy came up in our rear. Our gallant Gen. J.B. Palmer, seeing the situation, escaped by the way we came with the larger part of the brigade having his horse shot under him as he passed between the two lines of the enemy.
>
> The eighty of us, who were the last to leave the works, were cut off from the only avenue of escape.[8]

Among this group were many 3rd Tennesseans. Ogilvie's original manuscript had the section describing Palmer's retreat crossed out. Palmer's stampede to the rear and his abandonment of eighty of his men was not the recollection most Confederates wanted to pass to posterity .

While Palmer's Brigade retreated to the west, a portion of the Tennessee regiment, still commanded by Anderson Searcy, set off to the east. This created a new set of problems as it put them on a collision course with Sherman's other wing. Ogilvie continued.

> Finding the enemy all about us, in the bushes, we kept dodging them, picking up three or four prisoners at a time until we had twelve to take care of. We marched out to the east, with our prisoners, literally surrounded by the enemy, and not even

hoping to escape. We moved to the right end of their works, and continued in that direction, through the swamps nearly knee deep, passing near their ordnance trains.

During the night a lieutenant of the 3rd Tennessee who was severely wounded walked between two of his comrades, until coming to a dry lake where some bark had been stripped from a tree, the gallant fellow asked his supporters to leave him, feeling that he was a burden, and that we could not escape with him. His comrades carried him [and] seeing a light in the distance they carried him to a residence and left him.[9]

Ogilvie did not mention the name of this wounded 3rd Tennessean, but his identity can be narrowed to two possibilities. W.D. Suttle of Company A is listed in the Rollbook as having been killed at Bentonville, but Suttle shows no record of having been promoted past the rank of private.[10]

The other possibility is F.M. Bunch. Bunch was first sergeant in Company A, and he is the only man in the role book with a complete record of service through the Murfreesboro fight in December of 1864. Bunch could have been promoted to lieutenant by this time.[11]

Ogilvie continued:

When they returned we pursued the march till midnight not knowing where we were going. Because the enemy's fires were still in front of us, we passed the remainder of the night, and the next day, on a dry place in the swamp. We could hear the enemy riding about us and talking during the day.

A map of the country taken from the enemy was perused closely, and the plan of action was adopted by our officers ... Lieut. McFadden of the 45th and Captain Rhea of the 3rd took charge of the prisoners. We continued east until we got beyond the enemy, thence south two or three nights march, thence west crossing the Alamanche river and thence north to Raleigh.[12]

This is the same David Rhea who was assigned surrender duty by John C. Brown at the regiment's first big battle at Fort Donelson three years before. Rhea had missed most of the big fights in 1863 because of illness, but had returned in time to participate in the Atlanta campaign and this, the regiment's last hurrah. Rhea played a vital role in keeping this small group of survivors alive.

James David Rhea
Courtesy: Confederate Veteran

John Kennedy
Courtesy: Confederate Veteran

The route Ogilvie described meant that the Tennesseans circled Sherman's left wing, which was no mean feat since an army on the march could stretch out for twenty or more miles. The Yankees also had cavalry patrols extending for miles in all directions.

The men had numerous close calls as they made their way back to their lines. They would cross roads and streams by sprinting across in single file. At one point everyone had to lie flat in the woods while the Yankees drove a cattle herd past barely one hundred-fifty yards away. They had to take long detours around lines of Yankee campfires, and around unfordable streams. They were very concerned that their prisoners might give them away. Ogilvie said, "Our prisoners would have had us captured, but we had assured them that the two governments had recently agreed upon an exchange of prisoners [not true], and that they would be immediately exchanged. For extra insurance, the Confederates also emphasized that attempting to alert their comrades would threaten their own safety, a statement that could be taken several ways.[13]

When food ran out, Captain Rhea volunteered to go on a scout and was imminently successful. Scouring the woods, he discovered a 'red razor-back' hog wandering about, and to avoid alerting the Yankees, Rhea and a North Carolina soldier trapped the tusker in a fence corner where Rhea cut its throat with his knife. The hog was then divided into ninety-two equal portions. To their credit, the Confederates made sure their Federal prisoners ate as well as themselves.[14]

The men later found a buggy full of meat hidden in the woods. Not long after the owner showed up, and, apparently confused as to who was the prisoner of whom, professed that he was "the best Union man in the country." When the Tar Heel finally determined who was in charge, "he changed front" as Ogilvie put it. The man was retained as guide and led them to a crossing point on the Alamache River. The men later came upon an old mill which provided them a cornbread feast.[15]

When they finally entered friendly lines, the army was amazed that these tattered men could have come so far without being captured. They were welcomed like long lost brothers.

John C. Brown
Courtesy: Confederate Veteran

The man present at the birth of the 3rd Tennessee was also there at its end. John C. Brown had rejoined the army after his long convalescence and delivered a welcoming speech "in which he rated it [the men's escape] the greatest campaign of any war, comparing it to Napoleon crossing the Alps and other historical campaigns." Brown sounded as if he was campaigning for office.[16]

Bentonville was the last battle for the few 3rd Tennesseans still in the ranks, and within a few weeks after their odyssey behind Yankee lines, the war ended. On April 17th, four days after Abraham Lincoln was assassinated, Sherman pulled out a bottle of good whiskey, and as drinks were passed around, he and Joe Johnston worked out terms for the Army of Tennessee's surrender.

Like the Confederacy itself, the 3rd Tennessee had been worn down to little more than a pitiful remnant of a once powerful force. Of the more than 1200 men who served in its ranks, only seventy-nine men remained to muster out at Greensboro on April 26th. To say the least, the men faced an uncertain future; but with a bit of luck, and the political savvy of John C. Brown, the Tennesseans avoided much of the pain of reconstruction.

It was time for the ferocious men in tattered butternut uniforms, and their flag, to go home. To prevent capture by the enemy, John B. Kennedy of Company A, secreted the "blood stained, bullet-torn flag" under his clothing. Under Kennedy's care the flag was returned to Calvin Walker's widow in Lynnville. In a later year it was used to cover Walker's coffin at his reburial. Now it is displayed at the Tennessee State Museum.[17]

Notes for Chapter 21

1 *Battles and Leaders*, Vol.IV, pp. 696-700. Connelly, *Autumn of Glory*, p. 525.

2 *Ibid.* National Archives, Microfilm Publication Roll 134, File M268.

3 National Archives, *op. cit.*.

4 Connelly, *op. cit.,* pp. 526-527.

5 *Ibid.*, p. 526.

6 W.H. Ogilvie Memoir.

7 *Battles and Leaders*, Vol.IV, p. 703.

8 Ogilvie Memoir.

9 *Ibid.*

10 Rollbook, p. 273.

11 *Ibid.*, p. 260.

12 Ogilvie Memoir.

13 *Ibid.*

14 W.H. Ogilvie, *CV*, Vol. XV, p. 361 (editied version of the original).

15 *Ibid.*

16 Ogilvie Memoir.

17 *CV*, Vol. XXI, p. 240.

WIZARDS, GOBLINS, AND THE GOVERNOR

Slowly, but surely, by ones and twos, John C. Brown and the 3rd Tennessee arrived home. While the Federal army had shown generosity by allowing the immediate release on parole of the Confederates after their surrender, and had even broken bread with their former enemies, they made no arrangements for returning the men to Tennessee. The destitute former Rebels had to beg or steal enough food to stay alive as they hoofed back across former battlefields.

Once there, they found a countryside wreaked by marching armies, and few jobs. The situation was not helped by a tornado that devastated many of Giles County's best plantations later that December.

The 3rd Tennesseans also discovered that the 'institutions' they had fought four long years to defend were also undergoing radical change. Interestingly, these changes were not driven by the bluecoat army then occupying the state, or even by the radical Republican government then governing Tennessee. The instrument by which the North was busily unraveling the social fabric of old Tennessee society was a new agency called the Bureau of Freedmen, Refugees, and Abandoned Lands, or Freedmen's Bureau. Not content with simply setting the slaves free, in early 1865 hoards of idealistic Yankees from the Freedmen's Bureau descended on the Southland and set to teaching the newly emancipated blacks the responsibilities of citizenship, as well as the basic skills of reading, writing, and arithmetic. This direct assault on the "natural order of things" by these strange beings from the North created a general feeling of unease in Giles, Maury, and surrounding counties, especially since the ex-Confederates were still without the rights of citizenship themselves.[1]

The problem of citizenship was partially solved by the new president and fellow Tennessean, Andrew Johnson. On May 29th he issued a general amnesty proclaiming that ex-Confederate officials could regain their full rights of citizenship simply by making application. John C. Brown immediately asked Johnston for a pardon which the President quickly granted (Brown was fortunate. Robert E. Lee did not receive his pardon until the Jimmy Carter administration).[2]

There was another problem. Post war Tennessee was under the control of radical Republicans headed by the arch Confederate hater, Governor William G. Brownlow (Brownlow was also a Methodist minister, and seems to have equated secessionists with the worst kind of sinners). If Brownlow had his way, no Confederate would ever vote again, much less hold political office. This made for a volatile situation since the ex-Confederates were by far the most popular public figures in the state.

Then an event occurred in Pulaski during the spring of 1866, something quite innocent in its inception, but so terrible in its subsequent evolution that American society is still coping with its degrading impact on society.

Six young Confederate veterans, bored with the inactivity of civilian life after four years of the hard soldiering, were pondering how to add some excitement to their lives. Three of these men were former 3rd Tennesseans—Richard R. Reed, who joined the regiment sometime in its last year; John Lester, former commander of Company A; and John Kennedy, also of Company A, the same man that rescued the regimental flag. Lester suggested that they organize a club; all agreed that would be a capital idea.

They appointed a committee of three to come up with a name. This was a time of secret, ominous organizations such as the 'Know-Nothings' and 'Knights of the Golden Circle,' so the boys wanted a club name that sounded as sinister as possible. John Kennedy suggested the group adopt the Greek word for circle, or 'kuklos.' Then another member of the group, Jim Crowe, suggested they alter this to kuklux to add mystery to the meaning. Since the men were all Scotch-Irish, Kennedy suggested they add "klan" to the title. Lester loved it saying it reminded him of "bones rattling together."[3]

Next, they needed some impressive titles to go with their newly formed organization. Frank McCord got the top job of 'Grand Cyclops' probably because he had newspaper connections and could thereby propagate the 'aims' of the organization. As to just what these aims were, according to Lester, "There was entire unanimity among the members in regard to the end in view, which was diversion and amusement." John Kennnedy became 'Grand Magi' while John Lester was appointed a lowly 'Night Hawk.'[4]

These were very bright and energetic young men. Four would become lawyers, McCord a newspaper editor, and John Lester would become a state legislator. What transpired next bears all the markings of a college fraternity prank. That night, the men dawned sheets and pillow cases and went riding off through the streets of Pulaski whooping and hollering like mad men much to the amazement, and amusement, of the local citizens.

After the drabness of four years of grim war, the lunacy of the Pulaski Ku-Klux was wonderful comic relief; the men were the hit of Giles County. They soon were in big demand as entertainment for barbecues and other outdoor parties. They would swoop in on their horses in costumes even more outrageous than their original outfits, would dance with the girls, and speak in strange voices about ominous events in the future.

John Lester
Courtesy: KuKlux Klan: It's Origin, Growth, and Disbandment

The chief diversion for the group, however, was the initiation of new members. For this they devised an elaborate ceremony. Each new member was blindfolded and taken to an abandoned mansion a short distance west of Pulaski (one of those wrecked by the tornado the year before). A cap with large donkey ears was placed on the man's head, and he was then told to recite the following oath:

> O wad some power giftie gie us
> To see oursel's as ithers see us.

The blindfold was then removed as the man was standing before a large mirror. All present, including the initiate, would then break into great peals of laughter. Such was the comic relief provided by the original Ku Klux Klan.[5]

Among the new members quickly joining the Ku Klux were former 3rd Tennesseans: Robert A. Mitchell, former captain of Company B; Thomas E. McCoy, former captain of Company K; J.L. Nelson and John Moore, also of Company K; and C.C. Abernathy, formerly the regimental surgeon.[6]

For about a year, the Ku-Klux was relatively harmless. More and more men joined the Pulaski group. Imitation groups sprang up in central Tennessee, and in northern Alabama (since the

Ku-Klux had no stated purpose, the only qualification for forming a new 'Den' was to declare itself as such). Somewhere along the line, the organization took a mean turn.

The men first discovered that their group had an intimidating effect during the conduct of their initiation ceremonies. A costumed guard, or 'Lictor,' was placed along the road to the old mansion to insure privacy. "In a short time the Lictor of the Pulaski 'den' reported that travel along the road which he had his post had almost entirely stopped." These strange men with their strange doings were obviously making people uncomfortable.[7]

The group expanded their repertoire to include tricks aimed at the supposed superstitions of Blacks. Klansmen, claiming to be dead Confederate soldiers returned from some horrible battlefield, would suddenly remove a fake head or arm, or otherwise scare the newly freed individuals.

As the political climate heated up, more and more unsavory types joined the Ku-Klux seeing it as a vehicle for achieving more sinister aims. It was not long before the organization began to take on an entirely new purpose.

1867 was an election year for the Tennessee legislature. In preparation, Governor Brownlow tried to insure his own reelection first by granting Blacks the right to vote, and denying the same to all ex-Rebels. His opposition, a new party called the Conservatives, was made up of former Whigs such as John and Neill Brown, and former Democrats. Together these two groups contained most of the pre-war voting population of Tennessee. Under the new rules, most of these men were ineligible to vote. The Conservatives thought they could win anyway, assuming that most of the ex-slaves voting for the first time would abide by their former masters desires. They were wrong.

The Republicans won big in 1867. Not only that, the legislature approved the 14th Amendment to the U.S. Constitution making equal rights for the races the official law of the land. Although they did not realize it at the time, both of these events were a god-send to the long-range interests of the Conservatives in Tennessee.[8]

Having lost the 1867 elections, it suddenly dawned on Tennessee's white establishment that the Black population and their 'radical' friends were not wildly enthusiastic about returning to a pre-war status-quo. The Conservatives were in a state of near panic and desperately sought a means to regain some political power. It was at this moment that the interests of the white conservatives of Tennessee and the Ku-Klux Klan converged. The man largely responsible for main-streaming the Ku-Klux into the political process in Tennessee, and most other southern states, was Nathan Bedford Forrest came into the picture.[9]

During the summer of 1867, the Ku-Klux standardized its organization. A convention met in Nashville for this purpose, and adopted a set of rules and offices (which now included Goblins, Titans, Furies , Dragons, and Hydras). What the group really needed was a leader, or 'Grand Wizard' to give it some stature. That was where Forrest came in.

Forrest was working in Memphis as an insurance agent, and once he decided to join the group, was the perfect person to spread the group's message since, next to Robert E. Lee, he was probably the most admired ex-Confederate in the South. Forrest traveled as part of his business activities, and where he moved, Ku-Klux membership grew. By electing the old 'Wizard of the Saddle' to the office of 'Grand Wizard,' the Ku-Klux gained instant respectability. Citizens from the social mainstream, as well as political extremists, now became members, including John C. Brown. By the next year, 1868, Forrest estimated the group contained 40,000 members.[10]

The Klan's purpose was now political intimidation, and its targets were Blacks whom the Klan thought were becoming too independent, representatives of the Freedmen's Bureau, and especially members of the Union League, political activists for the Republican party active throughout the south.

For the next year, Tennessee simmered at the edge of anarchy. Brownlow's militia maintained nominal control, but the Klan ruled the night. Most of the population supported the rival conservative Democrats, and there was strong support for allowing ex-Confederates like Brown back into the political process. Tennessee teetered at the edge of a new civil war. A militia act was passed, and Brownlow immediately called its members into service declaring martial law in all counties where the Klan had been active. All out war appeared certain.

Despite the Klan's intimidation, one estimate by a Nashville newspaper claimed the Klan prevented 15,000 Giles County voters from participating in the election, the Republicans were victorious. Then, a remarkable thing occurred.

William Brownlow had made himself a candidate for senator in the election of 1868, and when the election ended, the new senator immediately departed for Washington.

He had hardly left the state when the crises ended.

Brownlow's handpicked successor for governor was DeWitt Senter. The best conclusion one can draw today is that Senter was a closet Conservative. The first words out of the new governor's mouth were conciliatory, and he immediately reversed most of the measures Brownlow had imposed against ex-Confederates just before he left office.

Sensing a change in the political wind, in March of 1869, John C. Brown and others convinced Forrest to officially disband the Ku-Klux. Most respectable citizens, including Forrest, were fed up with Klan violence by this time, so he readily complied. Brown then mustered a delegation of Giles County citizens and paid Senter a visit. Brown announced that the Giles County Ku-Klux was disbanded, and that the citizens of Giles County were ready to cooperate with the new governor. (Since Klan dens were independent, the organization continued to flourish in other locations anyway.)[11]

Soon after, the Tennessee Supreme Court re-enfranchised most of the ex-Confederates. With that Senter became even more conciliatory. In 1869, the Conservatives won control of the legislature. Since Tennessee had passed the 14th Amendment, the Federal government did not interfere. It was time for the old Confederates, and in particular, John C. Brown, to resume control in Tennessee politics.

John C. Brown was riding a wave of popularity at this point of his life. Not only was the Brown family still part of the social elite, not surprising that the Tennessee state constitutional convention elected John C. Brown its president and, indicating that his popularity crossed party lines, he was elected unanimously. In his opening speech, Brown set a moderate tone, and encouraged his fellow Tennesseans to adapt to the changes going on everywhere.

The challenge for Brown was finding a way to orchestrate the convention so power would be transferred back to the Conservative majority without incurring the wrath of the Republican Congress in Washington, and without inciting more violence at home.

The issue of restoring voting rights to ex-Conferderates was passed with little controversy, but there was also a strong movement to find a way to deny the vote to Blacks. Conservative delegates proposed a poll tax as an indirect means to achieve this end, one of the first of several methods southern states adopted to limit minority access to the ballot box.[12]

Brown came out of the convention with more prestige than ever. His moderation and evenhandedness throughout the rough and tumble debates made a positive impression on Conservatives and Republicans alike. He was at his peak of popularity (Brown had also mastered the politician's high art of issue straddling; he participated in only sixty-seven out of more than three-hundred and fifty votes taken during the course of the convention). Andrew Johnson later commented on Brown's political finesse: "He was a Whig, then he was a Know-Nothing, then he was a rebel, then a Greeley man ... . He is a Democrat! Why he is a perfect chameleon. When he is in the grass he's green, and when he is on the rail he is grey. Talk about such Democracy!" It was inevitable that he would be selected for high office.[13]

The Conservatives met in September of 1870, and by a unanimous vote, selected John C. Brown as their candidate for governor. For a platform, rather than proposing constructive policies to rebuild worn torn Tennessee, the Conservatives chose to denounce the Grant administration and its treatment of recalcitrant ex-Confederate states (who refused to endorse the Fourteenth, and newly proposed Fifteenth Amendments) and demanded that they be allowed back in the Union.

John C. Brown
Courtesy: Herb Peck, Jr.

Showing his usual political savvy, Brown ignored his party's inflammatory platform and championed progressive ideas like restoring the state's credit, building roads, and expanding educational opportunities. Brown won in a landslide.

While the election of Brown ended most of the political turmoil in Tennessee, the social turmoil continued. One of Brown's greatest challenges would be returning peace and harmony to the state in the midst of radical social change.

Memphis had been a hotbed of racial unrest since the war ended. Various white and black groups had divided themselves into armed camps, and perpetual violence was inevitable unless someone from outside the city took the initiative to bring the situation under control. By the start of Brown's second term, in 1873, U.S. Grant was prepared to do just that.

For several months Brown walked a tightrope, trying by various means to cajole city and county law enforcement agencies in Memphis to crack down on the Klan, offering rewards for the turning in of rioters, and even issuing a proclamation ordering all organized groups on both sides disbanded. Federal marshals began making arrests prompting Brown to protest directly to the president. Grant replied cordially but firmly that Brown was not to interfere with the enforcement of federal laws.[14]

It was in his dealings with the federal government that John C. Brown was at his political best. Brown brow-beat the Memphis law enforcement establishment into cracking down on ring leaders and eventually persuaded a local federal judge to grant the state of Tennessee jurisdiction. While the situation remained tense during Brown's entire administration, there was never a federal crackdown like those which occurred in some of the other Southern states.

Brown's biggest contribution as governor was probably in the advancement of public education. In the mid-1800s, the idea of universal education at public expense was a relatively novel idea. Brown, with his background as a teacher, believed absolutely that the key to Tennessee's future growth and prosperity was directly linked to public education. It took the better part of both his terms in office to get an education bill passed, but pass it did.

John's brother Neill was instrumental in convincing the legislature and the public that the bill was necessary. The fact that the definition of "everyone" included Blacks was undoubtedly the biggest problem, but the legislature resolved that issue by establishing "separate but equal" facilities for Negro children, creating another thorny problem for future generations.[15]

Brown was also a financial expert and eliminated most of the state's floating debt. Of course any new taxes created considerable hardship for post-war Tennessee, so, as Brown improved the financial condition of the state, his popularity diminished accordingly.

In 1874, Brown announced his intention of not seeking a third term as governor. Part of his decision was probably based on his reduced popularity. Though he had been accused of 'chameleon' behavior in the past, he had addressed Tennessee's problems head-on, and naturally had alienated large segments of the population in the process. The Nashville Banner said "John Brown is a dead cock in the pit." In Memphis, where Brown successfully locked up many of his old Klan cronies, a politician felt "Brown couldn't be elected to carry water to a kennel of sick dogs in any part of Shelby County."[17]

Brown still had friends in the Tennessee legislature, and since U.S. Senators were still chosen by the state senate in the 1870's, Brown decided to pursue that high office. The 1875 contest evolved into a three way race between Brown, Brown's old wartime comrade William Bate, and Brown's arch political enemy, Andrew Johnson. The legislature convened on January 20, 1875, to elect the new senator. It quickly split hopelessly into three factions with Johnson in the lead, but without sufficient support to win the majority. The session turned into a political brawl "beyond the limits of decorum," as the Speaker of the House put it. Brown and Bate supporters vied over who should be the Conservative candidate. Eventually Brown withdrew, but that still did not provide sufficient support to get Bate elected. Finally, after fifty-five ballots, Johnson was selected.[18]

That ended John C. Brown's active political career in Tennessee. However, he would have one more brush with raucous reconstruction politics. In 1876, Louisiana elected two complete state governments, and both attempted to rule the state simultaneously. Louisiana appeared to be on the verge of its own civil war. The federal government took action to head off the crisis, forming a commission to mediate. John C. Brown was selected as a distinguished Southern representative to give the commission more credibility.

The two sides were divided between the Democrats, or People's Party, and the Republicans, or 'carpetbag' element. Brown, always the compromiser, managed to get the two sides to agree that the Democratic governor would hold that seat while all Republicans properly elected according to parish rules would take their seats in the legislature. Once the legislature was seated, the conflict soon dissolved.[19]

Brown devoted the rest of his life to railroading. He first took a position as vice-president of the Texas and Pacific Railroad which had ambitions of being the first southern transcontinental line. With his southern background and his considerable experience with railroad financing as governor, Brown appeared to be an ideal choice to spearhead the project to the northern financiers backing the project. Brown's job was to obtain financial support from both Congress and the Texas legislature. This proved to be a daunting task.

Brown encountered strong opposition at both state and national levels from the already established transcontinental corporations, the Union Pacific and Central Pacific lines. A third company, the Southern Pacific, was also in direct competition with the Texas Pacific. Brown presented financial packages to congress at least three times, and got nowhere. Then in 1880, Jay Gould entered the picture. Gould purchased a controlling interest in the Texas Pacific and shortly after concluded a deal with the Southern Pacific. Together the two rail companies completed the new transcontinental line. Brown managed most of the Texas Pacific operations out of his headquarters in Marshall, Texas. In 1888, he became its president.[20]

The intense pressure of corporate management, the stress caused by several years of turbulent politics, and the deaths of two

John C. Brown's grave marker.
Courtesy: Author

of his daughters took their toll on the aging Tennessean, and in the spring of 1889, Brown resigned from the Texas Pacific. He returned to Nashville, where he built a his third new home since the end of the war.

It was not long before the always intense Brown tired of the quiet pace of retired life, and despite declining health, he accepted the presidency of the Tennessee Iron and Coal Company. In August, he visited his family vacationing in New Jersey. Upon returning home, after conducting some business in Birmingham, he decided to take some time off. He traveled to the health spa at Red Boiling Springs, Tennessee, where on the evening of August 16, 1889, he began coughing up blood. The local doctor did what little he could, including traveling to Gallatin to fetch some shaved ice which Brown had been accustomed to using to treat his ailment which appears to have been stomach ulcers. The doctor was not equipped to handle someone so desperately ill, and on August 17, Brown died. His final words, "I would give a thousand dollars to be in Nashville," reflect the spirit of the true capitalist the old warrior had become. While Yankee bullets could not kill Brown, Yankee capitalism could.[21]

Funeral services in Nashville were presided over by Bishop Quintard, one of Brown's comrades from the Army of Tennessee. He was buried in the family plot in Maplewood Cemetery in Pulaski. A life-sized marble statue of Brown in full military regalia marks his grave.

Thus ended the life of one of Tennessee's most colorful and controversial political figures, and one of its true warriors of the Civil War.

Notes for Chapter 22

1 Wyn C. Wade, *The Fiery Cross: The Ku Klux Klan in America*, pp. 12-14.

2 Butler, The Life of John C. Brown, p. 26.

3 John C. Lester and D.L. Wilson, *KuKlux Klan: Its Origens, Growth, and Disbandment*, pp. 21-23.

4 *Ibid.*

5 *Ibid.*, pp. 58-64.

6 *Ibid.*, pp. 21-23.

7 Wade, *op. cit.*, pp. 35-37.

8 P.M. Hamer, *Tennessee, A History, 1673-1932,* Vol. II, pp. 616-617.

9 Wade, *op. cit.*, pp. 16-17, 40-41.

10 Butler, *op. cit.*, pp. 31-34.

11 *Nashville Union and Dispatch*, November 10, 1868.

12 Journal of the Constitutional Convention of 1870, pp. 7-8.

13 *Knoxville Daily Chronicle*, December 13, 1871.

14 Butler, *op. cit.*, p. 66.

15 *Ibid.*, pp. 71-84.

16 John Allison, *Notable Men of Tennessee*, p. 102.

17 *Nashville Banner*, May 10, 1874.

18 Butler, *op. cit.*, pp. 107-108.

19 *Ibid.*, pp. 113-115.

20 *Ibid.*, pp. 111-112.

21 Margaret I. Phillips, The Governors of Tennessee, p. 94. Lewis K. Smith, "Historical Sketches and Traditions of Jackson County, Tennessee." White, *Speeches of the Governors of Tennessee*, Vol.VI, p. 116. Butler, *op. cit.*, pp. 117-118.

EPILOGUE

The 3rd Tennessee was composed of top quality human material, and like John C. Brown, many of the soldiers went on to successful post-war careers. William Polk, the regiment's first sergeant major, became a successful planter with large holdings in Mississippi. George McLaurine of Company B was equally successful planting cotton in Alabama as was James T. Henderson of Company K in Arkansas.

John S. Wilkes, the regimental commissary officer, wrote the official history of the regiment for the *Military Annals of Tennessee.* Wilkes, a close associate to Brown, was a brilliant accountant and was Brown's ex-officio attorney general for a while during Brown's stint as governor. He served as Brown's treasurer throughout his railroading career.

Alfred Jones, who started the war as second lieutenant of Company G, had possibly the most remarkable post-war career. Sometime after Fort Donelson Jones transferred to the 17th Tennessee and became regimental surgeon. When the war ended, he became a full time physician, then a professor of medicine at the University of Tennessee. He became a bank president in Cornersville, and later served terms in Tennessee's lower house and in its senate.

The youngest soldier in the regiment, Liles E. Abernathy of Company A, became president of the Commercial Bank and Trust in Pulaski.

But most of the men led ordinary lives as farmers and tradesmen, and for most of them the great War Between the States remained the peak experience in their lives. For well into the Twentieth Century, the veterans held frequent reunions. The commemorative ribbons the men wore, some with John C. Brown' s likeness inscribed on them, can still be found at Civil War shows. Brown's wife, Elizabeth, was prominent in post-war commemorative societies, and she was the second president of the United Daughters of the Confederacy.

As the years passed, the number of survivors from the regiment became less and less. One of the oldest survivors was W.F.(or W.J.) Tucker who lived to be 90 years old and died in 1928. Another was Lieutenant Alonzo Lindsey of Company I. A large cotton grower and grocery wholesaler, Lindsey died at age 91 in Lawrenceburg in 1932.

Not all of the regiment's survivors lived such long lives. In 1881, David Rhea was attempting to return to his farm from Pulaski, and in attempting to cross a swollen creek, he, his Black companion, buggy and all were swept down stream. Rhea was an expert swimmer and easily reached the shore with his friend in tow. Rhea saw that his horse was struggling and dove back into the water. In the process of attempting to save his horse he lost his life.[1]

In succeeding years, nearly every town contributing a company to the regiment erected a Confederate war memorial in its town square, the most visible manifestation of post-war Southern nostalgia. The dedication of the statue was always a major event, with some of the survivors as guests of honor. Walter Jennings, last commander of the 3rd Tennessee, was present for the dedication at Mount Pleasant, located in the Bigby Creek Valley of Maury County. Octavia Zollicoffer Bond reported some highlights:

> Neither delaying nor holding back the best, Bigby Valley ungrudgingly gave to the cause her sixteen-year-old boys of promise,

her choice young men of twenty-five. It was the hope and pride of each Bigby family who hastened in the early spring of 1861 to join the company being then organized in the village of Mt. Pleasant by Capt. (afterward Col.) Fount Wade under the name of 'Bigby Grays,' a picked band that was one of the first ten companies of Tennessee volunteers enlisted in the war. At Nashville on May 16 they were mustered in as Company C of the 3rd Tennessee Infantry.

From Donelson to Bentonville those youthful soldiers bore the hardships of march, bivouac, and battle with the fortitude of veterans. Under Gens. John C. Brown, Albert Sidney Johnston, Bragg, Polk, and Hood they were dedicated to Southern principles in the fires of Chickasaw Bayou, Port Hudson, Chickamauga, and holocausts around Atlanta. Few came back to the beautiful valley unmaimed or alive except as their memories persist in the hearts of their grateful countrymen...

It was her day of achievement when on the 27th of September, 1907, the monument was unveiled in ... the city of Mt. Pleasant on the spot where forty-seven years ago the 'Bigby Grays' had made their vows of war and accepted their virgin banner from the hands of a typical Bigby maiden, Miss Matt Dobbins [Mattie Dobbins was also at the ceremony]. It was a day of grace for all in the green lands of Big and Little Bigby when Capt. W.S. Jennings, a former commander of the 'Grays,' led a troop of mounted Veterans, and Sons of Veterans, flying the colors of the State and the Confederacy ... .

Thousands of hearts beat 'double-quick' when the Fayetteville band emerged from the train to the strains of "Dixie" ...[2]

They still do.

Notes for Epilogue

1 All data on individual soldiers compiled from *Confederate Veteran.*

2 *Confederate Veteran*, Vol.XVI, pp. 270-271.

ROSTER
3rd Tennessee Infantry
May 16, 1861 - Surrender

Notes on the Appendix

The following individual service records are based primarily on entries contained in the 3rd Tennessee Rollbook, the paroles issued to each surviving member of the regiment at the surrender of the Army of Tennessee near Greensboro, N.C., pension records, and other documents recording the service activities of the men recorded at various times after the war.

The primary source of information, the Rollbook, is divided into two parts. The first part records the activities of the men from the organization of the regiment on May 16, 1861, through the battle of Fort Donelson. The second part begins with the reorganization of the regiment on September 26, 1862, and ends with the conclusion of the war. The individual records are a consolidated summary of the information contained in both parts of the Rollbook. Each man is listed at the highest rank held during course of the war. Participation in minor skirmishes is not listed. It should be noted that few entries were made after commencement of the Atlanta campaign, so records from that point on are very sparse. Some of the entries detailing events from 1864 on are in the handwriting of someone who was obviously well along in years and were likely made well after the conclusion of the war.

Occasionally records will provide multiple spellings of service members' names. In these cases both versions are listed.

ROSTER

3rd Tennessee Infantry

* Died in service
** Killed in battle
# Present at final surrender
( ) Alternate spelling or initial

Command and Staff

Colonel

John Calvin Brown, elected May 16, 1861; commanded brigade at Fort Donelson; imprisoned at Fort Warren; promoted to brigadier general.

** Calvin H. Walker, commanded Company G at Fort Donelson; imprisoned at Camp Chase and Johnson's Island; exchanged Sep. 16, 1862; elected colonel Sep. 26, 1862; absent sick during Chickasaw Bayou battle; in command at Port Hudson, Raymond, Jackson; and Chickamauga; absent sick from Missionary Ridge; in command at Resaca and New Hope Church; killed at Kolb's Farm.

Lieutenant Colonel

Thomas M.L. Gordon, elected May 16, 1861; commanded regt. at Fort Donelson until wounded; resigned 1862.

** Calvin J. Clack, in command of Company A at Fort Donelson; imprisoned at Camp Chase and Johnson's Island; exchanged Sep. 16, 1862; elected lieutenant colonel Sep. 26, 1862; commanded regt. at Chickasaw Bayou; present at Port Hudson, Raymond, Jackson, and Chickamauga; commanded regt. at Missionary Ridge; present at Resaca, New Hope Church, and Kolb's Farm; commanded regt. at Atlanta and Jonesboro where he was killed.

Major

Nat. F. Cheairs, elected May 16, 1862; commanded regt. at Fort Donelson until wounded; imprisoned at Fort Warren; exchanged and resigned Aug., 1862.

** Thomas M. Tucker, appointed adjutant May 17, 1861; wounded Fort Donelson; imprisoned at Camp Chase and Fort Warren; exchanged Aug., 1862; elected major, Sep. 26, 1862; killed at Chickasaw Bayou Dec. 29, 1862.

** Flavel C. Barber, commanded Company K at Fort Donelson; imprisoned at Camp Chase and Johnson's Island; exchanged Sep. 16, 1862; present at Port Hudson, Raymond, and Jackson; on furlough during Chickamauga battle; present at Missionary Ridge; killed at Resaca.

Adjutant

David S. Martin, elected junior 2nd lieutenant of Company A; captured at Fort Donelson; imprisoned at Camp Chase and Johnson's Island; exchanged Sep. 16, 1862; appointed adjutant Sep. 26, 1862; present at Chickasaw Bayou, Port Hudson, and Raymond; commanded his old company (A) at Jackson; on furlough during Chickamauga; present at Missionary Ridge; surrendered at Greensboro, N.C..

Quarter Master

Ben P. Roy, appointed depot quartermaster at Bowling Green Nov. 19, 1861; became brigade quartermaster in Brown's Brigade Sep. 30, 1862.

J.L. Herron, appointed Jan., 1862 from Company I; present at Fort Donelson; imprisoned at Camp Chase and Fort Warren; exchanged Aug., 1862; resigned Oct. 20, 1862.

John D. Flautt, appointed Oct. 21, 1862; detailed to Commissary Dept. at Camp Cheatham; detailed to Quartermaster at Corinth Apr. 15, 1862; rejoined regt. Oct. 1, 1862.

Commissary

* B.L. Wilkes, appointed May 17, 1861; died at Camp Chase Mar., 1862.

John S. Wilkes (regimental historian), appointed commissary sergeant May 17, 1861; imprisoned Camp Douglas; exchanged Sep. 23, 1862; appointed commissary officer Sep. 26, 1862; on furlough Sep. 26 to Dec. 15, 1862; survived the war.

Surgeon

Saml. H. Stout, appointed May 17, 1861; transferred to Gordon Hospital, Nashville, Tenn., Nov. 11, 1861; post surgeon at Chattanooga; Director of Hospitals, Army of Tennessee, 1862.

James A. Bowers, appointed Nov. 11, 1861; escaped from capture at Fort Donelson Feb. 28, 1862; rejoined regt. Dec. 15, 1862; made chief surgeon of Gregg's Brigade; remained with wounded at Raymond; rejoined regt. in Jun., 1863, then made chief surgeon of Walker's Division.

Daniel F. Wright, assigned as surgeon, Jul. 3, 1863; resigned Dec. 1, 1863.

C.C. Abernathy, assigned Feb., 1864.

Assistant Surgeon

Wiley S. Perry, appointed May 17, 1861; missed Fort Donelson tending the sick at Russellville; resigned.

J.T.S. Thompson, appointed Sep. 26, 1862; detailed to Secret Service Feb. 22, 1864.

J.L. Lipford, appointed Jun. 1, 1863; relieved Jul. 1, 1863.

J.C. Henderson, appointed in 1863; relieved Feb. 5, 1864.

Thomas H. Moss, appointed Feb. 5, 1864.

Chaplain

Marcus Williams, appointed May 17, 1861; departed Fort Donelson with the wounded Feb. 14, 1862: never returned.

Thomas H. Deavenport, served as a private with Company G at Fort Donelson; imprisoned at Camp Douglas; exchanged Sep. 23, 1862; appointed chaplain at reorganizaton; resigned Apr., 1863 and went on leave of absence; no approval received so rejoined the regt. Jan. 25, 1864; surrendered at Greensboro, N.C..

Sergeant Major

William Polk, appointed May 17, 1861; wounded at Fort Donelson on Feb. 15, 1862, and sent home; appointed adjutant of 48th Tenn. at exchange.

John Phillips, present at Chickasaw Bayou, Port Hudson, Raymond, Jackson, and Chickamauga; absent sick from Missionary Ridge.

Quarter Master Sergeant

J.F. Alexander, detached at Bowling Green; remained in Quarter Master.

J.W. Littleton, appointed Jan., 1862; imprisoned Camp Douglas; exchanged Sep. 23, 1862.

Lewis Amos, as a private detailed to accompany corpse of Sergeant Simpson home during Fort Donelson battle; served in cavalry until exchange; appointed quarter master sergeant Dec. 15, 1862.

Commissary Sergeant

* R.S. Wilkes, appointed Dec. 15, 1862; took sick leave Jun. 23, 1863; died at Aberdeen, Miss..

S.S. Craig, appointed Sep., 1863; surrendered at Greensboro, N.C..

Ordnance Sergeant

Ben. S. Thomas, appointed Sep. 26, 1862; as a private present at Fort Donelson; imprisoned at Camp Douglas; exchanged Sep. 23, 1862; promoted to 3rd sergeant at reorganization; appointed ordnance sergeant Sep. 26, 1863; surrendered at Greensboro, N.C..

Hospital Steward

Eber Fry, appointed May 17, 1861; escaped from Fort Donelson after surrendered and never returned.

Robert P. Jenkins, appointed Sep. 26, 1862; present at Fort Donelson; imprisoned at Camp Douglas; exchanged Sep. 23, 1862; appointed hospital steward, Sep. 26, 1862.

Company A (later G)

Captain

David Rhea, as 1st lieutenant present at Fort Donelson; imprisoned at Camp Chase; escaped Mar., 1862; promoted to captain in Sep., 1862; commanded the company at Chickasaw Bayou; absent sick until the beginning of the Atlanta campaign; surrendered at Greensboro, N.C..

1st Lieutenant

(All appointed to this position were immediately appointed to higher office)

2nd Lieutenant

* Leonidas Black, sick at Fort Donelson but in the trenches; imprisoned at Camp Chase; died April 21, 1862.

John C. Lester, served as a private at Fort Donelson; imprisoned at Camp Douglas; exchanged Sep. 23, 1862; promoted to 2nd lieutenant at reorganization; present at Chickasaw Bayou; absent sick until Chickamauga; commanded company at Missionary Ridge; surrendered at Greensboro, N.C..

Junior 2nd Lieutenant

Wallace W. Rutledge, as 3rd sergeant present at Fort Donelson; imprisoned at Camp Douglas; exchanged Sep. 23, 1862; promoted to junior 2nd lieutenant at reorganization; absent sick until Port Hudson; commanded company at Raymond and was captured; imprisoned at Johnson's Island.

1st Sergeant

Joseph V. Cowan, detached to Porter's Battery at Fort Donelson; captured and escaped after the surrender; discharged Mar., 1862.

Francis M. Bunch, as a private present at Fort Donelson; imprisoned at Camp Douglas; exchanged Sep. 23, 1862; promoted to 1st sergeant at reorganization; present at Chickasaw Bayou and Port Hudson; wounded at Raymond; AWOL at Chickamauga parts of both days; present at Missionary Ridge, Resaca, New Hope Church, Atlanta, Jonesboro, and Murfreesboro.

2nd Sergeant

John Phillips, sick during Fort Donelson battle; imprisoned at Camp Douglas; exchanged Sep.23, 1862; no further record.

John D. Wright, as a private present at Fort Donelson; imprisoned at Camp Douglas; exchanged Sep. 23, 1862; promoted to 2nd sergeant at reorganization; present at Chickasaw Bayou, Port Hudson, Raymond, Jackson, Chickamauga, and Missionary Ridge. Survived the war.

3rd Sergeant

Thomas J. Wells, as a private present at Fort Donelson; imprisoned at Camp Douglas; exchanged Sep. 23, 1862; promoted to 3rd sergeant at reorganization; present at Chickasaw Bayou, Port Hudson, Raymond (infirmary corps), and Jackson; then detached.

4th Sergeant

Richard B. Buford, permanently detached to sappers and miners Oct., 1861.

John D. Reynolds, as a private absent sick during Fort Donelson; imprisoned at Camp Douglas; exchanged Sep. 23, 1862; promoted at reorganization; present at Chickasaw Bayou, Port Hudson and Raymond; then absent sick.

5th Sergeant

* William F. Simpson, transferred to 32nd Tenn. Dec., 1861; died soon after at Bowling Green.

William W. Smith, promoted Dec., 1861; present at Fort Donelson; imprisoned at Camp Douglas; exchanged Sep. 23, 1862.

J. Thomas Adams, as a private present at Fort Donelson; imprisoned at Camp Douglas; exchanged Sep. 23, 1862; promoted to 5th sergeant at reorganization; present at Chickasaw Bayou and Port Hudson; wounded at Raymond; absent thereafter.

1st Corporal

William McCallum, discharged for disability at Camp Trousdale Sep., 1861.

William Madison, promoted Sep., 1861; absent from Fort Donelson sick at Bowling Green; transferred to 35th Tenn. and made 2nd lieutenant.

John Kennedy, as a private present at Fort Donelson; imprisoned at Camp Douglas; exchanged Sep. 23, 1862; promoted to 1st corporal at reorganization; present at Chickasaw Bayou, Port Hudson, Raymond, and Jackson; wounded at Chickamauga; absent from Missionary Ridge due to wound; surrendered at Greensboro, N.C..

2nd Corporal

P. Bruce Plummer, detailed clerk to Col. Brown; left Fort Donelson with wounded and never returned to regt..

Enoch H. Bunch, as a private sick during Fort Donelson battle; imprisoned

at Camp Douglas; exchanged Sep. 23, 1862; promoted to 2nd corporal at reorganization; present at Chickasaw Bayou, Port Hudson, Raymond, and Jackson; AWOL part of both days at Chickamauga; absent sick at Missionary Ridge. Surrendered at Greensboro, N.C..

3rd Corporal

William R. Smith, promoted in 1861; present at Fort Donelson; imprisoned at Camp Douglas; exchanged Sep. 23, 1862.

Thomas J. Flippen, as a private present at Fort Donelson; imprisoned at Camp Douglas; exchanged Sep. 23, 1862; promoted to 3rd corporal at reorganization; present at Chickasaw Bayou, Port Hudson, Raymond,and Jackson; absent sick from Chickamauga; present at Missionary Ridge.

4th Corporal

A.S. Ayrnett, AWOL at Fort Donelson; captured and imprisoned at Camp Douglas; exchanged Sep. 23, 1862.

Spencer D. Clack, as a private sick during Fort Donelson battle; imprisoned at Camp Douglas; exchanged Sep. 23, 1862; promoted to 4th corporal at reorganization; captured at Springdale, Miss. Dec. 4, 1862; held at Alton, Ill.; exchanged at City Point, Va., May 11, 1863; present at Raymond; absent sick from Jackson; present at Chickamauga; on furlough during Missionary Ridge battle; surrendered at Greensboro, N.C..

Private

Abernathy, J.M., present at Fort Donelson; imprisoned at Camp Douglas; exchanged Sep. 23, 1862; absent inebriated during Chickasaw Bayou battle; absent sick from Raymond; present first day at Chickamauga, AWOL the second; AWOL from Missionary Ridge.

* Abernathy, L.D., present at Fort Donelson, imprisoned at Camp Douglas; exchanged Sep. 23, 1862; died at Jackson, Miss., Oct. 8, 1862.

Abernathy, Liles E., present at Fort Donelson; imprisoned and exchanged Sep. 23, 1862; discharged at Port Hudson as non-conscript Mar. 10, 1863.

Abernathy, T.O., sick in quarters at Fort Donelson;imprisoned at Camp Douglas; exchanged Sep. 23, 1862; present at Chickasaw Bayou and Port Hudson; absent sick from Raymond; present at Chickamauga and Missionary Ridge.

Abernathy, William J., present at Fort Donelson; imprisoned at Camp Douglas; exchanged Sep. 23, 1862; present at Chickasaw Bayou and Port Hudson; captured at Raymond; imprisoned at Fort Delaware and Point Lookout.

Adams, Lewis L., present at Fort Donelson, imprisoned at Camp Douglas; exchanged Sep. 15, 1862; absent sick from Chickasaw Bayou; present at Port Hudson; transferred to 1st Tenn. Cavalry Apr. 1, 1863.

Amis, Lewis, absent from Fort Donelson; detailed to accompany the corpse of Sgt. Simpson home; served in cavalry until exchanged and then rejoined.

Anderson, D.G., enlisted Oct. 26, 1862; absent sick from Chickasaw Bayou; present at Port Hudson, Raymond, Jackson, Chickamauga, and Missionary Ridge.

Anderson, J.P., enlisted Oct. 26, 1862; present at Chickasaw Bayou, Port Hudson, Raymond, and Jackson; absent sick from Chickamauga; present at Missionary Ridge.

Ayrnett, John M., absent from Fort Donelson, sick at Russelville; no further record.

Barber, Robert J., wounded at Fort Donelson; imprisoned at Camp Douglas, exchanged Sep. 23, 1862; captured at Oxford, Miss., Nov., 1862; exchanged Mar. 25, 1863; captured at Raymond; imprisoned at Fort Delaware and Point Lookout.

* Barnes, J.H., enlisted Dec. 17, 1862; substitute for J.L. Barnes; present at Chickasaw Bayou; died at Port Hudson, Feb., 1863.

Barnes, J. Luke, sick during Fort Donelson battle; imprisoned at Camp Douglas; exchanged Sep. 23, 1862; discharged for having provided a substitute Dec. 20, 1862.

* Bass, Nathan H., died at home Jul., 1861.

Beckham, Green B., absent Fort Donelson sick at Bowling Green; never returned.

* Bennett, J.M., died at home Sep., 1861.

Brister, W.T., present at Fort Donelson; imprisoned at Camp Douglas; exchanged Sep. 23, 1862; absent sick from Chickasaw Bayou; present at Port Hudson; wounded at Raymond; present at Jackson and Chickamauga; wounded at Missionary Ridge; survived the war.

Brown, Leon., present at Fort Donelson; imprisoned at Camp Douglas; exchanged Sep. 23, 1862; present at Chickasaw Bayou and Port Hudson; transferred to 1st Tenn. Cavalry, Apr. 26, 1863.

Buchanan, Chesley M., wounded at Fort Donelson; left behind and joined an Arkansas regiment where he became a lieutenant.

Buford, Charles, present at Fort Donelson; imprisoned at Camp Douglas; exchanged Sep. 23, 1862; on furlough during Chickasaw Bayou battle; present at Port Hudson, Raymond, Jackson, and Chickamauga; wounded at Missionary Ridge.

Buford, Eb. G., wounded at Fort Donelson and permanently diabled; rejoined regt. after exchange; discharged Oct., 1862.

Buford, Gilbert T., present at Fort Donelson; imprisoned at Camp Douglas: exchanged Sep. 23, 1862; on leave during Ckickasaw Bayou battle; present at Port Hudson and Raymond; detailed as cook at Jackson; went to the rear the first day at Chickamauga and did not return the second; absent sick at Missionary Ridge.

Bunch, Alexander, present at Fort Donelson; imprisoned at Camp Douglas; exchanged Sep. 23, 1862; present at Chickasaw Bayou, Port Hudson, and Raymond; captured at Canton, Miss., Jul., 1863; paroled Mar. 1, 1864.

** Bunch, James W., killed at Fort Donelson Feb. 15, 1862.

Bunch, T.J., enlisted Nov. 14, 1862; present at Chickasaw Bayou and Port Hudson; captured at Raymond; paroled and rejoined his company Oct. 1, 1863; present at Missionary Ridge; survived the war.

* Burton, William P., present at Fort Donelson; died at Camp Douglas May, 1862.

Carter, R.V., absent from Fort Donelson on detached duty with cavalry; entered cavalry permanently after regt. captured at Fort Donelson.

Causby, Thomas, discharged for disability at Camp Cheatham May 28, 1861.

Cosby, E.H.F., enlisted Nov. 10, 1862; present at Port Hudson; absent sick from Raymond; captured Jun, 1863, near Big Black, Miss..

Chamber, Ed., enlisted Nov. 10, 1862; present at Port Hudson; absent sick from Raymond and Jackson; present at Chickamauga; absent sick from Missionary Ridge; surrendered at Greensboro, N.C..

Chambers, William T., present at Fort Donelson; captured but released after he took the oath of alligience to the U.S. at St. Louis; rejoined the regt. after its exchange; absent sick from Chickasaw Bayou; present at Port Hudson and Raymond; wounded the first day at Chickamauga; absent sick at Missionary Ridge; survived the war.

\# Deavenport, H., enlisted Nov. 3, 1862; absent sick from Chickasaw Bayou, Port Hudson, Raymond, and Jackson; absent barefoot from Chickamauga; absent sick from Missionary Ridge; surrendered at Greensboro, N.C..

Dickson, James M., absent from Fort Donelson sick at home; served with cavalry until the regt. was exchanged; present at Port Hudson and Raymond; absent sick from Jackson, Chickamauga, and Missionary Ridge; survived the war.

Dyer, John W., absent from Fort Donelson sick at Russellville; served with cavalry until exchange; present at Chickasaw Bayou, Port Hudson, Raymond and Jackson; lost his left arm the first day at Chickamauga; permanently disabled.

Everly, John H., detailed as teamster during Fort Donelson battle; served in cavalry until exchange; absent sick from Chickasaw Bayou and Port Hudson; captured at Raymond.

Everly, William D., present at Fort Donelson; imprisoned at Camp Douglas; exchanged Sep. 23, 1862.

Flippen, Joseph, present at Fort Donelson; imprisoned at Camp Douglas; exchanged Sep. 23, 1862; present at Chickasaw Bayou, Port Hudson, and Raymond; captured at Jackson, Jul. 15, 1863.

Garner, J.K.P., present at Fort Donelson; imprisoned at Camp Douglas; exchanged Sep. 23, 1862; present at Chickasaw Bayou and Port Hudson; wounded at Raymond; captured at Jackson, Jul. 15, 1863.

** Goode, Patrick, present at Fort Donelson; imprisoned at Camp Butler, IL; exchanged Sep. 23, 1862; present at Chickasaw Bayou, Port Hudson Raymond, Jackson, Chickamouga, and Missionary Ridge; killed at Resaca, May 14, 1864.

** Gordon, Edward M., mortally wounded at Fort Donelson; died on way to Nashville.

Gordon, John A., transferred to Col. Biffle's cavalry at Bowling Green, Oct., 1861.

Grubbs, W.L., detailed as teamster; never rejoined regt..

Hainey, John L., absent from Fort Donelson, sick at Russellville; joined 1st Tenn..

Hall, James K.P., present at Fort Donelson; imprisoned Camp Douglas; exchanged Sep. 23, 1862; present at Chickasaw Bayou and Port Hudson; deserted May 4, 1863.

Hamlett, J.H., present at Fort Donelson; imprisoned at Camp Douglas; exchanged Sep. 23, 1862; present at Chickasaw Bayou and Port Hudson; captured at Raymond; imprisoned at Fort Delaware and Point Lookout.

Hancock, Enoch, present at Fort Donelson; imprisoned at Camp Douglas; escaped Jun. 19, 1862 and served in the cavalry until exchange; present at Chickasaw Bayou; absent sick from Port Hudson; present at Raymond, Jackson, Chickamauga, and Missionary Ridge.

* Hancock, Luke, died at home Aug. 16, 1861.

* Harwell, R.F., present at Fort Donelson; imprisoned at Camp Douglas; died in prison May 13, 1862.

** Haygood, G.W., present at Fort Donelson; imprisoned at Camp Douglas; exchanged Sep. 23, 1862; present at Chickasaw Bayou and Port Hudson; killed at Raymond.

Hickey, James, enlisted Sep. 7, 1863; substitute for George Short; deserted the same day.

Holt, Algernon S., present at Fort Donelson; imprisoned at Camp Douglas, exchanged Sep. 23, 1862; detached at Tippah Ford, La., Nov., 1862; captured at Vicksburg Jul. 4, 1863; paroled and deserted in Aug., 1863.

Holt, F.M., enlisted Nov. 15, 1862; absent sick from Chickasaw Bayou, Port Hudson, and Raymond; present at Jackson; deserted Aug. 1, 1863.

Holt, Thomas H., present at Fort Donelson; imprisoned at Camp Douglas; exchanged Sep. 23, 1862; present at Chickasaw Bayou, Port Hudson, Jackson, Chickamauga, and Missionary Ridge; surrendered at Greensboro, N.C..

Holt, Wyatt L., present at Fort Donelson; imprisoned at Camp Douglas; exchanged Sep. 23, 1862; present at Chickasaw Bayou and Port Hudson; captured at Raymond; was paroled but did not rejoin the company until Nov. 1, 1863; present at Missionary Ridge; survived the war.

Hopkins, Benjamin F., present at Fort Donelson; imprisoned at Camp Douglas; escaped May 31, 1862 and rejoined regt. after exchange; present at Chickasaw Bayou, Port Hudson, and Raymond; captured Jul. 15, 1863, at Jackson; escaped and rejoined company Nov. 17, 1863; present at Missionary Ridge.

** Jackson, Thomas L., present at Fort Donelson; imprisoned at Camp Douglas; exchanged Sep. 23, 1862; absent inebriated from Chickasaw Bayou; present at Port Hudson; killed at Raymond.

Jones, Thomas W., present at Fort Donelson; imprisoned at Camp Douglas; exchanged Sep. 23, 1862; present at Chickasaw Bayou; discharged as a non-conscript at Port Hudson, Mar. 10, 1863.

Kennedy, Joseph, wounded at Fort Donelson; sent home and entered Scott's Louisiana Cavalry.

Latta, William A., absent during Fort Donelson battle; joined the 1st Tenn. Cavalry; wounded and disabled at Corinth.

Lindsay, Thomas F, musician; wounded at Fort Donelson; sent home permanently disabled.

Lucy, W.H., detailed as teamster; missed Fort Donelson; rejoined regt. after exchange; present at Chickasaw Bayou; absent sick from Port Hudson; captured at Raymond and imprisoned at Fort Delaware and Point Lookout.

Macklin, M.M., present at Fort Donelson; imprisoned at Camp Douglas; exchanged Sep. 23, 1862; transferred to 53rd Tenn. Oct. 9, 1862.

Martin, John, enlisted Dec. 13, 1862; on detached duty until Mar. 8, 1864 when he rejoined the company at Dalton, Ga..

McCallum, James J., discharged for disability at Bowling Green, Oct., 1861.

McCracken, J.F., absent from Fort Donelson, sick at Russellville; served in cavalry until the regt. was exchanged; rejoined the regt. at Port Hudson; present at Raymond and Jackson; AWOL from Chickamauga; absent sick from Missionary Ridge; surrendered at Greensboro, N.C..

* McCracken, John W., present at Fort Donelson; imprisoned at Camp Douglas; exchanged Sep. 23, 1862; present at Chickasaw Bayou and Port Hudson; captured at Raymond; died at Fort Delaware.

McDonald, R.F., present at Fort Donelson; imprisoned at Camp Douglas; exchanged Sep. 23, 1862; present at Chickasaw Bayou and Port Hudson; absent sick from Raymond; captured the second day at Chickamauga.

McLaurine, W.J., discharged for disability at Bowling Green, Dec., 1861.

McRobert, John A., musician; discharged for disability at Bowling Green, Jul. 20, 1861.

Misenheimer, M.A., lost a leg at Fort Donelson; sent home and discharged by A.S. Johnston.

Mitchell, Philip B., wounded at Fort Donelson; sent home where he joined the cavalry.

Mitchell, Samuel C., present at Fort Donelson; imprisoned at Camp Douglas; exchanged Sep. 23, 1862; on detached duty during Chickasaw Bayou, Port Hudson, and Raymond battles; present at Jackson; went AWOL the second night at Chickamauga; absent from Missionary Ridge.

Neill, James B., present at Fort Donelson; imprisoned at Camp Douglas; exchanged Sep. 23, 1862; discharged for disability Oct. 12, 1862.

Nevils, Robert F., wounded at Fort Donelson; sent home and entered the cavalry.

Nipp, Andrew J., present at Fort Donelson; imprisoned at Camp Douglas; exchanged Sep. 23, 1862; present at Chickasaw Bayou and Port Hudson; on detached duty during Raymond and Jackson battles; wounded the second day at Chickamauga; detailed as teamster during Missionary Ridge battle; wounded at Atlanta; survived the war.

Pack, James F., present at Fort Donelson; imprisoned at Camp Douglas; exchanged Sep. 23, 1862; present at Chickasaw Bayou and Port Hudson; detailed as teamster during Jackson and Chickamauga battles; present at Missionary Ridge.

Parker, John W., present at Fort Donelson; imprisoned at Camp Douglas; escaped from prison May 18, 1862; never returned.

Perkins, Spencer, enlisted Oct. 17, 1863; joined company at Missionary Ridge but was absent sick from the battle.

Pittard, A.G., enlisted Nov. 3, 1862; present at Chickasaw Bayou; absent sick from Port Hudson, Raymond, Jackson, Chickamauga, and Missionary Ridge.

Pittard, John W., wounded at Fort Donelson; sent home; served in the cavalry until exchange; excused from Chickasaw Bayou by the surgeon; discharged for disability Feb., 1863.

Pittard, Thomas S., enlisted Nov. 3, 1862; present at Chickasaw Bayou; absent sick from Port Hudson, Raymond, Jackson, Chickamauga, and Missionary Ridge; survived the war.

Pitts, Andrew J., sick in quarters during Fort Doneslon battle; imprisoned at Camp Douglas; exchanged Sep. 23, 1862; present at Chickasaw Bayou, Port Hudson, Raymond, and Jackson; wounded the second day at Chickamauga; present at Missionary Ridge.

Pitts, S. Houston, sick at Russellville during Fort Donelson battle; served in cavalry until exchange; rejoined regt. at Port Hudson; wounded at Raymond; absent on account of wound thereafter.

Plummer, C.B., wounded at Fort Donelson; sent to Clarksville, Tenn., where he was captured and paroled; never returned.

Reed, Jesse J., absent sick at home during Fort Donelson; served in cavalry until exchange; present at Chickasaw Bayou, Port Hudson, Raymond, and Jackson; wounded the first day at Chickamauga; present at Missionary Ridge.

Reed, Richard R., discharged for disability at Bowling Green, Oct., 1861.

Reynolds, David O., absent sick at home during Fort Donelson battle; rejoined regt. after exchange; absent sick from Chickasaw Bayou; present at Port Hudson; captured at Raymond; paroled and deserted Jul., 1863.

** Reynolds, E.L., enlisted Nov. 1, 1862; present at Chickasaw Bayou; absent sick from Port Hudson, Raymond, and Jackson; present at Chickamauga; present at Missionary Ridge; killed at New Hope Church (more likely at Kolb's Farm).

** Reynolds, James L., present at Fort Donelson; imprisoned at Camp Douglas; exchanged Sep. 23, 1862; present at Chickasaw Bayou, Port Hudson, Raymond, and Jackson; killed at Chickamauga the first day.

Reynolds, Leroy W., absent sick at home during Fort Donelson battle; rejoined regt. after exchange; present at Chickasaw Bayou and Port Hudson; wounded at Raymond; absent on account of wound thereafter.

Rodgers, Henry, wounded at Fort Donelson; imprisoned at Camp Douglas; exchanged Sep. 23, 1862; present at Chickasaw Bayou, Port Hudson, Raymond, and Jackson; wounded the second day at Chickamauga; AWOL from Missionary Ridge.

* Russell, William A., present at Fort Donelson; imprisoned at Camp Douglas; exchanged Sep. 23, 1862; present at Chickasaw Bayou, Port Hudson, and Raymond; absent sick from Jackson; died at Lauderdale Springs, Miss., Sep. 2, 1863.

Short, George E., enlisted Nov. 15, 1862; present at Chickasaw Bayou, Port Hudson, Raymond, and Jackson; discharged Sep. 7, 1863, for having provided a substitute.

Short, James B., wounded at Fort Donelson; sent home; discharged on account of wounds at Jackson Miss..

Smith, W.R., joined company at reorganization; present at Chickasaw Bayou, Port Hudson, and Raymond; on detached duty during Jackson, Chickamauga, and Missionary Ridge; survived the war.

Smith, W.W., joined company at reorganization; present at Chickasaw Bayou, Port Hudson, Raymond, Jackson, Chickamauga, and Missionary Ridge.

** Steele, Nathaniel G., wounded at Fort Donelson; imprisoned at Camp Douglas; exchanged Sep. 23, 1862; present at Chickasaw Bayou, Port Hudson, and Raymond; killed at Jackson Jul. 11, 1863.

Stevenson, Thomas L., present at Fort Donelson; escaped after the surrender served with 44th Tenn. until exchange; rejoined the regt. at Port Hudson; present at Raymond and Jackson; present the first day at Chickamauga but AWOL the second; AWOL from Missionary Ridge; survived the war.

Strong, J.P., enlisted Feb., 1863; present at Port Hudson, Raymond, and Jackson; deserted Jul. 30, 1863.

Suttle, Leroy W., absent sick at home during Fort Donelson battle; served in cavalry until exchanged; sick, on detail, or in the hospital during every engagement thereafter; survived the war.

** Suttle, William D., present at Fort Donelson; imprisoned at Camp Morton; exchanged Sep. 15, 1862; absent sick from Chickasaw Bayou; present at Port Hudson; captured at Raymond; paroled and rejoined regt. Jan. 20, 1864, after six months AWOL; killed at Bentonville, N.C..

Taylor, Rory, discharged for disability at Camp Trousdale, Aug., 1861.

Thompson, Peter, enlisted Mar. 1, 1863; present at Port Hudson and Raymond; captured at Jackson.

Tinnery, E.K.P., sick during Fort Donelson battle; imprisoned at Camp Douglas; exchanged Sep. 23, 1862; present at Chickasaw Bayou, Port Hudson, Raymond, and Jackson; captured the second day at Chickamauga.

** Tinnery, Pleasant H., sick during Fort Donelson battle; imprisoned at Camp Douglas; exchanged Sep. 23, 1862; present at Chickasaw Bayou and Port Hudson; wounded at Raymond; present at Jackson; killed at Chickamauga the second day.

Tinnery, Robert M., sick during Fort Donelson battle; imprisoned at Camp Douglas; exchanged Sep. 23, 1862; on detached duty during Chickasaw Bayou battle; present at Port Hudson, Raymond, and Jackson; wounded the first day at Chickamauga; absent from Missionary Ridge on account of wound. Survived the war.

Webb, E., transferred from 1st Tenn. Cavalry by order of Gen. Bragg in Nov., 1863; immediately deserted from Lookout Mountain.

Webb, Frank M., wounded at Fort Donelson; sent home and joined the cavalry.

Wilkinson, Tyree R., present at Fort Donelson; imprisoned at Camp Morton; exchanged Sep. 15, 1862; on detached duty during Chickasaw Bayou battle; present at Port Hudson, Raymond, and Jackson; present at Chickamauga the first day, AWOL from then on.

** Williams, B.F., home sick during Fort Donelson; joined 5th Tenn.; killed at Farmington, Miss..

Williams, Gatewood, discharged for disability at Camp Cheatham, Jun. 1, 1861.

Worsham, J.H., enlisted Nov., 1862, substitute for W.J. Lewis; present at Chickasaw Bayou; absent sick from Port Hudson, Raymond, Jackson, Chickamauga, and Missionary Ridge.

Wright, J.R., present at Fort Donelson; imprisoned at Camp Douglas; exchanged Sep. 23, 1862; discharged for disability Oct. 12, 1862.

Company B

Captain

H.F. Gordon, commanded company at Fort Donelson; imprisoned at Camp Chase and Johnson's Island; exchanged Sep. 16, 1862; not re-elected and dropped from the rolls.

Robert A. Mitchell, as 1st lieutenant present at Fort Donelson; imprisoned at Camp Chase and Johnson's Island; exchanged Sep. 16, 1862; elected captain at reorganization; absent from Chickasaw Bayou due to serving on a court martial; on sick leave during Port Hudson battle; commanded the company at Raymond and Jackson; absent sick from Chickamauga; commanded the company at Missionary Ridge; surrendered at Greensboro, N.C..

1st Lieutenant

** J.M. Thompson, as 3rd sergeant present at Fort Donelson; imprisoned at Camp Douglas; exchanged Sep. 23, 1862; elected to 1st lieutenant at reorganization; commanded the company at Chickasaw Bayou; present at Raymond; absent sick from Jackson; died at Enterprise, Miss., Sep. 8, 1863.

M.T. West, as a private present at Fort Donelson; imprisoned at Camp Douglas; exchanged Sep. 23, 1862; elected to 2nd lieutenant at reorganization; present at Chickasaw Bayou, Port Hudson, and Raymond; commanded the company at Chickamauga where he was wounded the second day; present at Missionary Ridge; promoted 1st lieutenant on the death of J.M. Thompson.

2nd Lieutenant

William M. Brickeen, AWOL during Fort Donelson battle; imprisoned at Camp Chase and Johnson's Island; exchanged Sep. 16, 1862; not re-elected and dropped from the rolls.

William T. Mitchell, as junior 2nd lieutenant sick in quarters during Fort Donelson; imprisoned at Camp Chase and Johnson's Island; exchanged Sep. 16, 1862; replaced M.T. West as 2nd lieutenant; present at Chickasaw Bayou, Port Hudson, Raymond, Jackson, and Missionary Ridge.

Junior 2nd Lieutenant

J.M. Knox, as a private present at Fort Donelson; imprisoned at Camp Douglas; exchanged Sep. 23, 1862; present at Chickasaw Bayou; Port Hudson, Raymond, Jackson, Chickamauga, and Missionary Ridge; elected junior 2nd lieutenant, Nov. 29, 1863; surrendered at Greensboro, N.C..

1st Sergeant

R.W. Westmoreland, sick in quarters during Fort Donelson; imprisoned at Camp Douglas; exchanged Sep. 23, 1862; returned to the ranks at reorganization; AWOL from Chickasaw Bayou; present at Port Hudson, Raymond, Jackson, Chickamauga, and Missionary Ridge.

Robert V. Griffis, as 5th sergeant present at Fort Donelson; imprisoned at Camp Douglas; exchanged Sep. 23, 1862; promoted to 1st sergeant at reorganization; present at Chickasaw Bayou and Port Hudson; wounded at Chickamauga the second day; absent from Missionary Ridge because of wound; survived the war.

2nd Sergeant

Joseph Goldman, present at Fort Donelson; imprisoned at Camp Douglas; escaped Mar., 1862 and rejoined regt. after exchange; returned to the ranks at reorganization; present at Chickasaw Bayou; Port Hudson, Raymond, and Jackson; wounded at Chickamuaga; absent from Missionary Ridge because of wound.

John G. Caldwell, joined the company at the reorganization; present at Chickasaw Bayou, Port Hudson, and Raymond; absent sick from Jackson and Chickamauga; present at Missionary Ridge.

3rd Sergeant

J.W. Franks, as a private present at Fort Donelson; imprisoned at Camp Douglas; exchanged Sep. 23, 1862; promoted to 3rd sergeant at reorganization; present at Chickasaw Bayou, Port Hudson, and Raymond; absent sick from Chickamauga; on detached duty during Missionary Ridge.

4th Sergeant

J.T. Moore, present at Fort Donelson; imprisoned at Camp Douglas; exchanged Sep. 23, 1862; returned to the ranks at reorganization; present at Chickasaw Bayou, Port Hudson, Raymond, Jackson, Chickamauga, and Missionary Ridge; survived the war.

Maxwell Daugherty, as a private wounded at Fort Donelson; imprisoned at Camp Couglas; exchanged Sep. 23, 1862; present at Chickasaw Bayou, Port Hudson, Raymond, and Jackson; wounded at Chickamouga and Missionary Ridge; surrendered as a sergeant at Greensboro, N.C.

1st Corporal

** Carter Davis, present at Fort Donelson; escaped after capture; rejoined regt. after exchange; returned to the ranks at the reorganization; present at

Chickasaw Bayou, Port Hudson, Raymond, and Jackson; killed at Chickamauga the second day.

A.R.Cannon, as a private present at Fort Donelson; imprisoned at Camp Douglas; exchanged Sep. 23, 1862; promoted to 1st corporal at reorganization; present at Chickasaw Bayou and Port Hudson; absent sick from Raymond and Jackson; wounded at Chickamauga; absent from Missionary Ridge due to wound.

2nd Corporal

** J.B. Compton, killed while bearing the colors at Fort Donelson, Feb. 15, 1862.

** S.F. Sands, joined company at reorganization; present at Chickasaw Bayou, Port Hudson, Raymond, and Jackson; killed at Chickamauga the first day.

3rd Corporal

G.T. McLaurine, detailed to commissary during Fort Donelson battle; rejoined regt. after exchange; returned to the ranks at the reorganization; present at Chickasaw Bayou and Port Hudson; captured at Raymond and imprisoned at Fort Delaware and Point Lookout.

J.H. Reynolds, as a private present at Fort Donelson; imprisoned at Camp Douglas; exchanged Sep. 23, 1862; promoted to 3rd corporal at reorganization; present at Chickasaw Bayou and Port Hudson; wounded at Raymond; absent from Jackson and Chickamauga because of wound; AWOL from Missionary Ridge.

4th Corporal

M.L. Seagraves, as a private present at Fort Donelson; imprisoned at Camp Douglas; exchanged Sep. 23, 1862; promoted to 4th corporal at reorganization; present at Chickasaw Bayou and Port Hudson; captured at Raymond and imprisoned at Fort Delaware and Point Lookout.

Privates

Agnew, J.F., present at Fort Donelson; took oath of allegiance to U.S. at St. Louis; was released and rejoined regt. after exchange; wounded himself in the hand and missed Chickasaw Bayou battle; AWOL from Port Hudson, Raymond, and Jackson; deserted from the hospital at Newton, Miss., Aug. 14, 1863.

* Alderson, M.L., died at Bowling Green, Oct. 13, 1861.

Bailey, T.B., sick in quarters during Fort Donelson battle; imprisoned at Camp Douglas; exchanged Sep. 23, 1862; present at Chickasaw Bayou; absent sick thereafter until he deserted from Lauderdale Springs, Miss., Sep., 1863.

Batson, J.J., present at Fort Donelson; imprisoned at Camp Douglas; exchanged Sep. 23, 1862; detailed as teamster after reorganization; deserted from Canton, Miss., Jun., 1863.

\# Batte, G., wounded at Fort Donelson; imprisoned at Camp Douglas; exchanged Sep. 23, 1862; present at Chickasaw Bayou, Port Hudson, Raymond, and Jackson; wounded at Chickamauga; present at Missionary Ridge; surrendered at Greensboro, N.C..

* Batte, Henry, present at Fort Donelson; imprisoned at Camp Douglas; exchanged Sep. 23, 1862; absent sick from Chickasaw Bayou; died at Port Hudson Jan. 26, 1863.

Beal, John M., present at Fort Donelson; escaped after capture; served as partisan, then rejoined regt. after exchange; present at Chickasaw Bayou, Port Hudson, Raymond, and Jackson; detailed as teamster during Chickamauga and Missionary Ridge battles.

** Bearden, Henry, present at Fort Donelson; imprisoned at Camp Douglas; exchanged Sep. 23, 1862; present at Chickasaw Bayou, Port Hudson, Raymond and Jackson; killed at Chickamauga the first day.

Bearden, W.C., AWOL from Fort Donelson; imprisoned at Camp Douglas; exchanged Sep. 23, 1862; absent sick from Chickasaw Bayou; present at Port Hudson; wounded at Raymond; absent from Jackson and Chickamauga because of wound; deserted at Chattanooga, Nov. 2, 1863.

Boatwright, James M., present at Fort Donelson; imprisoned at Camp Douglas; exchanged Sep. 23, 1862; present at Chickasaw Bayou and Port Hudson; absent sick from Raymond; present at Jackson, Chickamauga, and Missionary Ridge.

Boatwright, Thomas R.E., present at Fort Donelson; imprisoned at Camp Butler; exchanged Sep. 23, 1862; present at Chickasaw Bayou, Port Hudson, Raymond, Jackson, and Chickamauga; absent sick from Missionary Ridge; surrendered at Greensboro, N.C..

Braden, J.W., present at Fort Donelson; imprisoned at Camp Douglas; exchanged Sep. 23, 1862; present at Chickasaw Bayou and Port Hudson; wounded at Raymond; absent thereafter due to wound.

Branch, M.P., present at Fort Donelson; escaped from Camp Douglas, Apr., 1862.

* Brickeen, A.J., present at Fort Donelson; imprisoned at Camp Douglas; exchanged Sep. 23, 1862; present at Chickasaw Bayou and Port Hudson; captured at Raymond and died in prison.

Brickeen, M.F., AWOL from Fort Donelson; imprisoned at Camp Douglas; exchanged Sep. 23, 1862; AWOL from Chickasaw Bayou; present at Port Hudson and Raymond; absent sick from Jackson; AWOL from Chickamauga; absent sick from Missionary Ridge; surrendered at Greensboro, N.C..

* Briggs, W.W., died at Nashville, Nov. 5, 1861.

Brown, Robert M., present at Fort Donelson; imprisoned at Camp Douglas; exchanged Sep. 23, 1862; absent sick from Chickasaw Bayou; present at Port Hudson; absent sick from Raymond and Jackson; present at Chickamauga and Missionary Ridge.

Brown, Thomas A., present at Fort Donelson; imprisoned at Camp Douglas; exchanged Sep. 23, 1862; present at Chickasaw Bayou and Port Hudson; wounded at Raymond; absent from Jackson due to wound; present at Chickamauga and Missionary Ridge; surrendered at Greensboro, N.C..

* Bugg, George B., enlisted Oct. 19, 1862; present at Chickasaw Bayou; died at Port Hudson Feb. 25, 1863.

Caldwell, W.H., present at Fort Donelson; imprisoned at Camp Douglas; exchanged Sep. 23, 1862; present at Chickasaw Bayou, Port Hudson, Raymond, Jackson, and Chickamauga; absent sick from Missionary Ridge.

Calvert, L.N., enlisted Oct. 31, 1862; present at Chickasaw Bayou, Port Hudson, Raymond, and Jackson; wounded at Chickamauga; absent from Missionary Ridge due to wound; surrendered at Greensboro, N.C..

** Calvert, W.H., present at Fort Donelson; captured, then released after taking the oath of allegiance at St. Louis; rejoined regt. after its exchange;

present at Chickasaw Bayou, Port Hudson, and Raymond; killed at Jackson, Jul. 11, 1863.

** Cannon, S.H., enlisted Nov. 1, 1862; present at Chickasaw Bayou and Port Hudson; killed at Raymond, May 12, 1863.

Cochran, J.J., detailed as nurse in hospital at Russellville during Fort Donelson battle; never rejoined regt..

Coker, W.J., present at Fort Donelson; imprisoned at Camp Douglas; exchanged Sep. 23, 1862; present at Chickasaw Bayou, Port Hudson, Raymond, and Jackson; wounded at Chickamauga; AWOL from Missionary Ridge.

** Compton, J.L., enlisted Nov. 3, 1862; present at Chickasaw Bayou and Port Hudson; killed at Raymond, May 12, 1863.

** Compton, J.S., present at Fort Donelson; escaped after the surrender; rejoined the regt. after exchange; present at Chickasaw Bayou, Port Hudson, Raymond, and Jackson; killed at Chickamauga the second day.

Couch, William, absent sick from Fort Donelson; joined 11th Tenn. Cav..

Erwin, J.W., present at Fort Donelson; imprisoned at Camp Douglas; exchanged Sep. 23, 1862; present at Chickasaw Bayou; discharged as non-conscript at Port Hudson, Mar. 5, 1863.

Farley, A.J., present at Fort Donelson; escaped after the surrender; joined the 1st Tenn. Cavalry.

Farley, W.L., wounded at Fort Donelson; sent home; served in the cavalry until exchange; officially joined 1st Tenn. Cavalry, Dec., 1862.

Fitzpatrick, John, absent from Fort Donelson sick; rejoined the regt. after exchange; joined the 1st Tenn. Cavalry, Nov., 1862.

Fry, J.M., sick in quarters during Fort Donelson battle; imprisoned at Camp Douglas; exchanged Sep. 23, 1862; deserted at Oxford, Miss., Nov., 1862; joined Holman's Battalion of Tenn. Cavalry.

Fry, M.M., discharged at Bowling Green, Dec. 17, 1861; then joined the cavalry.

Fry, W.B., present at Fort Donelson; imprisoned at Camp Douglas; exchanged Sep. 23, 1862; dicharged for disability at Jackson, Miss., Sep. 29, 1862.

Fry, W.E., enlisted Nov. 5, 1862; absent sick from Chickasaw Bayou, Port Hudson, and Raymond; captured at Jackson, Jul. 15, 1863, and imprisoned at Camp Morton.

Fry, W.P., present at Fort Donelson; imprisoned at Camp Douglas; exchanged Sep. 23, 1862; captured at Springdale, Miss., Dec. 3, 1862; imprisoned at Alton, Ill., penitentiary; exchanged Apr., 1863; present at Raymond, Jackson, Chickamauga, and Missionary Ridge.

Garrett, D.B., present at Fort Donelson; imprisoned at Camp Douglas; exchanged Sep. 23, 1862; present at Chickasaw Bayou, Port Hudson, Raymond, Jackson, and Chickamauga; absent sick from Missionary Ridge; survived the war.

Giesler, F., present at Fort Donelson; imprisoned at Camp Douglas; exchanged Sep. 23, 1862; absent sick from Chickasaw Bayou; present at Port Hudson; captured at Raymond; imprisoned at Fort Delaware where he deserted to the enemy.

* Glenn, J.B., died at Camp Cheatham Jun. 19, 1861.

Goldman, J., joined company after reorganization; present at Chickasaw Bayou and Port Hudson, Raymond, and Jackson; wounded at Chickamauga; absent from Missionary Ridge due to wound.

Green, J.S., on furlough during Fort Donelson battle; discharged from service as non-conscript.

Griffin, O.R., present at Fort Donelson; imprisoned at Camp Douglas; exchanged Sep. 23, 1862; present at Chickasaw Bayou; discharged as non-conscript at Port Hudson, Mar. 5, 1863.

Griffis, W.W., enlisted Nov. 5, 1862; absent sick from Chickasaw Bayou; present at Port Hudson; absent sick from Raymond; present at Jackson, Chickamauga, and Missionary Ridge.

* Grigsby, F.M., died at Camp Trousdale, Sep. 15, 1861.

Grigsby, J.N., absent from Fort Donelson sick; served in cavalry until exchange; present at Chickasaw Bayou and Port Hudson; wounded at Raymond; absent from Jackson, Chickamauga, and Missionary Ridge due to wound; survived the war.

Grigsby, M.G., enlisted Oct. 19, 1862; present at Chickasaw Bayou, Port Hudson, Raymond, Jackson, Chickamauga, and Missionary Ridge.

Griswell, W.R., present at Fort Donelson; imprisoned at Camp Douglas; exchanged Sep. 23, 1862; absent sick from Chickasaw Bayou; present at Port Hudson; absent sick from Raymond; present at Jackson; absent sick from Chickamauga; present at Missionary Ridge.

** Hackney, W.F., present at Fort Donelson; imprisoned at Camp Douglas; exchanged Sep. 23, 1862; AWOL from Chickasaw Bayou; present at Port Hudson; killed at Raymond, May 12, 1863.

Harris, G.W., present at Fort Donelson; escaped after the surrender; joined 1st Tenn. Cavalry.

** Harwell, W.M., present at Fort Donelson; imprisoned at Camp Douglas; exchanged Sep. 23, 1862; on detached duty during Chickasaw Bayou battle; present at Port Hudson, Raymond, Jackson, Chickamauga, and Missionary Ridge; killed at Resaca.

* Helmick, Hiram, present at Fort Donelson; died at Camp Douglas, Mar. 21, 1862.

* Henderson, J.S., present at Fort Donelson; died enroute to prison at St. Louis, Mar. 16, 1862.

Higdon, J.C., present at Fort Donelson; escaped after the surrender; joined the 41st Miss..

\# Hobbs, Caleb, present at Fort Donelson; imprisoned at Camp Douglas; exchanged Sep. 23, 1862; AWOL from Chickasaw Bayou; present at Port Hudson and Raymond; on detached duty during Jackson battle; AWOL from Chickamauga; present at Missionary Ridge; surrendered at Greensboro, N.C..

Hodge, J.M., enlisted Nov. 1, 1862; on detached duty during Chickasaw Bayou battle; present at Port Hudson, Raymond, and Jackson; absent sick from Chickamauga; present at Missionary Ridge.

Hodge, S.W., present at Fort Donelson; imprisoned at Camp Douglas; exchanged Sep. 23, 1862; present at Chickasaw Bayou, Port Hudson, and Raymond; absent sick from Jackson and Chickamauga; present at Missionary Ridge.

* Hodge, W.A., died at Bowling Green, Jan. 28, 1862.

* James, Thomas, died at home, Aug 1, 1861.

James, W.N., present at Fort Donelson; imprisoned at Camp Douglas; exchanged Sep. 23, 1862; present at Chickasaw Bayou and Port Hudson; captured at Raymond and imprisoned at Fort Delaware and Point Lookout; exchanged Jan. 1, 1864.

Jones, James L., absent sick from Fort Donelson; joined the 1st Tenn. Cavalry; rejoined the regt. Nov. 19, 1863; absent sick from Missionary Ridge.

Kerr, W.G., present at Fort Donelson; escaped from Camp Douglas, Jun. 3, 1862; returned to regt. after exchange.

Knox, Henry M., present at Fort Donelson; imprisoned at Camp Douglas; exchanged Sep. 23, 1862; present at Chickasaw Bayou, Port Hudson; Raymond, Jackson, and Chickamauga; absent sick from Missionary Ridge; surrendered at Greensboro, N.C..

Kosier, Daniel, present at Fort Donelson; imprisoned at Camp Douglas; exchanged Sep. 23, 1862; discharged for disability, Sep., 1862; then rejoined the regt. as a substitute at Port Hudson in Feb., 1863; captured at Raymond and imprisoned at Fort Delaware and Point Lookout.

Laird, R.M., transferred from Co. K; present at Fort Donelson; imprisoned at Camp Douglas; exchanged Sep. 23, 1862; present a Chickasaw Bayou, Port Hudson, Raymond, Jackson, and Chickamauga; absent sick from Missionary Ridge.

Lambert, J.L., detailed as teamster during Fort Donelson battle; rejoined regt. after exchange; absent sick from Chickasaw Bayou; transferred to Company F (E) at Port Hudson; no further entries in Rollbook..

Lowry, T.J., present at Fort Donelson; escaped from Camp Douglas, Jun. 21, 1862; joined the 11th Tenn..

Mantlo, W., detailed as teamster during Fort Donelson battle; joined the cavalry.

Martin, C.W., wounded at Fort Donelson; imprisoned at Camp Douglas; exchanged Sep. 23, 1862; after reorganization detailed as teamster until he deserted, Jun., 1863.

** Martin, Felix G., present at Fort Donelson; escaped from Camp Douglas Apr. 6, 1862; rejoined regt, after exchange; present at Chickasaw Bayou and Port Hudson; killed at Raymond.

Martin, N.E., sick in quarters during Fort Donelson; imprisoned at Camp Douglas; exchanged Sep. 23, 1862; no further entries in Rollbook.

Maxey, S (I). H., present at Fort Donelson; imprisoned at Camp Douglas; exchanged Sep. 23, 1862; wounded at Springdale, Miss., Dec. 3, 1862; absent from Chickasaw Bayou because of wound; furloughed home, Feb. 25, 1863, and never returned.

** McCarter, Thomas, present at Fort Donelson; imprisoned at Camp Douglas; exchanged Sep. 23, 1862; wounded at Springdale, Miss., Dec. 3, 1862, and died from wound Dec. 20.

McKnight, J.W., detailed as teamster during Fort Donelson battle; joined the 53rd Tenn..

Mitchell, J.O., enlisted Oct. 31, 1862; present at Chickasaw Bayou, Port Hudson, Raymond, and Jackson; AWOL from Chickamauga; present at Missionary Ridge.

Mitchell, J.W., present at Fort Donelson; imprisoned at Camp Douglas; exchanged Sep. 23, 1862; present at Chickasaw Bayou and Port Hudson; wounded at Raymond; absent thereafter due to wound.

Mitchell, M.M., conscripted Nov. 9, 1862; present at Port Hudson; absent sick from Raymond, Jackson, and Chickamauga; captured at Missionary Ridge.

Newlin, W.J., present at Fort Donelson; imprisoned at Camp Douglas; exchanged Sep. 23, 1862; on detached duty during Chickasaw Bayou battle; present at Port Hudson; captured at Raymond and imprisoned at Fort Delaware.

Page, D.G., present at Fort Donelson; imprisoned at Camp Douglas; exchanged Sep. 23, 1862; on detached duty during Chickasaw Bayou battle; discharged at Port Hudson as a non-conscript, Mar. 5, 1863.

Pate, J.M., present at Fort Donelson; imprisoned at Camp Douglas; exchanged Sep. 23, 1862; on detached duty during Chickasaw Bayou and Port Hudson battles; excused from duty thereafter due to defective vision.

* Reynolds, G.I., died at home, Aug., 1861.

\# Richardson, W.J., present at Fort Donelson; imprisoned at Camp Douglas; exchanged Sep. 23, 1862; present at Chickasaw Bayou, Port Hudson, Raymond, and Jackson; absent sick from Chickamauga; present at Missionary Ridge; surrendered at Greensboro, N.C..

* Rutledge, J.D., present at Fort Donelson; died at Camp Douglas, Apr. 6, 1862.

Sands, J.E., enlisted Oct. 30.1862; present at Chickasaw Bayou, Port Hudson, Raymond, Jackson, and Chickamauga; deserted at Chattanooga, Nov. 5, 1863.

Sands, S.F., present at Fort Donelson; imprisoned at Camp Douglas; exchanged Sep. 23, 1862; no further record.

Sands, W.P., enlisted Oct. 30, 1862; present at Chickasaw Bayou, Port Hudson, Raymond, Jackson, Chickamauga, and Missionary Ridge.

Scruggs, L.S., detailed as blacksmith during Fort Donelson battle; on detached duty to Confederate government blacksmith shops; deserted at Atlanta.

Shannon, M.J., present at Fort Donelson; took the oath of alliegience to the U.S. at St. Louis; rejoined the regt. after exchange; present at Chickasaw Bayou, Port Hudson, Raymond, Jackson, Chickamauga, and Missionary Ridge.

* Simmons, M.M., died at Camp Cheatham, Jun. 29, 1861.

Simmons, W.W., present at Fort Donelson; imprisoned at Camp Douglas; exchanged Sep. 23, 1862; present at Chickasaw Bayou, Port Hudson, and Raymond; absent sick from Jackson; wounded at Chickamauga; absent from Missionary Ridge due to wound.

Smith, J.S., sick at home during Fort Donelson; served in Hill's regt. until exchange; absent sick from Chickasaw Bayou; present at Port Hudson; wounded at Raymond; absent thereafter due to wound.

Spivey, W.H., sick at home during Fort Donelson battle; served in the 1st Tenn. Cavalry until exchange; present at Farmington, Iuka, and Corinth; absent sick from Chickasaw Bayou; present at Port Hudson, Raymond, and Jackson; absent sick from Chickamauga; absent barefoot from Missionary Ridge.

\# Stewart, J.W., present at Fort Donelson; imprisoned at Camp Douglas; exchanged Sep. 23, 1862; absent sick from Chickasaw Bayou; present at Port Hudson; on furlough during Raymond battle; present at Jackson, Chickamauga, and Missionary Ridge; surrendered at Greensboro, N.C..

Stroud, G.W., present at Fort Donelson; imprisoned at Camp Douglas; exchanged Sep. 23, 1862; present at Chickasaw Bayou; furloughed home, Feb. 25, 1863, for 30 days from Port Hudson; present at Missionary Ridge.

Thompson, A.C., enlisted Nov. 4, 1862; present at Chickasaw Bayou, Port Hudson, and Raymond; absent sick from Jackson and deserted from hospital, Sep., 1863.

Thompson, H.L., present at Fort Donelson; imprisoned at Camp Douglas; exchanged Sep. 23, 1862; absent sick from Chickasaw Bayou; present at Port Hudson; deserted Apr., 1863.

Thompson, H.S., conscripted Jan. 28, 1863; present at Port Hudson and Raymond; absent sick from Jackson and deserted from hospital, Sep., 1863.

Thompson, J.L., present at Fort Donelson; imprisoned at Camp Douglas; exchanged Sep. 23, 1862; present at Chickasaw Bayou and Port Hudson; wounded at Raymond; absent from Jackson due to wound; took leave Sep. 3, 1863, and was captured at home; present at final surrender near Greensboro, N.C...

Thorp, C.F.M., sick in quarters during Fort Donelson battle; imprisoned at Camp Douglas; exchanged Sep. 23, 1862; present at Chickasaw Bayou, Port Hudson, Raymond, Jackson, Chickamauga, and Missionary Ridge.

Thorp, J.P., enlisted Nov. 3, 1862; absent sick from Chickasaw Bayou; present at Port Hudson; absent sick from Raymond; present at Jackson and Chickamauga; absent sick from Missionary Ridge.

Waldrup, A.J., enlisted Oct. 30, 1862; present at Chickasaw Bayou, Port Hudson, Raymond, Jackson, and Chickamauga; detailed as teamster during Missionary Ridge battle.

Waldrup, D., enlisted Nov. 1, 1862; AWOL from Chickasaw Bayou and all battles thereafter.

Waldrup, G.M., present at Fort Donelson; imprisoned at Camp Douglas; exchanged Sep. 23, 1862; present at Chickasaw Bayou, Port Hudson, Raymond, Jackson, Chickamauga, and Missionary Ridge.

* Waldrup, J.M., present at Fort Donelson; died at Camp Douglas, Mar. 26, 1862

Waldrup, T.J., enlisted Oct. 30, 1862; present at Chickasaw Bayou, Port Hudson, Raymond, Jackson, and Chickamauga; absent sick from Missionary Ridge; surrendered at Greensboro, N.C..

Walker, T.B., present at Fort Donelson; imprisoned at Camp Douglas; exchanged Sep. 23, 1862; present at Chickasaw Bayou and Port Hudson; absent sick from Raymond; present at Jackson; absent sick from Chickamauga and Missionary Ridge.

Wells, R.L., AWOL during Fort Donelson battle; captured and took oath of alliegience to the U.S. at St. Louis; rejoined the regt. after exchange; present at Chickasaw Bayou, Port Hudson, Raymond, Jackson, Chickamauga, and Missionary Ridge.

Wilkes, James, wounded at Fort Donelson; imprisoned at Camp Douglas; exchanged Sep. 23, 1862; discharged for disability, Sep., 1862.

Willeford, H.C., enlisted Oct. 30, 1862; present at Chickasaw Bayou, Port Hudson and Raymond; absent sick from Jackson; went on furlough in Sep., 1863, and never returned.

Williams, Thomas, detached as blacksmith during Fort Donelson battle; never rejoined regt..

Wilson, W.B., present at Fort Donelson; imprisoned at Camp Douglas; exchanged Sep. 23, 1862; discharged for disability, Oct., 1862.

Company C (later D)

Captain

Daniel F. Wade, in command and wounded Feb. 15 at Fort Donelson; sent home; not re-elected at reorganization and dropped from the rolls.

Walter S. Jennings, promoted to 2nd lieutenant from junior 2nd lieutenant Sep. 14, 1861; present at Fort Donelson; imprisoned at Camp Chase and Johnson's Island; exchanged Sep.16, 1862; elected captain at reorganization; commanded company at Chickasaw Bayou, Port Hudson, Raymond, and Jackson; on furlough from Chickamauga; commanded company at Missionary Ridge; last acting commander of the regiment; survived the war.

1st Lieutenant

* James D. Moss, died at home, Sep. 4, 1861.

Johnston Long, promoted from 2nd lieutenant Sep. 14, 1861; present at Fort Donelson; imprisoned at Camp Chase and Johnson's Island; not re-elected after exchange, resigned, and dropped from the rolls.

W.C. Dunham, promoted to 4th sergeant from 1st corporal, Sep. 14, 1861; present at Fort Donelson; imprisoned at Camp Douglas; exchanged Sep. 23, 1861; promoted to 1st lieutenant at reorganization; present at Chickasaw Bayou, Port Hudson, Raymond, and Jackson; on detached service from Chickamauga and Missionary Ridge.

2nd Lieutenant

R.R. Williams, as a private present at Fort Donelson; imprisoned at Camp Douglas; exchanged Sep. 23, 1862; elected 2nd lieutenant at reorganization; present at Chickasaw Bayou, PortHudson, Raymond, and Jackson; commanded company at Chickamauga and Missionary Ridge.

Junior 2nd Lieutenant

James Giddens, Jr., promoted from 4th Sergeant Sep. 14, 1861; present at Fort Doneslon; imprisoned at Camp Chase and Johnson's Island; not re-elected after exchange and dropped from the rolls.

* Y.R. Watkins, as a private present at Fort Donelson; imprisoned at Camp Douglas; exchanged Sep. 23, 1862; elected to junior 2nd lieutenant at reorganization; present at Chickasaw Bayou and Port Hudson; furloughed Apr. 14, 1863 and died at home, May 16, 1863.

Walter M. (W.) Warren, as a private present at Fort Donelson; imprisoned at Camp Douglas; exchanged Sep. 23, 1862; present at Chickasaw Bayou, Port Hudson, and Raymond; elected Junior 2nd Lieutenant Jun. 15, 1863; present at Jackson, Chickamauga, and Missionary Ridge; survived the war.

1st Sergeant

John S. Hunter, present at Fort Donelson; took the oath of allegience at St. Louis and released from captivity in Mar., 1862; discharged as non-conscript, Mar., 1863.

John A. Jackson, as a private present at Fort Donelson; imprisoned at Camp Douglas; exchanged Sep. 23, 1862; promoted to 1st sergeant at reorganization; absent inebriated from Chickasaw Bayou; present at Port Hudson; wounded at Raymond; absent thereafter because of wound.

2nd Sergeant

J. Fount Ingram, detached to Sappers and Miners, Oct., 1861; joined the 1st Tenn. Cavalry.

Mumford Smith, joined company at reorganization; present at Chickasaw Bayou and Port Hudson, captured at Raymond; paroled Aug. 15, 1863; absent sick from Chickamauga; present at Missionary Ridge; surrendered at Greensboro, N.C..

3rd Sergeant

C. Fletcher Barnes, present at Fort Donelson; escaped from Camp Douglas, Jun.1, 1862; joined the cavalry.

Charles Kelly, as a private present at Fort Donelson; imprisoned at Camp Douglas; exchanged Sep. 23, 1862; pomoted to 3rd sergeant at reorganization; present at Chickasaw Bayou, Port Hudson, and Raymond; absent sick from Jackson; present at Chickamauga; absent sick from Missionary Ridge; captured on the retreat to Dalton, Nov. 26, 1863.

4th Sergeant

Thomas M. Tune, as a private present at Fort Donelson; imprisoned at Camp Douglas; exchanged Sep. 23, 1862; promoted to 4th sergeant at reorganization; on detached duty during Chickasaw Bayou battle; absent sick from Port Hudson; on detached duty during Raymond battle; present at Jackson; absent sick from Chickamauga; present at Missionary Ridge.

5th Sergeant

Mark Cartwright, absent from Fort Donelson due to accidental wound; joined the cavalry.

M.H. Barnes, as a private present at Fort Donelson; imprisoned at Camp Douglas; exchanged Sep. 23, 1862; promoted to 5th sergeant at reorganization; present at Chickasaw Bayou, Port Hudson, Raymond, Jackson, Chickamauga, and Missionary Ridge.

1st Corporal

P.H. Edwards, as a private present at Fort Donelson; imprisoned at Camp Douglas; exchanged Sep. 23, 1862; promoted to 1st corporal at reorganization; present at Chickasaw Bayou, Port Hudson, Raymond, Jackson, Chickamauga, and Missionary Ridge; surrendered at Greensboro, N.C..

2nd Corporal

James E. Craig, as 2nd corporal present at Fort Donelson; imprisoned at Camp Douglas; exchanged Sep. 23, 1862; returned to ranks at reorganization; absent sick from Chickasaw Bayou; present at Port Hudson and Raymond; absent sick from Jackson; present at Chickamauga the first day but AWOL the second; present at Missionary Ridge.

B.E. Perkinson, as a private present at Fort Donelson; imprisoned at Camp Douglas; exchanged Sep. 23, 1862; promoted to 2nd corporal at reorganization; present at Chickasaw Bayou, Port Hudson, Raymond, and Jackson; furloughed Aug. 11, 1863 and was captured at home in Sep., 1863.

3rd Corporal

* W.A. Kittrell, present at Fort Donelson; died at Camp Douglas, Apr. 1, 1862.

T.J. Hall, as a private present at Fort Donelson; imprisoned at Camp Douglas; exchanged Sep. 23, 1862; promoted to 3rd corporal at reorganization; present at Chickasaw Bayou and Port Hudson; wounded at Raymond; absent thereafter due to wound.

4th Corporal

** William M. Bynum, present at Fort Donelson; imprisoned at Camp Douglas; exchanged Sep. 23, 1862; returned to the ranks at reorganization; present at Chickasaw Bayou, Port Hudson, and Raymond; mortally wounded at Jackson, Jul. 11, 1863, and died at Point Clear Hospital near Mobile, Sep. 23, 1863.

H.A. Stockard, joined company at reorganization; present at Chickasaw Bayou, Port Hudson, Raymond, Jackson, Chickamauga, and Missionary Ridge.

Privates

Alley, William A.(R.), present at Fort Donelosn; imprisoned at Camp Douglas; exchanged Sep. 23, 1862; present at Chickasaw Bayou and Port Hudson; captured at Raymond and imprisoned at Fort Delaware and Point Lookout.

Barnes, Joel L., present at Fort Donelson; imprisoned at Camp Douglas; exchanged Sep. 23, 1862; present at Chickasaw Bayou, Port Hudson, Raymond, Jackson, Chickamauga, and Missionary Ridge; survived the war.

* Bell, Valentine, died in Lewis County, Tenn., Jul. 15, 1861.

Bell, William, present at Fort Donelson; imprisoned at Camp Douglas; exchanged Sep. 23, 1862; present at Chickasaw Bayou and Port Hudson; absent footsore from Raymond; present at Jackson and Chickamauga; absent sick from Missionary Ridge.

** Benderman, John W., present at Fort Donelson; imprisoned at Camp Douglas; exchanged Sep. 23, 1862; present at Chickasaw Bayou and Port Hudson; mortally wounded at Raymond and died there, May 13, 1863.

Boggus, R.B., present at Fort Donelson; imprisoned at Camp Douglas; exchanged Sep. 23, 1862; present at Chickasaw Bayou, Port Hudson, Raymond, and Jackson; left the field without leave the first day at Chickamauga; absent sick from Missionary Ridge.

** Bond, B.W., killed at Fort Donelson.

Bond, John H., enlisted Nov. 1, 1862; AWOL from Chickasaw Bayou; present at Port Hudson; discharged Apr., 1863, for providing a substitute.

Brennen, D., present at Fort Donelson; imprisoned at Camp Douglas; took the oath of alliegience to the U.S. in August 1862, and never returned.

Bryson, J.H., wounded at Fort Donelson and sent home; rejoined regiment at Port Hudson; present at Raymond; absent sick thereafter.

Bryson, John J., present at Fort Donelson, imprisoned at Camp Douglas; exchanged Sep. 23, 1862; present at Chickasaw Bayou, Port Hudson, Raymond, Jackson, Chickamouga, and Missionary Ridge; surrendered at Greesboro, N.C..

Buford, Edward C., present at Fort Donelson; imprisoned at Camp Douglas; exchanged Sep. 23, 1862; present at Chickasaw Bayou, Port Hudson, Raymond, and Jackson; absent from Chickamauga with sprained ankle; present at Missionary Ridge; survived the war.

* Burkett, Caleb, died at home, Aug. 27, 1861.

** Burkett, W. Edward, present at Fort Donelson; imprisoned at Camp Butler; exchanged Sep. 23, 1862; present at Chickasaw Bayou, Port Hudson, and Raymond; killed at Chickamauga the first day.

** Bynum, John W., present at Fort Donelson; imprisoned at Camp Douglas; exchanged Sep. 23, 1862; present at Chickasaw Bayou, Port Hudson, Raymond, and Jackson; mortally wounded at Chickamauga the second day and died at a field hospital there, Oct. 8, 1863.

* Childers, John, died at Camp Trousdale, Sep. 5, 1861.

* Clanton, A.C., present at Fort Donelson; died at Camp Douglas, Jul. 28, 1862.

* Clanton, T.J., died in Maury County, Tenn., Sep. 4, 1861.

Coleburn, T.J., carried the flag at Fort Donelson; took the oath of allegiance at Camp Douglas and released; rejoined regt. after exchange at Missionary Ridge, then absent sick; surrendered at Greensboro, N.C..

Collins, John C., present at Fort Donelson; imprisoned at Camp Douglas; exchanged Sep. 23, 1862; discharged for disability, Oct. 10, 1862.

* Copeland, Anderson, died at Russellville, Feb., 1862

Cox, W.J., present at Fort Donelson; imprisoned at Camp Douglas; exchanged Sep. 23, 1862; present at Chickasaw Bayou and Port Hudson; captured at Raymond and imprisoned at Alton, Ill.; exchanged at City Point and rejoined regt. Aug. 11, 1863; present at Chickamauga and Missionary Ridge.

Craig, John B., discharged for disability at Bowling Green, Dec., 1861.

Craig, R.F., present at Fort Donelson; imprisoned at Camp Douglas; exchanged Sep. 23, 1862; present at Chickasaw Bayou, Port Hudson, Raymond, Jackson, and Chickamauga; absent sick from Missionary Ridge; survived the war.

Cross, Shelton H., enlisted Nov. 1, 1862; present at Chickasaw Bayou, Port Hudson, and Raymond; absent sick from Jackson; AWOL from Chickamauga; absent sick from Missionary Ridge; survived the war.

Dawson, Mann, present at Fort Donelson; imprisoned at Camp Douglas; exchanged Sep. 23, 1862; present at Chickasaw Bayou, Port Hudson, Raymond, and Jackson; wounded at Chickamauga the first day and left the field; present at Missionary Ridge.

Dotson, Alexander, present at Fort Donelson; imprisoned at Camp Douglas; exchanged Sep. 23, 1862; present at Chickasaw Bayou, Port Hudson, Raymond, and Jackson; absent sick from Chickamauga; present at Missionary Ridge.

Douglas, H.B., present at Fort Donelson; imprisoned at Camp Douglas; exchanged Sep. 23, 1862

Dycus, James Q.A., joined company at reorganization; present at Chickasaw Bayou, Port Hudson, Raymond, Jackson, and Chickamauga; AWOL from Missionary Ridge; survived the war.

Dycus, Joseph, present at Fort Donelson; imprisoned at Camp Douglas; exchanged Sep. 23, 1862; present at Chickasaw Bayou and Port Hudson; captured at Raymond and imprisoned at Fort Delaware and Point Lookout; surrendered at Greensboro, N.C..

Edwards, J.J., detached to Quartermaster Department during Fort Donelson battle; joined the cavalry.

Ellett, J.H., enlisted Nov. 1, 1862; absent sick from Chickasaw Bayou; present at Port Hudson, Raymond and Jackson; AWOL from Chickamauga; absent sick from Missionary Ridge.

* Fisher, George W., present at Fort Donelson; died at Camp Douglas, Mar. 1, 1862.

Fisher, William, present at Fort Donelson; imprisoned at Camp Douglas; exchanged Sep. 23, 1862; captured at Water Valley, Miss., Dec. 4, 1862, and imprisoned at Alton, Ill.; exchanged at City Point May 1, 1863; present at Raymond and Jackson; absent barefoot at Chickamauga; present at Missionary Ridge.

Gannon, Patrick, present at Fort Donelson; took the oath of allegience to the U.S. at Camp Douglas Jun. 4, 1862; joined the enemy.

George, John H., transferred to 26th Tenn., Dec., 1861.

Goodloe, H.G., enlisted Nov. 1, 1862; present at Chickasaw Bayou, Port Hudson, Raymond, and Jackson; absent barefoot from Chickamauga; AWOL from Missionary Ridge.

Goodloe, John P., joined company Dec. 7, 1862; AWOL from Chickasaw Bayou; present at Port Hudson; left the field without leave at Raymond and Jackson; injured at Enterprise, Miss. in Aug., 1863; absent thereafter because of hurt.

* Goodloe, Rufus T., died in Maury County, Jun. 11, 1861.

Gordon, J.F., present at Fort Donelson; imprisoned at Camp Douglas; exchanged Sep. 23, 1862; present at Chickasaw Bayou and Port Hudson; wounded at Raymond; absent due to wound from Jackson; on furlough during Chickamauga; absent sick from Missionary Ridge.

Gordon, Jonathan, discharged for disability, Sep., 1861.

Granberry, John J., wounded at Fort Donelson; sent home and discharged.

Grimes, J.P., discharged for disability, Aug., 1861.

Grimes, John F., wounded at Fort Donelson; sent home; rejoined regt. after exchange; present at Chickasaw Bayou and Port Hudson; wounded at Raymond; absent from Jackson and Chickamauga due to wound; present at Missionary Ridge.

** Guthrie, Fleming, killed at Fort Donelson, Feb. 15, 1862.

Hall, G.M., transferred from 9th Tenn. Cavalry Battalion Mar. 14, 1863; absent sick from Raymond; present at Jackson; absent sick from Chickamauga and Missionary Ridge; captured on the retreat to Dalton, Nov. 27, 1863.

Hall, T.A.M., enlisted Nov. 1, 1862; absent sick from Chickasaw Bayou; present at Port Hudson, Raymond, and Jackson; wounded at Chickamauga the first day; left the field without leave at Missionary Ridge.

Harris, W.B., present at Fort Donelson; imprisoned at Camp Douglas; exchanged Sep. 23, 1862; absent sick from Chickasaw Bayou; present at Port Hudson and Raymond; transferred to 9th Tenn. Cavalry, Jun. 23, 1863.

Henshaw, John F., present at Fort Donelson; imprisoned at Camp Douglas; exchanged Sep. 23, 1862; present at Chickasaw Bayou, Port Hudson, and Raymond; detailed as teamster during Jackson and Chickamauga battles; present at Missionary Ridge.

Hoge, G.S., enlisted Nov. 1, 1862; present at Chickasaw Bayou; absent sick from Port Hudson; present at Raymond and Jackson; AWOL from Chickamauga; absent sick from Missionary Ridge.

Holden, David, present at Fort Donelson; imprisoned at Camp Douglas; exchanged Sep. 23, 1862; present at Chickasaw Bayou, Port Hudson, Raymond, and Jackson; absent sick from Chickamauga and Missionary Ridge; surrendered at Greensboro, N.C..

* Howard, Joseph C., died at home, Sep., 1861.

* Howard, William, died at home, Sep., 1861.

Howell, M., detailed as teamster during Fort Donelson battle; deserted to enemy, Mar., 1862.

Hunter, James B, discharged for disability at Bowling Green, Nov., 1861.

Ingram, J.G., detached to Sappers and Miners, Dec., 1861

Ingram, W.C., sick during Fort Donelson battle and sent off with wounded; rejoined regt. after exchange; AWOL from Chickasaw Bayou; present at Port Hudson; left the field early at Raymond; absent sick from Jackson; AWOL from Chickamauga and Missionary Ridge.

Irwin, G.W., detached to Quartermaster Dept., Nov., 1861.

Jackson, R.C., detached to Commissary Dept. during Fort Donelson battle; took oath of alliegence to U.S. in Maury County, then rejoined regt. after exchange; detached to Quartermaster Dec. 15, 1862, and assigned to Atlanta.

* Jennings, Ben. E., enlisted Nov. 1, 1862; present at Chickasaw Bayou, Port Hudson, and Raymond; absent sick thereafter until he died, Dec. 5, 1863.

Jewell, W.A., present at Fort Donelson; imprisoned at Camp Douglas; exchanged Sep. 23, 1862; on detached duty during Chickasaw Bayou battle; present at Port Hudson, Raymond, and Jackson; wounded the first day at Chickamauga and left field; present at Missionary Ridge; surrendered at Greensboro, N.C..

Johns, A.J., present at Fort Donelson; imprisoned at Camp Douglas; exchanged Sep. 23, 1862; present at Chickasaw Bayou and Port Hudson; on detached duty from Raymond; deserted at Cane Creek, Miss., Jul. 5, 1863.

* Kennedy, William L., died at home, Jul. 22, 1861.

Keyton, Larry, detached to Sappers and Miners, Oct., 1861

** King, E.A., wounded at Fort Donelson; sent home and became a lieutenant in the C.S. Regular Army; mortally wounded at Corinth.

* King, Robert, present at Fort Donelson; died at Camp Douglas, Jul. 23, 1862.

Kittrell, J.H., present at Fort Donelson; imprisoned at Camp Douglas; exchanged Sep. 23, 1862; absent sick from Chickasaw Bayou; present at Port Hudson and Raymond; lost right arm at Jackson, Jul. 13, 1863; discharged Sep. 10, 1863.

Kittrell, J.R., present at Fort Donelson; imprisoned at Camp Douglas; exchanged Sep. 23, 1862; AWOL from Chickasaw Bayou; discharged as non-conscript, Mar. 8, 1863.

Langford, Joseph, present at Fort Donelson; imprisoned at Camp Douglas; exchanged Sep. 23, 1862; present at Chickasaw Bayou, Port Hudson, and Raymond; captured at Jackson May 15, 1863; exchanged and rejoined regt. at Missionary Ridge, Oct. 1, 1863, and present for battle.

Langley, J.A., detached as teamster during Fort Donelson battle; rejoined regt. after exchange; present at Chickasaw Bayou and Port Hudson; on detached duty from Raymond; present at Jackson; deserted Sep. 6, 1863.

Langley, Thomas H., detached as teamster during Fort Donelson battle; discharged May, 1862.

Lindsay, James M., present at Fort Donelson; imprisoned at Camp Douglas; exchanged Sep. 23, 1862; present at Chickasaw Bayou; transferred to 48th Tenn., Mar. 1, 1863.

Long, Albert, discharged for disability, Sep., 1861.

Long, Henry, transferred to 1st Tenn. Cavalry, Nov., 1861.

Mack, John B., sick at home during Fort Donelson battle; rejoined regt. after exchange; wounded and captured at Springdale, Miss., Dec. 3, 1862; exchanged and rejoined the regt. at Port Hudson; transferred to 9th Tenn. Cavalry Battalion, Apr. 9, 1863.

Matthews, J.C., enlisted Nov. 1, 1862; present at Chickasaw Bayou and Port Hudson; absent sick from Raymond and Jackson; wounded at Chickamauga the first day; absent sick from Missionary Ridge; captured in Maury County, Tenn..

* Matthews, John T., present at Fort Donelson; imprisoned at Camp Douglas; exchanged Sep. 23, 1862; present at Chickasaw Bayou and Port Hudson; absent sick from Raymond; died at Lauderdale Springs, Miss., Jul. 4, 1863.

Matthews, N.J., present at Fort Donelson; imprisoned at Camp Douglas; exchanged Sep. 23, 1862; present at Chickasaw Bayou, Port Hudson, Raymond, Jackson, Chickamauga, and Missionary Ridge.

\# Matthews, R.H., wounded at Fort Donelson; sent home; rejoined regt. after exchange; present at Chickasaw Bayou, Port Hudson, Raymond, and Jackson; wounded at Chickamauga the first day and absent from Missionary Ridge due to wound; surrendered at Greensboro, N.C..

Matthews, S.E.S., present at Fort Donelson; imprisoned at Camp Douglas; exchanged Sep. 23, 1862; present at Chickasaw Bayou and Port Hudson; absent on guard duty during Raymond battle; present at Jackson; wounded at Chickamauga the first day; absent from Missionary Ridge due to wound.

Maxwell, J.L., present at Fort Donelson; imprisoned at Camp Butler; exchanged Sep. 23, 1862; present at Chickasaw Bayou and Port Hudson; absent on guard duty during Raymond battle; present at Jackson, Chickamauga, and Missionary Ridge; survived the war.

McClain, Martin, wounded at Fort Donelson; sent home; joined 48th Tenn..

McKnight, D.A., present at Fort Donelson; imprisoned at Camp Douglas; exchanged Sep. 23, 1862; present at Chickasaw Bayou and Port Hudson; captured at Raymond and imprisoned at Fort Delaware and Point Lookout.

\# Moss, J.A., present at Fort Donelson; imprisoned at Camp Douglas; exchanged Sep. 23, 1862; present at Chickasaw Bayou and Port Hudson; absent guarding baggage during Raymond battle; present at Jackson, Chickamauga, and Missionary Ridge; surrendered at Greensboro, N.C..

Moss, Thomas G., discharged for disability, Aug. 1, 1861.

** Nelson, B.H., present at Fort Donelson; imprisoned at Camp Douglas; exchanged Sep. 23, 1862; present at Chickasaw Bayou and Port Hudson; killed at Raymond.

Nelson, William D., wounded at Fort Donelson; sent home and discharged.

* Norwood, N.A., wounded at Fort Donelson; sent home; rejoined regt. after exchange; absent inebriated from Chickasaw Bayou; present at Port Hudson, Raymond, and Jackson; died at Lauderdale Springs, Miss., Sep. 11, 1863.

* Pickard, Y.S., present at Fort Donelson; died at Camp Douglas, Apr. 8, 1862.

Porter, John, discharged for disability, Aug., 1861.

* Robinson, William R., present at Fort Donelson; imprisoned at Camp Douglas; exchanged Sep. 23, 1862; died at Jackson, Miss., Dec. 21, 1862.

Smith, J.E., enlisted Nov. 1, 1862; joined regt. Dec. 31, 1862; present at Port Hudson; absent sick from Raymond and Jackson; present at Chickamauga and Missionary Ridge.

Stewart, J.P., joined company at reorganization; absent from Chickasaw Bayou; present at Port Hudson, Raymond, and Jackson; absent sick from Chickamauga; present at Missionary Ridge.

Stockard, D.F., present at Fort Donelson; imprisoned at Camp Douglas; exchanged Sep. 23, 1862; present at Chickasaw Bayou and Port Hudson; wounded at Raymond; absent thereafter due to wound; survived the war.

Thompson, N.A., deserted to the enemy at Camp Cheatham, Jun., 1861.

Tune, William H., fought at Fort Donelson; imprisoned at Camp Douglas; exchanged Sep. 23, 1862; no further entries in Rollbook.

Tune, William T., sick in Dover during Fort Donelson battle; imprisoned at Camp Butler; exchanged Sep. 23, 1862; present at Chickasaw Bayou and Port Hudson; on detached duty during Raymond battle; present at Jackson; wounded at Chickamauga the first day; absent from Missionary Ridge due to wound.

Walker, J.F., present at Fort Donelson; imprisoned at Camp Douglas; exchanged Sep. 23, 1862; present at Chickasaw Bayou, Port Hudson, Raymond, Jackson, and Chickamauga; absent sick from Missionary Ridge.

Watkins, Isaac J., present at Fort Donelson; imprisoned at Camp Douglas; exchanged Sep. 23, 1862; present at Chickasaw Bayou and Port Hudson; absent sick from Raymond; present at Jackson; wounded the second day at Chickamauga; absent from Missionary Ridge due to wound.

Watkins, Samuel, transferred to 1st Tenn., May, 1861.

Watkins, W.W., enlisted Nov. 1, 1862; present at Chickasaw Bayou, Port Hudson, and Raymond; absent sick from Jackson; present at Chickamauga; absent sick from Missionary Ridge.

** Weaver, William, killed at Fort Donelson, Feb. 15, 1862.

Williams, D.W., present at Fort Donelson; imprisoned at Camp Douglas; exchanged Sep. 23, 1862; absent from Chickasaw Bayou; present at Port Hudson; left field without leave at Raymond; absent sick thereafter.

Williams, T.J., detached as teamster during Fort Doneslon battle; never rejoined the regt..

Wooten, A.W., present at Fort Donelson; imprisoned at Camp Douglas; exchanged Sep. 23, 1862; present at Chickasaw Bayou, Port Hudson, and Raymond; captured at Jackson; paroled and deserted Jun. 1, 1863, at Demopolis, Al..

Company E (later F)

Captain

H.P. Pointer, commanded company at Fort Donelson; imprisoned at Camp Chase and Johnson's Island; exchanged Sep. 16, 1862 and re-elected Captain, then resigned Sep. 26, 1862; joined the cavalry.

R.B McCormick, replaced Childers as 3rd corporal in 1861; present at Fort Donelson; imprisoned at Camp Douglas; exchanged Sep. 23, 1862; elected captain upon resignation of Pointer; on sick leave during Chickasaw Bayou battle; present at Port Hudson, Raymond, and Jackson; absent sick from Chickamauga; present at Missionary Ridge; surrendered at Greensboro, N.C..

1st Lieutenant

Campbell Brown, transferred to the Army of Northern Virginia, Jun., 1861.

E.E. Crawford, promoted from 3rd sergeant Jun., 1861; detached to Sappers and Miners and never returned.

** D.G. Stevenson, as 2nd sergeant present at Fort Donelson; imprisoned at Camp Douglas; exchanged Sep. 23, 1862; promoted to 1st lieutenant at reorganization; commanded company at Chickasaw Bayou; present at Port Hudson, Raymond, and Jackson; mortally wounded at Chickamauga the second day and died that September in Marietta, Ga..

2nd Lieutenant

Thomas Thompson, as a private detailed to Quartermaster Dept. during Fort Donelson battle; rejoined regt. after its exchange and promoted to 2nd lieutenant; initially went on recruiting service; present at Chickasaw Bayou, Port Hudson, and Raymond; absent sick from Jackson; present at Chickamauga and Missionary Ridge.

Junior 2nd Lieutenant

J.T.S. Thompson, present at Fort Donelson; escaped after the surrender and rejoined the regt. after its exchange; resigned and dropped from company rolls after reorganization.

G.P. Straley, as a private present at Fort Donelson; imprisoned at Camp Douglas; exchanged Sep. 23, 1862; elected junior 2nd lieutenant, Sep. 30, 1863; present at Chickasaw Bayou and Port Hudson where he reported sick, Apr. 15, 1863; never returned.

J.H. Reams, as a private present at Fort Donelson; escaped from Camp Douglas, Jun. 5, 1862; rejoined regt. after its exchange; present at Chickasaw Bayou and Port Hudson; absent footsore from Raymond; present at Jackson and Chickamauga; elected junior 2nd lieutenant upon desertion of Straley; present at Missionary Ridge; surrendered at Greensboro, N.C..

1st Sergeant

W.D. Rountree, present at Fort Doneslon; imprisoned at Camp Douglas; exchanged Sep. 23, 1862; not re-elected, then discharged as a non-conscript, Sep., 1862.

Alon. McKissack, as a private present at Fort Donelson; imprisoned at Camp Douglas; exchanged Sep. 23, 1862; promoted to 1st sergeant at reorganization; present at Chickasaw Bayou and Port Hudson; captured at Raymond and imprisoned.

2nd Sergeant

T.B. Tucker, as a private present at Fort Donelson; imprisoned at Camp Douglas; exchanged Sep. 23, 1862; promoted to 2nd sergeant at reorganization; present at Chickasaw Bayou, Port Hudson, Raymond, and Jackson; captured at Chickamauga the second day; escaped and rejoined company Oct. 1, 1863; present at Missionary Ridge.

3rd Sergeant

T. (J.) B. Terrell, as a private present at Fort Donelson; imprisoned at Camp Douglas; exchanged Sep. 23, 1862; promoted to 3rd sergeant at reorganization; present at Chickasaw Bayou, Port Hudson, Raymond, and Jackson; absent sick from Chickamauga; deserted from Missionary Ridge, Nov. 25, 1863.

Isaac K. Cowsert, sick during Fort Donelson battle; joined the 47th Tenn.; rejoined the regt. at Dalton, Ga., Jan. 1, 1864; immediately promoted to 3rd sergeant; survived the war.

4th Sergeant

T.B. Wade, present at Fort Donelson; escaped from Camp Douglas, May 1, 1862; joined Holman's Battalion of cavalry.

J.W. Alexander, as a private present at Fort Donelson; imprisoned at Camp Douglas; exchanged Sep. 23, 1862; present at Chickasaw Bayou, Port Hudson, and Raymond; wounded at Jackson; absent from Chickamauga due to wound; present at Missionary Ridge.

5th Sergeant

** T.J. Bond, present at Fort Donelson; imprisoned at Camp Douglas; exchanged Sep. 23, 1862; returned to ranks at reorganization; present at Chickasaw Bayou and Port Hudson; killed at Raymond.

T.V. Ferguson, present at Fort Donelson; imprisoned at Camp Douglas; exchanged Sep. 23, 1862; promoted to 5th sergeant at reorganization; captured at Springdale, Miss., Dec. 3, 1862; took the oath of allegience to the U.S. at Oxford, Miss., then joined the 1st Tenn. Cavalry.

1st Corporal

R.L. Wilson, detached as harness maker; never returned.

J.D. Blanton, present at Fort Donelson; imprisoned at Camp Douglas; exchanged Sep. 23, 1862; returned to ranks at reorganization; present at Chickasaw Bayou, Port Hudson, Raymond, and Jackson; wounded at Chickamauga the first day; absent from Missionary Ridge due to wound.

** Horace Williams, as a private present at Fort Donelson; imprisoned at Camp Douglas; exchanged Sep. 23, 1862; promoted to 1st corporal at reorganization; present at Chickasaw Bayou and Port Hudson; wounded at Raymond and died there from wound, Jun. 20, 1863.

* J.T. Clark, present at Fort Donelson; imprisoned at Camp Douglas; exchanged Sep. 23, 1862; present at Chickasaw Bayou, Port Hudson, and Raymond; promoted to corporal, Jul. 3, 1863; wounded at Jackson and died at Lauderdale Springs, Miss., Aug. 1, 1863.

W.T. Edwards, present at Fort Donelson; escaped from Camp Douglas Jun. 20, 1862; rejoined regt. after its exchange; present at Chickasaw Bayou, Port Hudson, Raymond, Jackson, Chickamauga, and Misssionary Ridge; promoted to corporal, Dec. 1, 1863; survived the war.

2nd Corporal

J.W. Buford, sick at Russellville during Fort Donelson battle; joined the cavalry.

W.T. Beasley, as a private present at Fort Donelson; imprisoned at Camp Douglas; exchanged Sep. 23, 1862; promoted to 2nd corporal at reorganization; absent sick from Chickasaw Bayou; present at Port Hudson and Raymond; absent sick from Jackson and Chickamauga; present at Missionary Ridge.

3rd Corporal

J.V. Childers, detached as assistant surgeon in Nashville; promoted to surgeon.

J.H. Denton, as a private present at Fort Donelson; imprisoned at Camp Douglas; exchanged Sep. 23, 1862; promoted to 3rd corporal at reorganization; present at Chickasaw Bayou, Port Hudson, Raymond, and Jackson; AWOL from Chickamauga; present at Missionary Ridge; survived the war.

4th Corporal

T.F. Dunlap, present at Fort Donelson; escaped from Camp Douglas, Jun. 7, 1862; rejoined regt. after its exchange; returned to the ranks; AWOL from Chickasaw Bayou; present at Port Hudson; absent footsore from Raymond; present at Jackson; AWOL from Chickamauga the second day; present at Missionary Ridge; transferred to 48th Tenn., Jan. 15, 1864.

James W. Newcomb, as a private present at Fort Donelson; imprisoned at Camp Douglas; exchanged Sep. 23, 1862; promoted to 4th corporal at reorganization; wounded at Springdale, Miss., and missed Chickasaw Bayou battle due to wound; deserted from Port Hudson Mar. 30, 1863; arrested and rejoined regt. Apr. 28, 1863; absent from Raymond under arrest; absent sick from Jackson; AWOL from Chickamauga; deserted to the enemy at Chattanooga, Nov. 7, 1863.

L.V. Dowell, present at Fort Doneslon; imprisoned at Camp Douglas; exchanged Sep. 23, 1862; present at Chickasaw Bayou and Port Hudson; captured at Raymond, exchanged and rejoined the regt. Oct., 1863; present at Missionary Ridge; promoted to corporal, Dec 1, 1863.

Privates

Bailey, A.M., sick in Dover during Fort Donelson battle; escaped from Camp Douglas Jun.7, 1862; rejoined the regt. after its exchange; present at Chickasaw Bayou and Port Hudson; wounded at Raymond; furloughed home until Feb. 11, 1864; detached to Secret Service, Mar. 1, 1864.

Blair, T.W., present at fort Donelson; escaped from Camp Douglas Jun. 5, 1862; joined Bartow's Cavalry.

Brown, W.H., discharged for disability at Bowling Green, Dec. 1, 1861.

Buchanan, R., discharged at Camp Cheatham, Jul. 8, 1861.

Bunch, J., present at Fort Donelson; imprisoned at Camp Douglas; exchanged Sep. 23, 1862; transferred to 48th Tenn. at reorganization.

Caldwell, W.A., wounded at Fort Donelson; sent home and joined the 48th Tenn.; rejoined the regt. Dec. 27, 1862; present at Port Hudson, Raymond, and Jackson; AWOL from Chickamauga the second day; absent barefoot from Missionary Ridge.

Campbell, J.B., present at Fort Donelson; imprisoned at Camp Douglas; exchaged Sep. 23, 1862; present at Chickasaw Bayou, Port Hudson, Raymond, and Jackson; absent barefoot from Chickamauga; present at Missionary Ridge.

Cash, T.W., detached to the Quarter Master Dept. at Bowling Green; rejoined the regt. after its exchange; present at Chickasaw Bayou and Port Hudson; discharged as non-conscript, Apr., 1863.

Cavin, R.B., sick at home during Fort Donelson battle; rejoined regt. after its exchange; present at Chickasaw Bayou and Port Hudson; furloughed Apr. 1, 1863, and never returned.

** Chatham, W.T., killed at Fort Donelson, Feb. 15, 1862.

Clark, J.S., detailed as teamster; rejoined regt. after its exchange

Cooper, J.O., present at Fort Donelson; imprisoned at Camp Douglas; exchanged Sep. 23, 1862; present at Chickasaw Bayou; deserted from Port Hudson, Apr. 12, 1863.

Crump, G.K., present at Fort Donelson; escaped from Camp Douglas, Jun. 5, 1862; rejoined the regt. Dec. 27, 1862; deserted from Port Hudson, May 3, 1863.

Curtis, W.W., present at Fort Donelson; imprisoned at Camp Douglas; exchanged Sep. 23, 1862; present at Chickasaw Bayou, Port Hudson, Raymond, and Jackson; went on furlough, Aug., 1863, and then deserted.

Dabney, N.I., sick during Fort Donelson battle; discharged at Decatur, Alabama, Apr., 1861.

Davis, W.M., sick at Russellville during Fort Donelson battle; rejoined regt. after its exchange; AWOL from Chickasaw Bayou; present at Port Hudson; absent sick from Raymond and Jackson; deserted Sep. 18, 1863.

Dobbins, J.J., sick during Fort Donelson battle; joined the 48th Tenn..

Eddington, H.L.W., present at Fort Donelson; took the oath of alliegence to the U.S. at Camp Douglas and deserted to the enemy.

Erskine, H.C., detailed as nurse in Russellville; joined 17th Tenn; rejoined regt. at Port Hudson, Jan. 20, 1863; on guard duty during Raymond battle; present at Jackson; wounded at Chickamauga; present at Missionary Ridge.

* Golden, T.V., present at Fort Donelson; killed by fellow prisoner W.H. Kilpatrick at Camp Douglas in Apr., 1862.

Grant, G.F., deserted from Camp Trousdale, Aug. 12, 1862.

Hargrove, J.N., AWOL during Fort Donelson battle; imprisoned at Camp Douglas; exchanged Sep. 23, 1862; detailed as teamster during Chickasaw Bayou and Port Hudson battles; under arrest during Raymond battle; on detached duty as teamster thereafter.

** Hassel, James, sick during Fort Donelson battle; rejoined regt. after its exchange; present at Chickasaw Bayou, Port Hudson, and Raymond; absent sick from Jackson; killed at Chickamauga the first day.

Hays, J.L., present at Fort Donelson; escaped after the surrender and joined the cavalry.

* Holland, W.J., present at Fort Donelson; imprisoned at Camp Douglas; exchanged Sep. 23, 1862; died at Jackson, Miss., Oct., 1862.

Hutchcraft, W.B., present at Fort Donelson; imprisoned at Camp Douglas; exchanged Sep. 23, 1862; present at Chickasaw Bayou and Port Hudson; captured at Raymond and then paroled; never returned.

Jackson, S.A., present at Fort Donelson; imprisoned at Camp Douglas; exchanged Sep. 23, 1862; present at Chickasaw Bayou and Port Hudson; wounded at Raymond; furloughed Aug., 1863, and never returned.

** Johnson, H., sick during Fort Donelson battle; joined the cavalry and was killed at Rickmond, Ky..

Johnson, V.B., discharged for disability at Camp Trousdale, Aug. 15, 1861.

Johnson, W.D., present at Fort Donelson; imprisoned at Camp Douglas; exchanged Sep. 23, 1862; present at Chickasaw Bayou, Port Hudson, Raymond, and Jackson; AWOL from Chickamauga the second day; present at Missionary Ridge.

* Johnson, W.J.L., died at Bowling Green, Jan.1, 1862.

Kilpatrick, William H., musician; present at Fort Donelson; imprisoned at Camp Douglas; imprisoned at the Illinois State Penitentiary for one year for the murder of T.M. Golden; never rejoined the regt..

* Lamb, J.T., died at Nashville, Oct., 1861.

Leftwich, T.J., present at Fort Donelson; imprisoned at Camp Douglas; exchanged Sep. 23, 1862; present at Chickasaw Bayou, Port Hudson, Raymond, Jackson, Chickamauga, and Missionary Ridge; captured on the retreat to Ringold, Nov. 26, 1863.

Lockridge, G.B., present at Fort Donelson; took the oath of allegience to the U.S. at St. Louis; rejoined regt. after its exchange; present at Chickasaw Bayou, Port Hudson, Raymond, and Jackson; wounded at Chickamauga the first day; absent sick from Missionary Ridge; survived the war.

Lockridge, J.W., present at Fort Donelson; took the oath of allegience to the U.S. at St. Louis; rejoined regt. after its exchange; absent injured from Chickasaw Bayou; present at Port Hudson, Raymond, and Jackson; wounded at Chickamauga the first day; absent sick from Missionary Ridge; surrendered at Greensboro, N.C..

McCarroll, James, detailed as an apothecary; rejoined regt. after its exchange; absent from Chickasaw Bayou due to being unarmed; discharged for disability at Port Hudson, Feb., 1863.

* Meece, O., present at Fort Donelson; imprisoned at Camp Douglas; exchanged Sep. 23, 1862; died in hospital at Jackson, Miss., Oct. 30, 1862.

Moore, T.J., present at Fort Donelson; escaped from Camp Douglas Jun. 5, 1862, and never returned.

Morris, J.P., present at Fort Donelson; imprisoned at Camp Douglas; exchanged Sep. 23, 1862; present at Chickasaw Bayou, Port Hudson, Raymond, and Jackson; AWOL from Chickamauga; deserted from Lookout Mountain, Nov. 24, 1863.

Murphy, Pat, present at Fort Donelson; imprisoned at Camp Douglas; exchanged Sep. 23, 1862; detached as blacksmith to government works, Sep. 26, 1862.

Nelums, D.A., present at Fort Donelson; imprisoned at Camp Douglas; exchanged Sep. 23, 1862; discharged for disability, Sep., 1862.

Nichol, N.M., sick at Russellville during Fort Donelson battle; rejoined regt. after its exchange; present at Chickasaw Bayou; discharged as non-conscript, Feb., 1863.

Orman, R.L., present at Fort Donelson; imprisoned at Camp Douglas; exchanged Sep. 23, 1862; present at Chickasaw Bayou, Port Hudson, Raymond, and Jackson; AWOL from Chickamauga; deserted from Missionary Ridge, Nov. 25, 1863.

Orman, W.E., discharged for disability at Camp Cheatham, Jun., 1861; rejoined the regt. at Vicksburg, Dec. 27, 1862; detached to surgeon; discharged for disability, Mar., 1863.

** Owen, A.J., present at Fort Donelson; imprisoned at Camp Douglas; exchanged Sep. 23, 1862; present at Chickasaw Bayou and Port Hudson; absent sick from Raymond and Jackson; wounded at Chickamauga the first day and died at Atlanta, Oct. 9, 1863.

Owen, R.W., present at Fort Donelson; imprisoned at Camp Douglas; exchanged Sep. 23, 1862; absent from Chickasaw Bayou due to being unarmed; present at Port Hudson, Raymond, and Jackson; absent barefoot from Chickamauga; on detached duty during Missionary Ridge battle.

Owen, W.J., present at Fort Donelson; imprisoned at Camp Douglas; exchanged Sep. 23, 1862; present at Chickasaw Bayou and Port Hudson; captured at Raymond, paroled, and rejoined the regt. in May, 1863; present at Jackson; present at Chickamauga the first day; present at Missionary Ridge; survived the war.

* Parham, E.J., sick during Fort Donelson battle; rejoined company Dec. 1, 1862; present at Chickasaw Bayou and Port Hudson; captured at Raymond and imprisoned at Fort Delaware and Point Lookout where he died.

* Parham, E.T., sick during Fort Donelson battle; rejoined company Dec. 1, 1862; present at Chickasaw Bayou, Port Hudson, Raymond, and Jackson; absent sick from Chickamauga; died at Marion, Al., Oct. 16, 1863.

** Pope, W.A., sick during Fort Donelson battle; joined another regt. and was killed at Shiloh.

Reynolds, J.H., present at Fort Donelson; imprisoned at Camp Douglas; exchanged Sep. 23, 1862; present at Chickasaw Bayou, Port Hudson, Raymond, and Jackson; AWOL from Chickamauga; deserted from Lookout Mountain, Nov. 24, 1863.

Rountree, J.A., permanently detailed as harness maker.

Rountree, T.J., sick at home during Fort Donelson battle; rejoined regt. after its exchange; present at Chickasaw Bayou and Port Hudson; captured at Raymond and imprisoned at Fort Delaware and Point Lookout.

Rumage, A.J., sick at Bowling Green during Fort Donelson battle; joined an Arkansas regt..

Sharp, J.J., sick during Fort Donelson battle; rejoined regt. after its exchange; present at Chickasaw Bayou and Port Hudson; absent sick from Raymond and Jackson; AWOL from Chickamauga; deserted from Lookout Mountain, Nov. 24, 1863.

* Sharp, M.V., died at Camp Trousdale.

Spratt, A.J., present at Fort Donelson; imprisoned at Camp Douglas; exchanged Sep. 23, 1862; present at Chickasaw Bayou, Port Hudson, and Raymond; absent sick thereafter; survived the war.

Spratt, C.B., sick during Fort Donelson battle; discharged.

Stanfield, W.R., present at Fort Donelson; imprisoned at Camp Douglas; exchanged Sep. 23, 1862; present at Chickasaw Bayou and Port Hudson; captured at Raymond and imprisoned.

Thom, Edward C., present at Fort Donelson; imprisoned at Camp Douglas; exchanged Sep. 23, 1862; present at Chickasaw Bayou, Port Hudson, Raymond, and Jackson; on detached duty thereafter.

Thompson, J.A., present at Fort Donelson; imprisoned at Camp Douglas; exchanged Sep. 23, 1862; present at Chickasaw Bayou, Port Hudson, Raymond, and Jackson; AWOL from Chickamauga; present at Missionary Ridge.

* Thompson, J.T., present at Fort Donelson; died at Camp Douglas, Mar. 18, 1862.

Tucker, J.M (D.), fought at Fort Donelson; imprisoned at Camp Douglas; exchanged Sep. 23, 1862; AWOL from Chickasaw Bayou, Port Hudson, and Raymond; present at Jackson, Chickamauga, and Missionary Ridge; survived the war.

Watson, James, present at Fort Donelson; imprisoned at Camp Douglas; exchanged Sep. 23, 1862; captured at Springdale, Miss., Dec. 3, 1862; took the oath of allegiance to the U.S. and deserted.

Watson, S., present at Fort Donelson; imprisoned at Camp Douglas; exchanged Sep. 23, 1862; absent sick from Chickasaw Bayou; present at Port Hudson; captured at Raymond and imprisoned.

White, W.W., present at Fort Donelson; imprisoned at Camp Douglas; exchanged Sep. 23, 1862; no further company record.

Company F (later E)

Captain

George W. Jones, commanded company at Fort Donelson; imprisoned at Camp Chase and Johnson's Island; exchanged Sep. 16, 1862; commanded company at Chickasaw Bayou, Port Hudson, and Raymond; absent sick thereafter.

1st Lieutenant

James B. Murphy, present at Fort Donelson; imprisoned at Camp Chase and Johnson's Island; exchanged Sep. 16, 1862; present at Chickasaw Bayou and Port Hudson; captured at Raymond and imprisoned at Johnson's Island.

2nd Lieutenant

Benjamin G. Darden, present at Fort Donelson; imprisoned at Camp Douglas; exchanged Sep. 16, 1862; present at Chickasaw Bayou and Port Hudson; wounded at Raymond; absent from Jackson due to wound; furloughed Jul. 1, 1863; surrendered at Greensboro, N.C..

Junior 2nd Lieutenant

J.T. Williamson, wounded at Fort Donelson; sent home; joined the cavalry.

J.F. Matthews, as a private present at Fort Donelson; imprisoned at Camp Douglas; exchanged Sep. 23, 1862; promoted to junior 2nd lieutenant at reorganization; present at Chickasaw Bayou, Port Hudson, Raymond, and Jackson; absent sick thereafter.

1st Sergeant

L.J. Mash, resigned and returned to the ranks Aug. 5, 1861; present at Fort Donelson; imprisoned at Camp Douglas; exchanged Sep. 23, 1862; present at Chickasaw Bayou; discharged at Port Hudson as non-conscript, Mar. 5, 1863.

M.P. Taylor, replaced Mash; present at Fort Donelson; imprisoned at Camp Douglas; exchanged Sep. 23, 1862; no additional enties.

** N.G. Walker, as a private present at Fort Donelson; imprisoned at Camp Douglas; exchanged Sep. 23, 1862; promoted to 1st sergeant at reorganization; present at Chickasaw Bayou and Port Hudson; killed at Raymond.

E.Y. Murphy, as a private present at Fort Donelson; imprisoned at Camp Douglas; exchanged Sep. 23, 1862; present at Chickasaw Bayou and Port Hudson; wounded at Raymond; promoted to 1st sergeant, Jul. 1, 1863; present at Chickamauga and Missionary Ridge.

2nd Sergeant

Thomas Putnam, discharged for disability, Jan. 25, 1862.

A.F. Thompson, as a private present at Fort Donelson; imprisoned at Camp Douglas; exchanged Sep. 23, 1862; promoted to 2nd sergeant at reorganization; on detached duty during Chickasaw Bayou battle; present at Port Hudson, Raymond, and Jackson; absent sick thereafter.

3rd Sergeant

* J.R. Good, died at Camp Cheatham, Aug. 7, 1861.

S. Garrett, promoted upon Good's death; wounded at Fort Donelson; sent home; rejoined regt. after its exchange

4th Sergeant

M.B. Tomlinson, present at Fort Donelson; imprisoned at Camp Douglas; exchanged Sep. 23, 1862; transferred to 48th Tenn., Sep. 28, 1862; made lieutenant.

John T. Goodrich, as a private present at Fort Donelson; imprisoned at Camp Douglas; exchanged Sep. 23, 1862; promoted to 4th sergeant at reorganization; present at Chickasaw Bayou, Port Hudson, and Raymond; wounded at Jackson; present at Chickamauga and Missionary Ridge; survived the war.

5th Sergeant

W.A. Henderson, sick at home during Fort Donelson battle; entered the cavalry; rejoined the regt. at Port Hudson and returned to the ranks; present at Raymond, Jackson, and Chickamauga; absent sick from Missionary Ridge.

H.A. Martin, as a private present at Fort Donelson; imprisoned at Camp Douglas; exchanged Sep. 23, 1862; promoted to 5th sergeant at reorganization; present at Chickasaw Bayou and Port Hudson; captured at Raymond; paroled and then deserted, Jul. 1, 1863.

R.R. Jones, as a private present at Fort Donelson; imprisoned at Camp Douglas; exchanged Sep. 23, 1862; present at Chickasaw Bayou and Port Hudson; promoted to 5th sergeant Apr. 5, 1863; present at Raymond and Jackson; on detached duty thereafter.

Color Sergeant

J.H. Hogan, as a private present at Fort Donelson; imprisoned at Camp Douglas; exchanged Sep. 23, 1862; AWOL from Chickasaw Bayou; present at Port Hudson, Raymond, and Jackson; appointed color sergeant, Sep. 10, 1863; present at Chickamauga and Missionary Ridge.

1st Corporal

A.E. Crews, wounded at Fort Donelson; sent home and rejoined the regt. after its exchange

** John Holt, as a private present at Fort Donelson; imprisoned at Camp Douglas; exchanged Sep. 23, 1862; promoted to 1st corporal at reorganization; present at Chickasaw Bayou, Port Hudson, Raymond, and Jackson; killed at Chickamauga the first day.

2nd Corporal

** J.H. Crews, killed at Fort Donelson, Feb. 15, 1862.

J.A. Richardson, as a private present at Fort Donelson; imprisoned at Camp Douglas; exchanged Sep. 23, 1862; promoted to 2nd corporal at reorganization; present at Chickasaw Bayou, Port Hudson, Raymond, and Jackson; captured at Chickamauga the first day and never returned.

3rd Corporal

J.J. Beaty, wounded at Fort Donelson; sent home and joined the 17th Tenn..

** J.R. Taylor, as a private present at Fort Donelson; imprisoned at Camp Douglas; exchanged Sep. 23, 1862; promoted to 3rd corporal at reorganization; present at Chickasaw Bayou and Port Hudson; killed at Raymond.

4th Corporal

J.G. Holding, present at Fort Donelson; imprisoned at Camp Douglas; exchanged Sep. 23, 1862; returned to the ranks at reorganization; present at Chickasaw Bayou and Port Hudson; on detached duty to Ordnance Dept. until deserting to the enemy at Lookout Mountain, Nov. 24, 1863.

G.D. Matthews, as private, wounded at Ft. Donelson; present at exchange; joined company at reorganization; present at Chickasaw Bayou and Port Hudson; captured at Raymond; exchanged and rejoined the regt. Sep. 10, 1863; captured at Chickamauga the first day; escaped and rejoined the regt. Oct. 1, 1863; surrendered at Greensboro, N.C..

Robert Galloway, enlisted Nov. 10, 1862; present at Chickasaw Bayou and Port Hudson; absent sick from Raymond; present at Jackson, Chickamauga, and Missionary Ridge; promoted to corporal, Dec. 1, 1863.

Privates

Amis, M.C., sick at home during Fort Donelson battle; never rejoined the regt..

Aydelotte, J.P., detailed as teamster during Fort Donelson battle; rejoined regt. after its exchange; absent sick from Chickasaw Bayou; discharged as non-conscript, Mar., 1863.

Branch, John T., present at Fort Donelson; escaped from Camp Douglas, Jun. 1, 1862; joined the cavalry.

Bryant, T.H., present at Fort Donelson; imprisoned at Camp Douglas; exchanged Sep. 23, 1862; present at Chickasaw Bayou and Port Hudson; wounded at Raymond; absent from Jackson due to wound; furloughed Aug., 1863, and never returned.

* Cheatham, Polk, present at Fort Donelson; died at Camp Douglas, Mar. 10, 1862.

Cheek, R.N., detailed as teamster during Fort Donelson battle; served in the cavalry; rejoined the regt. after its exchange; on detached duty during Chickasaw Bayou battle; present at Port Hudson; captured at Raymond and imprisoned at Fort Delaware.

Childrey, R.B., present at Fort Donelson; imprisoned at Camp Douglas; exchanged Sep. 23, 1862; present at Chickasaw Bayou, Port Hudson, Raymond, and Jackson; absent sick at Chickamauga and Missionary Ridge; surrendered at Greensboro, N.C..

* Coffey, J.F., died at Bowling Green, Nov. 20, 1861.

* Coffey, J.M.G., present at Fort Donelson; imprisoned at Camp Douglas; exchanged Sep. 23, 1862; present at Chickasaw Bayou and Port Hudson; died at Clinton, La., Apr., 1863.

Coffey, T.J., present at Fort Donelson; imprisoned at Camp Douglas; exchanged Sep. 23, 1862; present at Chickasaw Bayou, Port Hudson, Raymond, and Jackson; absent sick from Chickamauga; on detached duty during Missionary Ridge battle.

Courtney, J.H., present at Fort Donelson; imprisoned at Camp Douglas; exchanged Sep. 23, 1862; present at Chickasaw Bayou and Port Hudson; captured at Raymond; paroled and deserted Jul. 1, 1863.

Craig, D.A., present at Fort Donelson; imprisoned at Camp Douglas; exchanged Sep. 23, 1862; present at Chickasaw Bayou and Port Hudson; lost right arm at Raymond and became permanently disabled.

Craig, James F., transferred to regt. from the 32nd Miss., Mar. 1, 1864.

Craig, W.J., present at Fort Donelson; imprisoned at Camp Douglas; exchanged Sep. 23, 1862; present at Chickasaw Bayou, Port Hudson,

Raymond, and Jackson; wounded at Chickamauga the first day; absent from Missionary Ridge due to wound.

Crews, A.E., joined the company Dec. 7, 1862; on detached duty during Chickasaw Bayou battle; present at Port Hudson; captured at Raymond; paroled and deserted Jul. 1, 1863.

** Crews, P.L., enlisted Nov. 10, 1862; present at Chickasaw Bayou, Port Hudson, Raymond, and Jackson; killed at Chickamauga the first day.

Crews, R.T., enlisted Nov. 10, 1862; absent sick from Chickasaw Bayou; present at Port Hudson; absent sick from Raymond and Jackson; absent barefoot from Chickamauga; deserted from Lookout Mountain, Nov. 24, 1863.

** Crews, W.J., killed at Fort Donelson, Feb. 15, 1862.

Cross, J.M., enlisted Nov. 10, 1862; present at Chickasaw Bayou and Port Hudson; wounded at Raymond; absent from Jackson due to wound; deserted Sep. 1, 1863.

Cross, S.S., enlisted Nov. 10, 1862; present at Chickasaw Bayou, Port Hudson, and Raymond; absent sick from Jackson; on detached duty to Commissary Dept. thereafter; survived the war.

** Davis, A.B., killed at Fort Donelson, Feb. 15, 1862.

Davis, A.C., sick at home during the Fort Donelson battle; deserted to the enemy.

Davis, Black, enlisted Nov. 10, 1862; present at Chickasaw Bayou, Port Hudson, and Raymond; deserted Jul. 4, 1863.

Davis, H.B., present at Fort Donelson; escaped after the surrender and joined the cavalry.

Davis, J.H., present at Fort Donelson; escaped from Camp Douglas, Apr. 15, 1862; joined the cavalry.

* Davis, R.C., died at Bowling Green, Dec. 15, 1861.

Davis, William, enlisted Nov. 10, 1862; present at Chickasaw Bayou, Port Hudson, and Raymond; deserted Jul. 4, 1863.

Ellis, R.B., present at Fort Donelson; imprisoned at Camp Douglas; exchanged Sep. 23, 1862; on detached duty during Fort Donelson battle; discharged at Port Hudson as non-conscript, Mar. 5, 1863.

Faulkner, F., detached as nurse to a hospital in Nashville; never returned.

Fitzpatrick, M.J., present at Fort Donelson; escaped from Camp Douglas, Aug., 1862; joined the cavalry.

* Galloway, E.S., present at Fort Donelson; imprisoned at Camp Douglas; exchanged Sep. 23, 1862; detached as butcher fro Tilghman's Division in Nov., 1862; wounded and captured at Vicksburg; furloughed home and died Oct. 17, 1863.

Garrett, J.S., present at Fort Donelson; escaped after the surrender and never returned.

Gifford, Frank, present at Fort Donelson; imprisoned at Camp Douglas; exchanged Sep. 23, 1862; on detached duty during Chickasaw Bayou battle; discharged at Port Hudson as non-conscript, Mar. 5, 1863.

Gilmore, John, enlisted Nov. 10, 1863; never reported.

Graves, Frank, enlisted Nov. 10, 1862; transferred to regt. from 48th Tenn. at Port Hudson in Apr., 1863; present at Raymond; deserted Jul. 4, 1863.

Graves, P.P., present at Fort Donelson; imprisoned at Camp Douglas; exchanged Sep. 23, 1862; present at Chickasaw Bayou and Port Hudson; absent sick thereafter.

Henderson, J.F., enlisted Nov. 10, 1862; absent sick from Chickasaw Bayou; present at Port Hudson and Raymond; absent sick from Jackson, Chickamauga, and Missionary Ridge; permanently detached to hospital duty, Jan. 4, 1864.

Holt, I.A., wounded at Fort Donelson; sent home; rejoined regt. at Port Hudson; absent sick from Raymond; permanently detached to the hospital at Enterprise, Miss., Aug. 5, 1863.

Howlett, J.S., present at Fort Donelson; imprisoned at Camp Douglas; exchanged Sep. 23, 1862; detached as assistant surgeon to the 12th Arkansas, Oct. 5, 1862; deserted Nov., 1862.

Hubbell, B.R., present at Fort Donelson; imprisoned at Camp Douglas; exchanged Sep. 23, 1862; wounded at Springdale; AWOL from Chickasaw Bayou; discharged at Port Hudson as non-conscript Mar. 5, 1863.

* Hughes, A.B., died at Bowling Green, Oct.3, 1861.

Irvin, W.M., transferred to regt. from 48th Tenn., Jan. 7, 1864.

James, David, present at Fort Donelson; imprisoned at Camp Douglas; exchanged Sep. 23, 1862; present at Chickasaw Bayou and Port Hudson; discharged for disability, Mar., 1863.

* Jarrett, Jeff, died at Russellville, Feb. 20, 1862.

* Jarrett, P., died at Russellville.

Jarrett, William, discharged for disability at Camp Cheatham, Jul. 20, 1861.

Kannon, E.D., present at Fort Donelson; took the oath of alliegience to the U.S. at St. Louis and released; joined the cavalry.

Lamar, J.W., present at Fort Donelson; imprisoned at Camp Douglas; exchanged Sep. 23, 1862; present at Chickasaw Bayou and Port Hudson; wounded at Raymond; absent thereafter due to wound; survived the war.

\# Lamar, L.S., present at Fort Donelson; imprisoned at Camp Douglas; exchanged Sep. 23, 1862; present at Chickasaw Bayou, Port Hudson, Raymond, Jackson, Chickamauga, and Missionary Ridge; surrendered at Greensboro, N.C..

Lamar, W.B., detached as teamster; joined the 32nd Tenn.; rejoined the regt. Jan. 1, 1864.

Leneave, T.M., present at Fort Donelson; imprisoned at Camp Douglas; exchanged Sep. 23, 1862; discharged for disability, Sep. 28, 1862.

London, C.C., present at Fort Donelson; imprisoned at Camp Douglas; exchanged Sep. 23, 1862; present at Chickasaw Bayou and Port Hudson; captured at Raymond and imprisoned at Fort Delaware.

* London, J.M., present at Fort Donelson; imprisoned at Camp Douglas; exchanged Sep. 23,1862; present at Chickasaw Bayou and Port Hudson; on detached duty during Raymond battle; captured at Jackson May 14, 1863; paroled and rejoined regt. Aug. 20, 1863; died at Enterprise, Miss., Sep. 15, 1863.

Mack, W.R.C., present at Fort Donelson; imprisoned at Camp Douglas; exchanged Sep. 23, 1862; absent sick from Chickasaw Bayou; present at Port Hudson; on detached duty during Raymond battle; absent sick from Jackson; on detached duty thereafter.

Mahoney, Thomas, present at Fort Donelson; imprisoned at Camp Douglas; exchanged Sep. 23, 1862; present at Chickasaw Bayou, Port Hudson, and Raymond; detailed as teamster thereafter.

* Martin, G., died at Camp Cheatham, Jul. 7, 1861.

Martin, James, present at Fort Donelson; imprisoned at Camp Douglas; exchanged Sep. 23, 1862; no further entries.

** Mash, W.R., present at Fort Donelson; imprisoned at Camp Douglas; exchanged Sep. 23, 1862; present at Chickasaw Bayou and Port Hudson; killed at Raymond.

McCain, H.M., discharged for disability at Camp Cheathm, Jul. 1, 1861; rejoined the regt. at Grenada, Miss., Dec. 7, 1862; present at Chickasaw Bayou; discharged for disability at Port Hudson, Mar. 5, 1863..

* McKnight, G.W., enlisted Nov. 10, 1862; present at Chickasaw Bayou; absent sick from Port Hudson; died at Clinton, La., Mar. 24, 1863.

McKnight, J.S., present at Fort Donelson; imprisoned at Camp Douglas; exchanged Sep. 23, 1862; present at Chickasaw Bayou and Port Hudson; on detached duty during Raymond battle; present at Jackson; absent barefoot from Chickamauga; deserted from Lookout Mountain, Nov. 24, 1863.

Neely, R.B., present at Fort Donelson; imprisoned at Camp Douglas; exchanged Sep. 23, 1862; present at Chickasaw Bayou, Port Hudson, and Raymond; wounded at Jackson; absent sick thereafter.

Paul, Uriah, present at Fort Donelson; escaped after the surrender; rejoined regt. after its exchange; AWOL from Chickasaw Bayou; present at Port Hudson; wounded at Raymond; absent from Jackson due to wound; deserted Aug. 1, 1863.

** Pullen, E.T., present at Fort Donelson; imprisoned at Camp Douglas; exchanged Sep. 23, 1862; present at Chickasaw Bayou, Port Hudson, and Raymond; killed at Jackson, Jul. 11, 1863.

Pullen, G.W., enlisted Nov. 10, 1862; present at Chickasaw Bayou and Port Hudson; absent footsore from Raymond and Jackson; AWOL from Chickamauga; deserted from Lookout Mountain, Nov. 24, 1863.

Pullen, J.T., discharged for disability at Bowling Green.

* Refrow, Barclay, died at Russellville, Feb. 6, 1862.

* Ramsay, G.E., died at Russellville, Feb. 14, 1862.

Renfrow, B.W., present at Fort Donelson; imprisoned at Camp Douglas; exchanged Sep. 23, 1862; present at Chickasaw Bayou; discharged at Port Hudson as non-conscript, Mar. 5, 1863.

Renfrow, R.T., absent from Fort Donelson detailed to accompany his brother's corpse home; joined the cavalry.

Renfrow, W.P., present at Fort Donelson; escaped from Camp Douglas, Jun. 1, 1862; rejoined regt. after its exchange; present at Chickasaw Bayou and Port Hudson; left the field without leave at Raymond; present at Jackson and Chickamauga; absent sick from Missionary Ridge;

Richardson, J.D., present at Fort Donelson; imprisoned at Camp Douglas; exchanged Sep. 23, 1862; present at Chickasaw Bayou, Port Hudson, Raymond, and Jackson; wounded at Chickamauga; present at Missionary Ridge; transferred to 48th Tenn., Jan. 1, 1864.

* Russell, G.W., present at Fort Donelson; imprisoned at Camp Douglas; exchanged Sep. 23, 1862; absent sick from Chickasaw Bayou; present at Port Hudson and Raymond; died at Canton, Miss., Jun. 23, 1863.

Russell, H.W., AWOL during Fort Donelson battle; imprisoned at Camp Douglas; exchanged Sep. 23, 1862; discharged for disability, Sep. 28, 1862.

* Scott, A.P., died at Camp Cheatham, Aug. 12, 1861.

Scott, C.S., present at Fort Donelson; imprisoned at Camp Douglas; exchanged Sep. 23, 1862; present at Chickasaw Bayou, Port Hudson, Raymond, Jackson, and Chickamauga; absent sick from Missionary Ridge.

Scott, D.C., enlisted Nov. 10, 1862; absent sick from Chickasaw Bayou; present at Port Hudson; wounded at Raymond; absent thereafter due to wound.

Scott, H.E., enlisted Nov. 10, 1862; present at Chickasaw Bayou and Port Hudson; absent sick from Raymond, Jackson, and Chickamauga; present at Missionary Ridge; surrendered at Greensboro, N.C..

Scott, Henry, enlisted Nov. 10, 1862; joined regt. at Port Hudson; present at Raymond, and Jackson; wounded at Chickamauga the second day; absent from Missionary Ridge due to wound; surrendered at Greensboro, N.C..

** Scott, J.K.P., sick at home during Fort Donelson battle; joined 48th Tenn.; killed at Richmond, Ky..

* Street, Alex., transferred to the regt. from the 48th Tenn., Mar. 1, 1863; present at Port Hudson; absent sick from Raymond; present at Jackson and Chickamauga; transferred to Company B in Apr., 1863; absent sick from Missionary Ridge; died in Marietta, Ga., Apr. 25, 1864.

* Taylor, William, present at Fort Donelson; imprisoned at Camp Douglas; exchanged Sep. 23, 1862; absent sick from all battles until he died at Lauderdale Springs, Miss., Jul. 1, 1863.

* Thomas, J.E., present at Fort Donelson; died in prison at St. Louis, Mar. 10, 1862.

Thompson, A.H., present at Fort Donelson; imprisoned at Camp Douglas; exchanged Sep. 23, 1862; present at Chickasaw Bayou, Port Hudson, Raymond, and Jackson; absent sick thereafter.

Thompson, J.W., enlisted Nov. 10, 1862; present at Chickasaw Bayou and Port Hudson; absent sick from Raymond and Jackson; present at Chickamauga and Missionary Ridge.

Vincent, J.A., present at Fort Donelson; escaped after surrender; rejoined regt. after its exchange; AWOL from Chickasaw Bayou; present at Port Hudson; absent sick from Raymond and Jackson; deserted Aug. 1, 1863.

Walker, W.R., enlisted Nov. 10, 1862; absent sick from Chickasaw Bayou; present at Port Hudson; discharged for disability, Mar. 20, 1863.

Wells, J.F., present at Fort Donelson; imprisoned at Camp Douglas; exchanged Sep. 23, 1862; present at Chickasaw Bayou, and Port Hudson; captured at Raymond and imprisoned at Fort Delaware.

Wells, Jeff, enlisted Nov. 10, 1862; deserted from Grenada in Dec., 1862, then rejoined the regt. at Port Hudson; present at Raymond; deserted Jul. 15, 1863.

Wells, W.T., enlisted Nov. 10, 1862; present at Chickasaw Bayou and Port Hudson; absent sick thereafter.

Williamson, James, sick at home during Fort Donelson battle; joined another command and became a lieutenant.

Company G (later H)

Captain

James S. Walker, as regimantal ordnance sergeant captured at Fort Donelson; imprisoned at Camp Douglas; exchanged Sep. 23, 1862; elected captain of the new Company H at reorganization; absent sick from Chickasaw Bayou, commanded company at Port Hudson; wounded while commanding company at Raymond; commanded company at Jackson; wounded while commanding company the first day at Chickamauga; absent sick from Missionary Ridge; surrendered at Greensboro, N.C..

1st Lieutenant

E.C.L. Bridges, present at Fort Donelson; imprisoned at Camp Chase and Johnson's Island; exchanged Sep. 16, 1862; not re-elected, resigned, and dropped from the rolls.

J.B. McCanless, appoined 1st sergeant, Aug. 25, 1861; present at Fort Donelson; imprisoned at Camp Douglas; exchanged Sep. 23, 1862; elected 1st lieutenant at reorganization; commanded company at Chickasaw Bayou; present at Port Hudson, Raymond, and Jackson; absent sick from Chickamauga; commanded company at Missionary Ridge; survived the war.

2nd Lieutenant

Alfred Jones, assistant surgeon at Fort Donelson; escaped from Camp Chase in Mar., 1862; joined 17th Tenn. as assistant surgeon.

J.A. Ralston, as a private present at Fort Donelson; imprisoned at Camp Douglas; exchanged Sep. 23, 1862; promoted to 2nd lieutenant at reorganization; present at Chickasaw Bayou, Port Hudson, Raymond, and Jackson; on detached duty thereafter.

Junior 2nd Lieutenant

E.W. Harmond, present at Fort Donelson; imprisoned at Camp Chase and Johnson's Island; exchanged Sep. 16, 1862; not re-elected, resigned, and dropped from the rolls; joined 11th Tenn. Cavalry.

Calvin J. Orr, as a private present at Fort Donelson; imprisoned at Camp Douglas; exchanged Sep. 23, 1862; elected to junior 2nd lieutenant at reorganization; present at Chickasaw Bayou, Port Hudson, Raymond, and Jackson; on furlough during Chickamauga battle; present at Missionary Ridge; survived the war.

1st Sergeant

* Thomas H. Chiles, died at Camp Trousdale, Aug. 21, 1861.

\# Thomas G. McMahon, as a private present at Fort Donelson; imprisoned at Camp Douglas; exchanged Sep. 23, 1862; promoted to 1st sergeant at reorganization; present at Chickasaw Bayou and Port Hudson; wounded at Raymond; absent due to wound the remainder of 1863; surrendered at Greensboro, N.C..

2nd Sergeant

G.W. Taylor, AWOL from Fort Donelson; imprisoned at Camp Douglas; exchanged Sep. 23, 1862; returned to the ranks at reorganization; AWOL from every battle except Missionary Ridge where he was detailed as teamster.

James B. Orr, as a private present at Fort Donelson; imprisoned at Camp Douglas; exchanged Sep. 23, 1862; promoted to 2nd sergeant at reorganization; present at Chickasaw Bayou and Port Hudson; mortally wounded at Raymond and died there May 14, 1863.

3rd Sergeant

Levi Eslick, as a private present at Fort Donelson; imprisoned at Camp Douglas; exchanged Sep. 23, 1862; promoted to 3rd sergeant at reorganization; transferrred to 1st Tenn. Cavalry, Dec. 24, 1862.

D.W. Kincaid, present at Fort Donelson; imprisoned at Camp Douglas; exchanged Sep. 23, 1862; present at Chickasaw Bayou; promoted to sergeant, Jan. 15, 1863, at Port Hudson; present at Raymond and Jackson; present at Chickamauga the first day, AWOL the second; present at Missionary Ridge.

4th Sergeant

S.M. Clayton, wounded at Fort Donelson; imprisoned at Camp Douglas; exchanged Sep. 23, 1862; returned to ranks at reorganization; present at Chickasaw Bayou, Port Hudson, and Raymond; detached as ambulance driver, Jun.20, 1863; rejoined company Feb. 28, 1864.

* J.A. McMahon, as a private present at Fort Donelson; imprisoned at Camp Douglas; exchanged Sep. 23, 1862; promoted to 4th sergeant at reorganization; sent home on recruiting duty in Oct., 1862, and died at home Oct. 29, 1862.

W.B. Chiles, as a private present at Fort Donelson; imprisoned at Camp Douglas; exchanged Sep. 23, 1862; promoted to 3rd corporal at reorganization; present at Chickasaw Bayou, Port Hudson, Raymond, and Jackson; promoted to sergeant, Jan., 1863; on furlough during Chickamauga battle; present at Missionary Ridge.

5th Sergeant

W.M. Dabney, as 3rd sergeant sick in quarters during Fort Donelson battle; imprisoned at Camp Douglas; exchanged Sep. 23, 1862; reduced to 5th sergeant at reorganization; present at Chickasaw Bayou, Port Hudson, and Raymond; captured at Raymond and imprisoned at Camp Morgan.

\# John B. Rodgers, present at Fort Donelson; imprisoned at Camp Douglas; exchanged Sep. 23, 1862; present at Chickasaw Bayou, Port Hudson, and Raymond; promoted to sergeant Jun. 25, 1863; present at Jackson, Chickamauga, and Missionary Ridge; surrendered at Greensboro, N.C..

1st Corporal

\# W.S. King, sick at Russellville during Fort Donelson battle; rejoined regt. after its exchange; returned to the ranks at reorganization; present at Chickasaw Bayou and Port Hudson; wounded at Raymond; absent remainder of 1863 due to wound; surrendered at Greensboro, N.C..

William M. Martin, as a private present at Fort Donelson; imprisoned at Camp Douglas; exchanged Sep. 23, 1862; present at Chickasaw Bayou and Port Hudson; wounded at Raymond; present at Jackson, Chickamauga, and Missionary Ridge.

2nd Corporal

* Robert Kincaid, died at Camp Cheatham, Jun. 15, 1861.

W.R.B. Wade, replaced Kincaid; present at Fort Donelson; imprisoned at Camp Douglas; exchanged Sep. 23, 1862; appointed regimental wagonmaster at reorganization; detached as brigade wagon master in Jun., 1863; rejoined company Feb. 24, 1864.

** E.C. Chafin, as a private present at Fort Donelson; imprisoned at Camp Douglas; exchanged Sep. 23, 1862; promoted to 2nd corporal at reorganization; present at Chickasaw Bayou and Port Hudson; killed at Raymond.

** J.P. Ezell, present at Fort Donelson; imprisoned at Camp Douglas; exchanged Sep. 23, 1862; present at Chickasaw Bayou, Port Hudson, and Raymond; promoted to corporal, Jun. 25, 1863; present at Jackson; killed at Chickamauga the first day.

3rd Corporal

J.F. Freeman, present at Fort Donelson; imprisoned at Camp Douglas; exchanged Sep. 23, 1862; returned to the ranks at reorganization; present at Chickasaw Bayou, Port Hudson, and Raymond; captured at Jackson.

W.G. Collins, as a private present at Fort Donelson; imprisoned at Camp Douglas; exchanged Sep. 23, 1862; present at Cd to 4th corporal at reorganization; present at Chickasaw Bayou, made corporal at Port Hudson, present at Raymond, and Jackson; present at Chickamauga the first day, AWOL the second; AWOL from Missionary Ridge.

4th Corporal

W.A. Beaver, present at Fort Donelson; imprisoned at Camp Douglas; exchanged Sep. 23, 1862; returned to the ranks at reorganization; detached as brigade carpenter Nov. 1862.

J.H. Burgess, as a private present at Fort Donelson; imprisoned at Camp Douglas; exchanged Sep. 23, 1862; promoted to 4th corporal at reorganization; present at Chickasaw Bayou, Port Hudson, Raymond, and Jackson; absent barefoot from Chickamauga, AWOL from Missionary Ridge; deserted at Dalton, Dec. 1, 1863.

Private

Anderson, E., musician; present at Fort Donelson; escaped after the surrender; served in 5th Tenn.; rejoined regt. after its exchange; with the band in every engagement; surrendered at Greensboro, N.C..

Anderson, Joel, sick at Russellville during Fort Donelson battle; joined 5th Tenn.; never rejoined the regt..

** Bearden, W.V.S., present at Fort Donelson; imprisoned at Camp Douglas; exchanged Sep. 23, 1862; present at Chickasaw Bayou and Port Hudson; killed at Raymond.

Beaver, J.S.M., enlisted Nov. 10, 1862; present at Chickasaw Bayou; deserted at Vicksburg, Jan. 5, 1863.

* Bevils, B.G., enlisted Nov. 10, 1862; present at Chickasaw Bayou and Port Hudson; captured at Raymond and imprisoned at Fort Delaware where he died.

** Boyett, Robert, sick at Bowling Green during Fort Donelson battle; joined 5th Tenn.; killed at Perryville, Ky..

* Burgess, G.B., died at Bowling Green, Nov. 26, 1861.

Burgess, H.L., transferred to Regt. from 32nd Tenn., Oct., 1863; present at Missionary Ridge.

Burgess, J.C.J., present at Fort Donelson; imprisoned at Camp Douglas; exchanged Sep. 23, 1862; discharged for disability, Oct. 1, 1862.

Capps, W.R., present at Fort Donelson; imprisoned at Camp Douglas; exchanged Sep. 23, 1862; absent sick from Chickasaw Bayou; present at Port Hudson and Raymond; no further record.

Chiles, James, sick at home during Fort Donelson battle; joined 5th Tenn.; wounded at Richmond, Ky.; rejoined regt. at Port Hudson; absent sick from Raymond; present at Jackson, Chicamauga, and Missionary Ridge.

Claxton, M.D., enlisted Nov. 1, 1862; present at Chickasaw Bayou, Port Hudson, and Raymond; absent sick thereafter.

** Claxton, W.L., enlisted Nov. 10, 1862; present at Chickasaw Bayou and Port Hudson; killed at Raymond.

* Clift, Thomas, died at Bowling Green, Jan. 1, 1862.

Clift, W.P., sick at home during Fort Donelson battle; joined 5th Tenn., then 32nd Tenn.; rejoined regt. Sep. 22, 1863 at Missionary Ridge; AWOL from Missionary Ridge battle; deserted Dec. 1, 1863.

Compton, Jeff, discharged for disability at Bowling Green, Oct. 6, 1861.

Cook, W.R., present at Fort Donelson; imprisoned at Camp Douglas; exchanged Sep. 23, 1862; absent sick from Chickasaw Bayou; discharged for disability, Mar. 12, 1863.

Cox, P.J., present at Fort Donelson; imprisoned at Camp Douglas; exchanged Sep. 23, 1862; discharged for disability, Oct. 6, 1862.

Dabney, J.H., present at Fort Donelson; imprisoned at Camp Douglas; exchanged Sep. 23, 1862; present at Chickasaw Bayou, Port Hudson, Raymond, and Jackson; AWOL from Chickamauga; ran at Missionary Ridge.

Davis, A.C., sick at home during Fort Donelson battle; joined 5th Tenn. and made lieutenant; never returned.

Deavenport, J.D., present at Fort Donelson; imprisoned at Camp Douglas; exchanged Sep. 23, 1862; present at Chickasaw Bayou, Port Hudson, Raymond, Jackson, Chickamauga, and Missionary Ridge.

Doss, W.B., sick in quarters at Fort Donelson; imprisoned at Camp Douglas; exchanged Sep. 23, 1862; present at Chickasaw Bayou and Port Hudson; lost his left arm at Raymond; premanently disabled.

Downing, J.G., enlisted Oct. 28, 1862; present at Chickasaw Bayou; transferred to 41st Tenn., Mar., 1863.

Emberson, B.F., present at Fort Donelson; imprisoned at Camp Douglas; exchanged Sep. 23, 1862; present at Chickasaw Bayou and Port Hudson; wounded at Raymond; absent from Jackson due to wound; absent sick from Chickamauga; on detached duty during Missionary Ridge battle.

Erwin, W.C., present at Fort Donelson; imprisoned at Camp Douglas; exchanged Sep. 23, 1862; present at Chickasaw Bayou; missed all subsequent battles sick, then transferred to 32nd Tenn., Oct., 1863.

Foster, F.S., enlisted Nov. 10, 1862; present at Chickasaw Bayou, Port Hudson, Raymond and Jackson; AWOL from Chickamauga; deserted Oct. 27, 1863.

Foster, W.A., present at Fort Donelson; imprisoned at Camp Douglas; exchanged Sep. 23, 1862; present at Chickasaw Bayou, Port Hudson, Raymond, and Jackson; absent sick thereafter.

Foster, W.T., detailed as teamster; joined the 1st Tenn. Cavalry and never returned.

Franks, W.H, present at Fort Donelson; imprisoned at Camp Douglas; exchanged Sep. 23, 1862; present at Chickasaw Bayou; transferred to Company B, Jan. 3, 1863; present at Port Hudson, Raymond, Jackson, Chickamauga, and Missionary Ridge.

Freeman, John, present at Fort Donelson; took the oath of allegiance to the U.S. at Camp Douglas; upon release joined the 32nd Tenn.; rejoined the regt. Sep. 22, 1863; deserted Nov. 1, 1863.

Garrett, S.L.P., present at Fort Donelson; imprisoned at Camp Douglas; exchanged Sep. 23, 1862; present at Chickasaw Bayou; transferred to 41st Tenn., Mar. 12, 1863.

Garrett, W.T., sick at home during Fort Donelson battle; joined 1st Tenn. Cavalry; never returned.

Goodnight, R.A., enlisted Nov. 10, 1862; present at Chickasaw Bayou, Port Hudson, Raymond, and Jackson; present at Chickamauga first day only, AWOL the second; absent sick from Missionary Ridge.

Griggs, R.P., wounded at Fort Donelson; sent home and joined the cavalry; rejoined regt. after its exchange; present at Chickasaw Bayou, Port Hudson, Raymond, Jackson, and Chickamauga; absent barefoot from Missionary Ridge.

* Griggs, Y.M., present at Fort Donelson; died at Camp Douglas, Mar. 26. 1862.

Hamlin, W.T., present at Fort Donelson; imprisoned at Camp Douglas; exchanged Sep. 23, 1862; absent sick from Chickasaw Bayou; present at Port Hudson, Raymond, and Jackson; AWOL from Chickamauga and Missionary Ridge; survived the war.

Harris, J.A., wounded at Fort Donelson; sent home and joined the 32nd Tenn.; rejoined the regt. Sep. 22, 1863; on furlough during Missionary Ridge battle.

Hays, W.F., present at Fort Donelson; imprisoned at Camp Douglas; exchanged Sep. 23, 1862; present at Chickasaw Bayou and Port Hudson where he was left behind when the regt. marched to Mississippi, captured at Port Hudson in Jul., 1863.

* Hobbs, William, died at Nashville, Nov. 25, 1861.

Holly, J.P. detailed at teamster; joined 1st Tenn. Cavalry; rejoined regt. at reorganization and again detailed as teamster..

Hudson, J.M., discharged for disability at Bowling Green.

Jackson, John M., sick at home during Fort Donelson battle; joined 1st Tenn. Cavalry; rejoined regt. after its exchange; present at Chickasaw Bayou, Port Hudson, Raymond, Jackson, and Chickamauga; absent sick from Missionary Ridge.

James, W.R., present at Fort Donelson; imprisoned at Camp Douglas; exchanged Sep. 23, 1862; present at Chickasaw Bayou; discharged as non-conscript, Feb. 16, 1863.

Kimbrough, D.L., present at Fort Donelson; took the oath of allegience to the U.S. at St. Louis and was released; joined Morgan's Cavalry; never returned.

Mantlo, J.J., present at Fort Donelson; imprisoned at Camp Douglas; exchanged Sep. 23, 1862; present at Chickasaw Bayou; absent sick from Port Hudson and Raymond present at Jackson; wounded at Chickamauga the second day; absent from Missionary Ridge due to wound.

** Marsh, R.J., wounded at Fort Donelson; sent home; rejoined regt. after its exchange; present at Chickasaw Bayou, Port Hudson, Raymond, and Jackson; killed at Chickamauga the second day.

McCanless, S.H., lost his right arm at Fort Donelson; sent home; rejoined regt. after its exchange; discharged for disability, Dec. 23, 1862.

McClelland, F.S., detached to Ordnance Dept.; never returned.

McClure, L.B., present at Fort Donelson; imprisoned at Camp Douglas; exchanged Sep. 23, 1862; present at Chickasaw Bayou, Port Hudson, Raymond, Jackson, and Chickamauga; absent sick from Missionary Ridge.

McGaugh, B.F., lost his right arm at Fort Donelson; sent home; rejoined regt. after its exchange; discharged for disability, Dec. 23, 1862.

** McGaugh, N.C., present at Fort Donelson; imprisoned at Camp Douglas; exchanged Sep. 23, 1862; present at Chickasaw Bayou, Port Hudson, Raymond, and Jackson; killed at Chickamauga the second day.

* McMillion, J.P., present at Fort Donelson; died in prison at St. Louis, Mar., 1862.

McMillion, J.P., enlisted Nov. 10, 1862; present at Chickasaw Bayou, Port Hudson, Raymond, and Jackson; AWOL from Chickamauga; deserted from Chattanooga Valley, Oct. 27, 1863.

McMillion, S.B., enlisted Nov. 10, 1862; present at Chickasaw Bayou, Port Hudson, Raymond, and Jackson; AWOL from Chickamauga and Missionary Ridge; deserted from Dalton, GA., Dec. 1, 1863.

* McMullin, James, died at home, Aug. 5, 1861.

Murry, H.L., wounded at Fort Donelson; sent home and joined the cavalry; never returned.

Nance, J.R., enlisted Nov. 4, 1862; absent sick from Chickasaw Bayou, Port Hudson, Raymond, and Jackson; ran at Chickamauga; deserted Nov. 20, 1863.

* Nevils, John, died at Nashville, Jun., 1861.

Newton, William J., enlisted Nov. 10, 1862; present at Chickasaw Bayou, Port Hudson, and Raymond; deserted May 29, 1863.

Newton, Willis J., enlisted Dec. 10, 1862; present at Chickasaw Bayou, Port Hudson, and Raymond; deserted May 29, 1863.

Orr, C.J., sick at home during Fort Donelson battle; served in 5th Tenn.; rejoined regt. after its exchange; present at Chickasaw Bayou, Port Hudson, Raymond, Jackson, Chickamauga, and Missionary Ridge; survived the war.

Orr, W.W., enlisted Oct. 28, 1862; present at Chickasaw Bayou, Port Hudson, Raymond, and Jackson; wounded at Chickamauga the second day; absent from Missionary Ridge due to wound; surrendered at Greensboro, N.C..

Park, I.M., AWOL from Fort Donelson until the night of Feb. 15; imprisoned at Camp Douglas; exchanged Sep. 23, 1862; absent drunk from Chickasaw Bayou; present at Port Hudson; absent drunk from Raymond; on detached duty during Jackson battle; absent barefoot from Chickamauga; captured while drunk on Lookout Mountain, Nov. 24, 1863; imprisoned at Rock Island, Ill..

Park, J.L., present at Fort Donelson; imprisoned at Camp Douglas; exchanged Sep. 23, 1862; present at Chickasaw Bayou, Port Hudson, Raymond, Jackson, and Chickamauga; on furlough during Missionary Ridge battle.

Parsons, J.B., present at Fort Donelson; imprisoned at Camp Douglas; exchanged Sep. 23, 1862; present at Chickasaw Bayou; on furlough from Port Hudson, Raymond and Jackson; present at Chickamauga the first day, AWOL the second; AWOL from Missionary Ridge.

Paxton, J.A., transferred to regt. from 41st Tenn. at Port Hudson in Mar, 1863; present at Raymond; deserted Jun. 12, 1863.

Paxton, L., transferred to regt. from 41st Tenn.at Port Hudson in Mar., 1863; fought in the ranks at Raymond; with the band thereafter.

Phillips, D.B., present at Fort Donelson; imprisoned at Camp Douglas; exchanged Sep. 23, 1862; present at Chickasaw Bayou, Port Hudson, Raymond, and Jackson; on detached duty during Chickamauga battle; AWOL from Missionary Ridge.

Porch, J.F., present at Fort Donelson; imprisoned at Camp Douglas; exchanged Sep. 23, 1862; present at Chickasaw Bayou, Port Hudson, Raymond, and Jackson; wounded at Chickamauga the second day; absent from Missionary Ridge due to wound.

* Powers, B.F., died at Camp Cheatham, Jun. 1, 1861.

Rainey, G.W., sick at Russellville during Fort Donelson battle; never returned.

Rainey, T.J., sick at Russellville during Fort Donelson battle; joined the 5th Tenn.; never returned

Rhea, F.M., present at Fort Donelson; imprisoned at Camp Douglas; exchanged Sep. 23, 1862; AWOL from every battle until he deserted, Jun. 5, 1863.

Rhodes, G.F., wounded at Fort Donelson but stayed on the field; imprisoned at Camp Douglas; exchanged Sep. 23, 1862; AWOL from Chickasaw Bayou; present at Port Hudson, Raymond, and Jackson; wounded at Chickamauga the first day; present at Missionary Ridge.

Rhodes, John A., present at Fort Donelson; imprisoned at Camp Douglas; exchanged Sep. 23, 1862; present at Chickasaw Bayou; discharged as nonconscript, Mar. 7, 1863.

Roberts, Monroe, sick at home during Fort Donelson battle; joined Anderson's Cavalry Regiment; rejoined regt. after its exchange; absent sick from every battle.

Roberts, Noah, enlisted Nov. 5, 1862; present at Chickasaw Bayou and Port Hudson; ran from the field at Raymond; present at Jackson; AWOL from Chickamauga and Missionary Ridge; surrendered at Greesboro, N.C..

** Roberts, Thomas, present at Fort Donelson; imprisoned at Camp Douglas; exchanged Sep. 23, 1862; present at Chickasaw Bayou and Port Hudson; wounded at Raymond and died there from his wounds.

** Rodgers, J.T., enlisted Oct. 25, 1862; present at Chickasaw Bayou and Port Hudson; killed at Raymond.

Rothrock, G.M., present at Fort Donelson; escaped from Camp Douglas, Jun. 5, 1862; joined the 1st Tenn. Cavalry; never returned.

Silas, John, present at Fort Donelson; escaped from Camp Douglas, Mar., 1862; never returned.

Smith, E.H., present at Fort Donelson; imprisoned at Camp Douglas; exchanged Sep. 23, 1862; appointed bugler at reorganization; no further entries.

Smoot, Richard, present at Fort Donelson; escaped from Camp Douglas, Jul. 4, 1862; rejoined regt. after its exchange; present at Chickasaw Bayou; discharged for disability, Jan. 12, 1863.

Swinea, Bryant, sick at home during Fort Donelson battle; never returned.

Taylor, J.B., enlisted Oct. 30, 1862; present at Chickasaw Bayou and Port Hudson; wounded at Raymond; absent due to wound thereafter.

Taylor, J.H.C., enlisted Oct. 23, 1862; present at Chickasaw Bayou, Port Hudson, Raymond, and Jackson; wounded at Chickamauga the second day; absent from Missionary Ridge due to wound.

** Taylor, John, home sick during Fort Donelson battle; rejoined regt. after its exchange; present at Chickasaw Bayou, Port Hudson, Raymond, and Jackson; on detached duty during Chickamauga battle; present at Missionary Ridge; killed at Resaca, May 14, 1864..

Tucker, Matthew, wounded at Fort Donelson; sent home and never returned.

Ussery, G.H., present at Fort Donelson; imprisoned at Camp Douglas; exchanged Sep. 23, 1862; present at Chickasaw Bayou and Port Hudson; absent sick from Raymond, Jackson, and Chickamauga; detailed as teamster during Missionary Ridge battle.

Van Cleave, T.Y., sick at home during Fort Donelson battle; joined 5th Tenn.; rejoined regt. after its exchange; present at Chickasaw Bayou; transferred to 41st Tenn., Mar. 6, 1863.

Webb, Jesse, enlisted Nov. 10, 1862; present at Chickasaw Bayou, Port Hudson, and Raymond; captured at Jackson, Jul. 15, 1863.

Webster, William, enlisted Nov. 3, 1862; present at Chickasaw Bayou and Port Hudson; wounded at Raymond; absent from Jackson due to wound; ran from the field at Chickamauga; deserted Oct. 27, 1863.

White, W.W., discharged for disability at Camp Trousdale, Aug. 1, 1861.

Whittaker, C.M., nurse to the sick at Fort Donelson; imprisoned at Camp Douglas; exchanged Sep. 23, 1862; accidentally wounded and furloughed in Dec., 1862; never returned.

Whittaker, W.A., sick in quarters at Fort Donelson; imprisoned at Camp Douglas; exchanged Sep. 23, 1862; furloughed Sep. 26, 1862; never returned.

Williams, A.J., transferred into regt. from 41st Tenn. on Mar. 5, 1863, at Port Hudson; present at Raymond; captured at Jackson, Jul, 1863; paroled and never returned.

Williams, C.L., transferred into regt. from 41st Tenn. on Mar. 5, 1863, at Port Hudson; present at Raymond; captured at Jackson, Jul. 15, 1863.

Williams, Grogan, present at Fort Donelson; imprisoned at Camp Douglas; exchanged Sep. 23, 1862; absent sick from Chickasaw Bayou; present at Port Hudson, Raymond, Jackson, and Chickamauga; absent sick from Missionary Ridge.

\# Williams, M.P., sick at Russellville during Fort Donelson battle; joined 5th Tenn.; wounded at Perryville, Ky.; rejoined regt. at Enterprise, Miss., Aug., 1863; on detached duty during Chickamauga and Missionary Ridge Battles; surrendered at Greensboro, N.C..

Williams, W.A., sick at Russellville during Fort Donelson battle; never returned.

Wood, J.H., sick during Fort Donelson battle; joined 1st Tenn. Cavalry; never returned.

Woodward, John, sick at home during Fort Donelson battle; rejoined regt. at Port Hudson and detailed as nurse; on detached duty during Raymond battle; deserted Jun. 5, 1863.

Young, A.A., present at Fort Donelson; imprisoned at Camp Douglas; exchanged Sep. 23, 1862; discharged for disability, Sep. 26, 1862.

* Young, Thomas, died at home, Aug. 25, 1861.

Company H (later C)

Captain

S.L. Tarrent, traded positions with 2nd lieutenant R.T. Cooper at Camp Cheatham; resigned commission Nov., 1861; present as a private at Fort Donelson; imprisoned at Camp Douglas; exchanged Sep. 23, 1862; discharged for disability.

** Robert T. Cooper, promoted from 2nd lieutenant May 28, 1861; commanded company at Fort Donelson; imprisoned at Camp Chase and Johnson's Island; exchanged Sep. 16, 1862; commanded company at Chickasaw Bayou; on furlough during Port Hudson battle; killed at Raymond.

J.A. Doyel, as junior 2nd lieutenant AWOL at Fort Donelson; imprisoned at Camp Chase and Johnson's Island; exchanged Sep. 16, 1862; AWOL from Chickasaw Bayou; present at Port Hudson; left the field without leave at Raymond; promoted to 1st lieutenant, May, 1863, and to captain in Jun., 1863; furloughed in Aug., 1863, and never returned.

1st Lieutenant

O.T. Plummer, resigned Nov., 1861.

William J. Harden, promoted from 1st sergeant Dec., 1861; present at Fort Donelson; imprisoned at Camp Chase and Johnson's Island; exchanged Sep. 16, 1862; present at Chickasaw Bayou and Port Hudson; resigned Mar. 25, 1863, due to disability.

Samuel D. Strickland, promoted from private to 2nd sergeant, Aug., 1861; present at Fort Donelson; imprisoned at Camp Douglas; exchanged Sep. 23, 1862; present at Chickasaw Bayou and Port Hudson; elected 2nd lieutenant, May, 1863; present at Raymond; elected 1st lieutenant, Jun. 1863; commanded company at Jackson; on detached duty during Chickamauga and Missionary Ridge battles.

2nd Lieutenant

R.M. Plummer, promoted from 4th Sergeant, Dec., 1861; present at Fort Donelson; imprisoned at Camp Chase and Johnson's Island; exchanged Sep. 16, 1862; present at Chickasaw Bayou; resigned at Port Hudson, Feb. 19, 1863, due to disability.

M.H. Johnson, as a private present at Fort Donelson; imprisoned at Camp Douglas; exchanged Sep. 23, 1862; present at Chickasaw Bayou, Port Hudson, and Raymond; elected junior 2nd lieutenant Jun. 19, 1863; present at Jackson, Chickamauga, and Missionary Ridge; promoted to 2nd lieutenant, Dec., 1863.

* S.K. Johnston, promoted to 4th corporal, Feb., 1862; present at Fort Donelson; imprisoned at Camp Douglas; exchanged Sep. 23, 1862; returned to the ranks at reorganization; present at Chickasaw Bayou and Port Hudson; elected junior 2nd lieutenant, Apr., 1863; present at Raymond and Jackson; promoted to 2nd lieutenant, May, 1863; died Sep. 6, 1863.

Junior 2nd Lieutenant

Jesse Turner, promoted from private to 4th sergeant Feb., 1862; present at Fort Donelson; imprisoned at Camp Douglas; exchanged Sep. 23, 1862; present at Chickasaw Bayou, Port Hudson, Raymond, Jackson, and Chickamauga; elected junior 2nd lieutenant upon Johnston's promotion; present at Missionary Ridge.

1st Sergeant

J.M. Gillmer (Gillmore), promoted from 3rd Sergeant Dec., 1861; present at Fort Donelson; imprisoned at Camp Douglas; exchanged Sep. 23, 1862; returned to the ranks at reorganization; present at Chickasaw Bayou and Port Hudson; captured at Raymond.

J.L. Lawhorn, as a private present at Fort Donelson; imprisoned at Camp Douglas; exchanged Sep. 23, 1862; present at Chickasaw Bayou and Port Hudson; promoted to sergeant, Apr., 1863; present at Raymond, Jackson, Chickamauga, and Missionary Ridge; promoted to 1st sergeant, Jan., 1864.

2nd Sergeant

Charles Steward, discharged for disability at Camp Trousdale, Aug., 1861.

3rd Sergeant

J.W. Hensley, replaced Gillmer Dec., 1861; present at Fort Donelson; imprisoned at Camp Douglas; exchanged Sep. 23, 1862; reduced to 5th sergeant at reorganization; present at Chickasaw Bayou and Port Hudson; captured at Raymond and never returned.

W.B. Harder, as a private present at Fort Donelson; imprisoned at Camp Douglas; exchanged Sep. 23, 1862; on detached duty during Chickasaw Bayou battle; present at Port Hudson, Raymond, and Jackson; promoted to sergeant, Jul., 1863; present at Chickamauga and Missionary Ridge; survived the war.

4th Sergeant

** J.D. Flanigan, as a private present at Fort Donelson; imprisoned at Camp Douglas; exchanged Sep. 23, 1862; promoted to 4th sergeant at reorganization; present at Chickasaw Bayou, Port Hudson, Raymond, and Jackson; killed at Chickamauga the first day.

William Mayfield, as 3rd corporal present at Fort Donelson; imprisoned at Camp Douglas; exchanged Sep. 23, 1862; returned to the ranks at reorganization; present at Chickasaw Bayou and Port Hudson; on detached duty during Raymond battle; present at Jackson and Chickamauga; promoted to sergeant, Oct. 31, 1863; present at Missionary Ridge.

5th Sergeant

G.F.M. Davis, appointed Oct., 1861; present at Fort Donelson; imprisoned at Camp Douglas; exchanged Sep. 23, 1862; returned to the ranks at reorganization; present at Chickasaw Bayou and Port Hudson; absent thereafter due to accidental wound.

Henry Clayton, as a private present at Fort Donelson; imprisoned at Camp Douglas; exchanged Sep. 23, 1862; present at Chickasaw Bayou, Port Hudson, Raymond, Jackson, Chickamauga, and Missionary Ridge; promoted to 5th sergeant Oct. 31, 1863.

1st Corporal

** D.P. Garrett, as a private present at Fort Donelson; imprisoned at Camp Douglas; exchanged Sep. 23, 1862; promoted to 1st corporal at reorganization; present at Chickasaw Bayou, Port Hudson, Raymond, and Jackson; killed at Chickamauga the first day.

2nd Corporal

A.J. Strickland, as a private present at Fort Donelson; imprisoned at Camp Douglas; exchanged Sep. 23, 1862; promoted to 2nd corporal at reorganization; present at Chickasaw Bayou, Port Hudson, Raymond, Jackson, and Chickamauga; absent sick from Missionary Ridge.

3rd Corporal

William Sisco, as a private present at Fort Donelson; imprisoned at Camp Douglas; exchanged Sep. 23, 1862; promoted t 3rd corporal at reorganization; absent from Chickasaw Bayou; present at Port Hudson; wounded at Raymond; absent from Jackson and Chickamauga due to wound; on detached duty during Missionary Ridge battle.

4th Corporal

* A.C. Westbrook, AWOL from Fort Donelson battle; demoted; imprisoned at Camp Douglas; exchanged Sep. 23, 1862; furloughed Sep. 30, 1862; died at home, Oct., 1862.

P.F. Fite, as a private present at Fort Donelson; imprisoned at Camp Douglas; exchanged Sep. 23, 1862; promoted to 4th corporal at reorganization; absent sick from Chickasaw Bayou; present at Port Hudson, Raymond, and Jackson; on furlough during Chickamauga battle; present at Missionary Ridge.

J.H. Hamrick, as a private present at Fort Donelson; imprisoned at Camp Douglas; exchanged Sep. 23, 1862; present at Chickasaw Bayou, Port Hudson, Raymond, and Jackson; wounded at Chickamauga; absent from Missionary Ridge due to wound; promoted to 4th corporal, Oct. 31, 1863.

Private

* Aydelotte, G.P., present at Fort Donelson; died at Camp Douglas Mar. 3, 1862.

* Barr, Isaac, present at Fort Donelson; imprisoned at Camp Douglas; exchanged Sep. 23, 1862; present at Chickasaw Bayou, Port Hudson, and Raymond; died at Lauderdale Springs, Miss., Jun., 1863.

Bogus, Alexander, discharged for disability at Bowling Green Oct., 1861.

Brewer, R.W., present at Fort Donelson; imprisoned at Camp Douglas; exchanged Sep. 23, 1862; absent sick from Chickasaw Bayou; present at Port Hudson, Raymond, and Jackson; AWOL from Chickamauga; present at Missionary Ridge.

Campbell, A.J., present at Fort Donelson; imprisoned at Camp Douglas; exchanged Sep. 23, 1862; present at Chickasaw Bayou, Port Hudson, Raymond, Jackson, Chickamauga, and Missionary Ridge.

Christian, N.J., sick in quarters during Fort Donelson battle; imprisoned at Camp Douglas; exchanged Sep. 23, 1862; transferred to 48th Tenn., Sep., 1862.

* Clayton, Francis, died at Bowling Green Dec. 14, 1861.

Clayton, George, present at Fort Donelson; imprisoned at Camp Douglas; exchanged Sep. 23, 1862; present at Chickasaw Bayou and Port Hudson; wounded at Raymond; absent thereafter due to wound.

Combs, Charles; present at Fort Donelson; took the oath of allegience to the U.S. at Camp Douglas and joined the Federal army; was drummed out of the Federal army and returned to prison; exchanged Sep. 23, 1862; absent from Chickasaw Bayou under arrest; present at Port Hudson; transferred to McNally's Battery, May 4, 1863.

Conder, G.H., present at Fort Donelson; imprisoned at Camp Douglas; exchanged Sep. 23, 1862; present at Chickasaw Bayou and Port Hudson; captured at Raymond, escaped, and deserted, Jun., 1863.

Conder, J.W., present at Fort Donelson; imprisoned at Camp Douglas; exchanged Sep. 23, 1862; present at Chickasaw Bayou and Port Hudson; wounded at Raymond; absent thereafter due to wound.

Conder, M.L., present at Fort Donelson; imprisoned at Camp Douglas; exchanged Sep. 23, 1862; AWOL from Chickasaw Bayou; present at Port Hudson; captured at Raymond, escaped and rejoined the regt. Jul. 30, 1863; deserted, Sep. 6, 1863.

Conder, W.J., joined company at reorganization; furloughed home and deserted, Sep. 30, 1862.

* Cooper, Alex D., died at home Jul. 10, 1861.

Cooper, J.H., present at Fort Donelson; imprisoned at Camp Douglas; exchanged Sep. 23, 1862; discharged for disability, Oct., 1862.

Cooper, L.B., present at Fort Donelson; imprisoned at Camp Douglas; exchanged Sep. 23, 1862; present at Chickasaw Bayou and Port Hudson; wounded at Raymond; absent thereafter due to wound.

* Cooper, Samuel G., present at Fort Donelson; died at Camp Douglas Apr. 24, 1862.

** Cooper, T.M., mortally wounded at Fort Donelson; died enroute to Nashville.

Dabbs, J.C., present at Fort Donelson; imprisoned at Camp Douglas; exchanged Sep. 23, 1862; discharged for disability, Oct. 8, 1862.

Davis, J.S., discharged for disability at Bowling Green, Oct., 1861.

Davis, W.S., on furlough during Fort Donelson battle; entered cavalry.

Deen, J.G.B., present at Fort Donelson; imprisoned at Camp Douglas; exchanged Sep. 23, 1862; discharged for disability, Oct., 1862.

Deen, M.L., AWOL during Fort Donelson battle; imprisoned at Camp Douglas; exchanged Sep. 23, 1862; present at Chickasaw Bayou and Port Hudson; wounded at Raymond; absent thereafter due to wound until discharged, Dec. 28, 1863.

Deen, M.L. Junior, AWOL during Fort Donelson battle; imprisoned at Camp Douglas; exchanged Sep. 23, 1862; present at Chickasaw Bayou; discharged as non-conscript, Feb. 22, 1863.

Deen, N.M., AWOL during Fort Donelson battle; imprisoned at Camp Douglas; exchanged Sep. 23, 1862; AWOL from Chickasaw Bayou; present at Port Hudson; captured at Raymond, escaped, and deserted, Jun., 1863.

Deen, W.W., AWOL during Fort Donelson battle; imprisoned at Camp Douglas; exchanged Sep. 23, 1862; discharged for disability, Oct., 1862.

Dodson, John, present at Fort Donelson; imprisoned at Camp Douglas; exchanged Sep. 23, 1862; present at Chickasaw Bayou, Port Hudson, Raymond, and Jackson; deserted Sep. 6, 1863.

Doyel, J.H., discharged for disability at Bowling Green, Jan., 1862.

Fite, Elias, discharged for disability at Bowling Green, Dec., 1861.

Fite, W.F., present at Fort Donelson; imprisoned at Camp Douglas; exchanged Sep. 23, 1862; present at Chickasaw Bayou, Port Hudson, Raymond, Jackson, and Chickamauga; absent sick from Missionary Ridge.

** Gentry, H.D., present at Fort Donelson; imprisoned at Camp Douglas; exchanged Sep. 23, 1862; present at Chickasaw Bayou and Port Hudson; killed at Raymond.

* Goodman, C.H., present at Fort Donelson; died at Camp Douglas, Mar. 14, 1862.

Goodman, H. (W.) E., present at Fort Donelson; imprisoned at Camp Douglas; exchanged Sep. 23, 1862; discharged for disability, Oct., 1862.

Grimes, S.H., present at Fort Donelson; imprisoned at Camp Douglas; exchanged Sep. 23, 1862; absent sick from Chickasaw Bayou; present at Port Hudson; on detached duty during Raymond battle; present at Jackson; absent barefoot from Chickamauga; present at Missionary Ridge.

** Grinder, Henry, present at Fort Donelson; imprisoned at Camp Douglas; exchanged Sep. 23, 1862; present at Chickasaw Bayou, Port Hudson, Raymond, and Jackson; killed at Chickamauga the second day.

* Grinder, J.C., present at Fort Donelson; died at Camp Douglas, Jul. 2, 1862.

** Grinder, William, present at Fort Donelson; imprisoned at Camp Douglas; exchanged Sep. 23, 1862.; present at Chickasaw Bayou, Port Hudson, Raymond, and Jackson; killed at Chickamauga the second day.

Helton, T.B., present at Fort Donelson; imprisoned at Camp Douglas; exchanged Sep. 23, 1862; AWOL from Chickasaw Bayou; present at Port Hudson, Raymond, and Jackson; absent sick from Chickamauga; absent barefoot from Missionary Ridge.

Henley, J. Samuel, present at Fort Donelson; imprisoned at Camp Douglas; exchanged Sep. 23, 1862; present at Chickasaw Bayou, Port Hudson, Raymond, and Jackson; absent sick from Chickamauga; absent barefoot from Missionary Ridge; survived the war.

Hensley, A.S., present at Fort Donelson; took the oath of allegience to the U.S. at Camp Douglas and never returned.

* Hensley, E.B., died at home Aug. 17, 1861.

Hickerson, William, joined company at reorganization; on detached duty as cook during Chickasaw Bayou battle; discharged as non-conscript, Feb. 22, 1863.

Hinson, David, present at Fort Donelson; imprisoned at Camp Douglas; exchanged Sep. 23, 1862; discharged for disability, Oct., 1862.

Hinson, J.F., present at Fort Donelson; imprisoned at Camp Douglas; exchanged Sep. 23, 1862; furloughed Sep. 30, 1862, and never returned.

Hinson, J.P., present at Fort Donelson; imprisoned at Camp Douglas; exchanged Sep. 23, 1862; present at Chickasaw Bayou, Port Hudson, Raymond, and Jackson; captured at Chickamauga the second day.

Kelly, G.W., detailed as teamster; served in cavalry; rejoined the regt. Dec. 7, 1862; present at Chickasaw Bayou, Port Hudson, Raymond, and Jackson; absent sick from Chickamauga and Missionary Ridge.

Keutch, J.P., transferred to regt. from 1st Tenn. Cavalry, Nov. 1, 1863; present at Missionary Ridge.

Langford, N.B., present at Fort Donelson; took the oath of allegience to the U.S. at Camp Douglas and never returned.

* Langford, Samuel, died at Camp Cheatham, Jul. 6, 1861.

Langford, W.B., present at Fort Donelson; took the oath of allegience to the U.S. at Camp Douglas and never returned.

Matthews, W.H., present at Fort Donelson; imprisoned at Camp Douglas; exchanged Sep. 23, 1862; present at Chickasaw Bayou, Port Hudson, Raymond, and Jackson; AWOL from Chickamauga; absent barefoot from Missionary Ridge.

Mayfield, J.G., detailed as teamster; rejoined regt. after its exchange; absent sick from Chickasaw Bayou; present at Port Hudson; captured at Raymond and never returned.

Morris, E.T., AWOL during Fort Donelson battle; took oath of allegience to the U.S. at Camp Douglas and released; rejoined regt. after its exchange; present at Chickasaw Bayou; discharged as non-conscript, Feb. 22, 1863.

Napier, R.R., wounded at Fort Donelson; imprisoned at Camp Douglas; exchanged Sep. 23, 1862; absent from all battles except Port Hudson due to Fort Donelson wound.

** Peaveyhouse, F.M., present at Fort Donelson; imprisoned at Camp Douglas; exchanged Sep. 23, 1862; present at Chickasaw Bayou and Port Hudson; killed at Raymond.

** Peaveyhouse, J.N., present at Fort Donelson; imprisoned at Camp Douglas; exchanged Sep. 23, 1862; present at Chickasaw Bayou and Port Hudson; killed at Raymond.

* Peaveyhouse, W.P., detailed as nurse at Fort Doneslon; imprisoned at Camp Douglas; exchanged Sep. 23, 1862; died at Jackson, Miss., Nov. 14, 1862.

* Pope, Alexander, present at Fort Doneslon; died at Camp Douglas Jul. 30, 1862.

* Pope, B.L., present at Fort Donelson; imprisoned at Camp Douglas; exchanged Sep. 23, 1862; present at Chickasaw Bayou, Port Hudson, and Raymond; absent sick from Jackson; died at Yazoo City, Miss., Aug., 1863.

* Pope, D.R., died at Bowling Green, Dec. 4, 1861.

Pope, J.T., discharged for disability at Camp Trousdale Aug., 1861; returned to the regt. at reorganization; present at Chickasaw Bayou and Port Hudson; wounded at Raymond; absent from Jackson and Chickamauga due to wound; present at Missionary Ridge.

Quillin, Willis, present at Fort Donelson; imprisoned at Camp Douglas; exchanged Sep. 23, 1862; present at Chickasaw Bayou, Port Hudson, Raymond, Jackson, Chickamauga, and Missionary Ridge; survived the war.

* Sharp, J.F., present at Fort Doneslon; died at Camp Douglas, Mar. 22, 1862.

** Sharp, J.G., present at Fort Doneslon; imprisoned at Camp Douglas; exchanged Sep. 23, 1862; present at Chickasaw Bayou and Port Hudson; killed at Raymond.

Sharp, J.H., on furlough during Fort Donelson battle; entered the cavalry.

* Sims, George, died at home, Jan. 21, 1862.

Sims, J.W., present at Fort Donelson; imprisoned at Camp Douglas; exchanged Sep. 23, 1862; present at Chickasaw Bayou and Port Hudson; wounded at Raymond; absent thereafter due to wound.

* Sims, W.F., died at home, Sep. 20, 1861.

** Smith, James, present at Fort Donelson; imprisoned at Camp Douglas; exchanged Sep. 23, 1862; present at Chickasaw Bayou, Port Hudson, Raymond, and Chickamauga; mortally wounded at Missionary Ridge and died Jan. 20, 1864.

Smith, Martin, transferred to regt. from 48th Tenn., Apr., 1863; present at Raymond, Jackson, Chickamauga, and Missionary Ridge.

Strickland, B.J., present at Fort Donelson; imprisoned at Camp Douglas; exchanged Sep. 23, 1862; present at Chickasaw Bayou; discharged as non-conscript, Feb. 22, 1863.

Turnbow, Calvin, present at Fort Donelson; imprisoned at Camp Douglas; exchanged Sep. 23, 1862; present at Chickasaw Bayou, Port Hudson, Raymond, and Jackson; wounded at Chickamauga; absent from Missonary Ridge due to wound.

* Turnbow, George, present at Fort Donelson; imprisoned at Camp Douglas; exchanged Sep. 23, 1862; present at Chickasaw Bayou

Turner, George, present at Fort Donelson; imprisoned at Camp Douglas; exchanged Sep. 23, 1862; no further record.

* Turner, Samuel, present at Fort Donelson; died at Camp Douglas, May 5, 1862.

** Vincent, George, present at Fort Donelson; imprisoned at Camp Douglas; exchanged Sep. 23, 1862; present at Chickasaw Bayou, Port Hudson, Raymond, and Jackson; killed at Chickamauga the second day.

Vincent, John, transferred to regt. from 1st Tenn. Cavalry, Dec., 1862; present at Chickasaw Bayou, Port Hudson, Raymond, Jackson, Chickamauga, and Missionary Ridge.

Westbrook, J.N., AWOL during Fort Donelson battle; imprisoned at Camp Douglas; exchanged Sep. 23, 1862; absent sick from Chickasaw Bayou; present at Port Hudson, Raymond, and Jackson; absent sick from Chickamauga; absent barefoot from Missionary Ridge.

Company I (later K)

Captain

Ben F. Matthews, commanded company at Fort Donelson; imprisoned at Camp Chase and Johnson's Island; exchanged Sep. 16, 1862; commanded company at Chickasaw Bayou, Port Hudson, Raymond and Jackson; on furlough during Chickamauga battle; commanded company at Missionary Ridge.

1st Lieutenant

J.C. Chaffin, wounded at Fort Donelson; escaped after the surrender and never returned.

\# John Hildreth, as a private present at Fort Donelson; imprisoned at Camp Douglas; exchanged Sep. 23, 1862; promoted to 1st lieutenant at reorganization; present at Chickasaw Bayou, Port Hudson, and Raymond; wounded at Jackson, Jul. 11, 1863; absent from Chickamauga due to wound; present at Missionary Ridge; surrendered at Greensboro, N.C..

2nd Lieutenant

* B.W. Evans, accidentally killed by musket shot at Camp Trousdale, Aug., 1861.

\# Alonzo Lindsay, promoted from 1st corporal in Aug., 1861; present at Fort Donelson; imprisoned at Camp Chase and Johnson's Island; exchanged Sep. 16, 1862; absent sick from Chickasaw Bayou; present at Port Hudson, Raymond, and Jackson; commanded company the first day at Chickamauga, absent the second due to sprained ankle; absent sick from Missionary Ridge; surrendered at Greensboro, N.C..

Junior 2nd Lieutenant

C.F. Herron, on furlough during Fort Donelson battle; never returned.

* J.H. Hagan, as 3rd sergeant present at Fort Donelson; imprisoned at Camp Douglas; exchanged Sep. 23, 1862; promoted to junior 2nd lieutenant at reorganization; absent sick from Chickasaw Bayou and Port Hudson; present at Raymond; absent sick thereafter; died at home in Lawrence County, Tenn., Feb. 9, 1864.

\# J.W. Childress, as 4th corporal present at Fort Donelson; imprisoned at Camp Douglas; exchanged Sep. 23, 1862; promoted to 2nd corporal at reorganization; present at Chickasaw Bayou, Port Hudson, Raymond, Jackson, Chickamauga, and Missionary Ridge; elected junior 2nd lieutenant, Mar., 1864; surrendered at Greensboro, N.C..

1st Sergeant

M.V. Bentley, present at Fort Donelson; took the oath of office to the U.S. at Fort Donelson, released, and never returned.

C.W. Tidwell, as a private present at Fort Donelson; imprisoned at Camp Douglas; exchanged Sep. 23, 1862; promoted to 1st sergeant at reorganization; present at Chickasaw Bayou and Port Hudson; on detached duty during Raymond battle; absent due to sore eyes thereafter.

2nd Sergeant

M.C. Abernathy, present at Fort Donelson; imprisoned at Camp Douglas; exchanged Sep. 23, 1862; returned to the ranks at reorganization; deserted Dec. 25, 1862.

W.H. Childress, as a private present at Fort Donelson; imprisoned at Camp Douglas; exchanged Sep. 23, 1862; promoted to 2nd sergeant at reorgani zation; present at Chickasaw Bayou and Port Hudson; wounded at Raymond; present at Jackson; absent sick from Chickamauga; present at Missionary Ridge.

3rd Sergeant

T.B. Kelly, as a private present at Fort Donelson; imprisoned at Camp Douglas; exchanged Sep. 23, 1862; promoted to 3rd sergeant at reorganization; absent sick from Chickasaw Bayou; present at Port Hudson, Raymond, and Jackson; AWOL from Chickamauga and Missionary Ridge.

4th Sergeant

A.W. Bentley, discharged for disability at Camp Trousdale, Aug., 1861.

W.R. Smith, as a private present at Fort Donelson; imprisoned at Camp Douglas; exchanged Sep. 23, 1862; promoted to 4th sergeant at reorganization; present at Chickasaw Bayou, Port Hudson, Raymond, and Jackson; absent sick thereafter; survived the war.

5th Sergeant

H.W. Emerson, present at Fort Donelson; escaped after the surrender; rejoined regt. at Port Hudson in Apr., 1863; transferred to 48th Tenn., May 2, 1863.

J.E. Carothers, as 2nd corporal present at Fort Donelson; imprisoned at Camp Douglas; exchanged Sep. 23, 1862; promoted to 5th sergeant at reorganization; present at Chickasaw Bayou, Port Hudson, Raymond, and Jackson; AWOL from Chickamauga; present at Missionary Ridge.

1st Corporal

V.A.S. Green, as a private present at Fort Donelson; imprisoned at Camp Douglas; exchanged Sep. 23, 1862; promoted to 1st corporal at reorganization; present at Chickasaw Bayou, Port Hudson, and Raymond; absent sick thereafter.

2nd Corporal

(All persons holding this rank were subsequently promoted.)

3rd Corporal

* J.G. Robards, died at Camp Cheatham, Jul., 1861.

J.L. McLean, as a private present at Fort Donelson; imprisoned at Camp Douglas; exchanged Sep. 23, 1862; promoted to 3rd corporal at reorganization; present at Chickasaw Bayou and Port Hudson; wounded at Raymond; absent due to wound thereafter.

4th Corporal

W.F. Norman, as a private present at Fort Donelson; imprisoned at Camp Douglas; exchanged Sep. 23, 1862; promoted to 4th corporal at reorganization; present at Chickasaw Bayou and Port Hudson; wounded at Raymond; absent from Jackson due to wound; absent from Chickamauga and Missionary Ridge due to sore eyes; surrendered at Greensboro, N.C..

Private

Abernathy, L.E., present at Fort Donelson; imprisoned at Camp Douglas; exchanged Sep. 23, 1862; AWOL from Chickasaw Bayou; present at Port Hudson, Raymond, and Jackson; absent sick from Chickamauga and Missionary Ridge; survived the war.

Alford, R.N., on furlough during Fort Donelson battle; joined the cavalry.

Angel, J.M., detailed as teamster; joined the cavalry.

Anthony, W.W., present at Fort Donelson; took the oath of allegience to the U.S. at Camp Douglas; never returned.

Bailey, J.E., present at Fort Donelson; imprisoned at Camp Douglas; exchanged Sep. 23, 1862; furloughed, then deserted to cavalry during reorganization.

Bennett, S.B., present at Fort Donelson; imprisoned at Camp Douglas; exchanged Sep. 23, 1862; present at Chickasaw Bayou, Port Hudson, and Raymond; absent sick from Jackson and Chickamauga; deserted from Lookout Mountain, Nov. 24, 1863.

Brashears, Robert, present at Fort Donelson; took the oath of allegiance to the U.S. at Camp Douglas; rejoined regt. after its exchange; present at Chickasaw Bayou and Port Hudson; wounded at Raymond, captured, and parolled; never returned.

Busby, J.J., detailed to Provost Martial at Bowling Green; joined 48th Tenn..

Byrd, William, present at Fort Donelson; took the oath of allegience to the U.S. at Camp Douglas; never returned.

* Callahan, S.V., died at Camp Trousdale, Aug. 20, 1861.

Caputon (Caperton), F.G., present at Fort Donelson; imprisoned at Camp Douglas; exchanged Sep. 23, 1862; AWOL from Chickasaw Bayou; present at Port Hudson; wounded at Raymond; AWOL from Jackson and Chickamauga; present at Missionary Ridge; deserted from Dalton, Ga., Nov. 30, 1863.

Cobb, P.F., present at Fort Donelson; took the oath of allegience to the U.S. at Camp Douglas; joined the cavalry.

Cobb, William, present at Fort Donelson; imprisoned at Camp Douglas; exchanged Sep. 23, 1862; present at Chickasaw Bayou, Port Hudson, Raymond, and Jackson; on detached duty during Chickamauga and Missionary Ridge battles.

Cook, S.G., detailed as teamster; joined the cavalry.

* Defoe, J.C., present at Fort Donelson; died at Camp Douglas, May, 1862.

Dial, J.D., sick during Fort Donelson battle; imprisoned at Camp Douglas; exchanged Sep. 23, 1862; on detached duty until discharged as non-conscript, Mar. 5, 1863.

Durbin, J.A., present at Fort Donelson; excaped after the surrender; joined the 48th Tenn..

Edmiston, J.N., present at Fort Donelson; imprisoned at Camp Douglas; exchanged Sep. 23, 1862; present at Chickasaw Bayou, Port Hudson, and Raymond; absent sick from Jackson; furloughed to hospital Aug.1, 1863, and never returned.

* Ellison, J.D., present at Fort Donelson; imprisoned at Camp Douglas; exchanged Sep. 23, 1862; furloughed in Sep., 1862, and died in Oct..

Faust, J.M., AWOL from Fort Donelson; imprisoned at Camp Douglas; exchanged Sep. 23, 1862; AWOL from all battles until deserting, Jul. 20, 1863.

Faust, Richard, present at Fort Donelson; imprisoned at Camp Douglas; exchanged Sep. 23, 1862; absent sick from Chickasaw Bayou; present at Port Hudson; absent sick from Raymond and Jackson; present at Chickamauga; absent sick from Missionary Ridge.

Ferguson, G.M., present at Fort Donelson; imprisoned at Camp Douglas; exchanged Sep. 23, 1862; present at Chickasaw Bayou; discharged as nonconscript, Mar. 5, 1863.

Ferguson, W.A., present at Fort Donelson; imprisoned at Camp Douglas; exchanged Sep. 23, 1862; present at Chickasaw Bayou, Port Hudson, and Raymond; absent sick from Jackson; present at Chickamauga; AWOL from Missionary Ridge.

* Fisher, J.D., present at Fort Donelson; died at Camp Douglas, Apr. 23, 1862.

Foster, John, discharged for disability at Camp Cheatham, Jul., 1861.

Freeman, Fuller, hurt in accident pror to Fort Donelson; sent home and never returned.

Freeman, H.J., enlisted Nov. 12, 1862; absent sick from Chickasaw Bayou; present at Port Hudson; captured at Raymond and never returned.

** Freeman, J.L., presant at Fort Donelson; imprisoned at Camp Douglas; exchanged Sep. 23, 1862; present at Chickasaw Bayou and Port Hudson; killed at Raymond.

Garrett, W.R.M., present at Fort Donelson; imprisoned at Camp Douglas; exchanged Sep. 23, 1862; present at Chickasaw Bayou and Port Hudson; wounded at Raymond; absent from Jackson due to wound; absent sick from Chickamauga and Missionary Ridge.

Green, J.L., present at Fort Donelson; imprisoned at Camp Douglas; exchanged Sep. 23, 1862; present at Chickasaw Bayou, Port Hudson, Raymond, and Jackson; absent sick thereafter.

Green, John, present at Fort Donelson; imprisoned at Camp Douglas; exchanged Sep. 23, 1862; present at Chickasaw Bayou, Port Hudson, and Raymond; on detached duty during Jackson battle; deserted Jul. 20, 1863.

Green, William Allen, present at Fort Donelson; imprisoned at Camp Douglas; exchanged Sep. 23, 1862; present at Chickasaw Bayou and Port Hudson; wounded at Raymond; absent due to wound thereafter; survived the war.

* Hardin, J.M., died at Bowling Green, Nov., 1861.

Hare, F.A., present at Fort Donelson; imprisoned at Camp Douglas; exchanged Sep. 23, 1862; present at Chickasaw Bayou, Port Hudson, and Raymond; absent sick from Jackson; present at Chickamauga; deserted from Lookout Mountain, Nov. 24, 1863.

Harwell, B.W., discharged for disability at Camp Trousdale, Aug., 1861.

Harwell, J.M., AWOL during Fort Donelson battle; imprisoned at Camp Douglas; exchanged Sep. 23, 1862; ran in every battle; deserted near Dalton, Nov. 30, 1863.

Hatley, J.M., enlisted Nov. 1, 1863; joined regt. at Dalton, Ga., Dec. 18, 1863; deserted Jan. 31, 1864.

Herrin, B.F., enlisted Nov. 22, 1862; present at Chickasaw Bayou and Port Hudson; wounded at Raymond; absent from Jackson and Chickamauga due to wound; discharged for disability, Sep. 30, 1863.

* Holt, V.B., died at Camp Cheatham, Jul. 10, 1861.

Howard, Aaron, enlisted Nov. 1, 1863; joined regt. at Dalton, Ga., Dec. 18, 1863.

Hubbard, J.R., present at Fort Donelson; took the oath of allegience to the U.S. at Camp Douglas; rejoined the regt. after its exchange; absent sick from Chickasaw Bayou; discharged as non-conscript at Port Hudson, Mar. 5, 1863.

Hubbard, R.M., present at Fort Donelson; imprisoned at Camp Douglas; exchanged Sep. 23, 1862; present at Chickasaw Bayou, Port Hudson, Raymond, and Jackson; deserted Jul., 1863.

Hubbard, W.J., present at Fort Donelson; imprisoned at Camp Douglas; exchanged Sep. 23, 1862; present at Chickasaw Bayou, Port Hudson, Raymond, and Jackson; deserted Jul., 1863.

** Hudson, J.S., present at Fort Donelson; imprisoned at Camp Douglas; exchanged Sep. 23, 1862; present at Chickasaw Bayou and Port Hudson; killed at Raymond.

Hughes, S.D., AWOL during Fort Donelson battle; escaped after the surrender; never returned.

Johnson, D.T., present at Fort Donelson; took the oath of allegience to the U.S. at Camp Douglas; rejoined regt. after its exchange; present at Chickasaw Bayou and Port Hudson; wounded at Raymond; present at Jackson; deserted Aug. 12, 1863.

* Johnson, E.C., present at Fort Donelson; died at Camp Douglas, May, 1862.

Johnson V.A., carried the colors at Fort Donelson after Compton fell; imprisoned at Camp Douglas; exchanged Sep. 23, 1862; furloughed because of illness at reorganization and never returned.

Jones, Anderson, present at Fort Donelson; took the oath of allegiance to the U.S. at Camp Douglas in Aug., 1862; never returned.

Jones, J.S., present at Fort Donelson; took the oath of allegiance to the U.S. at Camp Douglas in Aug., 1862.

Jones, S.B., enlisted Nov. 16, 1862; transferred to Company K from Company H at Port Hudson; captured at Raymond and never returned.

* Keaton, J.H., wounded at Fort Donelson; sent home; rejoined regt. after its exchange; absent sick from Chickasaw Bayou and Port Hudson; died at Jackson, La., Apr., 1863.

Laymaster, W.H., detailed as teamster; never returned.

Lewellyn, J.H., present at Fort Donelson; imprisoned at Camp Douglas; exchanged Sep. 23, 1862; absent sick thereafter.

Liles, John. L., present at Fort Donelson; imprisoned at Camp Douglas; exchanged Sep. 23, 1862; detailed as teamster thereafter except Chickamauga when absent sick.

Liles, L.L., present at Fort Donelson; imprisoned at Camp Douglas; exchanged Sep. 23, 1862; present at Chickasaw Bayou and Port Hudson; wounded at Raymond; absent thereafter due to wound.

** Littleton, C.F., present at Fort Donelson; imprisoned at Camp Douglas; exchanged Sep. 23, 1862; present at Chickasaw Bayou and Port Hudson; killed at Raymond.

Littleton, J.M., sick during Fort Donelson battle; imprisoned at Camp Douglas; exchanged Sep. 23, 1862; furloughed at reorganization and deserted to cavalry.

Littleton, J.W., joined company at reorganization; present at Chickasaw Bayou and Port Hudson; wounded at Raymond; absent thereafter due to wound.

Littleton, R.S., Assistant Surgeon at Fort Donelson; imprisoned at Camp Douglas; exchanged Sep. 23, 1862; transferred to 27th Ala., Oct., 1862.

Loveless, B.F., enlisted Mar. 19, 1863 at Port Hudson; present at Raymond and Jackson; captured at Chickamauga and never returned.

* Lytle, Frank, detailed as teamster during Fort Donelson battle; rejoined regt. after its exchange; present at Chickasaw Bayou, Port Hudson, and Raymond; died at Canton, Miss., Jun. 27, 1863.

Maxey, J.C., discharged for disability at Camp Cheatham, Jun., 1861.

** May, T.B., present at Fort Donelson; imprisoned at Camp Douglas; exchanged Sep. 23, 1862; present at Chickasaw Bayou and Port Hudson; killed at Raymond.

McAllister F.L., present at Fort Donelson; imprisoned at Camp Douglas; exchanged Sep. 23, 1862; present at Chickasaw Bayou and Port Hudson; ran at Raymond; present at Jackson; ran at Chickamauga and Missionary Ridge; deserted at Dalton, Ga., Nov. 30, 1863.

** McAllister, N.A., enlisted Nov. 12, 1862; present at Chickasaw Bayou and Port Hudson; killed at Raymond.

McAllister, O.H.P., present at Fort Donelson; imprisoned at Camp Douglas; exchanged Sep. 23, 1862; present at Chickasaw Bayou, Port Hudson, Raymond, and Jackson; AWOL from Chickamauga; present at Missionary Ridge.

* McAllister, W.A., died at Camp Trousdale, Aug. 17, 1861.

McMillan, A.H., present at Fort Donelson; imprisoned at Camp Douglas; exchanged Sep. 23, 1862; absent sick until Chickamauga; absent barefoot from Missionary Ridge; survived the war.

Miles, F.M., present at Fort Donelson; imprisoned at Camp Douglas; exchanged Sep. 23, 1862; present at Chickasaw Bayou, Port Hudson, Raymond, Jackson, and Chickamauga; AWOL from Missionary Ridge.

** Miles, N.F., enlisted Nov. 12, 1862; present at Chickasaw Bayou, Port Hudson, Raymond, and Jackson; killed at Chickamauga the second day.

Morris, J.L., present at Fort Donelson; escaped from Camp Douglas, Mar. 31, 1862; joined the cavalry.

Neal, W.W., discharged for disability at Camp Cheatham, Jun., 1861.

Nelson, Charles W., enlisted at Dalton, Ga., Jan. 18, 1864; survived the war.

** Nowlin, D.L., present at Fort Donelson; imprisoned at Camp Douglas; exchanged Sep. 23, 1862; present at Chickasaw Bayou, Port Hudson, Raymond, and Jackson; killed at Chickamauga the second day.

* Osborn, James, died at Camp Cheatham, Jun. 6, 1861.

* Paine, J.A., died at home, Aug., 1861.

** Parker, W.R., present at Fort Donelson; imprisoned at Camp Douglas; exchanged Sep. 23, 1862; present at Chickasaw Bayou and Port Hudson; killed at Raymond.

Pillow, R.A., present at Fort Donelson; took the oath of allegiance to the U.S. at Camp Douglas; never returned.

Pryor, W.J., present at Fort Donelson; imprisoned at Camp Morton; took the oath of allegiance to the U.S.; never returned.

Ray, Thomas, transferred to regt. from 48th Tenn. at Port Hudson; absent barefoot from Raymond; present at Jackson; deserted Aug. 12, 1863.

* Richardson, A.J., present at Fort Donelson; imprisoned at Camp Douglas; exchanged Sep. 23, 1862; present at Chickasaw Bayou; died at Port Hudson, Feb. 11, 1863.

Riddle (Reddell), J.A., present at Fort Donelson; imprisoned at Camp Douglas; exchanged Sep. 23, 1862; present at Chickasaw Bayou, Port Hudson, Raymond, Jackson, Chickamauga, and Missionary Ridge; survived the war.

Scott, F.P., present at Fort Donelson; imprisoned at Camp Douglas; exchanged Sep. 23, 1862; furloughed at reorganization and deserted to the cavalry.

Shannon, A.J., AWOL during Fort Donelson battle; imprisoned at Camp Douglas; exchanged Sep. 23, 1862; absent sick from Chickasaw Bayou; present at Port Hudson; captured at Raymond, parolled, went home and was captured again; never returned.

Shields, J.T., present at Fort Donelosn; imprisoned at Camp Douglas; exchanged Sep. 23, 1862; present at Chickasaw Bayou and Port Hudson; captured at Raymond and imprisoned at Fort Delaware.

Smith, B.F., detailed as teamster.

Smith, G.B., present at Fort Donelson; imprisoned at Camp Douglas; exchanged Sep. 23, 1862; present for every battle but always missing at the end; deserted from Lookout Mountain, Nov. 18, 1863.

Smith, Jacob, present at Fort Donelson; took the oath of allegiance to the U.S. at Camp Douglas.

Springer, Aaron, present at Fort Donelson; imprisoned at Camp Douglas; exchanged Sep. 23, 1862; furloughed at reorganization and never returned.

* Springer, Ananias, died at Camp Cheatham.

* Stewart, William, died at Camp Cheatham, Nov. 9, 1861.

Stribling, J.B., present at Fort Donelson; imprisoned at Camp Douglas; exchanged Sep. 23, 1862; present at Chickasaw Bayou, Port Hudson, Raymond, and Jackson; AWOL during most of Chickamauga battle; present at Missionary Ridge.

Tanner, H.J., detailed as teamster during Fort Donelson battle; rejoined regt. after its exchange; present at Chickasaw Bayou, Port Hudson, Raymond, Jackson, Chickamauga, and Missionary Ridge.

Tayes, J.P., present at Fort Donelson; imprisoned at Camp Douglas; exchanged Sep. 23, 1862; present at Chickasaw Bayou; discharged as non-conscript, Mar. 5, 1863.

Tracy, N.F., present at Fort Donelson; imprisoned at Camp Douglas; exchanged Sep. 23, 1862; present at Chickasaw Bayou; transferred to 48th Tenn., Apr., 1863.

* True, N.P. absent sick from Fort Donelson; died at home, Mar., 1862.

Vaughn, T.D., present at Fort Donelson; imprisoned at Camp Douglas; exchanged Sep. 23, 1862; present at Chickasaw Bayou, Port Hudson, Raymond, and Jackson; absent sick thereafter.

Walker, J.T., present at Fort Donelson; imprisoned at Camp Douglas; exchanged Sep. 23, 1862; captured near Holly Springs, Miss., Nov., 1862; exchanged and rejoined regt. May 9, 1863; AWOL from Raymond; present at Jackson; deserted Aug. 12, 1863.

Walters, George, discharged for disability at Camp Trousdale, Aug., 1862.

Weatherford, M., present at Fort Donelson; imprisoned at Camp Douglas; exchanged Sep. 23, 1862; present at Chickasaw Bayou and Port Hudson; captured at Raymond; rejoined the regt. Jun., 1863; present at Jackson; wounded at Chickamauga the first day; present at Missionary Ridge.

* Welch, J.W., present at Fort Donelson; imprisoned at Camp Douglas; exchanged Sep. 23, 1862; died at Jackson, Miss., Oct., 1862.

* Williams, R.H., present at Fort Donelson; died at St. Louis, Feb. 25, 1862.

* Willis, J.H., sick at home during Fort Donelson battle; died at home, Apr., 1862.

Wilson, S.H., detailed as teamster; joined the cavalry.

Wisdom, J.L., present at Fort Donelson; imprisoned at Camp Douglas; exchanged Sep. 23, 1862; present at Chickasaw Bayou, Port Hudson, Raymond, and Jackson; furloughed Aug. 10, 1863, and never returned.

Wisdom, J.M., enlisted Apr.5, 1863; present at Raymond and Jackson; deserted Aug. 12, 1863.

Wisdom, J.W.F., present at Fort Donelson; escaped from Camp Douglas Mar. 31, 1862; rejoined regt. at Port Hudson, Feb., 1863; present at Raymond and Jackson but left the field early each battle; deserted Aug. 12, 1863.

Company K (later A)

Captain

Thomas E. McCoy, elected junior 2nd lieutenant Nov. 26, 1861; present at Fort Donelson; imprisoned at Camp Chase and Johnson's Island; exchanged Sep. 16, 1862; elected 1st lieutenant at reorganization; present at Chickasaw Bayou; promoted to captain Dec. 29, 1862; commanded company at Port Hudson; absent sick from Raymond; commanded company at Jackson and the first day at Chickamauga until wounded; commanded company at Missionary Ridge.

1st Lieutenant

Willis H. Jones, as 2nd lieutenant present at Fort Donelson; imprisoned at Camp Chase and Johnson's Island; exchanged Sep. 16, 1862; present at Chickasaw Bayou; promoted to 1st lieutenant after Chickasaw Bayou battle; present at Port Hudson; on detached duty during Raymond battle; present at Jackson; commanded Company E at Chickamauga; on detached duty during Missionary Ridge battle; survived the war.

William J. Ridgeway, as 3rd sergeant present at Fort Donelson; imprisoned at Camp Douglas; exchanged Sep. 23, 1862; returned to the ranks at reorganization; present at Chickasaw Bayou; elected junior 2nd lieutenant, Feb. 12, 1863; present at Port Hudson; wounded at Raymond; absent from Jackson due to wound; promoted to 2nd lieutenant Aug. 7, 1863; absent from Chickamauga and Missionary Ridge due to wound.

2nd Lieutenant

William H. Hodge, as 3rd corporal sick in Dover during Fort Donelson battle; imprisoned at Camp Douglas; exchanged Sep. 23, 1862; promoted to 4th sergeant at reorganization; present at Chickasaw Bayou; elected junior 2nd lieutenant, Jan., 1863; promoted to 2nd lieutenant Feb. 1, 1863; present at Port Hudson; absent sick from Raymond; present at Jackson; resigned due to disability, Aug. 7, 1863.

Junior 2nd Lieutenant

O.P. Bruce, resigned Nov., 1861.

** James P. Bass, as a private present at Fort Donelson; escaped from Camp Douglas Jun. 18, 1862; promoted to junior 2nd lieutenant at reorganization; mortally wounded at Chickasaw Bayou; died in Vicksburg, Miss., Dec. 30, 1862.

Henry M. Beaty, as 1st sergeant present at Fort Donelson; imprisoned at Camp Douglas; exchanged Sep. 23, 1862; present at Chickasaw Bayou and Port Hudson; absent from Jackson due to wound; elected junior 2nd lieutenant Aug. 7, 1863; commanded company at Chickamauga after Captain McCoy was wounded; present at Missionary Ridge.

1st Sergeant

J.W. Whitfield, as a private present at Fort Donelson; imprisoned at Camp Douglas; exchanged Sep. 23, 1862; present at Chickasaw Bayou, Port Hudson, Raymond, and Jackson; promoted to 1st sergeant, Aug. 7, 1863; present at Chickamauga and Missionary Ridge; surrendered at Greensboro, N.C..

2nd Sergeant

Wade L. Hargrove, present at Fort Donelson; imprisoned at Camp Douglas; exchanged Sep. 23, 1862; returned to the ranks at reorganization; present at Chickasaw Bayou, Port Hudson, Raymond, and Jackson; wounded at Chickamauga the first day; absent from Missionary Ridge due to wound; surrendered at Greensboro, N.C..

Jesse A. Holland, as 1st corporal present at Fort Donelson; imprisoned at Camp Douglas; exchanged Sep. 23, 1862; promoted to 2nd sergeant at reorganization; transferred to 1st Tenn. Cavalry, Dec. 15, 1862.

** Samuel H. Abernathy, as 2nd corporal sick in hospital during Fort Donelson battle; imprisoned at Camp Douglas; exchanged Sep. 23, 1862; promoted to 3rd sergeant at reorganizaton; AWOL from Chickasaw Bayou; present at Port Hudson; promoted to 2nd sergeant Apr. 12, 1863; killed at Raymond.

3rd Sergeant

Thomas W. Wren, reduced to the ranks, Jun., 1861; injured at Bowling Green, Sep. 18, 1861, removing flag from roundhouse; hospitalized at Nashville where he was captured ; imprisoned at Camp Chase; exchanged Sep. 16, 1862; discharged for disability, Sep. 29, 1862.

James H. Sims, replaced Wren but then reduced to ranks himself; absent sick at Bowling Green during Fort Donelson battle; rejoined regt. in time for Chickasaw Bayou; discharged as non-conscript Mar. 1863.

Henry W. Watson, as a private present at Fort Donelson; imprisoned at Camp Douglas; exchanged Sep. 23, 1862; promoted to 3rd corporal at reorganization; present at Chickasaw Bayou, Port Hudson, and Raymond; promoted to 3rd sergeant, Jun. 3, 1863; present at Jackson; AWOL from Chickamauga from the end of the first day; present at Missionary Ridge; surrendered at Greensboro, N.C..

4th Sergeant

Felix G. Wilson, sick at Nashville during Fort Donelson battle; detached to Medical Department; never returned.

John F. Simpson; as a private present at Fort Donelson; imprisoned at Camp Douglas; exchanged Sep. 23, 1862; present at Chickasaw Bayou, Port Hudson, Raymond, Jackson, and Chickamauga; absent sick from Missionary Ridge; promoted to sergeant, Feb., 1863; surrendered at Greensboro, N.C..

5th Sergeant

W.F. Tucker, as a private present at Fort Donelson; imprisoned at Camp Douglas; exchanged Sep. 23, 1862; promoted to 5th sergeant at reorganization; present at Chickasaw Bayou and Port Hudson; captured at Raymond and imprisoned at Fort Delaware and Point Lookout; never returned.

1st Corporal

William E. Garrison, as a private present at Fort Donelson; imprisoned at Camp Douglas; exchanged Sep. 23, 1862; promoted at 1st corporal at reorganization; present at Chickasaw Bayou and Port Hudson; absent sick from Raymond; captured at Raymond and parolled; present at Chickamauga; transferred to 32nd Tenn., Oct., 1863.

2nd Corporal

Larkin Cardin, as a private present at Fort Donelson; imprisoned at Camp Douglas; exchanged Sep. 23, 1862; promoted to 2nd corporal at reorganization; absent sick from Chickasaw Bayou; present at Port Hudson; on detached duty during Raymond battle; captured and parolled prior to Jackson battle; present at Chickamauga and Missionary Ridge.

3rd Corporal

J.P. Henderson, enlisted Nov. 3, 1863; as a private present at Chickasaw Bayou, Port Hudson, Raymond, and Jackson; wounded at Chickamauga the second day; promoted to corporal, Nov. 1, 1863; present at Missionary Ridge; surrendered at Greensboro, N.C..

4th Corporal

Thomas Reed, sick in Dover hospital during Fort Donelson battle; imprisoned at Camp Douglas; exchanged Sep. 23, 1862; returned to the ranks at reorganization; present at Chickasaw Bayou and Port Hudson; captured at Raymond and imprisoned at Fort Delaware and Point Lookout; never returned.

J.L. Abernathy, as a private present at Fort Donelson; imprisoned at Camp Douglas; exchanged Sep. 23, 1862; promoted to 4th corporal at reorganization; present at Chickasaw Bayou, Port Hudson, Raymond, Jackson, Chickamauga, and Missionary Ridge; survived the war.

Private

Abernathy, J.P., present at Fort Donelson; imprisoned at Camp Douglas; exchanged Sep. 23, 1862; present at Chickasaw Bayou and Port Hudson; wounded in the arm at Raymond; present at Jackson; wounded in the arm at Chickamauga; present at Missionary Ridge; survived the war.

Abernathy, M.T. (or L.), present at Fort Donelson; imprisoned at Camp Douglas; exchanged Sep. 23, 1862; present at Chickasaw Bayou; discharged as non-conscript, Mar. 5, 1863; reenlisted Aug. 4, 1863; present at Chickamauga and Missionary Ridge; survived the war.

** Arthurs, William H., present at Fort Donelson; imprisoned at Camp Douglas; exchanged Sep. 23, 1862; wounded at Sprindale, Miss.; absent from Chickasaw Bayou due to wound; present at Port Hudson and Raymond; killed at Chickamauga the first day.

Atkins, William J., present at Fort Donelson; imprisoned at Camp Douglas; exchanged Sep. 23, 1862; present at Chickasaw Bayou, Port Hudson, Raymond, and Jackson; absent barefoot from Chickamauga; present at Missionary Ridge.

Bass, John Ball, present at Fort Donelson; imprisoned at Camp Douglas; exchanged Sep. 23, 1862; present at Chickasaw Bayou and Port Hudson; wounded at Raymond; absent thereafter due to wound; survived the war.

* Bass, John M., present at Fort Donelson; died at Camp Douglas, Mar. 11, 1862.

Beaty, Thomas B., present at Fort Donelson; imprisoned at Camp Douglas; exchanged Sep. 23, 1862; on detached duty during Chickasaw Bayou battle; present at Port Hudson, Raymond, and Jackson; wounded at Chickamauga the first day; present at Missionary Ridge.

\# Biles, S.J., present at Fort Donelson; imprisoned at Camp Douglas; exchanged Sep. 23, 1862; present at Chickasaw Bayou and Port Hudson; on detached duty during Raymond battle; present at Jackson, Chickamauga, and Missionary Ridge; surrendered at Greensboro, N.C..

* Birdwell, Blooming, present at Fort Donelson; died at Camp Douglas, Sep. 27, 1862

\# Birdwell, J.F., present at Fort Donelson; imprisoned at Camp Douglas; exchanged Sep. 23, 1862; present at Chickasaw Bayou and Port Hudson; wounded in the arm at Raymond; present at Jackson; wounded in the arm at Chickamauga; present at Missionary Ridge; surrendered at Greensboro, N.C..

Birdwell, S.C., transferred to regt. from 32nd Tenn., Nov. 1, 1863; present at Missionary Ridge.

* Boswell, D.B., sick in quarters at Fort Donelson; died at Camp Douglas, Mar. 7, 1862.

\# Bowers, E.D., enlisted Nov. 8, 1862; present at Chickasaw Bayou and Port Hudson; absent sick from Raymond; no additional battle entries; surrendered at Greensboro, N.C..

Brachine, G.S., enlisted Nov. 3, 1862; present at Chickasaw Bayou, Port Hudson, Raymond, Jackson, and Chickamauga; on detached duty during Missionary Ridge battle.

Brachine, J.G., present at Fort Donelson; imprisoned at Camp Douglas; exchanged Sep. 23, 1862; present at Chickasaw Bayou and Port Hudson; absent sick from Raymond and Jackson; present at Chickamauga and Missionary Ridge.

** Brachine, James, detailed as teamster during Fort Donelson battle; joined an Alabama regt.; killed near Richmond, Va..

** Bridgeforth, David J., discharged for disability at Camp Trousdale; joined the 9th Alabama and was killed near Richmond, Va., in Jun., 1862.

Bruce, George B., present at Fort Donelson; imprisoned at Camp Douglas; exchanged Sep. 23, 1862; present at Chickasaw Bayou and Port Hudson; captured at Raymond and imprisoned at Fort Delaware and Point Lookout; never returned.

Bruce, S.W., transferred to regt. from 32nd Tenn., Jan. 1, 1864.

Bruce, Thomas J., present at Fort Donelson; escaped from Camp Douglas, Jun. 18, 1862; joined 1st Tenn. Cavalry.

Buchanan, W.C., present at Fort Donelson; imprisoned at Camp Douglas; exchanged Sep. 23, 1862; detached as teamster shortly after reorganization; surrendered with Vicksburg garrison, Jul. 4, 1863; paroled but never returned.

** Bull, John W., present at Fort Donelson; imprisoned at Camp Douglas; exchanged Sep. 23, 1862; present at Chickasaw Bayou, Port Hudson, Raymond, and Jackson; killed at Chickamauga the first day.

* Caldwell, J.B., transferred to regt. from 53rd Tenn., Mar., 1863; died at Port Hudson, Apr., 1863.

Campbell, W.A., present at Fort Donelson; imprisoned at Camp Douglas; exchanged Sep. 23, 1862; present at Chickasaw Bayou; transferred to 53rd Tenn., Mar. 5, 1863.

Carter, Jonas, discharged for disability at Bowling Green, Nov., 1861.

Cheatham, A.W., AWOL at Fort Donelson battle; imprisoned at Camp Douglas; exchanged Sep. 23, 1862; present at Chickasaw Bayou; discharged as non-conscript, Mar. 5, 1863.

* Cheatham, W.H., died at Bowling Green, Dec. 25, 1861.

Childers, John W., sick during Fort Donelson battle; imprisoned at Camp Butler, exchanged Sep. 23, 1862; present at Chickasaw Bayou and Port Hudson; captured at Raymond and never returned.

** Childers, Robert H., enlisted Nov. 4, 1862; present at Chickasaw Bayou and Port Hudson; absent sick from Raymond and Jackson; mortally wounded at Chickamauga the second day.

Childs, G.W., present at Fort Donelson; escaped after the surrender; present at Shiloh; rejoined regt. after its exchange; present at Chickasaw Bayou; discharged as non-conscript at Port Hudson, Mar. 5, 1863.

Culps. R.L., sick at home during Fort Donelson battle; joined the 9th Alabama; wounded at Richmond, Va..

Davis, W.R., detached to hospital in Dover during Fort Donelson battle; imprisoned at Camp Butler; exchanged Sep. 23, 1862; present at Chickasaw Bayou; discharged as non-conscript at Port Hudson, Mar. 5, 1863.

DeGraffenreid, T.A., present at Fort Donelson; imprisoned at Camp Douglas; exchanged Sep. 23, 1862; present at Chickasaw Bayou and Port Hudson; wounded at Raymond; present at Chickamauga and Missionary Ridge.

Dougherty, M.A., present at Fort Donelson; imprisoned at Camp Douglas; exchanged Sep. 23, 1862; AWOL from Chickasaw Bayou; present at Port Hudson, Raymond, and Jackson; AWOL from Chickamauga the first day but present the second; present at Missionary Ridge.

Dungy, Abner, present at Fort Donelson; escaped after the surrender; rejoined regt. after its exchange; present at Chickasaw Bayou, Port Hudson, Raymond, and Jackson; on furlough during Chickamauga battle; present at Missionary Ridge; deserted from Rome, Ga., Feb. 14, 1864.

Dungy, F.M., present at Fort Donelson; imprisoned at Camp Douglas; exchanged Sep. 23, 1862; present at Chickasaw Bayou, Port Hudson, Raymond, Jackson, Chickamauga, and Missionary Ridge; surrendered at Greensboro, N.C..

Dungy, John, discharged for disability at Camp Trousdale, Aug., 1861.

Dyer, Zachariah T., present at Fort Donelson; imprisoned at Camp Douglas; exchanged Sep. 23, 1862; present at Chickasaw Bayou; discharged as non-conscript, Mar. 5, 1863.

Elder, G.W., transferred to regt. from 53rd Tenn., Mar. 5, 1863; present at Port Hudson, Raymond, Jackson, Chickamauga, and Missionary Ridge.

Elder, J.H., present at Fort Donelson; imprisoned at Camp Douglas; exchanged Sep. 23, 1862; present at Chickasaw Bayou, Port Hudson,

Raymond, and Jackson; present at Chickamauga the first day but AWOL the second; present at Missionary Ridge.

Estes, E.L.B., present at Fort Donelson; imprisoned at Camp Douglas; exchanged Sep. 23, 1862; present at Chickasaw Bayou, Port Hudson, Raymond, and Jackson; on furlough during Chickamauga battle; transferred to 32nd Tenn., Oct., 1863.

Ewing, J.C., enlisted Nov. 8, 1862; absent sick from Chickasaw Bayou; present at Port Hudson; wounded and captured at Raymond; paroled and went home; never returned.

* Ezell, J.P., died at home, Jul. 27, 1861.

Ferguson, Thomas, drummed out of service by court martial at Camp Cheatham, Jul., 1861.

** Franklin, W.L., present at Fort Donelson; escaped after the surrender; rejoined regt. after its exchange; present at Chickasaw Bayou and Port Hudson; killed at Raymond.

Fuller, A.B., present at Fort Donelson; imprisoned at Camp Douglas; exchanged Sep. 23, 1862; present at Chickasaw Bayou, Port Hudson, Raymond, Jackson, Chickamauga, and Missionary Ridge.

George, J.M.A., discharged for disability at Camp Trousdale, Aug., 1861; joined 41st Tenn..

Gibbs, W.H., sick at Nashville during Fort Donelson battle; joined the 44th Tenn. and made lieutenant.

* Gilbert, H.C., died at Camp Cheatham, Jun., 1861.

Grant, George H., sick at Bowling Green during Fort Donelson battle; never returned.

Hardiman, P.H., detailed as teamster during Fort Donelson battle; joined the cavalry.

* Hargrove, W.B., present at Fort Donelson; imprisoned at Camp Douglas; exchanged Sep. 23, 1862; detached as teamster during Chickasaw Bayou battle; present at Port Hudson; detached as teamster during Raymond and Jackson battles; absent sick from Chickamauga and Missionary Ridge; died at Lauderdale Springs, Miss., Apr. 10, 1864.

Hazlewood, H.V., present at Fort Donelson; imprisoned at Camp Douglas; exchanged Sep. 23, 1862; on detached duty during Chickasaw Bayou battle; present at Port Hudson; lost his right arm at Raymond; returned home but captured in Giles County, Tenn., Jan., 1864.

Henderson, T.B., present at Fort Donelson; imprisoned at Camp Douglas; exchanged Sep. 23, 1862; present at Chickasaw Bayou, Port Hudson, and Raymond; captured at Jackson and never returned.

* Holland, A.C., died at home.

** Holland, John W., present at Fort Donelson; imprisoned at Camp Douglas; exchanged Sep. 23, 1862; present at Chickasaw Bayou, Port Hudson, Raymond, and Jackson; killed at Chickamauga the first day.

** Hughes, James W., killed at Fort Donelson, Feb. 15, 1862.

Hughes, Thomas M., present at Fort Donelson; imprisoned at Camp Douglas; exchanged Sep. 23, 1862; on furlough during Chickasaw Bayou battle; present at Port Hudson, Raymond, and Jackson; AWOL from Chickamauga the first day, present the second; present at Missionary Ridge.

Hunnicutt, W.E., enlisted Nov. 8, 1862; absent sick from Chickasaw Bayou; discharged for disability, Mar. 5, 1863.

Hunter, F., sick at Nashville during Fort Donelson battle; joined the 17th Tenn., then the 44th Tenn..

Hunter, J.W., present at Fort Donelson; took the oath of allegience to the U.S. at St. Louis; joined the 17th Tenn., then the 44th Tenn..

* Johnson, Thomas F., sick during Fort Donelson battle; died in St. Louis Feb. 21, 1862.

Kennedy, W.P., present at Fort Donelson until the night of Feb. 15; imprisoned at Camp Butler; exchanged Sep. 23, 1862; on detached duty during Chickasaw Bayou battle; present at Port Hudson; on detached duty during Raymond battle; present at Jackson; on detached duty during Chickamauga and Missionary Ridge battles; transferred to 32nd Tenn., Feb. 25, 1864.

King, J.W., present at Fort Donelson; imprisoned at Camp Douglas; exchanged Sep. 23, 1862; present at Chickasaw Bayou, Port Hudson, and Raymond; captured at Jackson, Jul.. 15, 1863, and never returned.

* King, Thomas B., sick during Fort Donelson battle; died on board a steamboat on the Mississippi River Feb. 18, 1862; buried on shore.

Lauderdale, J.G., present at Fort Donelson; imprisoned at Camp Douglas; exchanged Sep. 23, 1862; present at Chickasaw Bayou; transferred to 53rd Tenn., 1863.

Madigan, Dennis, present at Fort Donelson; imprisoned at Camp Douglas; exchanged Sep. 23, 1862; transferred to 10th Tenn., Oct., 1862.

* Matthews, Edward H., died at Bowling Green, Oct., 1861.

McCallum, J.D., sick at Russellville during Fort Donelson battle; joined the 1st Tenn. Cavalry.

McCoy, J.W., enlisted Nov. 21, 1862; present at Chickasaw Bayou and Port Hudson; captured at Raymond and imprisoned at Fort Delaware and Point Lookout; never returned.

McCoy, Samuel H., lost an arm at Fort Donelson; imprisoned at Camp Douglas; exchanged Sep. 23, 1862; discharged for disability, Sep. 29, 1862.

* Merrill, George W., died at Camp Trousdale, Sep., 1861.

Mitchell, Thomas E., detailed as teamster during Fort Donelson battle; rejoined regt. after its exchange; detailed as teamster during Chickasaw Bayou battle; present at Port Hudson; detailed as teamster during Raymond, Jackson, and Chickamauga battles; present at Missionary Ridge.

Moore, John W., present at Fort Donelson; imprisoned at Camp Douglas; exchanged Sep. 23, 1862; present at Chickasaw Bayou and Port Hudson; wounded at Raymond; absent from Jackson due to wound; absent sick from Chickamauga; present at Missionary Ridge.

Nelson, C.H., sick at Nashville during Fort Donelson battle; joined the cavalry.

Nelson, J.H., detailed as nurse in a Nashville hospital during Fort Donelson battle; joined the cavalry.

\# Nelson, J.L., transferred to regt. from 32nd Tenn., Nov. 1, 1863; present at Missionary Ridge; surrendered at Greensboro, N.C..

Osborne, James A., present at Fort Donelson; imprisoned at Camp Douglas; exchanged Sep. 23, 1862; present at Chickasaw Bayou, Port Hudson, and Raymond; absent sick from Jackson; present at Chickamauga except the evening of the first day; present at Missionary Ridge.

Osborne, J.W., transferred to regt. from 32nd Tenn., Oct. 29, 1863; present at Missionary Ridge.

Pennington, Isaac, discharged for disability at Camp Trousdale, Aug., 1861.

Petty, Reps O., sick at home during Fort Donelson battle; never returned.

Pully, Isaac V., present at Fort Donelson; imprisoned at Camp Douglas; exchanged Sep. 23, 1862; present at Chickasaw Bayou, Port Hudson, and Raymond; absent sick from Jackson; wounded at Chickamauga the first day; present at Missionary Ridge; surrendered at Greensboro, N.C..

Ralls, J.H., enlisted Nov. 4, 1862; present at Chickasaw Bayou, Port Hudson, and Raymond; absent sick from Jackson; present at Chickamauga and Missionary Ridge.

Reed, A.J., enlisted Oct. 30, 1862; present at Chickasaw Bayou, Port Hudson, and Raymond; wounded at Jackson; absent thereafter due to wound.

Rowe, James H., sick at home during Fort Donelson battle; never returned.

Scruggs, William F., present at Fort Donelson; imprisoned at Camp Douglas; exchanged Sep. 23, 1862; captured at Springdale, Miss., and imprisoned at Alton, Ill.; exchanged and rejoined regt. Mar. 10, 1863; present at Raymond and Jackson; wounded at Chickamauga the second day; absent from Missionary Ridge due to wound.

Shapard (Shephard), James B., present at Fort Donelson; imprisoned at Camp Douglas; exchanged Sep. 23, 1862; AWOL from Chickasaw Bayou; present at Port Hudson, Raymond, and Jackson; on furlough during Chickamauga battle; present at Missionary Ridge; survived the war.

Smith Thomas J., enlisted Nov. 5, 1862; absent sick from Chickasaw Bayou; present at Port Hudson; absent sick at Raymond, Jackson, Chickamauga, and Missionary Ridge; surrendered at Greensboro, N.C..

Stanley, Henry M., enlisted Oct. 28, 1862; present at Chickasaw Bayou, Port Hudson, Raymond, Jackson, and Chickamauga; on detached duty during Missionary Ridge battle.

** Stepp, Logan, present at Fort Donelson; imprisoned at Camp Douglas; exchanged Sep. 23, 1862; present at Chickasaw Bayou, Port Hudson, Raymond, and Jackson; killed at Chickamauga the first day.

Stevenson, W.E.F., present at Fort Donelson; imprisoned at Camp Douglas; exchanged Sep. 23, 1862; on detached duty during Chickasaw Bayou battle; present at Port Hudson, Raymond, Jackson, Chickamauga, and Missionary Ridge; survived the war.

Stone, William H., present at Fort Donelson; imprisoned at Camp Douglas; exchanged Sep. 23, 1862; AWOL from Chickasaw Bayou; present at Port Hudson and Raymond; wounded at Jackson; absent thereafter due to wound.

Stout, C.C., discharged for disability at Bowling Green, Jan., 1862.

* Sullivan, Ambrose, sick at Nashville during Fort Donelson battle; died at home.

Sumner, G.W., discharged for disability at Camp Cheatham, Jun., 1861.

Swinea, Henry S., present at Fort Donelson; imprisoned at Camp Douglas; exchanged Sep. 23, 1862; present at Chickasaw Bayou, Port Hudson, Raymond, Jackson, and Chickamauga; absent sick from Missionary Ridge.

Swinea, S.W., enlisted Nov. 8, 1862; present at Chickasaw Bayou, Port Hudson, Raymond, and Jackson; wounded at Chickamauga the first day; went home without leave.

Swinea, W.F., enlisted Nov. 8, 1862; present at Chickasaw Bayou, Port Hudson, Raymond, and Jackson; AWOL from Chickamauga battle; present at Missionary Ridge; survived the war.

Sylvester, Thomas M., present at Fort Donelson; imprisoned at Camp Douglas; exchanged Sep. 23, 1862; absent sick until Chickamauga battle where he was sent to the rear due to exhaustion; absent sick from Missionary Ridge.

Taylor, Jno. W., enlisted Oct. 29, 1862; present at Chickasaw Bayou, Port Hudson, Raymond, and Jackson; wounded at Chickamauga the second day; absent from Missionary Ridge due to wound; furloughed from hospital in Dec., 1863; went home and surrendered.

* Tillery, W.H., enlisted Nov. 18, 1862; present at Chickasaw Bayou; absent sick from Port Hudson; died at Clinton, La., Mar. 27, 1863.

** Tucker, D.H., enlisted Oct. 27, 1862; present at Chickasaw Bayou, Port Hudson, Raymond, and Jackson; mortally wounded at Chickamauga and died at Marietta, Ga., Nov. 13, 1863.

Tucker, J.N., enlisted Oct. 27, 1862; never reported.

Watson, Daniel J., enlisted Nov. 18, 1862; AWOL from Chickasaw Bayou; present at Port Hudson and Raymond; captured at Jackson, Jul. 15, 1863; escaped and rejoined the regt.; AWOL from Chickamauga; shot himself in the hand and deserted shortly after the battle.

White, Thomas W., present at Fort Donelson; imprisoned at Camp Morton; exchanged Sep. 15, 1862; absent sick from Chickasaw Bayou; present at Port Hudson, Raymond,and Jackson; present for part of the Chickamauga battle; transferred to 32nd Tenn., Oct. 1, 1863.

White, Wiley P., enlisted Oct. 30, 1862; present at Chickasaw Bayou and Port Hudson; captured at Raymond.

Whitfield, W.S., present at Fort Donelson; imprisoned at Camp Douglas; exchanged Sep. 23, 1862; present at Chickasaw Bayou and Port Hudson; captured at Raymond and imprisoned at Fort Delaware and Point Look out; never returned.

Wilson, Vincent W., detached to hospital in Bowling Green during Fort Donelson battle; rejoined regt. after its exchange; detached to hospital after reorganization; never returned.

Bibliography

Primary Sources

Duke University, Durham, NC
3rd Tennessee Roll Book
Ira S. Doty Letters. Courtesy of Irene Doty
Georgia Archives and Library, Atlanta
The Confederate Veteran Magazine, Volumes I through XXIII.
Indiana University (Lilly Library), Bloomington
Flavel C. Barber Collection: Diary in four volumes, pocket Bible and photographs.
National Archives
Rolls of 4th Consolidated Regiment Tennessee Infantry, Roll 134, File M-268.
Tennessee State Library and Archives, Nashville
John C. Brown Autograph Book
Nathaniel F. Cheairs Memoir
B.F. Cheatham Papers
R.W. Colville Letters
Thomas H. Deavenport Diary
Enoch Hancock Letters
Giles County Census, 1860
Index to Confederate Pension Applications. 1964.
Journal of the Constitutional Convention of 1870
William L. McKay Memoir
W.H. Ogilvie Memoir
Smith, Lewis K., *Historical Sketches and Traditions of Jackson County, Tennessee.*

Books

Personal Accounts

Bierce, Ambrose. *Ambrose Bierce's Civil War.* Regnery Gateway: Washington, DC, 1988 (reprint from collected writings).

Bull, Rice., ed. by Jack K. Bauer. *Soldiering: The Civil War Diary of Rice Bull.* Presidio Press: San Rafael, Ca., 1977.

Hood, John Bell. *Advance and Retreat: Personal Experiences in the United States and Confederate States Armies.* Blue and Grey Press: Secaucus, NJ, 1985 (reprint of 1880 edition).

Lester, John C. and D.L. Wilson. *Ku Klux Klan: Its Origens, Growth, and Disbandment.* DeCapo Press: New York, 1973 (reprint of 1905 edition).

Longstreet, James. *From Manassas to Appomattox.* Blue and Grey Press: Secaucus, NJ, 1985 (reprint of 1896 edition).

Manigault, Arthur M. (Ed. by R. Lockwood Tower). *A Carolinian Goes to War.* University of South Carolina Press: Columbia, SC, 1983.

Watkins, Sam. *Co. Aytch.* Broadfoot Publishing Company: Wilmington, NC, 1882.

Secondary Sources

Allison, John. *Notable Men of Tennessee.* Southern Historical Assoc.: Atlanta, 1905.

Atlas to Accompany the Official Records of the Union and Confederate Armies. The Fairfax Press: Washington, D.C.. 1891-1895 (1983 reprint).

Battles and Leaders of the Civil War. Vols. I to IV, New York, 1887. Reprint, Castle: Secaucus, NJ, 1984.

Bearss, Edwin C.. *Hardluck Ironclad: The Sinking and Salvage of the Cairo.* Louisiana State University Press: Baton Rouge, LA, 1966.

Caldwell, Joshua. *Sketches of the Bench and Bar of Tennessee.* Ogden Brothers and Company: Knoxville, TN, 1898.

Castel, Albert. *Decision in the West: The Atlanta Campaign of 1864.* University Press of Kansas: Lawrence, KS, 1992.

Catton, Bruce. *The Coming Fury.* Doubleday: New York, 1961

__________. *Terrible Swift Sword.* Doubleday: New York, 1963.

__________. *This Hallowed Ground.* New York, 1956.

The Civil War: Master Index. Time-Life: Alexandria, VA, 1987.

Connelly, Thomas L.. *Army of the Heartland: The Army of Tennessee, 1861-1862.* Louisiana State University Press: Baton Rouge, LA, 1967.

__________. *Autumn of Glory: The Army of Tennessee, 1862-1865.* Louisiana State University Press: Baton Rouge, LA, 1971.

__________. *Civil War Tennessee: Battles and Leaders.* University of Tennessee Press: Knoxville, TN, 1979.

Cooling, Benjamin F.. *Forts Henry and Donelson: The Key to the Confederate Heartland.* University of Tennessee Press: Knoxville, TN, 1987.

Cozzens, Peter. *This Terrible Sound: The Battle of Chickamauga.* University of Illinois Press: Urbana, IL, 1992.

Daniel, Larry J., *Soldiering in the Army of Tennessee: A Portrait of Life in a Confederate Army.* University of North Carolina Press: Chapel Hill, NC, 1991.

Echoes of Battle: The Atlanta Campaign. Blue Acorn Press: Huntington, WV, 1991.

Faust, Patricia, et. al. *Historical Times Illustrated Encyclopedia of the Civil War.* Harper Perennial: New York, 1986.

Govan, Gilbert E. and James W. Livingwood. *A Different Valor: The Story of General Joseph E. Johnston, C.S.A..* Konecky & Konecky: New York, 1965.

Griffith, Paddy. *Battle in the Civil War.* Nottinghamshire, England, 1986.

Hamer, P.M.. *Tennessee: A History, 1673-1932.* Four Vols. The American Historical Society: New York, 1933.

Henry, Robert Selph. *First With the Most: Forrest.* Konecky & Konecky: New York, 1992.

Horn, Stanley F.. *The Army of Tennessee.* Broadfoot Publishing Company: Wilmington, NC, 1987 (reprint of 1941 edition).

Keegan, John. *The Face of Battle.* New York, 1976.

Korn, Jerry. *War on the Mississippi.* Alexandria, VA, 1985.

Losson, Christopher. *Tennessee's Forgotten Warriors: Frank Cheatham and His Confederate Division.* University of Tennessee Press: Knoxville, TN, 1989.

Marcot, Roy M., *Spencer Repeating Rifles.* Irvine, CA, 1983.????? Publisher???

Marshall, S.L.A., *Men Against Fire.* Gloucester, MA, 1978 (reprint of 1947 edition).

McDonough, James L. and Thomas L. Connelly. *Five Tragic Hours: The Battle of Franklin.* University of Tennessee Press: Knoxville, TN, 1983.

__________. *Stones River: Bloody River in Tennessee.* University of Tennessee Press: Knoxville, TN, 1980.

__________ and Thomas L. Connelly. *Five Tragic Hours: The Battle of Franklin.* University of Tennessee Press: Knoxville, TN, 1983.

McMurry, Richard M.. *John Bell Hood and the War for Southern Independence.* University Press of Kentucky: Lexington, KY, 1982.

McPherson, James M.. *Battle Cry of Freedom.* Oxford University Press: New York, 1988.

__________. *For Cause & Comrades: Why Men Fought in the Civil War.* New York: Oxford University Press, 1997.

McWhiney, Grady. *Braxton Bragg and Confederate Defeat.* University of Alabama Press (first published 1969).

The Military Annals of Tennessee. Ed. by John Barrien Lindsley. First Series: Embracing A Review of Military Operations, Regimental Histories and Memorial Rolls. Spartanburg, SC: LBroadfood Publications, 1974 (reprint).

Parks, Joseph H. *General Leonidas Polk, C.S.A.: The Fighting Bishop.* Louisiana State University Press: Baton Rouge, LA, 1960.

Patton, James M., *Unionism and Reconstruction in Tennessee, 1860-1869.* University of North Carolina Press: Chapel Hill, NC, 1934.

Phillips, Margaret I., *The Governors of Tennessee.* Pelican Publishing Company: Gretna, LA, 1978.

Roland, Charles P., *Albert Sidney Johnston: Soldier of Three Republics.* University of Texas Press: Austin, TX, 1964.

Sifakis, Stewart, *Who Was Who in the Civil War.* New York, 1988.

Sunderland, Glenn W., *Wilder's Lightning Brigade and Its Spencer Repeaters.* The Book Works: Washington, IL, 1984.

Sword, Wiley, *Embrace an Angry Wind: The Confederacy's Last Hurrah: Spring Hill, Franklin, and Nashville.* Harper-Collins: New York, 1992.

Tennessee Civil War Centennial Commission, *Tennesseans in the Civil War.* Civil War Centennial Commission: Nashville, TN, 1964.

Tucker, Glenn, *Chickamauga: Bloody Battle in the West.* Morningside Bookshop: Dayton, OH, 1984 (first published 1961)..

Wade, Wyn C., *The Fiery Cross: The Ku Klux Klan in America.* Simon & Schuster: New York, 1987.

The War of the Rebellion: A Compilation of the Official Records of Union and Confederate Armies (The Official Records). Washington, DC, 1880-1901, Volumes VII, XVI, XVII, XXIV, XXX, XXXI, XCIII.z

Wheeler, Richard, *The Siege of Vicksburg.* New York, 1978.

White, Robert H., *Messages of the Governors of Tennessee, 1869-1883,* Vol 6. Nashville, TN, 1963.

Wiley, Bell I., *The Life of Johnney Reb.* The Bobbs-Merrill Company: New York, 1943.

Woodworth, Steven E., *Jefferson Davis and His Generals: The Failure of Confederate Command in the West.* University Press of Kansas: Lawrence, KS, 1990.

Periodicals

Ambrose, Stephen E., Edwin C. Bearss, et. al., "Struggle For Vicksburg," *Civil War Times Illustrated.* 1967.

Ambrose, Stephen E., Thomas L. Connelly, et al., "The Campaigns for Fort Donelson." Acorn collection of *Civil War Times Illustrated* articles. 1983.

"The Battles for Chattanooga," *Civil War Times Illustrated.* August 1971.

Davis, Stephen, "Atlanta Campaign: Hood Fights Desperately," *Blue and Gray Magazine.* August 1989.

Kelly, Dennis, "Atlanta Campaign: The Battle of Kennesaw Mountain," *Blue and Gray Magazine.* June 1989.

McMurry, Richard M., "Atlanta Campaign: Sherman Plunges Into a North Georgia Hell Hole," *Blue and Gray Magazine*, April 1989.

Newspapers

Courier Journal (Louisville, Ky.), December 4, 1881.

Knoxville Daily Chronicle, October 30, 1874.

Knoxville Weekly Chronicle, December 13, 1871.

Nashville Banner, February 22, 1861; October 23, 1870; May 10, 1874; August 19, 1889.

Nashville Union and Dispatch, November 10, 1868.

Thesis

Butler, Margaret. "The Life of John C. Brown." Master's Thesis, University of Tennessee) Knoxville, 1936.

Index

(Names or initials in ( ) indicate an alternate spelling.)